$\frac{1}{97}$

£6-99

IN THE NAME
OF THE LAW

IN THE NAME
OF THE LAW

The Collapse of Criminal Justice

David Rose

JONATHAN CAPE

LONDON

First published 1996

1 3 5 7 9 10 8 6 4 2

© David Rose 1996

David Rose has asserted his right
under the Copyright, Designs and Patents Act, 1988
to be identified as the author of this work

First published in the United Kingdom in 1996 by
Jonathan Cape
Random House, 20 Vauxhall Bridge Road, London SW1V 2SA

Random House Australia (Pty) Limited
20 Alfred Street, Milsons Point, Sydney,
New South Wales 2061, Australia

Random House New Zealand Limited
18 Poland Road, Glenfield,
Auckland 10, New Zealand

Random House South Africa (Pty) Limited
PO Box 337, Bergvlei, 2012 South Africa

Random House UK Limited Reg. No. 954009

A CIP catalogue record for this book
is available from the British Library

Papers used by Random House UK Limited are natural,
recyclable products made from wood grown in sustainable forests.
The manufacturing processes conform to the environmental
regulations of the country of origin.

ISBN 0–224–03744–7

Printed and bound in Great Britain by
Mackays of Chatham PLC

For Shyama, Anyusha and Tushara
and in loving memory of Rhoda Green, 1928–95

Contents

Preface and Acknowledgments ix
1 The Old Regime and its Passing 1
2 Race, Class and Justice 51
3 The Rising Tide of Crime 87
4 The Retreat from Prosecution 114
5 The Problem of Organised Crime 165
6 The Culture of Policing 211
7 Policing the Police 260
8 The Collapse of Criminal Justice 306
Notes 339
Index 349

PREFACE AND ACKNOWLEDGMENTS

ENGLISH criminal justice is in a crisis without precedent, its solutions uncertain and its effects deeply damaging. At a time when the crime rate has reached an all time high, the system often fails to identify offenders: it locks up the innocent while the guilty go free. Often they are not prosecuted at all. Meanwhile, what passes for national debate on the subject becomes ever more shrill, its participants mired in cliché, ignorance and anachronism.

Since the early 1990s, when it seemed that barely a month went by without another bewildered victim emerging into the daylight from the Court of Appeal, the stream of reported miscarriages of justice seems to have slowed to a drip. But the myth that British justice is the finest in the world has suffered irreparable damage.

This book tries to examine the roots and context of this crisis. There is no simple recipe which will put things right. As faith is lost in the mechanisms of legal due process, we seem to be moving inexorably towards an atavistic form of justice, in which the dominant motive is revenge. The logical conclusion of this development is a twenty-first-century hell: a 30/30/40 society with guns and fortifications, in which notions of 'One Nation' are replaced by state and freelance vigilante violence.

Conservatives have never been good at accepting their part in creating a world whose dysfunctional aspects suddenly seem so overwhelming. In September 1985, touring Handsworth in Birmingham on the day after its bloody and destructive riot, the then Home Secretary Douglas Hurd insisted: 'These are not social phenomena, but crimes.' Prime Minister John Major went a step further with his extraordinary comments in an interview in February 1993: 'I feel strongly that society needs to condemn a little more and understand a little less.'

To condemn is easy, but without understanding, it is ultimately futile. In the debate on crime, the Left sometimes seems to deny the role of individual moral choice altogether, just as it refuses to accept that the weakening of family structures has brought any negative social effects. At the same time, the Right cannot confront the possibility that the reasons for the growth of what the Victorians called the criminal classes might be deprivation, unemployment and deepening inequality. The nineteenth-century writers Lombroso and Havelock Ellis, who believed you could identify criminals and their unlawful specialities by their physical appearance, are suddenly back in vogue, only this time, their heirs are looking for the tell-tale signs in offenders' DNA.

In the discussion of policing and the criminal process, a similar intellectual impasse is evident. On the one hand is a long politico-legal tradition, backed by impressive academic research, which claims that the police are and always must be inherently coercive, dismissive of suspects' rights, prone to widespread dishonesty and corruption and usually sexist and racist to boot. The reality of 'cop culture', as this tradition usually calls it, exposes 'community policing' as a public relations myth. As for the trial, it is always an unequal contest, with the balance permanently weighted against the hapless defendant.

Ranged against the civil libertarians, with their concern for the due process of law, is the crime control lobby. This says the time has come to give the police the tools they need to do their job. The real miscarriage of justice is the release of the guilty and is usually the work of unethical lawyers. In the middle is a criminal justice industry with an annual turnover of £20 billion, and rising, in which a sense of strategy or co-ordination is entirely absent.

Meanwhile, Britain remains a society for which crime has become an obsession. 'True Crime' paperbacks sell at every bookstall. There is almost no TV drama except drama about crime. The more expensive programmes centre on a modern-day Holmes, a brilliant detective such as Inspector Morse, Inspector Taggart, Inspector Wexford, Inspector Frost, to say nothing of Miss Marple and Hercule Poirot. There are series about every conceivable player in a criminal inquiry: the police surgeon, the

Crown prosecutor, the criminal psychologist and the defence QC. No doubt the BBC will soon launch an autumn season with a show called *Jury Usher*, or *Crown Court Canteen*. Some of these programmes provide excellent entertainment. None approach the unsatisfactory, unresolved and often boring reality of policing and criminal justice.

This book is the work of a journalist, not an academic, although at times it has been influenced by academic work. It makes no pretence at providing a complete or definitive account of how criminal justice works. Nor is it a comprehensive sociological analysis. But it does try to look at certain important themes and topics, and to provide analysis on the basis of some recent real cases. Its main focus is the police: their practice, policy and culture, but it tries to chart their relationship with the rest of the system, and with the formulation of law and policy.

I owe gratitude to many people without whom this project would not have become reality. Neil Belton, my editor at Jonathan Cape, inspired both its genesis and execution with his unfailing support, patience and encouragement. The *Observer* granted me generous leave of absence. Duncan Campbell of the *Guardian* allowed me to use his unpublished manuscript about the Torso Murders.

Carolyn Hoyle and Andrew Sanders at the Oxford Institute for Criminological Research helped me to explore some of the book's analysis and commented on the manuscript, as did Tom Williamson and Richard Wells. I wish to thank all those who agreed to be interviewed for this book, and those who gave me documentary materials. Not all their names can be found in the text.

Chapter Seven could not have been written without Raju Bhatt, who delved deep into his files. Special thanks are due to the officers of the Kilburn division of the Metropolitan Police, who cheerfully tolerated my presence on many occasions when it must have been inconvenient. Sergeant Steve Evans and his Community Action Team taught me more about the reality of policing than my previous seven years as a specialist reporter.

Above all, I must thank my family.

Throughout the text I have used the masculine pronoun for convenience.

David Rose
London, February 1996

CHAPTER ONE

The Old Regime and its Passing

TO DESTROY what was left of the old regime in criminal justice required five words. They were uttered at the Old Bailey by the Lord Chief Justice of England at midday on 19 October 1989. The words were: 'The officers must have lied.'

Lord Lane's comment on the Surrey police detectives who elicited confessions from the Guildford Four exploded like a depth-charge in a placid lake. His horror and cold fury were harbingers of tidal waves that have yet to subside.

Murder convictions had been set aside before. Police officers had been accused of serious malpractice, even by the Bench. But to free Gerard Conlon, Paul Hill, Patrick Armstrong and Carole Richardson after fifteen years in prison was something else again.

Their convictions, for planting the bomb in a Guildford pub which killed five people in October 1974, did not merely represent the outcome of a half-forgotten criminal trial. They were a key symbol of the British state's long struggle with Irish Republican terrorism, and of its ability to contain it.

The comments of their trial judge in sentencing set a bench-mark for the severity which the future perpetrators of such crimes could expect. He said:

You have been sentenced to life imprisonment for murder, and I want you to understand what this means. And I want your fellow members of the IRA and in particular those being sent to this country to commit these crimes to understand that these crimes have a very special feature.

You may think you can expect to be released in twelve to fifteen years. I want to spell out the facts. The idea that life means twelve to fifteen years dates from the days when the sentence for

murder was death. Only when there were extenuating circumstances was that commuted to life imprisonment. It was a reprieve,
and reprieved murderers were released after such a period. None
of you would have been in that category. You would have been
executed. Sentence of life imprisonment must have an entirely
different meaning.

The judge told Paul Hill: 'If as an act of mercy you are ever to be
released, it can only be because of great age or infirmity.' Armstrong
must serve not less than thirty-five years, Conlon not less than thirty.
Richardson, who was only seventeen at the time of the bombings,
and hence a juvenile, would be detained 'at Her Majesty's pleasure'.

By the time of the 1989 appeal, Sir John Donaldson, the judge
who had said these things, was Master of the Rolls, head of the civil
division of the Court of Appeal, one of the highest jurists in the land.
Among the officers who took part in the Guildford bombs inquiry
was Sir Peter Imbert, who by the time of the appeal was
Commissioner of the Metropolitan Police; the country's top
policeman. The Guildford Four were prosecuted by no less a figure
than Michael Havers, who went on to serve as Attorney-General
and Lord Chancellor, at the very pinnacle of the legal system.

In 1977, the four had fought and lost an appeal in the course of
which four other convicted terrorists claimed responsibility for their
crimes. Although this meant the three appeal judges had to accept
the collapse of important parts of the prosecution case, they refused
to quash the Guildford Four's convictions. The new evidence
simply meant the Guildford bombing 'team' was larger than
previously thought.

The forces ranged in support of the four were equally significant.
For years, newspaper and television journalists had been investigating the case. Yorkshire Television had broadcast three successive
documentaries; there had been two books about the case, and
countless articles in newspapers. By October 1989, the campaign to
persuade Home Secretary Douglas Hurd to refer the case back to the
Court of Appeal counted among its members two of his Labour
predecessors, Roy Jenkins and Merlyn Rees, the retired Law Lords
Devlin and Scarman, Cardinal Basil Hume, the head of the Roman

Catholic Church in Britain, and William Runcie, the Archbishop of Canterbury.

Hurd asked the Avon and Somerset police to re-examine all the evidence in 1987. As the results of their inquiries began to arrive at C3, the tiny Home Office department which dealt with alleged miscarriages of justice, Hurd was fully aware of how momentous the consequences of quashing the convictions would be. Much more than the liberty of four individuals was at stake.

Together with the case of the Birmingham Six (the men convicted of killing twenty-one people with bombs in Birmingham a few weeks after the Guildford outrage), the Guildford bombings had become the focus for a battle between two opposing visions of the British legal state. One held the police to be repressive, brutal and dishonest; the trial process hugely loaded against the defendant; and the judges of appeal incapable of admitting the system could err. The other view clung to the belief that British justice remained the finest and fairest in the world. Occasionally it might need fine-tuning or refreshment, but this could be organised from within.

There were two judgments in the Birmingham case which set out the enormity of what was at stake. In 1980, Lord Denning, then Master of the Rolls, blocked an action by the Birmingham Six for civil damages against police officers they claimed had beaten them, using the ancient power of 'estoppel'.[1] To allow it to continue would be a 'scandal' he said, explaining:

> If the six men win, it will mean the police were guilty of perjury, that they were guilty of violence and threats, that the confessions were involuntary and were improperly admitted in evidence, and that the convictions were erroneous. That would mean the Home Secretary would either have to recommend they were pardoned or he would have to remit the case to the Court of Appeal. That is such an appalling vista that every sensible person in the land would say: 'It cannot be right that these actions should go any further.'

Two years before the Guildford Four's release, Hurd had referred the Birmingham case to the Appeal Court, acting on a dossier of new evidence which included claims by former police officers that the men had been beaten to make them confess. In January 1988, the same Lord Lane delivered an adamantine judgment rejecting each and every point, accusing six new witnesses of lying. It concluded with words which, in the eyes of the media, came to represent his entire career: 'As has happened before in references by the Home Secretary to this court under section 17 of the Criminal Appeal Act 1968, the longer this hearing has gone on, the more convinced this court has become that the verdict of the jury was correct. We have no doubt the convictions were both safe and satisfactory.'

Both Denning and Lane had publicly expressed their low opinion of journalists who looked for evidence which called criminal convictions into question. In Lord Lane's view, 'television programmes are designed primarily to entertain. Entertainment and justice, or entertainment and truth, are not always compatible.' Lord Denning condemned journalism whose only effect was 'undermining public confidence in the system'.

In the winter of 1987–8, the Avon and Somerset inquiry into the Guildford convictions produced a steady stream of important evidence.[2] It included support for the alibis of Richardson, Hill and Conlon, and gave medical evidence about Richardson's suggestibility. As early as 25 May, the late Robert Baxter, C3's head, a man of supreme objectivity whose role in this and other miscarriages of justice has largely gone unsung, laid down a memorandum to Hurd recommending a fresh appeal.

It took another seven months, and the discovery of further cogent evidence, before Hurd felt ready to do so. The Home Secretary began a long correspondence with Baxter, in which his reluctance to act was manifest. At one stage, after it emerged that Richardson had been given an injection of the opiate drug pethidine before she made her confession, the Home Secretary suggested referring only her case back to the court. Baxter's exasperation leaps from the page. 'My main concern is with the importance of the confession evidence in this case,' he wrote to Hurd on 17 August. 'Information which casts doubt on the reliability of one may be seen as undermining the credibility of the others and this leads me to see the cases of all the Guildford Four as closely linked.'

By September 1988, Hurd had virtually made up his mind. Despite the stream of documents from C3, he intended to do nothing. He went to see Cardinal Hume and tried to explain his thinking: almost immediately, Hume and his distinguished allies redoubled their pressure.

Exactly what finally persuaded Douglas Hurd to change his mind is not publicly recorded. The delay is easy to understand. In the words of one of his most senior civil service advisers: 'It was a long, drawn out business. Hurd was no fool: he could see Denning's appalling vista only too clearly. He knew the consequences of the case unravelling were so awful that he didn't want to take these steps without being very, very sure.'[3] In the end, the official adds, a crucial argument had to be spelled out: 'We had to tell him, and in the end he accepted it, that the test for the Home Secretary, the question he has to ask is, "Is there a case here for the Court of Appeal?" It is not his job to usurp the court and decide whether a miscarriage of justice actually occurred.'

Hurd took the case papers home for Christmas. On 3 January 1989, he told his private office he had reached a decision: the Guildford Four would have a fresh appeal.

Its outcome was no foregone conclusion. The old regime remained determined to defend itself, and to resist the appeal. It might well have succeeded: there was the gloomy precedent of Lord Lane's Birmingham Six ruling in 1988, while the new evidence available was of a technical, perhaps inconclusive nature.[4]

Then, on the morning of 17 October, when all the journalists, lawyers, campaigners, police officers and defendants involved in the case had assumed there would not be any hearing until January 1990 at the earliest, the Crown Prosecution Service made an amazing announcement: 'Circumstances have recently come to the notice of the Director of Public Prosecutions which have caused him to conclude that it would be wrong for the Crown to sustain the convictions.' There would be a special session of the Court of Appeal, sitting at the Old Bailey, in forty-eight hours' time. At that hearing, the Guildford Four would be freed.

Outside a circle consisting of senior Avon and Somerset police officers, prosecution lawyers, the Prime Minister and a handful of officials and Ministers at the Home Office, at this point no one knew what had happened. On 19 October, when Roy Amlot QC, for the Crown, rose to his feet in a crammed, high-security Old Bailey courtroom, his words came as a profound shock. As he listened,

Lord Lane's face seemed to betray some of what he felt: anger and astonishment, and the crumbling of illusions which had sustained his long career.

Amlot told the court that in digging into the vast pile of documents extant from the 1974 inquiry, the Avon and Somerset police had found a set of draft *typewritten* records of the Surrey detectives' interviews with Patrick Armstrong. They were covered in corrections, additions, and rearrangements of material. When the police gave evidence at the Guildford Four trial in 1975, they had presented a set of *handwritten* notes, which, they said, were a verbatim, contemporaneous record made during the interview.

Amlot's stunning revelation was that the manuscript notes were identical to the draft typewritten version – in its altered, corrected form. It was difficult to see how the handwritten notes could have been taken during the interviews. The typescript must have preceded them. The detectives had recently been questioned, Amlot said, but could not provide any explanation: 'The inescapable conclusion is . . . that the officers seriously misled the court.'

Worse, they had colluded with each other in order to do so, he said: 'Because of the notes, preparation and statements they gave, clearly they agreed together to present their notes in this fashion.'

The Avon and Somerset officers had discovered further gaping holes in the evidence: undisclosed papers casting massive doubt on the confession taken from Hill. There would have to be a criminal inquiry. The case as a whole had been 'contaminated', Amlot concluded. The prosecution had 'depended entirely on the confessions,' he reminded the court, 'and in particular upon the integrity of the officers taking them'. If they had not been honest about the way they recorded confessions, their content could not be trusted.

Lord Lane, sitting with Lord Justice Glidewell and Lord Justice Farquharson, gave judgment immediately. He needed to add very little. The whole foundation of the convictions had 'disappeared'. He expressly rejected Amlot's anodyne expression, 'misleading the court', with the expression quoted above: the officers 'must have lied'. If they could lie about the details of their notes, 'then the whole of their evidence became suspect'. It was 'some comfort' to know that the Director of Public Prosecutions was now considering criminal charges against the police: 'May we express the hope that nothing will be allowed to stand in the way of the speedy progress of those proceedings.'

It all took barely two hours. Inside the court, despite the colossal impact of what was being said, reactions were muted. But outside, in a street sealed off to traffic, came the tumult. Conlon came out first to ecstatic pandemonium, the hundreds in the road augmented by crowds clinging to scaffolding on a building opposite the court.

Someone had set up a little row of microphones. Conlon stepped up to it, his eyes shining with anger and delight. He raised his arms above his head. 'I've been in prison for fifteen years for something I did not do,' he said. He seemed to know this was not going to be an isolated event: 'Let's hope the Birmingham Six are freed.'

★ ★ ★

There were some who, for a time, believed the damage to confidence in the English criminal justice would be limited: that the system, by belatedly correcting its own malfunction, had proven it was still essentially sound.

One such person was the great liberal jurist Lord Scarman. 'I have been convinced for a very long time there was a miscarriage of justice,' he said. The appeal would 'restore the faith of the Irish and the world in the British legal system. Now if the Prime Minister goes to Ireland and bangs her fist on the table about the impossibility of getting terrorists extradited from Ireland, she will not be open to the riposte they can't trust the British judicial system. The British legal system is showing it can correct miscarriages of justice when they occur.'[5]

However, even at this early stage, some commentators from outside the legal professions grasped the enormity of what had transpired. Writing in the *Guardian* a few days after the appeal, Hugo Young attacked the judges' 'complacency' in failing to apologise to the Guildford Four – a complacency which had to be remedied 'if the system is to be saved'. 'I do not think that even now, the full measure of Guildford has been taken,' he went on. 'It is nothing less than a catastrophe for the English judicial system . . . Guildford threatens the State because the State, through Parliament, is the inventor, repository and custodian of law. Law-and-order means law as well as order, reliable justice as well as a multiplied police force."[6]

In the Court of Appeal, the release of the Guildford Four brought about an immediate intellectual transformation. Judges who for years had solemnly expressed their reluctance to disturb the verdicts of juries suddenly *had* to recognise that police evidence might not always be true. The information on which trial juries had made their decisions was suddenly suspect. The most politicised cases, where previously the defence had laboured against almost impossible odds, were suddenly being thrown wide open. The court had started to realise that the political nature of these cases had placed immense pressure on the police at the time they made their inquiries, and had thus intensified the risk of wrongful convictions.

Like moles too long underground, the Birmingham Six came blinking into the daylight outside the Old Bailey at the start of 1991. Later that year, Winston Silcott, Engin Raghip and Mark Braithwaite won their appeals against their convictions for murdering PC Keith Blakelock during the 1985 Tottenham riots. In both cases, the recently-developed 'Esda' (electrostatic document analysis) test had destroyed the authenticity of confessions by suggesting the police records had not been made contemporaneously, as had always been claimed in court. With the Blakelock appeal, Lord Justice Farquharson set an important precedent, abandoning the old 'one bite of the cherry' principle, which said that evidence or legal submissions which could have been made in the original trial could not be considered on appeal. Unlike Lord Lane in Guildford, he also apologised to the defendants.[7]

The following year saw the release of Judith Ward, jailed for the 1974 M62 coach bomb, and the appeal of the tragic Stefan Kiszko, who had confessed sixteen years earlier to the sexual murder of a child. In both cases, the defendants were prevented from seeing vital evidence attesting to their innocence. The Maguire Seven, convicted of handling explosives just after the Guildford Four trial on the basis of nitroglycerine tests on their hands, also won an appeal. The court heard they could have been the victims of innocent contamination.

Numerous other convictions were quashed. Among the more significant was a series of fourteen appeals brought by people convicted of armed robberies on the basis of their confessions to officers from the West Midlands Serious Crime Squad. Most of these appeals were heard by Lord Lane, who now turned the contempt he had once reserved for investigative journalists to policemen who fabricated evidence.

Old, unjust ways of working were being discredited forever. In 1989, after the release of the Guildford Four, Home Secretary Douglas Hurd had established a judicial inquiry into the case under Sir John May. The Birmingham Six appeal provoked Hurd's successor, Kenneth Baker, to set up a full-blown Royal Commission on Criminal Justice. The Conservatives who won power in 1979 had until then eschewed Royal Commissions: attempts at objective inquiry by committees of the great and good did not suit Lady Thatcher's ideological approach to government. The resort to such a body was a marker of the depth of the perceived crisis.

Within newspaper and broadcasting organisations, the effects were also marked. For years, reporters interested in police malpractice and miscarriages of justice had to battle with the scepticism of media executives. In 1986, the BBC came close to killing off *Rough Justice*, its occasional programme which investigated wrongful convictions, because of criticism from Lord Lane. After Guildford, miscarriages of justice were suddenly hot property. Documentaries which once might not have been commissioned, and stories which would have had to fight for an obscure position on a quiet Monday, were getting prime-time slots and prominent displays on the front page.

The Guildford appeal and those which followed exposed failings in many organisations: the police, the forensic science service, the Bar and the judiciary. Yet as time went on, public blame for the crisis focused more and more on the police. Complaints against the service and cases where plaintiffs won civil damages against it were widely publicised. The huge investigation into the West Midlands Serious Crime Squad, supervised by the Police Complaints Authority, was a particular running sore.

In 1990, Lady Thatcher set the hares running with a proposal leaked to political journalists for a radical police reform – the establishment of an 'officer class'. The idea was that a service whose leaders rose from the ranks was incapable of restraining its own deviant behaviour: it needed a new breed, untarnished by policing's corrupt internal culture, to rein it in.

The proposal provoked a leading article in the *Independent* which represented a kind of nadir for the police. 'The institutional rot within the Metropolitan Police and other urban forces has developed over several decades,' it said. 'Although police are well paid and accelerated promotion is offered, it has proved impossible to recruit an officer class comparable in quality to that found in the armed forces. Able people with a choice of career opportunities look elsewhere for fulfilment.'

The article continued:

> As a result, the police have become an increasingly inward-looking group, insensitive to criticism, and too often aggressive and uncontrolled when dealing with trade unionists, members of ethnic minorities, young people or others of whom they do not approve. Again and again officers are found guilty of 'fitting up' those they believe to be criminals. Juries no longer accept automatically the word of a policeman or evidence from his notebook. Most members of the public have some story of casual offensiveness on the part of a police officer. When fish start to rot, they rot from the head.[8]

Criticism at this level of vehemence was nothing new from the Left. But the *Independent* of 1990 stood at the peak of its influence to date: it not only sold more than 400,000 copies a day, it was widely talked about as the 'new thunderer', as a newspaper which had replaced *The Times* as the authoritative voice of the Establishment. Nothing could have hurt more.

The Court of Appeal also played its part in limiting blame for the crisis to the police. In the Blakelock murder case, for example, the principal ground for quashing Winston Silcott's murder conviction was evidence that his police interview was fabricated. Nevertheless, the trial process was also at fault. The jurors heard a mass of highly prejudicial allegations against Silcott, including the claim he planned to parade PC Blakelock's head on a pole, which had been made by Jason Hill, a thirteen-year-old boy accused of the murder.

They knew the judge had ordered them to acquit Hill. But they were not in court to hear the judge dismiss Hill's account as 'fantasy', the result of days of oppressive and illegal treatment. (He had been held incommunicado for three days wearing only his underpants and a blanket, stained with his own vomit.) Hill's story must have weighed heavily on their minds. However, while Lord Justice Farquharson's appeal judgment concluded with understandable criticism of the police, this was coupled with exoneration of the rest of the criminal process: 'No system of trials is proof against perjury, but this will be of little comfort to its victims.'[9]

It has been fascinating to observe the changing reactions of senior police officers faced with this onslaught. At first, some made an unconvincing attempt to hold the line. Soon, however, they began to respond with qualified candour. Most were prepared to accept that officers had behaved badly in the past, but such methods were no longer tolerated. As time went on, they began to shift the blame to other parts of the system. From here, it was but a short step to the launch of a new offensive, based on the proposition that unwarranted legal restrictions were now causing justice to miscarry in a different way – by the wrongful acquittal of the guilty.

An example of the first kind of reaction came in September 1990, when Frank Wilkinson, the West Midlands Assistant Chief Constable, told a conference organised by the Association of Chief Police Officers that he was sure the Birmingham Six would soon be freed, because of the improper way they had been interrogated. I was present and recorded this entirely accurate prediction, together with his comment that this was one of several 'major disasters' and there was 'no point in being coy about it'.

My article in the *Observer* drew a furious reaction from Wilkinson's Chief Constable, Ron Hadfield. Obviously under severe pressure, Wilkinson first claimed he had been misquoted; then, when the typescript of his speech demonstrated the accuracy of the report, he insisted on withdrawing it from the volume of papers published after the conference.[10] Later, long after the release of the Birmingham Six, when Hadfield announced that no one would be prosecuted as a result of a fresh investigation into the bombings, he also made the double-edged comment that the six were 'innocent as far as the courts of the land are concerned'. Questioned by reporters, he refused to be drawn further as to exactly what he meant.[11]

A few days after the Tottenham Appeal in 1991, John Smith, the Deputy Commissioner of the Metropolitan Police, adopted a more enlightened approach. He accepted that the Birmingham Six case was a serious blow to the service, and had disastrous effects. But he insisted that the inquiry would nowadays be done in a different fashion, with a 'minimal reliance on confession evidence'.

The following year, in September 1992, Sir John Woodcock, the Chief Inspector of Constabulary, went several stages further. In an early public statement of an analysis which has since come to dominate police arguments about criminal justice, he admitted that the artificial 'improvement' of evidence had been widespread. However it derived from the workings of the rest of the criminal justice system, he insisted, which had for decades connived in the practice. He coined a memorable phrase, 'noble cause corruption'; the idea held by some officers, that it was permissible for police to fabricate evidence or commit perjury in order to convict 'factually guilty' suspects who would otherwise be acquitted.

For example, before the compulsory introduction of contemporaneous note-taking in 1986, police officers had to tell the courts they had performed what Woodcock described as 'the amazing feat of memory', in recording complete conversations with a suspect verbatim, hours or days after the event. If interrogations were carried out with two officers present, both would routinely claim to have produced the same identical record – while maintaining they had not collaborated. Woodcock said that the toleration of such evidence by the courts had allowed officers to believe this was 'only part of the game', essential to shore up the judicial system's eccentricities.

'The result is malpractice,' Sir John went on, 'not out of malice or desire for personal gain, but which begins out of good intentions. Once an officer has lied in one case and got away with it, then he or she feels less compunction another time.'

The rules of evidence and other restrictions created further difficulties. Sometimes, an officer might resist the temptation to cut corners or exaggerate. But if he then saw an acquittal on purely technical grounds, it became only too easy to form the view that 'pettifogging procedures are preventing that offender from being locked away' – and steps should be taken to stop that happening.[12]

In March 1993, the new Metropolitan Commissioner, Paul Condon, gave evidence to the Commons Select Committee on home affairs, and as Woodcock had done, warned of the dangers of noble cause corruption. He insisted the service had 'moved on': police no longer relied upon confessions, and were not allowed to write up notes together after arrests.[13]

Ten days later, in a BBC *Panorama* documentary, Condon and other top officers admitted that noble cause corruption had been rife. According to the Commissioner, 'quite often the truth was the casualty' in the process of convicting criminals. 'I think there was a time when a minority of officers were prepared to bend the rules. I think they were prepared to massage the evidence . . . elaborating on things that were said in a way to make sure that the case had the strongest chance of going through to a conviction.'[14]

Keith Hellawell, the West Yorkshire Chief, admitted suspects used to be 'physically frightened' of being in a CID office. He had personally never used violence, but had exploited its potential threat: 'I was a very big officer, I was over eighteen stone in weight. All detectives in those days were big guys. I would take my coat off, the criminal would perceive that this act was going to be followed up by a thumping or a fist or something, and therefore that put that person ill at ease and certainly more likely to tell me what they wished to tell me.'

Echoing Woodcock the previous year, Charles Pollard, the Thames Valley Chief Constable, claimed: 'Everyone knew it happened like that, judges, magistrates, the whole criminal justice system had a sort of conspiracy . . . If you didn't do it that way, you couldn't actually convict guilty people and that needed to be done.' He was emphatic that these methods had vanished. Yet their demise had caused the conviction rate to fall, he added: new ways of working were 'ultimately less effective, but more honest'.

The themes outlined above continue to influence what passes for debate on criminal justice. On the one hand there is the view that the rest of the system caused or at least encouraged police malpractice; that it is now much more rare; and as Condon told the Select Committee in 1993, judges and juries have not appreciated that the police have changed. From this stems an argument now being made by police officers with ever-increasing vehemence, that unnecessary legal restraints designed to prevent unfair convictions have now loaded the system in favour of the suspect. It therefore needs radical change to 'restore the balance'.

In the spring of 1995, Pollard was at the forefront of a concerted push by chief constables to expound this argument. The BBC commissioned him to present a one hour documentary, in which he argued criminal justice had become a 'game' manipulated by defence lawyers. 'I have lost my faith in Britain's justice system,' he said. 'Trials are not concerned to search out the truth.' He claimed that dangerous criminals were regularly walking free, and called for sweeping changes to trial procedures and the rules of evidence.[15]

Sir Paul Condon suggested in an interview with the *Guardian* that without reform, corruption might make a come-back: 'If there isn't confidence in the system, then it is harder for people like me to hold the line on ethical standards, because street cops see what's happening to victims, they see villains escape time and time again from court hearings, and that's when you risk noble cause corruption.'[16]

Meanwhile, out in the political wilderness, disregarded both by Tory Home Secretaries and Tony Blair's New Labour, is the classic civil liberties, Left-Liberal position. Here legal constraints on policing are seen as the necessary remedy for, not the source of, 'noble cause corruption'. If the police cannot get convictions without resorting to false confessions or other fabricated evidence, that is down to their investigative incompetence, not the rules of legal process.

As he set out Labour's newly-developed credentials as the party of law and order in 1992–4, the then Shadow Home Secretary, Tony Blair, came up with a much-repeated soundbite: Labour, he promised, would be 'tough on crime, tough on the causes of crime'. As a means of consolidating an impressive opinion poll lead, this slogan proved highly effective. It did not, however, herald an attempt to locate the febrile national political discourse about criminal justice in a broader context. It did not invite discussion of the principles and working methods which characterise the present system. Nor did it mark the start of a debate about what purpose criminal justice – a burgeoning industry absorbing perhaps half a million people and £20 billion a year – might actually serve; let alone what its present weakness might tell us about the condition of British society.

Among historians of the eighteenth and nineteenth centuries, it has become commonplace to argue that criminal law and its practical operation reveals underlying aspects of the social structure. *Whigs and Hunters*, E.P. Thompson's classic study of the draconian anti-poaching 'Black Act', describes how the landed classes used the Act to enforce social control in the countryside during a period of immense dislocation and upheaval.[17] Other writers have examined the political function of the death penalty. To state that in early industrial England, crime and punishment reflected deeper conflicts, has long been a historical cliché.

For Thompson, the most humanist of Marxist historians, the fact that there was a close and causal relationship between law and order and the wider organisation of society was in no sense an excuse for describing law as a mere expression of the ruling class's interests. Indeed, the final chapter of *Whigs and Hunters* contains an impassioned polemic against this type of analysis. In and after the tumultuous struggles of the seventeenth century, the English legal system erected an ideology of fairness and equality before the law. However harshly events such as the passage of the Black Act might conflict with these principles, Thompson believed that the fact they actually existed at all meant that it was possible to achieve progressive change. The legal system could and did become the site for hard-fought battles, whose outcomes sometimes saw theory and practice brought more closely into line.

The evolution of criminal justice over the last 200 years has been a complicated process. It is as useless to reduce law to economic processes as it is to rely solely on the seamless tradition of case law, Acts and legal tests.

For all that, in the closing years of the twentieth century, the details of what the law in the books actually says and its day-to-day application on the streets and in court still matter. However, at the same time, the bigger social picture seems to have receded entirely from view.

From time to time, usually on the publication of criminal statistics, some discussion on the reasons why people offend is still to be heard, usually from the standpoint of two well-worn positions. In simple terms, the Right considers crime to be what 'bad people' do; the Left holds that it is what otherwise good, well-meaning people are forced to do by economic circumstance and Governmental neglect. Only one thing is certain: nobody really knows the answer, and in its attempt to examine the question in Chapter Three, this book offers only the most tentative suggestions.

Yet there are other far-reaching questions which remain unasked. Criminal justice is state power in its rawest form, and on several levels, it is falling apart. Innocent people have served long gaol sentences, and some – too many – are still serving them. At the same time, it has become extremely difficult, if not impossible, to convict certain classes of very serious criminal. Kenneth Baker's Royal Commission on Criminal Justice was an opportunity to return to first principles, and to ask whether our 'adversarial' method of justice was up to the demands placed upon it.

Criminal justice is where deep-seated social pathologies present their symptoms, and its stylised, formulaic dramas reflect the more vivid realities of the streets. The signs of social stress are there in the police stations, courts and prisons when the media and politicians are looking the other way. The criminal justice system is the first and usually the only means of containing racism, sexual violence, and organised crime.

The Royal Commission report in 1993 ducked the challenge. What was needed was a holistic investigation which considered both the context of criminal justice and the interrelationships between its constituent agencies. Instead, the Commission preferred to produce an almost endless list of recommendations for administrative, piecemeal changes, many of which have been ignored.

Meanwhile, if E.P. Thompson could discern the operation of underlying principles of equality and fairness in the 1780s, the governing rules of criminal justice in the 1990s seem much weaker. One reason for the disappointing Royal Commission report was the absence of any theoretical consensus. In the eighteenth century, the arguments about law and society which accompanied the Civil War, the Protectorate and the Glorious Revolution were fresher in people's memories. Two hundred years later, the Charter 88 movement seemed, for a time, to have seized a historic moment, with its ambitious programme for replacing Britain's unwritten constitution with a Bill of Rights, a fair voting system and new mechanisms for ensuring the accountability of state institutions. But at the time of writing, that moment seems to have passed, with New Labour's commitment to rigorous constitutional reform apparently weakening with each passing month.

Behind Charter 88's exponential success in the first years after its foundation was a largely unarticulated collective desire to find ways of ensuring that the centralised, autocratic government of Margaret Thatcher must never be repeated. In the field of criminal justice, the enactment of its programme would have established standards which could not be breached. For example, the simplest way of establishing a Bill of Rights would be to 'incorporate' the European Convention on Human Rights – drafted by English lawyers and signed by the United Kingdom in 1951 – into domestic law, allowing domestic courts to apply its principles and, in certain circumstances, modify or strike down legislation. The Convention's protection of the right against self-incrimination alone would have nullified one of the key clauses of the 1994 Criminal Justice and Public Order Act – the effective abolition of the right to remain silent under questioning by police.

Yet unreformed our policy remains. The period after the appointment of the right-wing Conservative Home Secretary, Michael Howard, in 1993 saw the astonishingly rapid construction of a new authoritarianism governing the police, the courts and prisons. Amid a flood of tough-guy rhetoric, whole institutions – notably the old police authorities – were dismantled. Meanwhile, most of the real problems were not even addressed, and some of the most promising areas of good practice were ruthlessly starved or quashed.

★   ★   ★

The regime which produced the Guildford fiasco was already, by 1989, in a state of decay. Great changes in police practice were underway. The fierce debates now conducted on every front page had been going on in more limited circles for some time.

Nevertheless, there was a kind of historic logic behind Guildford's galvanising effect. Leaving aside, for the moment, the question of malpractice, the basic police method used in the Guildford bombs inquiry was absolutely typical of its time.

A retired Surrey detective who played an important part in the Guildford investigation – an officer whose conduct has not been called into question – made the point succinctly. 'I was taught in my training that a confession was about the strongest kind of evidence you could get from anyone,' he said. 'Getting a "cough" was vital to many investigations.'

However they may have gone about it, once the Surrey detectives had been fed the name of Paul Hill by intelligence sources in Ulster, they had one sole aim in mind: to make him talk, to confess to his own alleged role in the bombings, and to say who else was involved.

This had been the unquestioned mindset of the CID for decades. 'In some cases you didn't need an admission,' the Surrey detective went on, 'because there was fingerprint evidence, or surveillance. But in many cases, without an admission, you wouldn't have anything. You would obviously work much harder at the interview. There were occasions when you didn't get anywhere. But sometimes you did.'

Challenging police evidence of a confession was the staple of many trials. However, 'juries then were much more willing to believe police evidence than they are now'. As for the contemporaneous notes of Patrick Armstrong's interview which were to cause so many difficulties, the puzzling thing was that any such notes had been taken at all. The detective said: 'The word contemporaneous didn't figure in the sixties and seventies, at least in the provinces. If you'd have used it, most police officers would have had to look it up in a dictionary. You conducted your interview and then you got them to make a statement.'

Academic research from the period supports his argument. In 1980, John Baldwin and Michael McConville made a detailed analysis of nearly 1,500 Crown Court cases in Birmingham and London. They found about a third of all defendants made written statements amounting to a full admission, and 'only about a quarter of defendants reached the court without damaging statements of some kind having been recorded against them'. Nearly all the important admissions arose through formal interrogation at the police station. Only 12 per cent of all defendants had exercised their right to silence.

In 95 per cent of the cases, forensic science evidence was unavailable or unimportant. Contrary to what might have been expected, recidivists, who already had experience of police officers and prosecution, were more likely to confess than people without previous convictions. Even those deemed 'professional criminals' confessed at the same rate as other defendants.

In about half the cases, the confession was not essential to securing a conviction: there was other good evidence which meant admissions had 'no real bearing' on the outcome. However, in about a fifth of all cases, the prosecution would have been so weak without the confession that there would be no case to answer. Charges could not have been brought at all.

This represented only the extreme end of the spectrum. Without confessions, there would be still more cases in which a conviction would have been unlikely, even if there was a bare prima-facie case to answer. Baldwin and McConville made the conservative estimate that a further 5 per cent of convictions would not have been secured. In total, the number of convictions would have fallen by more than a quarter, across the whole spectrum of offences, if defendants had not made admissions.

Baldwin and McConville concluded their study by expressing deep misgivings about a system which relied on defendants' admissions to such an extent. At this time, there was virtually no control over the conditions in which interrogation was carried out. The 'Judges' Rules',[18] which in theory restricted the time suspects could be held, prohibited threats or violence and allowed suspects to have a solicitor present when they were questioned, did not have the force of statute law. There was a mass of evidence, going back many years, much it from the testimony of police officers, that the rules were frequently ignored.

They were disturbed that confession evidence had acquired 'an unchallengeable character which may not be justified on the facts. The secrecy that surrounds police interrogation readily creates a suspicion that the Judges' Rules are not merely being broken, but that interrogations themselves may be unfair and coercive.' Here they quoted the report of the Royal Commission on Police Powers, published as far back as 1929: 'We have received a volume of responsible evidence which it is impossible to ignore suggesting that a number of the voluntary statements now tendered in court are not "voluntary" in the strict sense of the word.'

In 1980 as in 1929, the innocent were not being protected. According to Baldwin and McConville: 'It is not sufficient to leave the matter to chance or to put absolute trust in the integrity of those involved. It is a dangerous delusion to imagine that the problem is solved by erecting sophisticated structures at the trial itself to assess the accuracy of what is in essence unverifiable.'[19]

Despite its pitfalls, the rigorous interrogation which characterised criminal investigation under the old regime was capable of producing valuable results: safe convictions in cases which aroused great public concern. Judge Bruce Laughland QC, who now sits at the Old Bailey, recalled a case he prosecuted as a barrister in the late 1970s – the murder of a prostitute whose body was found on the moors near Chesterfield. 'The police had no idea who was responsible,' he said. 'They interviewed half the town – bus drivers, publicans, anyone who might have had some connection to the victim. They took more than 10,000 statements. There was one chap whose name kept cropping up, so they pulled him in and questioned him for four days. Finally he admitted he had been on the moors with the girl and killed her. That evidence would never be admissible today. His detention would be considered oppressive. Yet I do think that in the end, his confession was true. It could not happen now: then it was commonplace. We thought nothing of it.'[20]

As Baldwin and McConville remarked, police stations were secret places, from which lawyers, to say nothing of journalists, were normally kept out. A study in 1983 by J. Walkley, based on interviews with a hundred detectives from twenty-five constabularies, suggested a variety of coercive practices was in regular use.[21] He found a 'significant minority' prepared to admit to having assaulted a suspect, while two-thirds had used 'mental pressure' or 'domineering behaviour' to make a suspect tell the truth. However, one third said they 'totally eschewed' this approach.

As for the supposed protection afforded by the Judges' Rules, his research vividly demonstrated just how weak that was. Every officer he interviewed said it was impossible to interrogate 'difficult suspects' successfully without breaking them. Only 7 per cent of Walkley's sample said they would go so far as giving a suspect 'a good hiding'. But he found 43 per cent agreed with the statement 'it is sometimes helpful to slap a suspect across the face' and 40 per cent that 'with some suspects, the only way of getting their respect is by using some form of physical force'. More than half, 60 per cent, agreed that 'I do, on occasions, hint to a suspect that I have the power to physically hurt him'.

Walkley said a good interrogator was like a salesman: he had to be able to read 'buy signs' in the guilty suspect who was ready to confess. But the subjective nature of this judgment implied great risks. If an officer wrongly decided that a suspect who was truthfully denying an offence was lying, then 'he may subject this innocent person to questioning of a type which may result in false confessions'. This type of false confession, though made under pressure, would nonetheless have been uttered by the suspect. In 1972, the historic Confait case thrust this problem to the forefront of public debate.

Maxwell Confait, a homosexual prostitute, was murdered, then incinerated in an arson attack at his home in London in 1972. Two boys, Ronald Leighton, then aged fifteen, and Colin Lattimore, eighteen, were charged both with his murder and arson, and a third, Ahmet Salih, aged fourteen, with the arson alone. Eventually all three were convicted of arson, Leighton of murder and Lattimore of manslaughter. All had low mental ages, verging on mental handicap, and the case against them rested on their confessions to police. In 1975, the Court of Appeal quashed the convictions after hearing new evidence, which suggested that Confait had died hours before the fire. The confessions claimed he was murdered only minutes before the blaze. Their content was thus exposed as totally unreliable.

After the appeal, the Labour Government set up a judicial inquiry under Sir Henry Fisher. In his evidence to Fisher, one of the defence counsel, Louis Blom-Cooper, set out precisely what was at issue. This was not a case where there had been a 'deliberately wicked concoction of a written record which was a travesty of what the youths said'. The problem here was one of psychology: the risk of false self-incrimination, especially by vulnerable suspects.

In 1978, the Government followed Fisher by setting up the Royal Commission on Criminal Procedure. By now, however, another issue was beginning to come to the fore: claims of outright *fabrication* of confessions by police.

Long before the Guildford Four, 'verbals', allegations that the police had made up records of self-incriminating statements, were the leitmotif of many criminal trials. In the absence of any requirement to write down interviews contemporaneously, the scope for producing such material was unlimited.

Defence lawyers seasoned in this period came to see verbals as a routine part of police work. In the 1960s and 70s, the Tory MP, Ivan Lawrence, QC, now the Chairman of the Commons home affairs select committee, defended in many important criminal trials. He said: 'The police made things up in a very large proportion of cases. I defended villains, heavy villains, including the Krays. And they were always being verballed, sometimes planted. Police officers were always lying. You would get notebooks which had been refitted with different pages inserted; you knew because the staples had been put in the wrong way round.' The Guildford and Birmingham cases were, he suggested, not exceptional but symptomatic: 'If you want a flavour of that time, look at the terrorist cases.'[22]

Some who served in the police at this time accept the truth of Lawrence's analysis. A former sergeant, now a defence solicitor, told me how 'noble cause corruption' worked at the sharp end. He said:

> I was an exceptionally good thief-taker. I was a shit nasty copper. I was fortunate enough to have joined the service when there were still a lot of ex-servicemen: they were disciplined professionals. They wouldn't take shit from anyone, and they knew right from wrong.
>
> I took the view that if someone had done something, then he should be brought to court and punished. I knew he would stand up and tell lies to get himself acquitted. I was taught from a very early stage that if I arrested someone for something, to do whatever was necessary to make sure the evidence was there,

otherwise they were going to walk free and it would be two fingers up at the door of the court and 'fuck off'.

The method was simple: 'Verbals, what else could you do? Written confessions, sign here, sign here. There's an art to statement-taking. You leave out the "wells", the "maybe's", the "perhaps". We justified that to ourselves as a moral service to the community.'

For experienced criminals, challenging verbals was extremely difficult. If they impugned the character of the officers giving evidence against them, the judge was almost certain to allow the jury to be told of their previous convictions. As one retired armed robber with more than twenty years in prison behind him put it, 'verbals were a godsend for the police. If you denied them, you ended up being retried for things that were over and done with.'

It is easy to find anecdotal evidence of the extent of such practices. Quantifying it in numerical terms is more difficult: in some cases involving verbals, defendants would accept the improbability of acquittal and plead guilty, in the hope of getting a lower sentence. However, there is significant evidence in Baldwin and McConville's 1980 survey of 1,500 trials. Analysis of its data reveals that large numbers of people whom the police alleged had confessed later tried to retract or deny their admissions. More than half of those who pleaded not guilty in Crown Courts began from the considerable disadvantage of having to retract a confession.

The crucial fact disclosed by the study was that in Birmingham, no fewer than 26 per cent of people who pleaded not guilty were supposed to have made complete or partial 'verbal admissions' – whose authenticity depended entirely on the word of the police. In distinct contrast to those who made or signed written statements after being interviewed, they had refused to sign the detectives' record of what they were supposed to have said. Often these 'verbatim' admissions were written down as lengthy dialogues, although the police would frequently accept they had not recorded them until long after the event. In London, even more defendants faced totally uncorroborated evidence of this kind: a staggering 44 per cent of all people pleading not guilty.[23]

Of course, not all these defendants would have been telling the truth. Some would have made exactly the comments attributed to them, and would have been trying to take advantage of the haphazard recording methods. Nevertheless, these figures demonstrate that claims of verballing were a dominant issue in Crown Court trials. Baldwin and McConville published some samples of these unsigned admissions. Reading them today, it is difficult to resist the conclusion that defendants' allegations must have all too often been justified. Typical examples include: 'Has Mickey grassed?' and 'So it's nicked, but I'm saying I found it. I've got too much too lose.'

These alleged verbals often appeared to be following a regular formula. Disputed statements would consist of remarks in which instead of issuing a denial, suspects supposedly told the police they could not prove the offence, or that the witnesses would never go to court to give evidence. Examples include: 'I've been expecting you, I'm saying nothing, you go ahead and charge me, you'll never prove it.' 'You can't prove anything. I shall say I couldn't have stolen it because I was never in the room on my own and you try to prove different. The old lady will never go to court anyway,' and 'What if I did nick it, you don't expect me to admit it, do you? You must think I'm stupid. I know the score. You prove it was me.'

Years later, scientific testing destroyed the credibility of admissions made by suspects to the West Midlands Serious Crime Squad. Many of them took this form. Another well-known example was Winston Silcott of the Tottenham Three. In his police interview, later thrown out by the Court of Appeal, he was supposed to have said: 'You ain't got enough evidence. Those kids will never go to court. You wait and see. No one else will talk to you. You can't keep me away from them . . . just take me down and charge me. I ain't saying no more.'

Verbals were the dark heart of the old regime in English criminal justice. Time and again, in the absence of other evidence, police extracted admissions through violence or threats, or made them up altogether. Defence lawyers could protest their clients' innocence until they were blue in the face, but faced with such evidence, their chances were poor. Baldwin and McConville found that only a third of those who pleaded not guilty after making unsigned verbal confessions were eventually acquitted in court. More than 90 per cent either pleaded guilty or were convicted by juries. Prosecutions based on signed confession statements were even more effective: in Birmingham, only 2.4 per cent were acquitted, and in London, 5.2 per cent.

It would be comforting to think that with the quashing of the Guildford convictions all the old miscarriages of justice which arose from this system have been dealt with, and that there are no more prisoners still serving life sentences on the basis of suspect confession evidence. Unfortunately, this is not the case.

★ ★ ★

The 'Torso Murders' case of 1977 exhibits many features of the old regime at its worst: not only unsigned, disputed admissions, but a supergrass who later admitted he lied, and the bizarre arrest and bail conditions applied to a defence witness, which prevented him giving evidence at the trial. As with the Guildford Four, when the Torso Murderers brought an appeal on the basis of new evidence which demolished important parts of the prosecution case, the Court of Appeal judges brushed it aside. In first the Torso and then the Guildford appeals, the court was led by Lord Justice Roskill.

After a trial lasting seven months – the longest murder trial in the Old Bailey's history – Reg Dudley and Bob Maynard were convicted of killing Billy Moseley and Micky Cornwall, and sentenced to life imprisonment. Their trial judge, Mr Justice Swanwick, called them 'brutal and cold-blooded', and recommended they should not be released for at least fifteen years. At the time of writing in 1995, both men have been in gaol since their arrest in 1976. They have no prospect of early release, although their behaviour in prison has always been exemplary. However, the Home Office considers that the protestations of innocence which they have made continuously since their arrest shows that they have not 'addressed their offending behaviour', and might therefore be a danger to the public if released. Aside from the implicit emotional blackmail this entails, the idea that they are dangerous desperadoes is a ridiculous notion. In 1995, Dudley, who suffers from sciatica, was seventy. Maynard, who had no previous convictions for violence, was fifty-six.

Both the convicted men and their alleged victims were professional criminals. Reg Dudley and Bob Maynard worked together as jewellery 'fences' in the big league, capable of moving stolen items worth thousands of pounds. Moseley, by contrast, was a petty thief. At the time of his death, he had just been released from an eighteen month sentence for organising a ring of female shoplifters. Cornwall was an armed robber.

Billy Moseley disappeared on 26 September 1974. He had been having an affair with Frankie Fright, the wife of a fellow north London criminal, Ronnie Fright, while Ronnie had been in prison. Moseley had agreed to meet Ronnie at a pub in Dalston. Within a fortnight, grisly segments of a dismembered body began washing up on the shore of the Thames between Rainham and Silvertown. There was no head. Eventually the remains were identified as Moseley's, by comparing their bone structure with X-rays taken before his death.

Nearly a year later, on 7 September 1975, the body of Moseley's friend Micky Cornwall was found in a shallow grave in Chalkdell Wood, near Hatfield, Hertfordshire. He had been shot through the head. The body was so badly decomposed that the police could only estimate the length of time it had been there.

The officer who led the inquiry was a significant figure in the history of policing: Commander Albert Wickstead of the Metropolitan Police. In the mid-1970s, the Scotland Yard Commissioner, Sir Robert Mark, was trying to cleanse the filthy stables of the London CID. He had made it his mission to root out bribery and financial corruption, hitherto endemic among plain-clothes officers. He set up a special internal investigation unit, A10, and during the five years of his leadership, nearly 500 detectives were sacked or forced to resign. A handful were prosecuted.

While this operation was in progress, someone still had to investigate serious crime. Experienced detectives untouched by allegations of graft were at a premium. Wickstead was among the most prominent, and he became the leader of an élite unit based at Loughton, Essex. He had the reputation of driving his teams relentlessly: he wanted results. Wickstead brought several well known 'firms' of armed robbers to justice, and his work in several cases had a distinguishing characteristic. When he interviewed

suspects their alleged comments would be recorded contemporaneously, in large, red notebooks, which Wickstead claimed were
'tamperproof'.

Jonathan Goldberg QC, who repeatedly found himself defending
clients accused by Wickstead, later recalled how Wickstead would
hold his suspects incommunicado, denying them contact with
solicitors or family until all interrogations were complete:

> Remarkably, there ensued unsigned verbal confessions by most if
> not all the defendants in all those famous cases. Invariably the
> defendants would decline to sign when offered the red book at the
> end, citing some reason as 'my brief would kill me' or 'I have said
> too much already, Mr Wickstead'. Not infrequently, a defendant
> would pay him the accolade in the red book of telling him what a
> fair man he was.[24]

Wickstead had known Reg Dudley for years. In 1955, as a
detective sergeant, he tried to persuade Dudley to become a police
informant. 'I told him to fuck off,' Dudley says, 'and he proceeded to
tell me what a bad person my wife was, who she'd been with while I
had been in prison.'[25] Ten years later, as a detective inspector based at
Stoke Newington, he tried again. 'This time it was my daughter he
was on about, just trying to wind me up, saying she was going out
with all the local villains and if I didn't help him, she'd be charged. I
gave him the same response.'

These ancient contretemps do not seem adequate explanations for
Wickstead's continuing interest in Reg Dudley. There was,
however, a further side to Dudley's activity which would, in the
mid-70s context, have made him a valuable prize. In addition to his
stolen jewellery business, he was known widely to criminals as a 'go-
between,' who could, for a suitable commission, arrange for corrupt
police officers to be bribed. 'I had one great contact,' Dudley recalls,
'who always knew someone, police colleagues in different areas,
who could have something done – for the right price. We had been
friends since the fifties. I was not his only outlet. He was making a
fortune.'

That contact was Alec Eist, who was later charged as part of
Mark's anti-corruption drive, although acquitted. Dudley says:

People knew I had this relationship with Eist. If they or their friends had been arrested, they'd come and see me. He could do everything from bail, to the withdrawal of important bits of evidence, to a complete 'out' – for enough money. A serious charge was serious money. There were of course taboo areas: robbing a pensioner, rape, murder. You wouldn't want to help anyone get out of that.

Dudley claims that in the decades of his friendship with Eist, he channelled hundreds of thousands of pounds his way. The trade was not always one way: 'If people had been caught, the gear would sometimes go missing: and so it would come to me from Eist – jewellery safe deposit boxes from bank raids. There was one occasion when he handed me some property from a raid and there was a lot of it. I gave him £60,000.'

In any event, the Hertfordshire police established that when Cornwall was released from prison, a few weeks after his friend Moseley's body began to emerge from the river, he became extremely upset, and tried hard to find out who was responsible. This gave them the 'link' between the two murders. A joint Hertfordshire–Metropolitan squad was set up under Wickstead's leadership. In January 1976, eighteen people, all of them friends or relatives of the victims, were arrested. Eventually a total of seven people were charged with a variety of offences, including Dudley and Maynard with the double murder.

The case as a whole was extremely complicated, and it will serve no purpose here to chart its labyrinthine detail. But in the end, as Jonathan Goldberg put it, 'the vast investigation in fact boiled down to a squabble over the verbals. That is the reality.'

The Crown alleged that Dudley and Maynard wanted Moseley dead because he had broken the criminal code by having an affair with Fright's wife, while he was in gaol. Cornwall had got too close to the truth, and so had to be killed as well.

There was no forensic science evidence. There were no witnesses to Moseley's abduction or to either death. But in Wickstead's big red notebooks, both Dudley and Maynard were alleged to have made unsigned admissions on the familiar and established pattern. Asked whether he had played a part in the killings, Maynard was supposed to have said: 'I'm not answering that, otherwise I'm finished.'

Micky Cornwall had had a brief affair with Dudley's daughter Kathy and the police claimed this gave Dudley another motive for wanting him dead. According to the notebook, Dudley said of Cornwall: 'He was a no-good loser . . . Take it from me, it's not on my conscience.' When Wickstead asked him: 'Did you murder Moseley?' the reply attributed to Dudley was: 'Prove it.'

Even by 1970s standards, this was not enough for a conviction. The key prosecution witness became Tony Wild, a serial armed robber, who claimed Dudley had given him a graphic account of the killings while they were both on remand in Brixton prison. In court, Wild claimed Moseley had been shot in the head. As for the mystery of the head's whereabouts, he said Dudley had taken it to Brighton, with bullet wound and all, and shown it to a publican there, Oliver Kenny. Later, he had thrown it into the sea. In his summing-up, Mr Justice Swanwick emphasised that Wild's story was central to the prosecution case: 'Without the evidence of the alleged oral confessions, there would not be evidence on which the Crown could ask you to convict.'

Wild's story about the head stood up for precisely six weeks after the end of the trial in June 1977. Then, a roadsweeper found it defrosting from its deep-frozen state in a public lavatory in Richmond Avenue, Islington. It had no bullet wound. Here was a vital – and it seems from this distance, utterly convincing – ground for appeal. But despite the stress the trial judge had placed on Wild's evidence, when it came to the appeal in 1979, Lord Justice Roskill refused to quash the convictions. While Wild was plainly 'a repellent character', whose evidence did not fit the discovery of the head, the trial judge had given 'ample warning of his character' to the jury. Their decision should therefore stand. Roskill added some petulant comments about the length of the trial, complaining that defence counsel had spent far too long attacking the integrity of admissions recorded by the police.

At the end of 1977, Wild was sentenced to nine years for his part in a series of armed robberies. His co-defendant got twenty years. However, Wild was released less than three years later. During this period of freedom, he was tracked down to a pub in Hove by

Duncan Campbell, then of *City Limits* magazine, now of the *Guardian*, and Graham MacLagan of the BBC. After checking he was not being tape-recorded, Wild told the two reporters he had 'made up' his evidence. He had been working from a 'script', he said. He could get Dudley and Maynard out of prison 'tomorrow', but would not do so, 'even for £50,000'. The journalists made statements about his claim to have fabricated his evidence. But Wild, interviewed again by the police, then retracted his remarks. In June 1995, Wild – now a born-again Christian – spoke again to Duncan Campbell. Once again, he insisted that his evidence against Dudley and Maynard had been untrue.

After the Torso Murder trial, Wild had resumed his trade of armed robbery, and continued to enjoy a charmed life. In 1983, he was convicted of another series of five robberies. On one of them, he fired several shots. However, despite the fact he committed these offences while still on parole, Mr Justice McCowan sentenced him to only ten years: in the circumstances, a remarkably lenient term. The judge said he did not regard Wild as a 'vicious or ruthless man'. He had used his pistol only to frighten people, and had 'no intention of harming anyone'.

There is one remaining puzzle about Wild's role in the case. He had claimed that Dudley showed Moseley's head to the Brighton publican, Oliver Kenny. If this were not true, why could the defence not have simply called Kenny as a witness?

The answer was discovered in 1994 by John Bray, a retired Gatwick airport bus driver who has investigated the case tirelessly since reading an *Observer* article about it in 1992. Kenny, who had no convictions, knew Dudley well: in fact, Dudley lent him £2,000 to help him buy his pub. A few weeks after Dudley's own arrest Kenny was arrested for his alleged part in a £1.5 million jewellery robbery which had taken place eleven years earlier, in 1965. After an unsigned interview conducted by Wickstead in which Kenny allegedly confessed to having received £30,000, sighed wistfully about his 'fine fucking friends' and vouchsafed the titbit that Dudley's nickname was the 'Boston strangler', Wickstead charged Kenny in person.

On 27 October 1976, Kenny was granted bail on sureties of £5,000 – an exceptional outcome for a robbery of this size. The tiny report in that day's *Brighton Evening Argus* recorded the conditions which the police asked the magistrates to attach to his bail. They were surely unprecedented in legal history: 'He must report daily to his local police station, and must not visit Brixton prison or the Central Criminal Court'. In other words, Kenny's bail prohibited him from visiting Dudley on remand, and from going to the Old Bailey where he might have heard or rebutted Wild's lies.[26]

After their convictions, Dudley and Maynard continued to campaign for their release. Maynard and Moseley had been best friends, and their families very close: the Moseleys could not accept Maynard might have been responsible for Billy's death, and supported him with petitions, pickets and appeals to the media. One possible opening was discovered by Dudley. He unearthed the fact that Micky Cornwall had been under surveillance by officers from the now-notorious West Midlands Serious Crime Squad after his release from prison in 1974. He succeeded in obtaining copies of their surveillance records. There were five separate entries purporting to describe his movements in May 1975 – when, according to the Crown in the murder case, Cornwall had been dead for eight months.

However, the most hopeful development came in the late 1980s, when the Court of Appeal accepted the validity of the 'Esda' (electrostatic document analysis) test in assessing the validity of confessions to police. Esda, developed at the London College of Printing, reveals the indentations left on documents when a sheet of paper overlying them is written on. It can therefore reveal whether a notebook, or in a fraud case, a chequebook or ledger, has been compiled in the correct order. When police have claimed a confession was recorded contemporaneously, Esda may be able to explode or verify their integrity. In 1989, as Esda tests were used to question the validity of several West Midlands Serious Crime Squad cases, it received a high media profile. That September, the then West Midlands Chief Constable, Geoffrey Dear, disabled the squad and launched the huge Police Complaints Authority investigation.

Summing up the Dudley-Maynard trial, Mr Justice Swanwick made comments which immediately recall Lord Denning's 'appalling vista' judgment against the Birmingham Six. 'If you think it really may be so that the confessions were fabricated,' he said, 'then it must mean that all those police officers are either very wicked or very weak men, and it would undermine the whole prosecution case.' But there was a clear alternative, which he seemed to prefer: 'The ganging up of prisoners in a series of plots to escape conviction.'

Esda might have sorted the matter out for good. In 1990, solicitors acting for Dudley and Maynard wrote to the Metropolitan Police, asking for the original police manuscript so that it could be tested. To their horror and amazement, they were told that the notes had been destroyed and only the typed-up text remained.[27]

What seemed inexplicable was that although the original interview notes had been shredded, many of the other police case papers had survived, and the destruction of the interview notes did not take place until September 1989 – *after* Dear confirmed Esda's place in history by disbanding the West Midlands Serious Crime Squad. A spokesman from the Metropolitan Police insisted that the notes fell into a different legal category from the rest of the case papers. The surviving documents, unlike the notes, were governed by the 1958 and 1967 Public Records Acts, which meant they did have to be kept for twenty-five years. The notes, on the other hand, were legally no different from police pocketbooks, which could be shredded after six years.

Yet it was admitted that when the outcome of a case was disputed, it was normal to retain interview notes, in case they were needed for an appeal. The destruction was the result of a 'misunderstanding' by a sergeant at the police property store, a huge warehouse in Cricklewood, north London. This individual had been 'under pressure from his superiors to clear space'. He should have checked with senior detectives, but instead only telephoned the Metropolitan Police solicitors' department. They told him that there were no legal proceedings pending. On that basis, he destroyed Dudley and Maynard's interview records. Crates of paperwork remained. But the property store had acquired valuable extra room previously taken up by two red notebooks.

Inadequate as the explanation may be, the destruction of the notes left Dudley and Maynard with few avenues of hope. In 1992, the *Observer* commissioned Dr Andrew Morton to examine the text of the interview notes. He has developed the 'cusum' test, which works on the principle that every individual possesses a unique verbal fingerprint, identifiable by computer analysis. His test can therefore ascertain whether utterances attributed to one individual have in fact been added to with the words of someone else. His work has been accepted as persuasive, although not conclusive, by the Court of Appeal.

Morton's conclusions were unequivocal. In relation to Dudley's admissions, his report stated: 'This is not the utterance of one person, it is the utterance of at least two people.' In relation to Maynard, he said: 'The signs of multiple origin are even more clearly visible.' Their admissions were therefore 'not acceptable' as evidence of their guilt. On that basis, Dudley and Maynard submitted a petition to the Home Secretary, asking him to refer the case back to the Court of Appeal. In January 1994, sixteen months later, Michael Howard turned them down, rejecting not only Morton but all the other areas of doubt raised by the case.

Six months later, they were told in a letter from the Home Office that although the 'tariff' of their sentence had expired, 'life sentence prisoners should not assume that once the minimum period fixed for retribution and deterrence has been served they will necessarily be released'. They had to satisfy the Parole Board and the Home Secretary they were no longer a danger to the public; and even if it could be assumed they were not, the Home Secretary could still block release indefinitely if he considered freeing them might cause a public outcry.

In practice, the power of Home Secretaries over 'lifers' is unlimited: a fundamental blurring of the judicial and executive role. Dudley and Maynard have been told repeatedly that their continued protestation of innocence is damaging their chance of freedom. Every year, on 22 January, the anniversary of his arrest, Maynard has gone to the punishment block of whatever gaol he happened to be in, because on that day he refuses to work. Usually, this has been met with tolerance: 'There have always been screws, and even governors, who believe me. I am bitter but I try not to show it.' In 1995, however, his protest earned him a transfer from an open prison in Derbyshire to Winson Green in Birmingham – one of the worst of Victorian gaols.

We are left with the image of two old men, alone in their cells, who have lost their wives, friendships and prospects for any kind of meaningful life. 'I've always said: if he'd come and fitted us up for a jewellery robbery, I would have accepted it,' Reg Dudley says. 'That was part and parcel of the game we were in. But to come and fit me up for murder and get me a life sentence while the people who did it walk free: that's different. That's final.'

It is not as if they are alone. In five years as a specialist Home Affairs reporter for the *Observer*, I have become almost inured to the pleas of innocence from men in gaol which regularly cross my desk. A few – a very few – soon reveal themselves as counterfeits, attempting to bamboozle the media as an alternative Court of Appeal, when it is rapidly clear on making cursory inquiries that no basis for quashing the conviction in question can be discerned. Sometimes there seems to be no evidence at all to support the claim of innocence and yet one can hardly fail to be struck by the vehemence with which it is made, in the knowledge that for life sentence prisoners, protesting innocence is a sure-fire way to remain in gaol forever. The inmate will be accused of having failed to 'address his offending behaviour', so making it impossible for the authorities to assess his future risk to the public.

However, the cases which really stick in one's mind are those where there appears to be strong and verifiable evidence that the prisoner is telling the truth, or where the original prosecution case was so manifestly inadequate, one wonders how a jury could ever have returned a conviction.

On investigating a case of this kind, one first fights to convince one's newspaper executive that the subject is worthy of space: a battle which, in the late 1990s, is increasingly hard to win, as miscarriages of justice no longer command the mainstream of political debate. At last the story is published: in the life of a prisoner, an event of incalculable significance. And then nothing, for years on end.

The victims of these miscarriages of justice are not famous and they do not have the infrastructure of support, the campaigning members of the establishment, which helped keep the hopes of the Guildford Four and the Birmingham Six alive. Frequently penniless and without entitlement to legal aid, they even lack a solicitor. There is no political pressure to put their cases right, and for these prisoners the wheels of justice turn at a fraction of their normal speed.

Even when the Home Office orders a new police investigation, it may take years, and it is likely to be carried out by the same force behind the original inquiry. The new independent commission set up by the 1995 Criminal Appeals Act does not, at the time of writing, seem likely to make much difference. It will have no independent investigatory squad of its own, while its structure has been conceived to resemble the Police Complaints Authority. This is not an encouraging model.

One case worthy of mention is that of Alf Fox, convicted and sentenced to life in 1980. Fox, from a mining family based near Rotherham, did not confess, and most of the evidence against him was circumstantial. At an early stage in the investigation, the police became convinced that Fox started the fire which killed his estranged wife and mother-in-law, because the killer spared his baby son, putting the cradle outside the back door of the house where the others died.

He had a partial alibi, and as in the case against the Guildford Four's Carole Richardson, the prosecution of Fox was flawed by almost impossibly tight restrictions on time. But there was one damning piece of testimony: the evidence of Myrtle Westhead, who owned a shop overlooking the house where the murders took place. She said she saw a car of the same kind Fox drove speeding to and from the house on the night in question. In 1992, Mike McColgan, Fox's solicitor, was given access to police documents which had not been disclosed at the time of Fox's trial. Fox's lawyers had never seen them before, nor been aware of their existence.

McColgan discovered an early statement by Mrs Westhead in which she said she saw a different car entirely, and then an instruction from a senior officer that detectives pay her a further visit to see if she might change her mind. She did not do so for more than a month.

In 1993, the Court of Appeal quashed the convictions of the sisters Michelle and Lisa Taylor for murdering the wife of Michelle's lover, after hearing that the police had not disclosed a document saying a vital Crown witness initially said he saw one white and one black girl leaving the murder scene. (Both sisters, as the witness eventually told the court, are of course white.) This, the Court held, was a 'material irregularity' which alone was enough to render the convictions unsafe, although there were several further grounds of appeal.

It might seem logical that the Taylor case would induce a sense of urgency in dealing with Fox. Yet, at the time of writing, he has been waiting nearly three years for a response by the Home Office to a petition from McColgan, which includes not only the new evidence about Mrs Westhead but important material adding strength to his alibi. Back in 1986, the BBC *Rough Justice* programme unearthed other, unrelated evidence which also supported his claim of innocence. When Fox petitioned the Home Office, the then Minister of State, John Patten, refused to refer the case back to the Court of Appeal on the basis that there was one witness whose evidence was of overwhelming importance and whose testimony had not been undermined – Myrtle Westhead.

Andy Evans is now in the twenty-fourth year of his sentence for killing a teenage girl. A failed boy soldier awaiting his army medical discharge from a barracks near Tamworth, Evans dreamt he saw the victim of a recent local murder, and walked into the local police station asking if he might see a photograph of her to put his mind at rest. He was already in the throes of a nervous breakdown and after three days in custody, all without the protection of a solicitor, he confessed to killing her. His confession contained important discrepancies with other known facts. While the killer would have been drenched in blood, there was none on Evans's uniforms. Moreover it is clear that today, after the passage of the 1984 Police and Criminal Evidence Act, no court would have admitted his confession at all.

By 1991, Evans – who had spent some years falsely admitting his guilt in order to progress through the system – was near to release. He was an inmate at Leyhill open prison near Gloucester, where he had been allowed to work outside the prison walls for two years. He had been given several home leaves. Then he grew sick of living a lie, and one morning calmly told the Governor he was innocent. By the afternoon of that day he was back in the high security conditions where he remains, with freedom deferred indefinitely.

The police are not the main agency at fault in all miscarriages of justice. Glen McCallion, currently resident at Wellingborough gaol in Northamptonshire, was imprisoned in 1985 for the murder of his girlfriend's three-year-old son. The boy died three days after McCallion spent a Friday evening looking after him while his girlfriend went out: the pathologist found that the boy had died from the effects of a tiny perforation in the bowel, caused by a blow to his stomach. To decide that McCallion hit the boy was a considerable inference by the Newcastle Crown Court jury – McCallion vehemently denied it. Several witnesses told the court of the close relationship between McCallion and the boy. Also, it was impossible to state exactly when the blow was struck. For the jury to infer that he had, as the law of murder requires, *intended* to kill or cause extremely serious harm was an even bigger step to take.

In 1995, following a decision by the House of Lords judges to give life sentence prisoners access to their own case files, McCallion discovered that his trial judge had been surprised by the verdict. In a letter to the then Lord Chief Justice, Lord Lane, the judge said he had expected at most a finding of manslaughter, for which he had planned to award a sentence of seven years. With remission, McCallion might then have expected to be released in 1989 or 1990.

In the early 1990s, McCallion's case was supported by the pressure group Justice, which commissioned an opinion from a retired High Court judge, the late Sir Brian McKenna. In his view, the trial judge had seriously misdirected the jury about the difference between murder and manslaughter – unintentional homicide. The judge had failed to point out that the fact that a blow had been struck with enough force to perforate a child's bowel could not on its own constitute evidence of intent to kill or maim. Assuming McCallion had struck the blow, he might have intended to *hurt* the child, but this did not mean he wished to cause him fatal or disabling injury. According to Sir Brian, the verdict of murder instead of manslaughter was a serious 'miscarriage of justice', brought about because 'the judge's directions on intent were very inadequate, and may well have been the cause of the jury convicting McCallion of murder'. This alone, Sir Brian went on, ought to be sufficient to persuade the Home Secretary to refer the case to the Court of Appeal.

This Kenneth Clarke refused to do, and when McCallion's lawyers challenged his decision in a High Court judicial review, it was Clarke's view which prevailed. But by now, McCallion's trial judge, Mr Justice Taylor, had risen in the profession. He was Lord

Taylor, Lord Chief Justice of England, and quashing a murder conviction on the basis of his judicial mistake was too much for the court to stomach.

★　★　★

The cases described could be taken as typical examples of the old regime at work. Meanwhile, we need to examine the intriguing claim first made by Sir John Woodcock. If 'noble cause corruption' was so common, can it really be true that the other players in the system – solicitors, Bar and judiciary – connived in malpractice? Was there, in fact, a hidden consensus by which this system was sustained?

Commander Michael Briggs, for several years an influential figure in the formation of Metropolitan Police policy, joined the force in 1961. He recalls court appearances in the early years of his service as an almost entirely ritualised game. The place of policing in society was uncontroversial, reflecting the broader post-war social consensus, and the dominant media image remained the avuncular, reassuring figure of Sergeant Jack Warner in Dixon of Dock Green. Factual reporting of crime and policing was typified by stories of dramatic murders, brilliantly solved by hero detectives who 'always got their man'. By contemporary standards, very little crime was being committed.

In the magistrates' courts – then usually known by the revealing term 'police courts' – the conviction rate was well over 90 per cent, and the niceties of evidence gathering barely registered. Briggs says:

> They all knew what was going on, but the legal clan, the middle-class people, they let the police go their merry way. You were expected to say you'd made your notes immediately after an incident; that you'd stood in a shop doorway in the dark, when everyone could see they were beautifully written. I remember a vice case, which had involved five days of surveillance. The magistrate interrupted me as I presented the first witness and said: 'When are we going to get to the bit where the money changed hands?' I timed the case: the whole thing took twenty-three minutes.

On another occasion, the then Sergeant Briggs had been patrolling by car when he arrested four men for public order offences. They pleaded not guilty, contesting his version of events. The magistrate interrupted their evidence, saying: 'I know Sergeant Briggs, and if he found it necessary to do a U-turn on a Friday night, then you must be guilty.'

Once a defendant appealed against a conviction for living on immoral earnings. Briggs says: 'The appeal was heard in the Crown Court before a judge and two lay assessors – one of whom turned out to be the very same magistrate who had heard the case in the lower court. As I got into the witness box he gave me a big wink. The conviction was upheld.'

Such examples, Briggs suggests, typified widely-held attitudes:

It was a paternalistic approach, in which all concerned believed they were acting in the best interests of society. The courts provided reassurance to police officers that they were doing the right thing, in the public interest. I never took a bent penny in my life. But looking back, I used to make sure that gaps in evidence had been filled or bridged. The messages in court were messages of reassurance – that 'you and your colleagues are looking after us all'.[28]

Chief Inspector Euan Read, of the Thames Valley police, joined the force in the latter days of the old regime, in 1978. Highly educated, he typifies a substantial layer of articulate, progressive officers now to be found in many constabularies. But as a young detective, 'my main aim was to get confessions. If I arrested you for burglary, I wanted you to cough not only to the burglary you had been nicked for, but other burglaries. I wanted TICs (offences taken into account) to boost the figures.' Interviews were 'badly planned', often carried out on a speculative basis: there had been virtually no evidence before the arrest. In Reading, where Read served, as elsewhere in the country,

it was standard practice to do a first interview, then go home, leaving the suspect locked up. It was no surprise that by morning, they were usually ready to cough. I never used violence. But verbal aggression was standard.

I think the people who confessed to me were guilty. But never once were the tactics I used to get those confessions seriously called into question. I speak from the perspective of a relatively honest officer. But you just imagine what you could do if you took the view that the people you nicked were 'scum' who 'needed nicking'. There were no contemporaneous notes; notebooks could be compiled days later. You assume any ability to be dishonest and the mind boggles. Documents could be changed and, sure, I saw people who'd been beaten up, threatened, told 'you fucking write this or else'.[29]

Barristers tell the same story from a different angle. According to Sir Ivan Lawrence,

Nobody had this intense preoccupation with civil liberties, human rights justice. When I started, Archbold, the textbook of criminal law, was two or three inches thick. Now, it's in several fat volumes. Villains used to accept the game had been played and lost. Now, many villains don't accept being convicted at all: as soon as the jury is out, they're getting everyone worked up for an appeal. If you look closely enough, you may well find something wrong and the Appeal Court will support you. In the old days, it was a rougher kind of justice.

In Lawrence's view, the wide use of verbals must be partly blamed on the judiciary. 'Police officers knew nothing would happen if they were caught out lying. There were a few judges who might have passed the papers over to the Director of Public Prosecutions, but they were few and far between. It was always shrugged off as just another silly jury. I think the judges thought: "If we don't hold the line, lawlessness is going to grow." So they would give the police the benefit of the doubt.'

Among defence lawyers, there was a kind of weariness, induced by the size of the battle of convincing people what was really happening:

Anyone who practised at the criminal Bar in the sixties and seventies knew what was going on. And they probably felt either powerless to do anything about it, or possibly they thought it was the side of right and justice which was doing it.

I don't think people had such deep concerns at the Bar in those days. You were just a cog in the machinery. You got worked up on behalf of your client in court, and then you just went home.

Criminals tell a similar story. George C., a retired armed robber, recalls:

In 1975, I was put on three ID parades for armed robberies which were unrelated to my actual criminal activity at the time. I wasn't picked out. I thought I was going home, so I sent my solicitor away. I was taken down to the cells; two hours later they drove me across London to another police station. I was charged with robbing Air India. Tapes and bits of packaging from the robbery had been planted in my car boot and in the pocket of my anorak. I was acquitted because I proved I had been planted, but the judge didn't want to know. He thought it was me, so he didn't care. It was the old principle: 'the police have got their man'.

I stood trial three times for offences I hadn't committed. I was convicted once. And when I say I wasn't guilty, I mean I had nothing to do with it. I got three years. I was one unhappy prisoner, I can tell you. Then, years ago, you couldn't call the police liars. Now you can. But the judges knew your background. They knew you had been up to no good and they didn't care if you got fucking framed. We know they knew. We can't prove it. But they knew.

Underlying the hidden consensus was an unspoken principle: a belief in the near-infallibility of police officers when it came to identifying criminals. Middle and upper-class lawyers trusted mainly working-class police officers' innate, almost mystic ability to get the right, usually working-class, man in the frame. Knowing what they did about the production of evidence, they needed such a belief to enable them to sleep at night.

Richard Wells, Chief Constable of South Yorkshire, says: 'For years, there was disbelief in the higher reaches of society, in social classes A and B, that anything could be wrong. The radical Left were regarded as destabilisers, troublemakers: and their claims couldn't be taken seriously. Police culture said that the end justified the means. From that one could draw down the fact that if the law was inadequate, the police had to fill the shortcomings.'

Nevertheless, throughout the 1970s, the consensus, and the police infallibility principle, were coming under mounting attack. In some quarters, the Confait case and the Royal Commission on Criminal Procedure began to foster grave doubt. Eventually they gave rise to the 1984 Police and Criminal Evidence Act.

Doubt was boosted by other factors. The 1960s' challenge to traditional, deferential attitudes began to find expression in court-rooms, as a younger generation of defence lawyers tackled alleged evidential corruption head-on. Their activities were enthusiastically reported, first in the alternative and left-wing press – the first articles about the Torso case were written in 1977 by Duncan Campbell for *Time Out* magazine – and then, increasingly, in more mainstream media outlets.

At the same time, the policing of political protest was marked by successive, violent confrontations: from the battle with anti-Vietnam war demonstrators in Grosvenor Square in 1968, to the death of Blair Peach in a fight with the Special Patrol Group at an anti-racist demonstration ten years later. Many of the participants in such demonstrations had absorbed a vehement, if sometimes less than rigorous, counter-cultural politics. Dixon of Dock Green had become dehumanised, reduced to the status of 'pig'. For a minority, violent attacks on police officers were a valid end in themselves. Inevitably, such attacks produced a response in kind, in the shape of increasingly combative public order policing – which only con-firmed the counter-cultural caricature.

A crucial aspect to this movement was its social base. Many of those who clashed with police at Grosvenor Square or on the Grunwick picket line were middle-class: people with a direct line to the formation of policy and public opinion.

Racism was a further element, helping to undermine public confidence in the system. Long before the 1980s cycle of inner city rioting burst into life with disturbances in Bristol in 1980, the discriminatory policing of black citizens was a matter for public concern. The 1824 Vagrancy Act, with its 'suspected persons' (sus) provisions, became the justification for arresting and charging black youths on the whim of individual officers. Convicted of 'loitering with intent', thousands of black youngsters found themselves being criminalised, their prospects ruined by removal to borstal or prison.

Finally, there was the disclosure of financial corruption in the CID, beginning with disclosures in *The Times* in 1968, followed by the Robert Mark purge – the so-called 'fall of Scotland Yard'. If police detectives could steal or take bribes, it did not take a vast leap of imagination to consider that they might also present evidence produced by fabrication or duress.

By the beginning of the 1980s, the consensus symbolised by the Dixon myth had been replaced by intense politicisation. The formation of the Greater London Council Police Committee in 1981, the year of riots in Brixton, Toxteth, Mosside and Handsworth, signified the creation of an apparently unbridgeable rift between the democratic Left and the police. The Metropolitan Police has no local elected police authority, and is answerable only to the Home Secretary: the committee was an attempt to create a form of *de facto* accountability. It funded several local 'monitoring groups' of widely varying competence, and produced a regular journal, *Policing London*, which criticised police in often strident terms.

Under Commissioner David McNee, the Metropolitan Police dug themselves deep into defensive bunkers. Similar conflicts were being played out on Merseyside, between the police authority doyenne Margaret Simey and Chief Constable Kenneth Oxford; and in Manchester, where James Anderton openly regarded critics of policing as godless subversives. With the breakdown of consensus over the basic legitimacy of policing, any parallel, hidden consensus over the mechanics of criminal justice was bound to come under attack.

Among the barristers whose career began to burgeon in this period was Ron Thwaites. Unlike some of his contemporaries, he made no attempt to locate his work in a wider political context. But if there was a secret consensus which sustained the old regime, he was one of a number of people who played an important role in its breakdown. He says:

In the sixties and seventies, it was unfashionable to attack the police. The police could not be accused of lying, and the Bar aided and abetted them. Because judges had much more power, the Bar was not truly independent: they would ostentatiously take notes of what you were saying to each witness, and jump down your throat if you put something slightly different. Often the judges would cap your cross-examination by asking police witnesses about their commendations for bravery. In that sort of atmosphere, there were very few barristers prepared to stand up and be counted.

Barristers were not supposed to defend vigorously. There was an approved way of putting questions in cross-examination. If clients said they had been verballed, counsel would say: 'On my client's instructions, officer, you do understand, I am acting on instructions, I must put it to you that you are lying.' Addressing the judge, they would always say, 'if it please your Lordship'. My view is, if it pleases your Lordship, it won't please my client.

So I became an expert in police procedure and I started to expose the discrepancies between what they said they had done and what they should have done. I discovered CID officers were supposed to keep diaries of their movements: I made such hay with this they abolished the diaries. I fought. And I got people off.

If the Bar and judiciary connived in police malpractice, it must be remembered that these institutions also played a role in actually *causing* the miscarriages of justice. In some cases, the defence was at fault. For example, the evidence which eventually demolished the prosecution of the Birmingham Six was an Esda test on an interview with the defendant Richard McIlkenny – curiously enough, the only interview in the entire case which was said to have been written down contemporaneously at the 1975 trial. It was also significant because Detective Chief Superintendent George Read, the officer in charge of the investigation, was present for a substantial part of it.

The police scribe told the court he had recorded everything said verbatim at normal conversational speed – in neat capital letters. All a more determined defence counsel would have had to do was to ask the officer to repeat this improbable feat in the witness box. (Normal conversational speed is 180–220 words per minute. Few people can

write capitals faster than twenty words per minute.) Yet the record
went unchallenged by McIlkenny's barrister, Michael Underhill QC.

Prosecution lawyers must also bear their share of blame. However, it is striking that while a number of police officers have faced
criminal charges arising from miscarriages of justice – albeit none of
them leading to convictions – the lawyers have continued to
prosper.

In the Guildford Four case, the police established that Carole
Richardson had been seen by numerous witnesses at a rock concert
in London within fifty-two minutes of supposedly planting a bomb
in Guildford. A fast police patrol car was commissioned to do a test
drive, and just managed to do the journey in the requisite time. But
from this distance, the whole story seems wildly improbable.
Richardson, an English girl of seventeen, was in London nearly an
hour before the bomb she was supposed to have just planted went
off, enjoying herself with friends, none of whom noticed anything
remotely amiss.

The police confirmation of Richardson's partial alibi was
damaging to the Prosecution's case. The Crown lawyers, led by
Michael Havers and supported by Michael Hill, now a distinguished
QC, elected not to withdraw the charges against her. Sir John May
concluded in his 1993 report: 'It was urged on the Court of Appeal
by Richardson's counsel in 1977 that there was an inherent weakness
in the case against her because of these tight timings . . . I consider
there was and is much force in that submission.'[30]

There was also the failure to reveal the possible alibi provided for
Conlon by Charles Burke, who told the police he spent the
afternoon of the bombing in a hostel with Conlon in Kilburn, north
London. Apart from anything else, Conlon's solicitors had tried
unsuccessfully to trace Burke themselves. Sir John May's report
concluded that this information should have been disclosed, but he
let the Crown lawyers off lightly. He said there was 'nothing sinister'
in the failure to supply Burke's statement and address; there had been
no 'deliberate suppression'.

However, the transcripts of the private hearings held by the May
inquiry in 1993 betray distinct unease on the part of the lawyers
when they were being examined. They had their own legal
representative, Simon Hawkesworth QC, who began one session

with a plaintive appeal to Sir John: 'The fact that potential criticisms have been hanging over surviving counsel now, who are distinguished, practising members of the Bar, for more than three years, is itself a considerable source of anxiety to them ... it is their professional reputations which are at risk.'[31]

The transcripts also reveal that the non-disclosure of Burke's possible alibi partly rested on a highly questionable value judgment made in secret by the lawyers. They believed he would not be of any use to Conlon, because another witness, a Mr Vine, contradicted what he said. However, having gone into both accounts exhaustively, May concluded: 'I think ... Burke is more likely to have been accurate.'

In his evidence to the inquiry, Michael Hill said the prosecution believed the defence did know about Burke's statement anyway, but had decided to drop him as a witness because they feared he might be undermined by Vine. This was an audacious claim, and there was no surviving documentation to support it. Pressed repeatedly, Michael Hill was vague about its provenance. Finally he was asked: 'You cannot help us on what the source of that information was, or the nature or quality of it?' He replied, simply, 'no'.[32]

Sir John May gave Hill and the other lawyers the benefit of the doubt in his report. The failure to disclose Burke was the consequence of their 'erroneous reliance' on their false belief, he said. Nevertheless: 'This failure was not sinister, but ought not to have occurred.'

The failure to disclose vital evidence dominated Stefan Kiszko's 1992 appeal against the sexual murder of Lesley Molseed, aged fifteen. Kiszko, who spent sixteen years in prison, had allegedly confessed, but had a zero sperm count: his lawyers were never told that tests on both his semen and semen found in the body proved he could not possibly be guilty. The hellish life of a sex offender in the British prison system drove him mad, and he died less than two years after his release.

Judith Ward, also freed in 1992, spent even longer in gaol for the 1974 M62 coach bombing. In her case, the Court of Appeal delivered a coruscating judgment which criticised non-disclosure by police, forensic scientists and Crown lawyers – both counsel and Michael Bibby, then a solicitor working for the Director of Public

Prosecutions. Bibby's career as a senior prosecutor with the Crown Prosecution Service continued.

Leading prosecution counsel against both Ward and Kiszko was Peter Taylor QC. By the time of their appeals, he had become Lord Lane's successor as Lord Chief Justice of England. The opprobrium surrounding the cases left him untouched. As far as Ward was concerned, his junior, Brian Walsh, absorbed the blame for instructing Bibby not to disclose a series of police interviews in which Ward had denied the bombing. We must accept that Walsh did not discuss the matter with the future Lord Chief Justice. In any event, Walsh too continued to prosper. He was in the news again in 1993, defending one of the boys who murdered the toddler James Bulger.

In the Kiszko case, a police officer and scientist were accused of perverting the course of justice, but later the charges were dropped. A thorough police inquiry lifted any cloud of suspicion which might have briefly lingered over Lord Taylor. The investigation was supervised by Brian Johnson, Chief Constable of Lancashire, who served as Taylor's police assessor in the 1985 inquiry into the Bradford football stadium fire. The case remains a mystery. We shall never know who was responsible for the wrongful conviction and the ruining of Kiszko's life.

★ ★ ★

Running through the English criminal justice system was a basic contradiction, between its rhetoric and reality. This was the ultimate significance of the Guildford Four appeal: that it exposed this gulf to the fiercest of public scrutiny. Yet at the same time, that exposure was limited and partial. Few commentators looked beyond first base. Taking their lead from Lord Lane, they considered only the officers who 'must have lied'.

Since the 1960s, academics have made use of a theoretical framework devised by the American Herbert Packer – the polarised dichotomy between the 'due process' and 'crime control' models of criminal justice.[33] According to Packer, the ethics of crime control are 'based on the proposition that the repression of criminal conduct is by far the most important function to be performed by the criminal process'. Crime control demands a high rate of conviction, and places a high degree of trust in the police: 'If there is confidence in the reliability of informal, administrative fact-finding activities that take place in the early stages of the criminal process, the remaining stages can be relatively perfunctory.' Police officers themselves are often unconscious, and sometimes conscious, advocates of the crime control model. They will tend to view acquittals as having been achieved on a 'technicality'.

Due process, in contrast, starts from the proposition that it is better to let ten guilty men go free than to convict a single innocent defendant: 'The aim of the process is at least as much to protect the factually innocent as it is to convict the factually guilty.' It cherishes the notion of equality before the law, and places great value in civil liberties. Due process also insists that one of the legal system's paramount goals is the protection of its own integrity. If evidence has been gathered by irregular means, it must be excluded, even if true. At the appeal stage, due process ideology says convictions, even of factually guilty people, must be quashed if there turns out to have been what English law terms a 'material irregularity'. Apart from anything else, this may rein in deviant police activity in the future.

Like all social science theories, Packer's model has its limitations, and is not applicable to each and every debate. In the real world, neither pole exists in its purest form. Under pure crime control the conviction rate would be 100 per cent. Pure due process would imply a system in which conviction demanded proof beyond any doubt at all, rather than the more accommodating test of proof beyond 'reasonable doubt'.[34] Nevertheless, Packer's dichotomy is a valuable analytical tool.

In the 1960s and 1970s, English (and indeed, Scottish) criminal justice operated under the guise of due process rhetoric. But as we have seen, in the most serious possible cases, its reality was crime control: the operation of a secret consensus which ignored the ways in which police gathered evidence, while clinging to blind faith in their ability to identify guilty suspects.

Writing at the start of the 1980s, Doreen McBarnet described this contradiction. 'The law on criminal procedure in its current form does not so much set a standard of legality from which the police deviate, as provide a licence to ignore it,' she said. The Judges' Rules erected various theoretical safeguards around the rights of suspects. But they did not have the force of law, and in practice were disregarded.[35] If, she went on, one brought the notion of due process down from the dizzy heights of abstraction and subjected it to empirical scrutiny, 'the conclusion must be that due process is *for* crime control'. Lawyers' and judges' due process rhetoric was only a mask for the system's crime control objectives.

She illustrated her argument with a 1967 judgment by the Scottish judge, Lord Wheatley. In relation to policing, 'fairness to the public is a legitimate consideration', he said. However, the courts had to remember that the police were primarily protecting the public. Judges should not be 'hamstringing the police in their investigation of crime with a series of academic vetos which ignore the realities and practicalities of the situation and discount entirely the public interest'.

McBarnet suggested the gulf between reality and rhetoric had a further effect: when things went wrong, the police shouldered blame which should have been shared. 'Focusing on the subversion of justice by its petty administrators, on the gap between the law in the books and the law in action, in effect whitewashes the law itself and those who make it,' she said. 'Front men like the police become the "fall guys" of the legal system, taking the blame for any injustices in the operation of the law.' As we have seen, after the Guildford appeal, this is precisely what happened.

McBarnet's analysis was an important departure from what was then, and still remains, the dominant view of public and academic debate. This view holds that rule-breaking and disregard for civil liberties evolve from the internal culture of policing, with its crime control emphasis on successful prosecutions and arrests. As the *Independent* put it after the Guildford case, the police are the source of justice's 'institutional rot'.

To sustain the secret consensus which characterised the old regime, to maintain its rhetoric-reality gulf, one thing was required above all other: public confidence. Lord Denning instinctively understood this when he described the collapse of the case against the Birmingham Six as an 'appalling vista'. Without public confidence, all that was solid would melt into air.

Meanwhile, the effects of the old regime's passing raise a final

uncomfortable question. If, as McBarnet says, it gave the police a
'licence to ignore' suspects' rights, one has to ask whether this had a
basic, functional purpose. According to some Left analysis, crime
control is merely an aspect of social control in general. Crime itself
only exists as the ideological construct of the state, periodically
emphasised by the 'moral panics' of the media.[36] If we took such a
view, everything would fall neatly into place. The job of the police
would not be to control crime but to enforce the existing class
structure, and the contradictions running through the old regime
would vanish.

But if we once, as this book does, accept that crime is a real
problem which damages real people's lives, another possible
function of the old regime is possible. Could it be that false
confessions and institutionalised malpractice existed because the
sytem's participants believed that without them, successful investigation would not be possible? That the proving of cases beyond
reasonable doubt could simply not be achieved?

These questions beg another, still less comfortable line of inquiry.
If that was what practitioners instinctively felt, could they, in fact,
have been right?

CHAPTER TWO

Race, Class and Justice

ON THE day the Deols opened their new supermarket for business, two of their staff resigned. It happened at about noon on a Thursday back in September 1989. In an area of high unemployment, the Abbey Hulton estate in Stoke-on-Trent, the two women, who had worked in the shop for years under its previous owner, could give no cogent reason for abandoning their jobs. It was only later the Deols learnt from some of their customers that the saleswomen felt they could not be seen working for the 'new Pakis'.[1]

Davinder Deol, known universally as Dave, his sister, Bali, and their brother, Lakhbir – 'Lucky' – were born in England to Sikh Punjabi parents. In the summer of 1989, Dave was only twenty-three, Bali eighteen and Lucky sixteen; yet when they first came to look at Abbey Hulton they had already achieved commercial success. In 1986, their father, a lorry driver, bought a moribund off-licence in Cwmbran, South Wales. His children's business diligence brought startling success and after less than three years' trading, the family managed to sell the off-licence with a profit of £93,000.

So they read the trade press magazines and looked for a bigger challenge. In the Abbey General Store, a post office-cum-grocery, they thought they had found it.

Abbey Hulton, a vast, low-rise sprawl housing more than 5,000 people, is an inconvenient bus ride from the nearest High Street shopping centre in Hanley: here was a market worth exploiting. The General Store had been run by the same couple for forty years, and it seemed ripe for development. The self-service revolution had passed it by and most of the stock was still stacked on shelves behind the counter. Inside, the shop was dingy, and food long past its sell-by date was stuck to the bottom of the freezer. The post office queues

were frequently so long that the former postmistress used to serve tea
to her customers as they waited in line on the pavement.

The Bank of Scotland, evidently taken with the Deols' energy,
agreed with their assessment, and lent them £186,000. The Post
Office was equally impressed, and made Dave sub-postmaster – at
twenty-three, the youngest in the country. On top of any trading
profit, this carried a guaranteed annual salary of £40,000.

The Deols had just one hint of possible trouble. A commercial
survey which they commissioned of the business contained a brief
warning: 'You may have to exercise caution in order to avoid any
racial prejudice which may exist.' They chose to disregard it. Their
experience in Cwmbran had made them bold. Like Abbey Hulton,
Cwmbran was an almost entirely white area, but they had found
rapid acceptance. On one occasion, a youth had entered the South
Wales shop, and threatened Dave and Bali with assault, shouting
racial abuse. They called the police, who arrived almost immediately
and arrested the youth. There was no repetition.

Physically, Abbey Hulton's 1930s and 40s housing is not
unattractive, although in some cases it is badly dilapidated. But with
hindsight, the Deols wish they had done some more research.
Locally, the estate was known as 'Little Chicago', and was reputedly
at the mercy of lawless teenage gangs. Unbeknown to the Deols, an
Asian called Sam Balu had opened a shop next door to the post office
in the early 1980s. In 1988, after his windows were repeatedly
broken, he sold up and left. His son, Rajkamal, recalls: 'I could not
work out the mentality of some of the people on Abbey Hulton. I
remember one man who was drunk headbutting the metal grille to
our shop, shouting abuse at my dad. The next day, this same person
came into the shop and acted in a normal manner.'

On the pavement outside the post office is a green British
Telecom junction box. Over a number of years, for some reason, it
was the meeting point for Abbey Hulton's white youth. The Balus
remember youths gathering there and hanging about, sometimes for
hours. Rajkamal says: 'Towards the weekend it used to get very
scary. There were drunken youths singing football songs and racist
chants: "The Union Jack ain't got no black, send them Pakis back." '

The youths were there on the Deols' first day. At that time, Lucky
and Dave wore turbans, and both youths and customers peered at

them through the windows as if they 'were from a different planet'. It was taunts from the youths that precipitated the walk-out by the two women staff, who had been 'inherited' from the previous owners.

By the end of that first day, the Deols were feeling tired and depressed. They were living in a flat above the shop, which still had bare walls and floorboards. 'Bali, Lucky and myself hardly said a word over our meal that night,' Dave says. There were already signs of more serious harassment: 'Even then, there were youths outside flicking stones at the windows and shouting. At that time, we thought it was just the novelty of us being the new owners.'

There were soon further blows. Another white saleswoman resigned, saying she didn't agree with what people were saying, but she couldn't take the pressure from some of her neighbours. Some customers let it be known that they had arranged to cash their benefit giros elsewhere because they didn't want to patronise the Deols. However, with other white residents, the Deols forged lasting friendships. Their cheerfulness and determination to offer good service were widely appreciated, and turnover began to rise rapidly. The family spent another £14,000 on refurbishment, gradually turning the shop into an efficient, modern supermarket. There were no more post office queues on the pavement.

Yet the nocturnal stonethrowing did not stop. The youths around the junction box were a constant, disquieting presence. They threw taunts and insults at the Deols and their customers; in the evenings, when those in work came back to the estate, their numbers would grow to twenty or more. Sometimes, after the Deols shut the shop for the night, they would bang on the doors and windows, or deliberately kick their footballs against the plate-glass. The first serious act of vandalism took place at about midnight on 16 October 1989, when someone heaved a slab of concrete through a large display window. A local man was arrested, but released without charge, due to lack of evidence. Repairing the damage cost nearly £300.

In those early months, Dave spoke frequently to the police. But he was told that unless there was evidence of an offence, nothing could be done. Once, a British National Party sticker was left on the window. However, Dave did not tell the police he believed the harassment had a racial motive. 'It seemed to me at the time that if I said the whole thing was racial, we'd be somehow giving in to the yobs,' he says. 'Somehow, I thought it would make it worse. I talked to the police about specifics.'

The Deols believed that despite their difficulties, in time they could make their business a success. They were prepared to make extraordinary sacrifices in order to fit in with the community. Before Christmas, Dave had a special greetings card printed and sent it to all their customers: the Deols received numerous cards in return. At the same time, he decided to remove his turban and cut his hair. This was a momentous step, and his father was so angry, he refused to speak to Dave for three months. However, to some extent, he says, it made relations with the people of 'the Abbey' easier. Yet there remained a hard core, 'who made it clear they would resent us, however we were dressed'.

The many social problems of Abbey Hulton were becoming apparent. Unemployment, drug and solvent abuse were rife; on numerous occasions, the Deols found used syringes thrown over the wall at the back of the shop. An off-licence in the same parade of shops experienced an armed robbery and there were many burglaries. After six months, Dave contacted an estate agent with a view to selling the business. He was told to do so would be financially disastrous at that stage: they would have to tough it out. Dave says: 'We learnt not to rise to the bait. We ignored racist comments and tried to do our best. I could not understand the mentality of these lads, who spent literally all day sitting outside our shop doing nothing. I remember once, it was raining very hard, and there were these two lads sitting on the cold pavement under a large green fishing umbrella.'

On six occasions in the first twenty months the Deols lived on the Abbey, their car or van was vandalised. The worst incident was on the evening of 13 May 1991. Lucky, Dave and Bali were upstairs in the flat, watching television, when they saw a youth they knew smash their car windscreen with a bottle. Dave rushed out to challenge him while Bali called the police. Officers arrived and spoke to the alleged assailant and his father – known locally as 'Psycho' – at his home. Dave and Lucky went to the house to offer their own version of events. The youth denied any involvement.

Nevertheless, Dave tried to remonstrate with the police, urging them to arrest him.

He says: 'The policeman told me to back off, and so I raised my arms in the air and walked away from the house, down the path. To my astonishment, I was arrested.' He was taken to Hanley police station and locked in a cell for two hours. 'I was furious and humiliated. We were the victims yet the police had refused to do anything; they seemed relieved not to have had to arrest "Psycho" or his son. I had never been arrested before; they both had criminal records. No one was charged with anything, but my confidence in the ability of the police to protect us had been badly shaken.'

Gradually, the Deols turned their premises into a fortress. First, they bought a German shepherd dog. Then they raised the height of the wall at the back by adding two layers of breeze blocks, and ran razor wire along the top. All the downstairs windows were equipped with steel bars, and the doors were reinforced. They added security cameras and a closed-circuit TV. 'The extra security added to our feeling of isolation,' Dave says. 'We found it almost impossible to relax. It seemed the shop was running our lives, not that we were running the shop.'

In May 1992, Dave married Baljinder, a British Sikh woman, but the stress of living in Abbey Hulton was a dismal start to married life. Soon, his GP referred him to a psychiatrist: 'I felt responsible for my wife and my sister. The stress was almost intolerable.' He drew some solace from a course of hypnotherapy, but it was clear that the root cause of his depression and anxiety was the shop. Three times in 1991 and 1992, he instructed commercial estate agents to try to sell it: each time, there were no takers.

The penultimate act in the Deol family drama began at about nine o'clock in the evening of 15 February 1993. Lucky had gone outside to get the car and go for a drink. Bali and Baljinder were cooking, and Dave was doing some paperwork. 'All of a sudden I heard Bali scream that Lucky was being attacked outside,' Dave says. 'I rushed downstairs.'

Kevin Copeland, aged seventeen, one of the most persistent of the family's tormentors, had Lucky by the neck, and was holding him against the shop-front. Blood was running from Lucky's nose, and his shirt was torn. Dave managed to separate them, and Copeland stood in front of the doorway shouting, 'Paki bastards, you should go home,' while Lucky retreated indoors. Lucky believes Copeland was high on drugs: 'His brother later said he was out of his tree.'

By ten o'clock that night, a crowd of about twenty youths had gathered outside the shop. Copeland shouted up to Lucky: 'Come on, I'll take you.' The Deols called the police, who for once arrived speedily at the scene. Copeland, still apparently intoxicated, was arrested. One of the officer's notebooks records what Copeland said as he was dragged away: 'It was that black idiot in there. They should not be here. It is my area and I will be back to burn them out.' As the police forced Copeland into a car, his friends surrounded it, kicked it and shouted abuse.

Copeland had convictions for theft, burglary and criminal damage. His family background was characterised by violence and emotional conflict. His mother, Marilyn, had divorced his father after years of violent abuse. His father had been in prison and by 1993, the family had been living entirely on state benefits for fifteen years. Kevin's only full-time work experience was when he was sixteen: two weeks on a Youth Training Scheme from which he dropped out.

Marilyn was later to make a statement to police saying that she was concerned about Kevin's behaviour, especially when he 'began to ride in stolen vehicles and assault people'. She added: 'I tried to talk to him about it, but it didn't seem to have any effect. Kevin did like to drink lager, and I caught him once last year smoking "draw", cannabis, in the living room. I wouldn't say he drank a lot because he couldn't afford it . . . I knew he was taking cannabis because he told me so.' In the early days of the Deols' management of the shop, when Kevin was fourteen, he worked for them as a paper delivery boy. They sacked him, because they believed he was selling some of his papers for personal profit. Lucky and Dave remained on good terms with his brother, John. But Kevin was an influential figure among the estate's listless youth and his dismissal gave the escalating campaign against the Deols a harder, personal edge.

The police never told the Deols what happened after Kevin's arrest on 15 February. It was not until many months later that they learnt he had appeared at Stoke Magistrates' Court, and received a conditional discharge for common assault. By then, Lucky was on remand for Kevin Copeland's murder.

After the February incident, Copeland and his friends stepped up their campaign of harassment. The abuse, door-banging and vandalism, which had previously seemed sporadic, now seemed 'orchestrated and predetermined', according to Dave and Lucky. They became aware that much older white men, some of whom had serious criminal records, were joining the youths in the harassment. The Deols' white staff and friends were also suffering. The business was increasingly successful, but according to Dave, 'our quality of life was so miserable, we had to sell, despite the fall in property values brought by the recession. We had improved the turnover substantially, but clearly there was no future for us in Abbey Hulton.' He put classified advertisements in the regional newspapers, and again instructed an estate agent – only this time, he and his family made clear they were prepared to make a considerable loss.

All through the spring and early summer, the Deols' harassment continued. At about midnight on 28 June, they heard a loud smashing downstairs. A lump of concrete had been put through one of the shop windows. Dave was especially concerned because the shop was on the market: no one would buy a business with boarded-up windows. He paid £318 for an emergency replacement window, but this time, he didn't bother to call the police at all. He had no evidence as to the identity of the attacker, and his experience since his arrest the previous year had induced an attitude of resigned despair.

One of Dave's saleswomen's daughters was a friend of Kevin Copeland, and the next day, she told him that Copeland had smashed the window. That night, Copeland and his friends hung around the shop late into the evening. Similar activity continued during the week.

At last, on 3 July, a Saturday, there seemed to be some respite. The Deols closed the shop as usual at 7 p.m., and decided to take a break by spending the night with their parents in Birmingham. They had driven no more than fifteen yards when they saw Copeland with a group of his friends, standing by the off-licence. Dave says: 'They had seen us leave the shop. Ordinarily when leaving the premises empty, we made sure no one was loitering about, in case they tried to take advantage of our absence. This time, without doubt, Copeland and his mates had seen us leave.'

Lucky, Dave, Bali and Baljinder were in two minds about whether to go to Birmingham at all. In the end, says Dave, 'we decided the shop mustn't rule our lives', and they continued. As soon as they arrived at his parents' house, Dave telephoned the Hanley police, warning them of his fears. His call was recorded at the police station at 9.09 p.m. A PC Martins told him there were no police patrolling on foot on the Abbey that night: it was a busy summer Saturday, and no officers were available. However, he promised a car would be sent to check the shop as soon as an opportunity arose.

Later, Dave and Lucky went out for a drink. While they were gone, Bali called the police again. By the time Lucky and Dave came back from the pub, their sister, mother and Baljinder were on their way back to Stoke-on-Trent. Their father told them he wasn't sure exactly what had happened, but it seemed all the windows in the shop and flat had been smashed.

Lucky and Dave got back to the Abbey at 12.30 a.m., to find a scene of devastation. Concrete slabs and bricks had shattered every window in their home and business, covering all the beds, stock and furniture with broken glass. Police officers were standing round outside the shop and there was a crowd of youths outside the chip shop, at the end of the parade. The police attempted to comfort the Deols, but said that they were unable to provide protection for the rest of the night. Soon the police left. The Deol women returned to Birmingham, leaving Lucky and Dave with £40,000 cash in the post office safe, stock on the shelves worth £15,000, and a building open to the elements.

This time, the Deols' home, which they had spent a lot of effort in making comfortable, had been violated. They were faced with the task of clearing up the mess by Monday morning: Monday was their busiest trading day, and there was always the chance of a sudden visit from a prospective buyer for the shop. There was, Dave says mildly, 'a degree of frustration at the police. We had warned them something like this would happen; now they were making no apparent effort to investigate the matter.' They seemed to have no interest in the Deols as victims of crime: 'No officer sat down with any member of the family to ask who we thought was responsible. I was surprised and frankly disappointed that no officer turned up on the Sunday to see how we were coping.'

With seven white friends from the estate, Dave and Lucky worked all day to put things right. After finishing, the Deol men took their friends for a drink in town, leaving the women in the flat. On their return at about eleven o'clock, they saw a group of youths in the alley next to the shop. Someone shouted 'go on, go on, do it!', then the youths saw the Deols and ran down the alley, towards a common. Dave and some of his friends gave chase; meanwhile Lucky and the others took the van and tried to head off the youths on the other side of the open ground. They drove round the area two or three times, but failed to find them. This time, at least, an attack had been prevented.

The Deols were open for business as usual on the Monday morning, 5 July. As usual, Copeland and his friends were loitering at the junction box. Dave and Lucky made no attempt to confront them: they knew they would simply deny smashing the windows, and they hoped against hope that the new pitch of attacks had been a phase which had passed. But within minutes of closing at seven, Baljinder saw the youths standing outside with bricks and concrete blocks. 'We simply knew our windows would be put in that night,' Dave says. 'It was only a question of when.'

The family had lived through the 1985 riot in Handsworth, Birmingham, in which two Asian brothers who ran a post office were burned alive, and damage worth £35 million was caused to a shopping parade. Dave says: 'The atmosphere on the Abbey that night was very similar. I was about eighteen during the riot and I remember very well the feeling of impending trouble.' As a precaution, Dave and Lucky asked some of their white friends to come to the flat for a drink. They hoped their presence might act as a deterrent: in the event of further trouble, they would be independent witnesses. Four men turned up. Dave says: 'We were afraid and very grateful.'

As darkness fell, the feeling of siege intensified. The Deols and their friends knew the youths were outside, waiting; but neither side had made a move. They turned out the lights, and removed the fluorescent tubes in the freezer cabinets, in order to be able to see out more clearly. At times, they could make out up to forty people on the pavement outside. The bolder ones pressed up to the glass, peering in. Occasionally they shouted racial taunts.

Still the Deols did not call the police: after their accumulated experience over the preceding four years, there seemed to be no point. 'I felt I was in a very bad dream,' Dave says. 'We didn't know what the crowd was going to do; we didn't know what they were capable of doing. I was afraid for the safety of the girls upstairs.' Lucky adds: 'It was clear something extraordinary was going to happen. They had all the appearance of an audience.' There were even children as young as nine or ten, wrapped up in quilts, waiting, says Lucky, 'as if for a favourite TV programme'. The Deols' memory of Handsworth intensified their terror. They imagined not just the breaking of windows, but an attack with petrol bombs, the looting and total destruction of their livelihood.

Shortly after 11 p.m., most of the crowd appeared to vanish, leaving only Copeland, Darryl Clarke, his closest friend, and one or two others. According to Dave, Copeland and Clarke could be very brave in a crowd, 'but on their own, they were as meek as lambs'. It was then, with ill-considered swiftness, that Dave and Lucky conceived the notion of a 'citizen's arrest'. Dave says:

> I genuinely thought if I could arrest them and get them away from the shop, it would prevent further damage and possible injury. They were boasting to people on the estate that they were responsible for the earlier attacks. I thought if they were isolated, they would readily admit it, and we could go to the police. At that moment, it seemed our only choice. We had to act swiftly and decisively.

The plan was that Lucky would get into the van, parked about fifteen yards from the door, drive round the block and then park as close as possible to the green box. Dave and the Deols' friends would stroll out nonchalantly as if Lucky were simply going to drive them home – then try to bundle Copeland and Clarke into the van, 'with minimum force'.

As arranged, Lucky left the shop and got into the van. As he did so, he heard Copeland snigger. 'I half expected to be jumped from behind as soon as I got outside the shop,' he says. He reversed away from the shop, and drove off. A few minutes later, at about 11.10 p.m., he was back. Copeland, Clarke and two others were still standing by the green box. No one else was in sight. He parked on the pavement, a few feet from the box, facing away from it, intending to make the 'citizen's arrest' as easy as possible. Dave and three of the Deols' friends had been standing just behind the shop-front door: as Lucky pulled in, they started walking slowly towards the green box.

The Deols' friends seized Clarke, opened the side door of the van and bundled him inside. At the same time, Dave went to grab Kevin Copeland. But his bomber jacket came away in Dave's hand; the youth span round, and escaped. Within seconds, Dave was fighting for his life.

With hindsight, the Deols believe the 'disappearance' of most of the crowd was merely a ploy to lure them out of the shop, with Clarke and Copeland as 'bait'. In any event, the 'citizen's arrest' had barely started before at least fifty Abbey Hulton youths came swarming from all directions: some from the alley beside the shop, others from the side of the parade; yet more from the road which faced it. They surrounded the van, banging it and rocking it from side to side. Lucky says:

The lads in the back were shouting, 'GO!' I could hear panic in their voices. I was bloody terrified. I was aware I hadn't heard Dave's voice: I expected him any second to jump into the passenger seat. I heard Clarke crying like a baby. I couldn't wait any longer, so I pulled off. When I was halfway round the traffic island at the junction facing the shop, I realised Dave was missing.

Dave was left in the middle of the angry crowd, which was still growing. He saw one man he knew with a huge white dog, which was barking loudly; he had barely time to register what was happening before the man dealt a stunning blow to his face with a baseball bat. Dave put his head down and tried to run, 'aware that if I fell to the floor, I would be kicked or beaten to death'. He felt blood running down the side of his face, soaking his shirt and trousers. Dave reached the traffic island and looked in vain for the van: instead he found himself facing a man with a long-bladed knife, screaming 'come on you black bastard, you Pakis have had it now'.

Lucky had turned round, driving back into the mob in order to rescue his brother. Amid the pools of streetlight were areas of darkness: at first he did not see Dave by the traffic island, and continued for another forty yards to the shop and green box. He heard the sound of breaking glass: yet again, missiles were being hurled against the shop and apartment windows. Lucky says: 'I drove towards the crowd where I had last seen Dave; my one thought was to get him in the van. I saw a number of people jump out of the way. I drove on to the kerb: people were banging their fists against the van. The crowd continued to pass on either side.'

At last he caught a glimpse of Dave and changed direction again, swinging off the pavement. Somewhere in the panic and confusion he felt a 'little bump': he knew he had hit someone with the vehicle. Back at the traffic island, Dave heard a scream from the direction of the green box. Suddenly, he was left alone. The van pulled up and he got in. 'Somebody handed me a towel,' he says, 'the pain from my wound was intense, searing. Lucky was in a state of shock and panic. I told him to drive away.'

Bewildered and frightened, they drove around the area, several times passing by the shop in the hope of preventing a murderous attack on those still inside. All the windows had been smashed. Finally they saw police cars. They drove into a pub car-park and, Dave says, 'with enormous relief' entrusted themselves to the forces of law and order. The police took them to Hanley police station, where they were cautioned and detained in the cells. It was not until the following morning that the duty solicitor arrived and informed them how serious the situation had become. Kevin Copeland was dead, and the police were treating his death as homicide.

★   ★   ★

The Deol family's nightmare intensified. On 7 July, Dave and Lucky were taken to Shrewsbury prison. While Lucky was eventually tried for murder, Dave faced charges of attempted kidnap. Three of the Deols' friends from the estate were also charged with kidnapping Darryl Clarke: they chose to plead guilty, and received short gaol sentences. Many of their fellow inmates came from Abbey Hulton and its environs, and as the brothers stepped on to the prison landing the following morning, they were met by a barrage of shouts: 'Murdering Paki bastards, you have messed with the wrong people now.' All day they faced similar threats. Late that evening, the governor decided to move them for their own protection, and they were driven down the motorway to Winson Green, in Birmingham.

There was, of course, no way any of the Deols could go on running the shop on the Abbey, much less live there. Immediately after Copeland's death, it was boarded up, and the family returned to their parents. Lucky was held on remand for sixteen months until the trial, but after a few weeks, Dave was granted bail. His bail conditions prevented him from going anywhere near Abbey Hulton, but something had to be done with the business. He arranged for a firm called Retail Relief Services to go in and run the shop until it could be sold.

On 14 August, Bali, her parents, Dave's wife Baljinder and three close male relatives returned to Stoke-on-Trent for the first time since Copeland's death. They planned to meet the team from Retail Relief and remove as much as they could of the family's possessions from the flat. Before the visit, they telephoned the Hanley police, who told them they did not expect trouble. They agreed to get a set of keys to the police, so the gates to the yard behind the shop could be left open, and the Deols could drive in without anybody realising they were there.

However, as they pulled up that Saturday afternoon, the gates were still shut. Bali says: 'There were two plain-clothes officers standing outside; we had to wait with them for five minutes, until the gates were unlocked. So we were seen. Inside, we realised at once the back door had been kicked in a few days earlier. We were totally paranoid.'

Within half an hour of the Deols' arrival, the shop was surrounded by a screaming mob, a hundred strong. This time, there were not only youths but their parents. Back in Birmingham, Dave spoke to his terrified wife on the telephone: 'Down the line I could hear them chanting, "Burn the Paki bastards, burn the Paki bastards out." She was speaking to me in what had been our bedroom. As we talked, a brick came through the window, missing her by inches, showering her with glass.'

It was a bad day to have chosen: Stoke City was playing at home to Millwall, notorious for its rowdy supporters, and the available police resources were concentrated at and around the football ground. A PC Riaz arrived, an Asian: he was spat at and abused. As the bombardment increased, it rapidly became clear that the family and the hapless team from Retail Relief Services were in danger and were going to have to escape.

At last a squad of police in riot gear arrived, with a helicopter hovering overhead. The police told the Deols' relatives to get in the van; and with wholly unintentional irony, to drive away as fast as possible, disregarding all obstacles. The immediate family were to be escorted to a squad car, with blankets over their heads. Both vehicles came under attack as they left, the boots of the mob leaving deep dents. The van was covered with saliva. Bali recalls: 'I didn't think we were going to get out alive. As we got in the car the engine was revving and we shot away, the wheels spinning. As soon as we reached the police station, my mother collapsed. For months afterwards, I was scared to go out. I kept an iron bar under my bed.'

Retail Relief Services, whose staff were also rescued by the police on that Saturday, made a valiant attempt to reopen the shop two days later, but by midday, they were forced to give up. Groups of youths stood on the pavement, threatening anybody who went near it. The following month, the shop went on sale for just £150,000 – £100,000 less than the Deols had paid, despite their many improvements. The business stayed boarded-up. By the end of November, the Bank of Scotland repossessed it. At the time of writing, bankruptcy proceedings against the Deols are in progress.

From the many houses overlooking the scene of the 5 July battle, the police investigating Copeland's death found not one witness prepared to make a statement. No one would say they had seen the gathering mob, the baseball bat attack on Dave, or the smashing of the windows. Virtually the only witnesses ready to talk had taken part in the assault on the shop, and most had criminal records.

Many of the youths had spent the hours after Copeland's death mourning their friend in a nearby house, comparing notes and concocting a wild story – that Lucky had driven straight at his victim, knocked him down, and then reversed over his body, just to make sure. It was this story which formed the basis of charging Lucky with murder, for which the law requires evidence of intent. When the case eventually came to trial, the claims melted into thin air. The Deols' solicitors, Howell and Co. of Birmingham, commissioned a report from a police traffic accident expert. He showed the suggestion that Lucky had reversed over Copeland could not possibly be true. It also emerged the police had sought forensic evidence to support the 'reversing' claim and failed to find any. The judge told the jury they should simply 'forget' the reversing story.

Those who stood up for the Deols on Abbey Hulton were brutally intimidated, with overt threats and extreme right-wing propaganda shoved through their letter-boxes. Eventually, three families had to be rehoused, so precarious had their situation become. One thirteen-year-old girl, driven to distraction by her schoolfriends' reaction to her parents' support for the family, made a serious suicide attempt. This happened after youths tried to run her father down in a car.

As the case made its way to trial via remand and committal hearings at the Magistrates' Court, there were further ugly clashes between the Abbey youths and the Deols within the court precincts. Opinion in Staffordshire remained bitterly polarised. In the summer of 1994, the Deols' lawyers twice applied to Mr Justice McKinnon, a High Court judge, to move the trial from Stafford Crown Court – where the population of the prospective jury's catchment area was almost one hundred per cent white – to Birmingham, where there was a greater prospect of a racially-mixed panel. They got written support for the move from Mark Fisher, the local Labour MP, and, most unusually, from the stipendiary magistrate who committed the case for trial.

Yet throughout the pre-trial period, both the police and the Crown insisted that race was simply not an issue. Repeatedly, they denied the attacks on the Deols had any racial motive. In view of their insistence, Mr Justice McKinnon ruled the trial would go ahead in Stafford, as planned.

Michael Stokes QC, who led the prosecution, took the same line when the case opened. Certainly, he told the court, the Deols had suffered much but not, however, due to racism. As Stephen Solley

QC and Ian MacDonald QC, counsel for Dave and Lucky, cross-examined the witnesses, this colour-blind approach fell apart. Darryl Clarke admitted in evidence he 'had it in for the Pakis'; Lisa Waterhouse, whose mother worked at the shop, told the court that on the day of the battle, Clarke called her 'scum' and Copeland shouted: 'Get a bath'. Finally, apparently exasperated, the judge, Mr Justice Kennedy, told the jury that the racial element in the Deols' persecution was 'as obvious as the noses on our collective faces'.

The jury acquitted the Deols after just two hours of deliberation on 18 October 1994, the foreman yelling the words across the court for emphasis. Even then, the 'no racism' myth refused to die. Next day, under the headline 'Our Kevin was just a clown prince, says his mum,' the local evening paper[2] quoted Marilyn Copeland saying: 'Kevin would use racist words, but only when talking about Lucky . . . it was not real racism, just categorising people.' Kevin's brother, John, added: 'A lot of people called them Pakis, but it was not racism. There was no malice meant.'

★ ★ ★

The futility of attempting to deny the vicious strand of racism which runs through the Deols' story seems very clear. This was not an 'ordinary' series of crimes (criminal damage, threatening behaviour, and assault) in which the victims just happened to be Asian. Racism gave the long months of harassment a special, loathsome horror; and as the incidents mounted in frequency and intensity, racism acted as a mobilising ideology. It gave apparent irrational acts an added rationale. For the Abbey youths, removing the Asians from the almost all-white estate became a subpolitical 'cause', which had the power to motivate them to commit acts of great violence. Casual vandalism does not possess this aura of warped glamour.

As Asian victims of racially-motivated crime, who were first left unprotected by the police and criminal justice system, then criminalised when they tried to retaliate, the Deols fit into a long and dismal tradition. A notorious example was the case of the four Virk brothers.[3]

One afternoon in April 1977, the Virks were working on their car in an east London street, when they were attacked by a gang of white youths. One brother went to call the police; the others tried to defend themselves as best they could. Eventually the police arrived. They allowed the whites who had started the incident to leave, but the Virks were arrested, and charged with assault and public order offences. When the case came to court, the judge said racial prejudice was 'irrelevant' to the points at issue. He strongly reprimanded defence lawyers for asking the attackers whether they were members of the overtly racist National Front – and this was during a period in which the popularity of the British extreme right was reaching its post-war electoral peak.

The perceived failure of the police to protect Asians from attack led in the early 1980s to the 'Bradford Twelve,' 'Newham Eight' and the 'Newham Seven' trials. All were groups of Asian teenagers who ended up charged with serious offences after taking the law into their own hands. In Bradford, they made petrol bombs after a spate of racial attacks. The Newham Eight physically tackled a gang responsible for repeated attacks on children outside a school. The Newham Seven organised their own 'raid' on a pub, later described in court as a 'fount' of racist violence; three of its regular white customers had kidnapped Asian boys and set about them with a claw-hammer in their car.[4] All these trials received wide publicity, and attained a symbolic, politicised importance.

The Newham Seven trial – which lasted nearly two months and cost, at 1985 prices, £500,000 – revealed bitter animosity between the defendants (who ended up with community service orders) and the investigating police. Referring to them and their local activist supporters (principally the Greater London Council-funded Newham Monitoring Project), Detective Constable Noel Bonczosek claimed relations between the police and minority community would be excellent if left to themselves. However, he added, 'time and again there are elements trying to stir up trouble'.[5] Detective Sergeant Gillie, who interviewed the suspects, implied racism was not a specific problem at all. If there were a high number of violent attacks on Asians, he said, this was simply because many Asians lived in the area. Those who criticised the police were merely 'lefty troublemakers'.[6]

If opinions such as these were common in this period, they had sometimes been fostered by the leadership of the service. One example was Metropolitan Commissioner Sir David McNee's annual report covering 1981. Published in March 1982, in the wake of Lord Scarman's criticisms of street policing in his report on the Brixton riot, it contained statistics suggesting most robberies were carried out by blacks. It was the cue for a virulent media campaign against the stereotypical black mugger.[7] In the same month, James Anderton, the Chief Constable of Greater Manchester, denounced critics of the police as 'an enemy more dangerous, insidious, and ruthless than any faced since World War II'.

McNee's report made no mention of racial attacks, racially-motivated crime or the generally high rate at which Asians and Afro-Caribbeans became crime victims.[8] This omission was all the more remarkable because a few months earlier, in the middle of the year covered by the annual report, an important, widely-reported Home Office survey concluded that Asians and Afro-Caribbeans were up to fifty times more likely to suffer assaults than white people.[9]

However, just a year or two later, a more enlightened approach was becoming evident, at least at the level of policy. From 1984, racial offences began to be recorded under criteria which stated that if the victim – or indeed, anyone else – said an incident had a racial element, then under that heading it would go. Street officers might still resent their 'unrepresentative' critics, but at Scotland Yard, these critics were being listened to and taken seriously. In 1985, Sir Kenneth Newman, McNee's successor, announced racial attacks were henceforth to be a 'force priority'. At the same time, his annual report for 1984 contained a frank admission: 'Some police officers have failed in the past to recognise the extent and degree of racial harassment.'

In the eyes of his critics, Newman's candour was spoilt by the sentence which followed: 'Some members of minority groups see racial affront where simply, crime or aggressiveness have struck at random.' But private police documents dating from this period also reveal a distinct change in emphasis. The 1986 internal force appraisal contained an entire section on racial attacks. It began: 'The implications for the force of failing to be seen to get to grips with this intractable problem are severe. First, the insidious nature of racially-motivated misbehaviour and its divisive product are clear. Secondly, perhaps cynically but nevertheless pragmatically, the force will be without political friends.'[10]

It discussed the need for more vigorous prosecution, noting that in Tower Hamlets, the heart of Britain's Bengali community, police were regularly charging perpetrators with the more serious crime of causing actual bodily harm, instead of common assault. In some areas, the police had tended to advise victims who were being harassed by their neighbours to take out civil actions: this was not satisfactory, the appraisal said – 'not least, because the victim is not entitled to the legal aid likely to be granted to a defendant. Fear and language difficulties are other obstacles to confront a victim "going it alone".' The document was also critical of a failure to communicate central policy decisions to divisional commanders and street patrols – echoing a charge often made by police critics. The section concluded:

The force is trying to gain credibility where there were mistakes of policy and attitude some years ago. Our policy, performance and attitude (particularly at divisional and street level) will be subject to the closest scrutiny. The force needs to speak with one voice and act vigorously and consistently, not only to refute our perpetual critics, but also to prevent some of our warmer friends from cooling.

In the mid-1980s, there were already signs that the intellectual direction being taken at the centre was having at least some effect at street level. In the twelve months before the Newham Seven trial, the local Newham police adopted a policy of sending CID officers to every alleged racial incident. There, and elsewhere in London, this produced a surge – in some places, of nearly 50 per cent – in the numbers of racial incidents reported. At 15 per cent, the arrest rate per 100 offences was very slightly higher than the overall Metropolitan average for all offences.

Yet these signs of improvement were limited. It was all too easy for the effect of better policy decisions to be dissipated. It was much easier to change official high-level policy than attitudes and behaviour on the street. In November 1985, a month after Newman first went on television to announce the new priority afforded to racial harassment, an editorial in *Police Review* claimed many attacks were trivial, or the result of internal community conflict. It added: 'Asians expect more than we can give ... there are a lot of factors within the Asian community that make it convenient for them to make allegations of racial motivation when it's simply caste or money at the root of the problem.'[11] It is therefore not surprising that black and Asian groups, and left-liberal commentators, have greeted successive public police campaigns with scepticism, even contempt.

One of the biggest initiatives came in 1987. Sir Kenneth Newman called a press conference to launch what he called 'an uncompromising and effective drive against a moral and social evil'. Racial violence was now to have still higher priority, he said, unveiling a package of leaflets and advertising aimed at victim groups. There was also to be a special CID squad devoted to the problem. The *Guardian* reported his initiative under the headline 'Yard scorned on race attacks'. It quoted Ealing councillor Valerie Vaz as saying the plan was 'too little, too late', and she called instead for 'a fundamental change in the racist and sexist attitudes of the police'.[12]

A 1987 article by Unmesh Desai, who founded the Newham Monitoring Project, among the most effective black pressure groups for the last fifteen years, illustrated the size of the mountain the police had to climb. 'A lot has been written about the police response to racial harassment,' he said. 'What we found, from our monitoring since 1980, is a police response which does not recognise the factor of racism. There is still, on the beat, the tendency to equate racial harassment with domestic disputes ... rank and file thinking is different from the highly-educated, media conscious flannel of senior police officers.'[13]

Just one badly-handled case can negate the effect of innumerable leaflets, policy statements and police campaigns. A disastrous example was the prosecution and acquittal of Mohammed Altaf, a Ford car worker accused in 1990 of wounding a Mr Dean Taylor with a knife – in, of all places, Newham. Altaf and his counsel, Courtenay Griffiths, were able to show a Snaresbrook Crown Court jury that he stabbed Taylor in self-defence, after Taylor and two other men chased him off the street into the home of his sister, Zahida Khan. His assailants were armed with a baseball bat and a knife. A doctor's report said Altaf bled copiously from blows to his mouth and nose, suffered severe bruising, and was slashed across the hand when he tried to ward off a knife attack.[14]

The police investigation appeared extremely one-sided. The officers who came to the incident took Taylor's claim that Altaf stabbed him in the street, without provocation, at face value. Yet the door to Zahida's home had been smashed in, and the floor was covered with blood. This blood was never tested: had it been shown to be Taylor's, it would have proved he was lying. The police did not search for weapons in the nearby house used by Taylor and his friends, although he and his friend Nigel Hayles had criminal records for violence.

Years of reporting racial harassment have taught me that incidents of this kind rapidly accrete strange stories, as perpetrators or their supporters try to justify what has happened. Zahida's neighbour, Lisa Rollingson, had a bitter row with Zahida over their respective children earlier in the day of the stabbing. Taylor also got involved: according to the prosecution, this was the trigger for the later, more serious attack. After the verdict, Rollingson expressed her sentiments in an interview with me. The real problem, she said, was the council housing Asians in the area. It was 'moving flotsam into the road, people who literally live like animals'. There were 'no rights for white people' any longer, as Altaf's acquittal proved.

I asked her how she thought Zahida's front door had been smashed in. She produced a truly fantastic explanation: that fifteen Asians from the Newham Monitoring Project had turned up in a van just after the stabbing, and ransacked the house in the minutes before the police arrived. Then, just in time, they had jumped over the garden fence and disappeared over a railway line. In court, Mrs Rollingson said she knew nothing of what had happened: she had been indoors the whole time, listening to Pavarotti.

The police reactions to this case amplified its intrinsic negative effect. At the time of the incident, the Metropolitan Police were in the middle of yet another expensive publicity campaign, aimed at persuading the victims of attacks to trust the police and come forward. It was based on an 'action guide' distributed by Saatchi & Saatchi, containing a personal message from Commissioner Sir Peter Imbert.

After Altaf's trial, Superintendent John Ball, the local community liaison officer, insisted the force had 'a sophisticated system for dealing with racial incidents which is working well'. He pointed out that juries found people not guilty 'all the time'. Chief Superintendent Patrick Pridige, the divisional chief officer, said the fault lay not with the police but the white witnesses: 'When we do these investigations, you have to accept we cannot make people tell us the truth.' In view of the distinct absence of proper investigation, his words carried unintentional irony.

★ ★ ★

By the beginning of the 1990s, police policies of the type pioneered in London had been adopted widely by constabularies throughout the country. The Staffordshire force which serves Stoke-on-Trent was no exception.

After the Deol family's trial, Chief Superintendent Keith Perrin, the county's chief community liaison officer, accepted that there had, after all, been a racial element to the case, despite the months of denial. He had not been able to say this before, he said, because it would not have been 'appropriate' with legal proceedings pending.[15] 'I don't know if there was a time when we could have interceded and stopped what happened,' he added. 'But maybe if we had had the full picture there were things we could have done. Hindsight is an exact science.' He had started a series of 'workshops' with Asian shopkeepers, with the intention of making them more secure and the police more aware of potential future attacks. But he maintained: 'What was really shocking about this case was that it happened in Stoke-on-Trent. I do believe that in general, Stoke provides a good picture of racial harmony.'

Was this mere complacency? The Stoke Labour MP, Mark Fisher, offered an important local perspective. Stoke-on-Trent, he said, was not a homogenous city, but an agglomeration of five towns and many villages, each with a discrete identity. There was a substantial Asian population: but until the Deols came along, none of this population was based on the Abbey Hulton estate. The police had developed sincere, effective policies in other districts, but were also 'oversensitive to it spreading'. If they confirmed the problem's existence by tackling it, they thought they would make it worse.

Thus they found themselves conditioned to ignore the evidence of racist violence in Abbey Hulton.[16]

As Asian victims of racially-motivated crime, the Deols were members of a subset of a larger group: victims of crime in general. In this lies a paradox of great importance, which has immense implications for the current state of impasse in the national debate about crime.

In discussing racial violence, something very strange happens to Left-Liberal critics. In dealing with almost every other type of crime, liberals instinctively argue for fewer police powers, less coercion: for the primacy of suspects' rights. They adopt, in other words, the due process model of criminal justice. In considering racial harassment, however, this position is often reversed, and Liberals and radicals find themselves making calls for more active policing, more vigorous prosecution: for crime control, not due process. Here is one group of offences where Left-Liberal commentators have even found themselves adopting the ultimate crime control position – attacking the validity of a white person's acquittal for an alleged racial attack.

An example came in January 1995, when John Rutter was cleared of participating in a brutal east London street beating which left Quddus Ali in a coma for months. The *Guardian* reported a series of reactions from 'Church and anti-racist groups' who 'criticised the weakness of the police evidence in the four-day trial'.[17] Kumar Murshid, of the Tower Hamlets Anti-Racist Committee, said: 'The criminal justice system is failing to respond to the rising curve of racist violence which is daily destroying lives.' Nasir Uddin, of Youth Connections, an umbrella organisation of Tower Hamlets youth groups, said: 'If this trial is the police and CPS attempting to stamp out racism, then it is not good enough.' David Haslam, of the Churches' Commission for Racial Justice, added: 'Somebody must know what went on. A wall of silence is not acceptable for the destruction of a family.'

Eight weeks earlier, the trial of Nicky Fuller, who was convicted of participating in the similar attack on Mukhta Ahmed, also produced furious reactions. Mukhta's scalp was almost removed from his skull in an attack in which almost every blow was a kick aimed at his head, but Fuller ended up pleading guilty only to the relatively minor offence of violent disorder. The much more serious charge of causing grievous bodily harm with intent was dropped by the Crown. As a result, the judge was obliged to let him walk free from court, because of the six months he had already spent in gaol on remand. This time, there were numerous calls for tougher penalties, possibly through new legislation.

Patrick Edwards, head of the race policy group GLARE, commented: 'For the assailant of such a brutal racist attack to be at liberty after conviction provides the clearest justification yet for a specific law against racial violence. Mukhta Ahmed was seized upon by a white gang and beaten severely. But yet again justice for the victim has not been forthcoming and the law failed to protect him.' Narendra Makanji, co-chair of the Anti-Racist Alliance, said:

> There need to be tougher and clearer laws on racial attacks and we are calling for the introduction of new legislation. We need a law that will make racial attacks a specific criminal offence. That would provide proper protection for black people and we will be stepping up our campaign for the new legislation. People are living in terrible fear but there is no protection for them under the law.[18]

The *Guardian*'s own leader columns have taken a similar line.

There is an analogy here with left-liberal responses to domestic violence. The barrister Helena Kennedy QC has written scathingly of the failure to investigate or prosecute domestic violence, and the consequent marginalisation of women in the criminal justice system: 'Many excuses given for failing to prosecute lack substance. Police officers fail to look for evidence that would support the complaint, particularly of a forensic nature, once an assault has been labelled "domestic" . . . In the few cases where they do go for trial, acquittal rates are high and fining is by far the most common disposal.'[19]

Kennedy draws conclusions about the system's failings in words which reveal a distinct crime control subtext:

> By supposedly creating equality between the parties the court reinforces inequality. The message to the defendant is that he is not accountable for his violence and the cycle is perpetuated . . .

There are a myriad ways in which the law can be reformed. Unfortunately, the knee-jerk response of most lawyers, even those with progressive attitudes, is to resist any change which might affect the position of a defendant.[20]

Demands for tougher legislation; more vigorous inquiry and prosecution; the imposition of harsher penalties. For liberals, this is unfamiliar language, even if they tend to apply it only to crimes committed against specific categories of vulnerable victims. That very act of discrimination implies a further departure from a basic due process principle – that of equality before the law. However, this is also the language of other types of crime victims and their supporters. In Abbey Hulton, it was in wide currency throughout the period the Deols were under attack.

There is an uncomfortable question arising from left-liberal critiques of the weakness of crime control as applied to racial and domestic violence. If the police and criminal justice system are inadequate at protecting these special categories of victim, are they any better at protecting everyone else?

According to the MP Mark Fisher, 'The policing on estates such as Abbey Hulton is derisory, because of underfunding; there aren't the resources to do it. It wasn't simply that the police didn't respond to Lucky and Dave. They can't respond to complaints of this kind at all. Five or six years ago, none of my constituents mentioned crime or law and order to me. Now, no one wants to talk about anything else.' The Asian taxi driver who took me to the Abbey in October 1994 made the same point another way: 'After the boy was killed, I stopped coming up here. Every time I did, my car would be stoned because of my colour. Now that's got better and every week I pick up an old lady, a white woman. You can see the fear in her eyes. Her windows have been broken, and she calls the police, and they say there's nothing they can do. And then the thugs come again. The thugs simply run this place.'

A trawl through back issues of the local paper reveals a dark history of intimidation. In October 1988, a local councillor, Brian Tinsley, claimed an experiment in 'community policing', based on the opening of an Abbey Hulton police office, had barely 'scratched the surface' of the estate's crime problems. He said the office had become merely 'a base to sup tea' with friendly residents, and even houses close to it were still being vandalised. In his view, the office, which was only open occasionally, was no substitute for 'more manpower' and regular patrols.[21]

In September 1991, more than 200 Abbey residents held a public meeting to put their concerns to the police. They told officers that teenagers were riding stolen motorbikes on the pavements at speeds of up to 70 m.p.h.; that gangs of up to sixty were congregating outside chip shops and off-licences, hurling abuse at passers by; and that a wave of burglaries and vandalism was not being contained. Chief Inspector Derek Haywood, the senior officer present, replied: 'I have been left in little doubt of the scale of the problem here, and we shall take action to deal with it.'[22]

If action was taken, it was not enough. The following January, the Abbey youths staged their own mini-riot. They overturned a car, set fire to a motorcycle and hurled bottles at the police who arrived to deal with the mayhem. Mr Haywood admitted: 'We did have extra patrols on duty on the estate, but they were initially overwhelmed and further men had to be drafted in.' Again he promised 'increased manning levels to achieve our objective'.[23] Two days later, none other than the Staffordshire Chief Constable, Charles Kelly, promised 'exceptional measures' to ensure the Abbey was adequately policed. Once again, these proved to be as ineffective at containing the wider problems as they were in assisting the Deols.[24]

In August of the same year, what the Evening Sentinel called 'desperate families' were driven to set up their own vigilante patrols with dogs, 'in a bid to stem a wave of drug-related incidents, vandalism, break-ins and car theft'. The immediate trigger was another public meeting called by residents to express their concern about crime. But this time, there were no promises of 'exceptional measures' or extra patrols. Instead, Chief Inspector Norma Cartwright, Haywood's successor, said: 'The simple fact is, there aren't enough policemen. There are not enough to go round. It's not just a local problem. Police forces nationwide are having the same difficulties.' Explaining the vigilante action, Alan Pomelli of the residents' association said: 'We know it's wrong and we shouldn't be doing it, but what else can we do? The police seem powerless to act.'

Ms Cartwright admitted: 'We are relying more and more on people like you to assist us when we are suffering from a lack of resources.'[25]

At the beginning of March 1993, three months before the death of Kevin Copeland, the *Sentinel* reported the vigilante squads were still in being, and enjoyed 'good relations' with the police.[26] However, they were not much of a deterrent to the estate's lawless minority. On 31 March, a delegation of fifty-three residents' association leaders, councillors and other community activists travelled to London by coach to lobby Mark Fisher and other MPs about crime in Abbey Hulton. When the last seven delegates were dropped off, they found themselves confronted by ten 'rowdy youths' who shouted abuse and called them 'grasses'. At 10 p.m. that night, they hurled a brick through the window of the association's van. A little later, a youth was disturbed as he crept towards the vehicle, carrying a petrol bomb.[27]

The Deol family always recognised that their ordeal was an intensified version of suffering being endured by many others. In the four-year period in which they ran the Abbey General Store, three other local shopkeepers gave up the struggle against vandalism and theft, and went out of business. Indeed, Dave says their passing may have been a factor in the escalation of attacks against the Deols in the spring of 1993. Racism, as we have seen, made the harassment of the Deols much worse and more organised. But the harassment of others was more bearable only by degree.

★   ★   ★

The ineffectiveness of the police and criminal justice at protecting victims of all races in places such as Abbey Hulton suggests another awkward challenge to standard left-liberal analysis. This assumes that the failure to bring racist attackers to justice is a function of police racism, which means they don't put enough effort into investigation or allocate enough resources. But is this always true? Or are there other failed inquiries where the prejudices of detectives play no part at all, but which nevertheless reveal some fundamental difficulties in the investigation of serious crime?

John Rutter, cleared of attacking Quddus Ali, and Nicky Fuller, convicted of joining the beating of Mukhta Ahmed, were both defended by the same east London solicitor, Joy Merriam. Part of her practice involves cases investigated by the Essex police, and she contrasts the 'huge resources' poured into the recent successful prosecution of an Essex car-theft ring with the less satisfactory outcome to the Ali and Ahmed inquiries. 'You do have to wonder if it is because the police are lax in investigating racist attacks,' she says.[28]

A letter to the *Guardian* about the Quddus Ali case from the Revd Kenneth Leech of St Botolph's church in Aldgate made a similar point, in familiar crime-control terms:

> After many months the only person charged with the appalling attack on Quddus Ali a few hundred yards from my home has been released for lack of evidence . . . The failure to find the perpetrators of yet another racist attack has left the Bengali community in this area feeling betrayed and deeply hurt. It is not as if this were the only attack or the only case where the criminals have not been found. Since the late 1960s when 'Paki bashing' was invented, we have had thousands of racist attacks in this area, including murders, and in most cases no one has been brought to justice.
>
> All this has led to a belief that attacks on Bengalis, and maybe Bengalis as persons, do not matter . . . The failure to treat such attacks seriously affects us all: an attack on one is an attack on all, human dignity is indivisible.[29]

With the wisdom of hindsight, it is logically possible to argue that the police investigating the attacks on both Quddus Ali and Mukhta Ahmed should have pursued other leads, and that these, if adopted, might have produced different final results. However, a dispassionate reading of the Quddus Ali and Mukhta Ahmed case papers leads inescapably to two conclusions. First, the police went to great, even unusual lengths in their hunt for the perpetrators of both attacks. Secondly, they faced enormous obstacles: the intimidation of witnesses, and the widespread refusal of the East End white community to co-operate with their investigations.

Merriam, who has worked in east London since 1979, says: 'There is a greater reluctance to help the police. There's never been a huge

willingness in the East End, but it has got much worse.' The gang
who nearly beat Mukhta to death late one night in February 1994, as
he made his way home after an evening with friends, had their own
means of intensifying such reluctance. The attack was the ninth of its
kind in the borough of Tower Hamlets within a few weeks, and this
escalation appeared to be linked with the recent election to the local
council of Derek Beackon of the racist British National Party. There
was, in other words, evidence of a new, organised aspect to racial
violence in the area, while reports suggested some of the attacks had
been carried out not by youths but by adults in their twenties and
thirties.

A squad of twenty detectives was formed to investigate the attack
on Mukhta. Within a few days, the police had arrested five people,
including Nicky Fuller, but he and the others were released because
there was insufficient evidence to bring a charge. One of the suspects
made extreme racist comments during his police interview, but no
one made admissions about the attack. There was a security video
taken in a nearby fast food outlet which showed a group of men and
youths leaving shortly before Mukhta was set upon: but without live
witnesses, it was useless – at best, it might have been supportive as
circumstantial evidence.

In the end, the prosecution was left with one material witness,
Nicky Fuller's ex-girlfriend, Kelly Turner, aged fifteen. Her story,
which she told to the *Daily Mirror*, gave more than a hint why
building a case against the other suspects had been so difficult, and it
had nothing to do with lax policemen. The *Mirror* reported:

> She has suffered a year of fear and violence for doing what no one
> else dared to do . . . She shopped her former boyfriend to the
> police for his part in a race hate attack . . . You would think
> Kelly's courage and integrity for standing up to such a violent thug
> would be applauded. Instead, she has been castigated and treated
> like a common criminal. Kelly has lost most of her friends, been
> bullied at school, followed in the street and received silent phone
> calls and chilling death threats.[30]

Kelly approached the police after attending a Valentine's party
with Fuller. He was so proud to have 'done a Paki' that he wore his

blood-stained trainers and showed them to Kelly: 'I was almost sick
when he showed me the blood which had congealed in between the
laces. He couldn't stop smiling and treated them like they were some
kind of trophy or memento.' Months of threatening phone calls and
abuse at school followed, much of it from her former closest friends.
She told the *Mirror*:

> I was having so many terrifying nightmares I had to have a baby
> monitor in my room so my mum could hear. I was too scared to
> go to school or even leave the house. I was bullied at school for
> seven months. People said they would pour petrol on me and set
> fire to it. I was called a Paki-lover, wog's mate, slag, slut every
> name you can think of. I wanted to curl up in a ball and make it all
> go away. I was also followed by my ex-boyfriend's friends, saying
> they were going to get me.

Finally, a week before the trial, she was attacked by an Afro-
Caribbean fellow pupil at school: 'He called me a bitch and slag for
sticking up for a "Paki" and then he punched me in the back of the
head with such force that I flew across the room. When I was on the
ground he started kicking my hands and arms which were around
my head. My friends and his had to pull him off me because he's so
huge.' She was left bruised and concussed, and said: 'I couldn't
believe I was being attacked by a black person after I stood up to
racists.'

It is perhaps not very surprising that the police found similar
difficulties in finding material witnesses prepared to give evidence
about the even more serious attack on Quddus Ali, which took place
a few months before that on Mukhta. As with the Mukhta case, they
had suspects but no immediate witnesses or admissions. Their one
substantial lead was a claim being made by local people who knew
the suspects that a few of the alleged attackers had confessed or
boasted about it to their friends.

In the event, of course, only one of those suspects, John Rutter,
then working as a council caretaker, ever faced trial. At the
Magistrates' Court committal stage, the Crown produced two of his
colleagues from work, to whom he was alleged to have made
admissions shortly after the beating. One of them dropped out

altogether by the time of the full Crown Court trial; the second was easily discredited by Rutter's defence – he had convictions for violence and dishonesty himself.

Joy Merriam remains a vehement advocate of Rutter's total innocence: not only was the prosecution case flawed, she says, but it was misconceived from the outset. Indeed, Rutter, tall, dark and thin, does not match the description given by some eyewitnesses of Ali's main assailants, who were said to be stocky and blond. He was not picked out by people who saw the attack at any of several identification parades.

The police may have been wrong: but they cannot be accused of being half-hearted. As with the Mukhta inquiry, there was a special squad, with an incident room, led by a Detective Superintendent from the east London 'Area Major Investigation Pool' – exactly as would have been the case with a murder investigation. They may not have produced a result, but the sheer volume of the paperwork their efforts generated is remarkable: many hundreds of statements, intelligence logs, and house-to-house inquiry forms, filling numerous binders, each four inches thick.

The officer who led the team, Detective Superintendent Michael Craik, was aware that Rutter's alleged 'third party' admissions were bound to be much less convincing than a confession to a police officer from Rutter's own mouth. To this end, Craik was prepared to employ controversial and expensive methods. In the spring of 1994, Rutter left his job in Tower Hamlets and together with other members of his family, went to work at a holiday camp in Norfolk. Three undercover officers were infiltrated into jobs at the camp with the task of befriending Rutter, in the hope he would drop his guard and admit to attacking Quddus Ali. The policemen were wired with secret tape-recorders. The results are revealed here for the first time.

As the days went by, Rutter made no admissions at all. But his brother, Neil, whom one of the officers, known as 'Ted', taped during a drive to London, did him no favours. At one stage, they discussed John's attitude to race relations, and Neil said: 'He hates Pakis . . . especially now.' They talked about John's pending trial, and Neil mentioned the recent successful murder appeal by the sisters Lisa and Michelle Taylor. Neil Rutter told Ted: 'They got put away for two years, and then they found out they was not guilty.

That the evidence they had against them was about two different girls totally . . . And then there's someone like me brother, *who did do it*, [author's italics] but the way it's going, hopefully get off with it.' But if John did go to prison, his brother added, 'then he got what he deserves, yeah, cos of what he's done.'

Under the rules of evidence, Neil's allegations against his brother could not be adduced in court. They were classed as hearsay: only if Neil had been willing to go into the witness box and accuse his own brother, on the basis that John had actually confessed to him, would they have had any legal value as evidence. Neil's claims might have been based on malice or sheer fantasy. In any event, the jury did not have an opportunity of hearing them and deciding whether they ought to carry any weight. The next part of the taped exchange suggests Neil's allegations might even have been wishful thinking: 'They arrested fifteen people, let them all off and now it's just me brother. I wouldn't mind if he killed him. But he didn't. I would have.'

★ ★ ★

Joy Merriam's conclusion about the inquiries into the Quddus Ali and Mukhta Ahmed beatings is harsh: 'The police line is, that unless people like Kelly Turner come forward they can't prosecute. It's crap, because they just don't investigate.'

Her comment begs a question. If witnesses are being intimidated, and there are no obvious scientific clues, what *can* they investigate? Can evidence be produced from thin air? Journalists get information because people give it to them, more or less freely: if that isn't happening, there is no story to write. Do not the same principles apply to the detection and prosecution of crime?

Earlier in this chapter, objective consideration of the victims of racial violence forced us to consider victims in general. In the same way, the problem of investigating racist attacks is a component of a wider problem: that of investigating serious crime. As the next chapter will demonstrate in detail, convictions have been falling, although crime rates have risen rapidly. The Ahmed and Ali cases point not to a mere local difficulty of racist or stupid detectives, but a broader, systematic impasse. Is criminal justice approaching some kind of collapse?

The left-liberal campaign for crime control to deal with racist violence presents a final paradox. Running throughout its rhetoric is an explicit warning: that if criminal justice will not protect the victims, they will sort things out for themselves. Uniting the campaigns for the Bradford Twelve, the Newham Eight and the Newham Seven was a potent slogan – 'self-defence is no offence'. 'Vigils and demos won't achieve anything,' one Asian youth worker told me after the attack on Mukhta Ahmed, 'the only thing that will do any good is to give the bastards a good hiding.' In other words: vigilantism, the conscious abandoning of the rule of law in the face of its perceived collapse.

This is, of course, exactly what happened in Abbey Hulton, when the white residents' association organised its dog patrols, and when Dave and Lucky Deol tried to grab Kevin Copeland to make their 'citizen's arrest'.

Vigilantism is spreading fast, often cheered on by the right-wing press. (It must also be said that Home Secretary Michael Howard's scheme for 'street watch' neighbourhood patrols, launched in autumn 1994 under the bizarre rubric of 'walking with a purpose', has done nothing to discourage it.) 'They have been pushed too far, too often,' the *Sunday Times* reported in February 1995. 'People throughout Britain are increasingly taking the law into their own hands and delivering summary justice to violent criminals by forming vigilante gangs.'[31] The article listed a series of examples, in Nottinghamshire, Cleveland and Birmingham, where citizens had variously 'restored order to a red light district', set up telephone hotlines, and dealt 'punishment beatings' to rowdy youths.

Participants in such 'schemes' justified their actions with enthusiasm. 'It does no harm to give these kids a few slaps to frighten them,' said a vigilante from Mansfield. His counterpart on Teesside, part of a group equipped with their own high-frequency walkie-talkie system, claimed: 'If these thugs draw weapons, my men will do likewise. We are just protecting our property. We have had enough.' A woman neighbour told the paper she found the patrols 'reassuring'.

In January 1995, Ted Newberry, 82, was given a suspended prison sentence for shooting a putative burglar through the wooden door of his allotment shed in Ilkeston, Derbyshire.[32] In the same county, at

New Mills, Andrew Robinson also got a suspended term for beating a youth over the head with a cane and kicking him in the face on the ground, so breaking his nose and blackening his eyes. The youth was one of a group of ten who, the *Daily Express* reported, ran through Mr Robinson's garden, singing football songs and abusing his wife. Mr Robinson, who lost his job as a result, was quoted as saying: 'I have ended up out of work with a criminal record while the yobs who caused this nightmare walked away scot-free. I have paid a heavy price for doing what I thought was right. Where is the justice in that?'[33] It is a matter for speculation whether the sudden rash of Derbyshire vigilantes is connected with the fact that years of cash starvation so denuded the county constabulary that it was denied Her Majesty's Inspectorate's 'certificate of efficiency' for three consecutive years, 1992–5.

There have always been 'have-a-go heroes' willing to risk their safety in pursuit of criminals; there have always been beefy householders ready to take on high-spirited young men with their fists. Pensioners letting 'chummy' have it with their shotguns and patrols of 'decent' citizens who tie young offenders to telegraph poles are something else again. Vigilantism ought not to be a source of amusement. In place of law and formal criminal justice, it heralds a return to the primitive: to justice defined by the temporary, local expediency of gangs and kinship clans. It is only one step away from the 'justice' meted out by the IRA to supposed car thieves in Belfast and Londonderry.

In an essay dating from 1915, the great sociological pioneer Max Weber suggested summary popular justice indicated a society in deep trouble: 'The state is an association that claims the monopoly of the legitimate use of violence, and cannot be defined in any other manner . . . where this factor is absent, the state is also absent.' The consequences, he added, would be escalating social violence: 'According to the inescapable pragmatism of all action, force and the threat of force inevitably breed more force.'[34]

Let there be no mistake: the position of Asians and other ethnic minorities is worse. They are more likely to be victims of assault and other types of harassment. A recent Policy Studies Institute study echoes much earlier research, finding the 10,000 racial incidents reported to police each year to be only 'the tip of the iceberg', and even the 130,000 suggested by the 1992 British Crime Survey to be a serious underestimate.[35] It rightly draws attention to the greater impact of 'low level harassment' such as verbal abuse when it comes loaded with racial hatred. But radicals and liberals cannot have it both ways. The white vigilante hardmen with their walkie-talkies and baseball bats also think self-defence is no offence.

At one point during the Deols' trial, defence counsel Stephen Solley made a curious remark. The sort of thing the jury had been hearing about, he said, 'does not go on in Kensington'. Indeed not: it happens where Britain's impoverished third lives, in the ruined cities which used to be centres of manufacturing, on council estates where the term 'inner city' has come to mean its opposite: communities on the margins and beyond. There the offenders live cheek by jowl with their victims.

Commenting on the Quddus Ali case in his letter to the *Guardian*, the Revd Leech said: 'From time to time the anger in inner city areas explodes in violence, and then all kinds of establishment figures descend and issue their single transferable speeches. And then it is business as usual: neglect, apathy, contempt, the rhetoric of the underclass, and continued violence.'

In 1987, A. Sivanandan, the director of the Institute of Race Relations, examined the bitter row which blew up when Maureen McGoldrick, a headteacher in the London Borough of Brent, was alleged to have asked the council not to send her any more black teachers. The parties to the ensuing conflict, Sivanandan wrote, completely lost sight of what should have been at stake. The real, underlying issue was not the provision of black teachers *per se*, but deep inequality in the provision of education. However, teachers, council and unions became locked in a futile struggle over the details of an anti-racist 'package' which existed all on its own. Racism had become disconnected from its historical and institutional contexts. The protagonists in the battle over McGoldrick had no answers to educational disadvantage. They preferred to concentrate on 'skin politics and white guilt-tripping'.

Beyond Sivanandan's analysis of education in Brent was a phrase full of insight with wider application: 'An issue of class was being fought out on the terrain of race.' Every fact had to be examined and analysed twice: 'Once on the touchstone of race, and once on the touchstone of class.'[36] That insight illuminates the paradoxes in left-liberal argument outlined above. Class has been excluded from the discourse. To restore it to its rightful place means accepting the plight of white crime victims, and accepting that most of them, like most offenders, are poor; that the absence of protection by the police and the difficulties in bringing successful prosecutions exist in circumstances other than racial violence; and that vigilantism poses a mortal threat to the rule of law.

To examine racist violence on the touchstone of class leads to conclusions we might prefer to ignore. For those who live outside the council tenanted archipelagos of the disenfranchised, it is easier and more convenient to consider racial violence only in 'skin politics' terms. It requires no deeper analysis of the causes of crime. It allows us to carry on blaming prejudiced policemen for failings which are not theirs alone.

On the Right, crime in general is blamed on the individual evil of demonised young thugs. For the Left, racist violence is simply the acts of demonised racist thugs. So the contradictions and paradoxes multiply. Once we bring class back into the picture, the crisis comes into sharper focus. If criminal justice is collapsing, it is only a part of a deeper social palsy.

CHAPTER THREE

The Rising Tide of Crime

MIDNIGHT in February on the Stonebridge Park estate, in Harlesden, north-west London; the end of a filthy Friday, teeming with rain. An Irish woman in her twenties kneels outside a ground-floor flat, battering the door with her fists, shouting incoherent obscenities. Her children stand around her in a sad little circle, their faces caught in the sodium glare. 'Let me in, you cow, you bitch, I haven't fucking finished with you!'

As the two policemen arrive, called by the occupants of the flat which the woman is trying to enter, she remains oblivious to their presence. Her elder son, who looks about seven, is at least fully-dressed. The girl, aged maybe five, has no shoes: her socks are black with mud. The younger boy, no more than three, is naked from the waist down. All the children are soaked.

Eventually, the mother's ex-husband, who was apparently telephoned at the same time as the police, arrives to collect his offspring. The woman staggers after them into the night. The officers go into the flat. Inside are a much bigger woman in her forties and her teenage son, who shrinks into the background, pretending to be absorbed in a television programme. She says:

> Officer, she is my best friend, or rather was. We were here having a drink and she suddenly went mad, just sort of flipped. She started blaming me for everything wrong in her life, and then she started kicking me: see, here are the bruises on my legs. So I had to throw them out: that's when I called you.
>
> We had only half a bottle of brandy each. To be honest we're all sick and tired of her drinking, and as you see she has kids. I'm worried about her drinking. I don't give a damn about her. What I give a damn about is those kids.

One of the PCs points out that sharing a bottle of brandy is an odd way to show concern for the children, let alone ejecting them into the rain. The woman will not accept it: 'She can drink a bottle of vodka tomorrow and be fine, but brandy is different. It does something to her.' There is nothing to be done, and we leave.

For six months, I was given unrestricted access to the London police division, Kilburn, whose 'ground' includes my home. I went on raids, patrolled on foot, sat in the back of 'instant response' cars and watched the treatment of prisoners. For journalists who specialise in crime and Home Affairs, it is easy to speak to senior officers, often at organised briefings. Unregulated contact with the service's 'ground floor', the PCs and sergeants, is more difficult to arrange. It gave this book a valuable perspective: the opportunity not only to observe, but to listen to what ordinary police officers think and say.[1]

In the course of the year before my first visit to Kilburn in October 1994, Michael Howard, the Conservative Home Secretary, had been busily moving the national debate on law and order far to the right. Howard's vision of policing was harsh and clearly defined. 'To those coppers who see their main job as clearing villains off the street, I have the simple message: carry on, constable, I will back you all the way,' he told the Commons after the 1993 Queen's Speech.

A few months later, Howard publicly attacked David Faulkner, who as Home Office Deputy Secretary 1982–92, had advised all Howard's Tory predecessors following Lady Thatcher's election victory. Howard accused Faulkner of being the architect of liberal theories which had 'held sway for too long in too many quarters'. To those such as Faulkner, who thought the job of the police was wider than simple law enforcement, Howard gave short shrift: 'We are getting back to basics and saying yes, the first duty of the police is to catch criminals.'[2]

Out on the ground, in the back of a squad car, things look different. With three police stations, Kilburn, Harlesden and Willesden, Kilburn division is one of the largest and busiest in the Metropolitan Police. Socially and ethnically mixed, with large Asian, Afro-Caribbean and Irish populations, it includes several big council estates with high levels of unemployment and deprivation. It has equally high rates for most types of crime. In 1994, Kilburn police dealt with fifty-eight reported rapes, against three in the central London division, Holborn, which covers the office where I work.

On the day I was shown round Kilburn station for the first time, two murder suspects were in the cells. There had been two homicides in the previous twenty-four hours. There is a lot of burglary and street robbery (mugging), much of it committed to finance the consumption of narcotics. On the division's big council estates, the scourge of crack cocaine has wrought incalculable human damage. There may be a lot of crime in Kilburn, but a high proportion of patrol officers' time is taken up with work which has little to do with it. When people cannot think of any other way of solving their problems, they call the police.

On another wet, winter evening, we go to the aid of Eugene, twenty, who has been been locked out of his flat. Eugene is a statistic: one of the 60 per cent of black males in London aged eighteen to twenty-four who have no job. 'I argued with my mother pretty badly this morning,' he says miserably. 'I went out for a walk to buy a paper and she'd gone, but she's changed the locks. I've nowhere else to go: I've sort of lost touch with a lot of my friends lately. I've been here five hours and I'm cold. I think my mum had a bag with her. I'm worried she's gone away.'

What Eugene wants is the law's help or approval in kicking in the door to his home. The police cannot supply it: 'If we smash down your door that will be criminal damage. You could do it yourself, but it's a question of whether you think you'll be able to square it with your mum later.' The temperature is dipping towards freezing, and Eugene wears only a shirt and thin blouson jacket. Through the door on the landing opposite wafts the unmistakable smell of cannabis. A man in dreadlocks opens it, takes in the officers and swiftly slams it shut. 'Doesn't look like the neighbours are going to be much help,' the PC says. 'This isn't picking up the pieces but just looking at them before putting them back.'

There is another common type of call which reduces the police to impotent, despairing rage. One night a message comes over the radio to go to an address on the fringes of the Stonebridge estate. There has been an 'abandoned call trace', meaning someone dialled 999, then left the receiver hanging, the line open but silent. Every call like that has to be checked: it might merely be naughty children; but it could be a murder in progress.

This one turns out to have been made by Sheila, a mountainous African woman in deep distress. 'Are you all right love?', asks PC Gordon, a rocksteady ex-miner from Derbyshire, who came south and joined the police when his colliery closed. 'No I'm not all right,' Sheila replies, bursting into tears. 'I'm hearing voices, I want to go to casualty, I want to be in hospital but there are no beds.' Around her sitting room, layered with grime, she has heaped huge, haphazard piles of money, ten and twenty pence pieces. 'Look, this is my collection,' Sheila says. 'Oh God, I want to be back in hospital. I only go in twice a week. Can't you see, I'm terrible. I've been crying. I'm so depressed. Why are you doing this to me?'

She has no recollection of dialling 999; no idea why she might have done so. As Gordon tries to calm her, suggesting a cup of tea, she suddenly flips into full-blown dementia. 'You've taken something from me! You've stolen my spirit! You came here to steal my spirit, I knew I should never have opened the door.' Abruptly, Sheila turns and flees, out of the room, down the stairs and out on to the pavement, shrieking all the while: 'Help me, they're trying to steal my spirit!'

We go. The sight of our departure reassures Sheila enough to go back inside. 'So there you have it,' says Gordon back in the car:

> Community care in action. There's a special crisis team which is supposed to help people like her: you can wait two hours for them to come, and by then the patient is lucid. Well, I checked the kitchen: she has food. She has warmth: the fire is on. She isn't in what they would call immediate need. She's in the community: they've saved the money by closing the hospital where she might have been. Some community, some care.

Dealing with people suffering severe mental illness has become so common in London that at the end of 1994, it was decided that every Metropolitan officer ought to be specially trained. But experience has taught the police there is little prospect of those who cry for help being admitted to hospital.

There are many cases worse than Sheila's. Four years ago,

Harlesden police disarmed a paranoid schizophrenic who was threatening people with a club while performing strange, T'ai Chi-style exercises in the Stonebridge shopping precinct. The psychiatric social worker and psychiatrist who saw him at the police station said there was no cause to 'section' him under the Mental Health Act: no cause to admit him to hospital as a danger to himself or others. Some months later, he murdered a young woman.

One day I arrived at Harlesden police station to find a sole topic of conversation – a young man who had been arrested the previous night during a 'domestic', a violent argument with his grandmother. 'I talked him down, I thought he was going to be fine, and then he leapt on her again,' the officer who dealt with the incident said. 'All this time he was stark, bollock naked. So we took him to the police station, called the doctors and they refused to admit him. There was no way we could let him go back to his grandmother. We kept him in the cells overnight for breach of the peace.'

Next morning, the magistrate had to let him go. An hour later the police got a call: a young man, naked, was threatening to jump off Neasden railway bridge on to the track. It was the same man. 'We go and get him and talk him down,' the officer said. 'We bring him back here; again no one will admit him. So we let him go again. He goes straight back to the railway and this time he climbs straight on to the parapet and jumps.' From the bridge to the track is about thirty feet. There was no train coming: he merely broke his back. He will spend the rest of his life in a wheelchair.

If the police often find themselves called upon as a social service of last resort, attending to the mentally ill or merely inadequate, it is a role they generally dislike – not because their only job is catching criminals, but because they know they cannot fulfil the social work role properly. Asked to fill gaps left by other agencies now cut to vestigial irrelevance, the police know they can provide no more than the most superficial kind of palliative care.

The measurement of crime is an imprecise science, and any discussion based upon criminal statistics must proceed with caution. But the evidence is convincing that the years since Lady Thatcher's first election victory in 1979 have seen a great surge in many kinds of offence. Certain categories, notably serious violence and burglary, have doubled. After so long in office, the proliferation of crime poses problems for Conservatism which it can barely confront. If Thatcher was responsible for an economic revolution, any suggestion of a causal link between crime and the social conditions which her revolution engendered has to be rejected. The standard Tory account cannot accept that deprivation causes crime, or that crime has risen because social divisions have deepened.

The then Home Secretary, Douglas Hurd, set the tone of subsequent ministerial reactions when he visited Handsworth in Birmingham on the day after the riot in September 1985. The events of the previous night, he said, were 'not social phenomena but crimes'. It was the individual moral choice which mattered, not the context in which it was made. Writing in 1992, the former Home Office Minister John Patten went so far as to blame crime on declining church attendance and the weakening fear of hell. He claimed: 'Dwindling belief in redemption and damnation has led to loss of fear of the eternal consequences of goodness and badness. It has had a profound effect on personal morality – especially on criminality.'[3]

It was not in the make-up of Prime Minister John Major to use such fundamentalist language. But the same analytical thread was evident in his remarks in a newspaper interview a few weeks after the murder of the toddler James Bulger at the beginning of 1993. Pledging to 'tackle the rising tide of crime threatening to engulf society', he said people had forgotten how to distinguish right and wrong: 'I believe they should condemn. If they do not condemn, they may appear to approve tacitly. Tacit approval will lead to repetition, and that is what we need to avoid. I feel strongly society needs to condemn a little more and understand a little less.'[4]

Home Secretary Michael Howard has also been assiduous in his search for non-economic causes of crime. 'We should have no truck with trendy theories that try to explain away crime by blaming socio-economic factors,' he proclaimed in November 1993. He went on to advance a bizarre alternative – the collapse of traditional values among young offenders' grandparents, who had raised their offspring in homes without fathers because the men were away fighting the Second World War.[5] Retreating to safer territory, in a speech in April 1994 Howard railed at 'the failure of some schools to instil discipline and respect'.[6]

Occasionally, there have been public hints of tension between the police and the Government, over the latter's evasion of macro-economic causes of crime. In February 1992, weeks before a general election in which crime was sure to figure, the Metropolitan Police Commander David Stevens claimed at a press conference: 'Social deprivation can be linked to most areas of crime, and the government must address the electorate in terms of a solution.' This was not appreciated by the Government. John Patten retorted: 'The majority of unemployed people are not criminals. Most people charged are in work. Low incomes or unemployment do not cause crime. There are no excuses for lawlessness and hooliganism.'[7]

Meanwhile, against these signs of desperation, the Shadow Home Secretary turned Labour Party Leader, Tony Blair, had only to repeat a single, brilliant soundbite, declaring his aim to be 'tough on crime, tough on the causes of crime'. Responding to Howard's lashing of the schools and grandfathers, he seemed to be speaking the most basic common sense. 'To draw a line under the causes of crime and say the family and the school matter, but broader social conditions like unemployment, levels of opportunity for our young people and poverty do not, is simply foolish.' His view coincided perfectly with the opinions of police officers, both cerebral high-flyers and the sages of the street.

★ ★ ★

To the officers who patrol places like the Stonebridge Park estate, the links between crime, mental illness and shattered families, and their well-springs in poverty and deprivation, seem blindingly obvious. Police officers' disillusion with 1990s Conservatism stems from their own, direct experience. Walking round the South Kilburn estate, another huge, high crime, low income enclave of poverty, a female beat officer said: 'You can look at this place and see the drug dealing, and the crime that goes on to support it. And you can also see that both the bad guys and their neighbours have enormous problems. Society marginalises the problems, and the people.' In Kilburn, as in Stoke's Abbey Hulton, offenders and victims live concentrated together, the poor robbing the poor. Some officers respond with bleak, cynical humour. In the words of a Harlesden CID man, 'here, even the victims are shit'.

'It's going to get worse: the rich are going to get richer and the poor will carry on sliding deeper into poverty,' one of Kilburn's sergeants said. 'Sooner or later, there's going to be an enormous punch-up between them.' Like many police officers, he said his long record of voting Conservative was at an end.

In Stonebridge Park, some of the enclosed corridors have been burnt out deliberately by residents desperate to move, in the vain hope that this might induce the council to rehouse them. Pools of solidified molten plastic lie on what remains of the flooring, and the walls have been left in a charred, blackened state. In the summer of 1994, a man opened the door of his flat unaware of the conflagration in progress outside. According to the officer who dealt with the body, 'he melted'. 'I was brought up in the Home Counties,' said the young PC who showed me round this devastation. 'Until I came here five years ago, I did not believe such places existed in our country. How can you expect people to live decent lives in this sort of place?'

Police officers share the sense of national disgust at contemporary Conservatism, which at the time of writing has fuelled a huge Labour opinion poll lead for many months. Amid the debris of the health and education services, Lady Thatcher's claim that 'there is no such thing as society' has been losing its allure. The outrage over huge pay rises enjoyed by the chairmen of privatised utilities has focused the growing public rejection of the Thatcherite morals of the eighties.[8]

Another Kilburn officer said: 'There is simply no way I'm going to vote Tory. I'm only just waking up to what the arrogant bastards have done.' He quoted Raymond Chandler: 'Crime isn't a disease, it's a symptom. Cops are like a doctor that gives you aspirin for a brain tumour.' A PC with 20 years' service identified two, related elements behind the rise in crime: the material and the moral.

Why do people commit crime? Come in Michael Howard: of course social deprivation plays a part. Yes, they're going to get their dole money. But these people have had their hope taken away.

Combine that with the fact that public morality just doesn't exist. Putting it bluntly, if someone's got a stolen telly in their front room, no one round here gives a shit. But why should they? If their father was on the dole, what do they know about anything except being on the dole? How can you expect people with no future, on the poverty line, to worry about a stolen telly when the Chairman of British Gas got his whopping pay rise and his millions in share options, while his own employees are getting the sack?

The rich are getting richer and the poor are getting poorer. And you see these so-called leaders of society, breaking the law and getting away with it. Major launched 'Back-to-Basics' and then half his own people turned out to be over the side.[9] The very fabric of society is in extreme danger. It goes all the way to the top: in fact, it starts at the top.

Researching his play *Murmuring Judges*, the playwright David Hare spent some time with the police in Clapham, south London. He found similar sentiments, and later wrote:

I did not know until I went out in the squad cars myself that so many policemen, patrolling the hopeless housing estates or trying to keep order on the lawless streets, had developed so clear an analysis of their own role. In their view, they were being used. The Conservative administrations of the eighties had gone hell for leather for economic policies which were crudely biased towards the rich. They had then turned to the police and blamed them for failing to cope with the huge social problems which the government itself had created.[10]

Elements of policing's upper echelons have, at least in private, been expressing for a decade the social awareness now to be heard from street officers. Commander Stevens's comments on crime and unemployment in 1992 were no isolated outburst. The confidential annual Metropolitan Police internal appraisal document provides a fascinating window into this thinking. The work of a Scotland Yard policy unit staffed by officers up to the rank of Commander, it includes each year a frank assessment of London's economic, political and social prospects, and their likely consequences for policing.

It was the 1986 appraisal which first raised the alarm about a deeply undesirable movement, which had become a powerful motor of crime – social polarisation, the widening of the gap between the rich and the poor. Already, the report said, it could be said that the Metropolitan Police had to cope with policing 'two Londons'.[11] It added that a close look at unemployment statistics 'reveals that in some parts of London, between a quarter and a third of young men aged nineteen to twenty-five are unemployed'. Meanwhile, 'the gap continues to widen between those in work and the unemployed. In the year to July 1986 the average person in employment had a pay rise of 7.5 per cent, which has not been reflected in benefit increases.'

As a result, London was under 'economic and political stress'. Developing the 'two Londons' concept, the document cited Cranham West in Havering as an example of the first, affluent, suburban London, where 'virtually everyone owns their house, and nine out of ten owns a car'. Only 3 per cent were out of work. In Spitalfields in the inner city, however, unemployment was at 22 per cent, 'virtually no one is a home owner and only one in five households has a car'. The mortality rate for people under forty-five was three times higher in Spitalfields than in Cranham West.

As far as inequality's effects on crime were concerned, it was necessary to come down to local level to see the differences which broad surveys could easily mask. 'Whilst fear of crime in the outer ring of more affluent boroughs is a pervasive problem,' the document said, 'the same fear is increasingly proximate to reality in the inner London "twilight boroughs".' There, if people were in fear of crime, it was because they were in genuine danger.

Both the level and the rate of increase in reported crime were much higher in the inner boroughs, the document went on. The 202 recorded offences per 100,000 inner London residents compared to a rate of 95 per 100,000 in the outer city. Burglary was two and a half times more prevalent in the inner boroughs, although people there had less to steal. In 1985–6, mugging rose 17 per cent in inner London, and only 1 per cent in the rich outer boroughs.

The following year's Metropolitan appraisal made similar points, quoting Disraeli, the Church of England's 'Faith in the City' report, Lord Scarman and others under the heading 'Polarisation and Deprivation'. Unless these issues were addressed, the document said, any progress in policing would be wasted; the conditions which had produced the 1981 inner city riots were burgeoning, instead of being alleviated.[12]

The 1987 Metropolitan document quoted the British Medical Association, saying that economic inequality was reflected in sickness and mortality rates, adding: 'Inequalities so severe as to give rise to pronounced effects on health are indefensible.' It published a list of comparative death rates, area by area, 'an analysis which brings home the effects of deprivation and illustrates social polarity'. This document, remember, was being written at the height of the Thatcher-Lawson 'economic miracle' – in the very year of the City of London's deregulation 'big bang', when the streets of London were supposed to be brimming with champagne-quaffing yuppies.

The internal appraisals continued to emphasise what the 1989 version called in a heading 'haves and have-nots'. In 1991, Commissioner Sir Peter Imbert organised a conference for senior officers to discuss policy issues. It was held in the pit of the recession which followed the Lawson boom. The briefing document for participants included the now-familiar pessimism. The economy was expected to pull out of recession soon, it said. But unemployment would stay high for years to come, although the well-off would quickly regain or surpass their old spending power. The poor 'will be the last to benefit from any recovery. This will serve only to emphasise the economic polarisation that has been taking place over the last decade. Whatever means of measurement are used, the top 20 per cent has been getting richer, and the bottom 20 per cent poorer.'[13]

By the spring of 1995, awareness of Thatcherism's downside had spread to the point where even Howard Davies, chairman of the CBI, could put his name to a Rowntree Foundation report which stated that the poorest fifth in society had felt none of the benefits of its economic miracle. Their incomes had stayed the same or diminished, while the richest tenth had seen their standard of living improve by 55 per cent. 'Just as in the last century it was in the interests of all to introduce public health measures to combat the spread of infectious diseases fostered by poverty' the report said, 'so in this century it is in the interests of all to remove the factors which are fostering drugs, crime, political extremism, and social unrest.'[14] In case his readers had not got the message, the *Financial Times* columnist Joe Rogaly commented: 'I am not asking you to express soppy sympathy for unmarried mothers in council flats. Just think about how safe you feel in certain streets at night. A divided society is insecure. This ultimately threatens everyone, including the middle classes.'[15]

It is significant and remarkable that thinkers in the Metropolitan Police – which the Left was then attacking as 'Mrs Thatcher's bootboys' – were reaching these conclusions almost a decade earlier.

In the wake of the Rowntree report, right-wing commentators attacked its methodology. It was claimed the poorest had not got poorer at all – for example, more had telephones and central heating than ever before. Absolute poverty – 'not a relative decline, nor statistical gymnastics, but actual drops in living standards' – was no worse, the *Sunday Telegraph* insisted. Even if the 'trickle down' from the self-enriching richest had been limited, it was absolute poverty which mattered.[16] Wishing the problem away by giving it new labels, Digby Anderson, director of the Social Affairs Unit, said that the rich and poor were better described as the 'reasonably affluent' and the 'extremely affluent'. David Green, director of health and welfare at the Institute of Economic Affairs, said: 'It doesn't matter about the gap between rich and poor so long as the bottom of the income range is not too low. I don't think it is. The main message of the report is: it pays to work.'[17] To which one might add: if you can.

Yet there was something shrill and unconvincing about the attempts to write off Rowntree's diagnosis. The prevalence of central heating makes a poor indicator of poor people's well-being. With the sale of older, more desirable (and gentrifiable) council housing, the poor have become overwhelmingly concentrated in post-war sink estates where central heating is a standard fitting. On the Stonebridge Park estate, for example, there are radiators in every dwelling. But a 1993 survey for the London borough of Brent found 64 per cent of tenants were on housing benefit. Nearly 30 per cent of the estate's potential breadwinners were unemployed, three times the London average; and 48 per cent of unemployed males had been out of work for more than a year.[18]

The link between crime and deprivation seemed pretty clear on the Stonebridge estate. Asked what they considered the disadvantages of the estate, nearly a quarter of residents said crime and vandalism – more than any other factor. Nineteen per cent had been crime victims in the preceding twelve months, of whom over half had been mugged. The survey asked residents 'what for you is the biggest advantage of living on the estate'. The most popular response, which attracted 45 per cent of replies, was: 'None'.

One of the few studies of the employment status of offenders was carried out in 1980 in Northumbria: a region blighted since the 1930s by the closure of its heavy industries: steel, shipbuilding and coal. It found that an unemployed man aged sixteen to twenty-nine was ten times more likely to have committed a crime than a person in work.[19]

The most authoritative research data on the connection between crime and the economy is a Home Office study by Simon Field, published in 1990. It contained a statistical model which Field said could be used to forecast future levels of crime, and when this was applied to the subsequent recession, it proved remarkably accurate. Throughout the twentieth century, Field found, property crime rose when economic consumption fell: when the economy was contracting in size.[20]

Falling consumption was likely to have rapid consequences for the employment of people most likely to commit offences, Field added. If they did have jobs, they tended to occupy 'weak or marginal' positions in the labour market, where overall economic changes had 'amplified effects'. Worsening business conditions would hit them and their jobs first. Field's work also suggested that 'unemployment and the relative deprivation associated with it' were conducive to violent crime.[21]

Ministerial rhetoric about the causes of crime sustained a further blow in October 1994, when the Home Office published details of a new formula for funding the police. Despite Michael Howard's claims that to place any blame on unemployment 'insulted the jobless who do not offend', the formula's two main elements were a 'disorder index' and a 'crime management index'. These were the means used to predict each constabulary's workload, and hence the funds they would need. The factors taken into account in the crime index were the number of single parent families, the number of people living in council estates, the proportion of people in rented accommodation, and, with heaviest weighting, the numbers of unemployed and long-term unemployed. The factors in the disorder index were identical, with the addition of the number of people who lived alone and in terraced housing.[22]

Meanwhile, the intellectual Right has focused on the weakening of family structures, and the increase in divorce rates and in single parenting as the principal cause of rising crime. Their most extreme exponent is the American, Charles Murray, who in a series of articles in the *Sunday Times* dating back to 1989, described the formation of an 'underclass' on the United States model. He blamed the 'dependency culture,' created by universal state benefits, for burgeoning hordes of never-married young mothers, whose children fall prey to drugs, truancy and crime. Illegitimate births were running at 45 per cent in Middlesbrough and only 15 per cent in Wokingham, he declared, and crime was worse in Middlesbrough – QED.[23]

Others have looked eagerly at the possibility of a 'crime gene'. Either way, the underlying message is the same: crime is what 'bad' people do. Each line of argument marks a return to ideas current at the beginning of the century: social Darwinism, and its obsession with 'national efficiency,' and eugenics. Then the trigger for this line of thought was the discovery that thousands of recruits applying to join the army to fight the Boer war were medically unfit, and the consequent fear that Britain's Imperial glory was threatened by its feeble national bloodstock. Now it is crime. Victorian England drew a rigid distinction between the 'deserving' and the 'undeserving' poor; between the feckless whose characters and habits made them irredeemable, and the honest, hard-working victims of circumstance. This distinction is making a comeback.

To support this position, Conservative commentators often repeat the fallacy that crime did not increase during the 1930s, which saw the deepest recession of the century. In fact, the biggest year-on-year percentage rise in recorded criminal statistics occurred in 1932. In the wake of the banking crisis and the collapse of the Labour

Government, unemployment tripled from one to three million. Crime increased (albeit from a much lower base) by 25 per cent. It went on going up throughout the Great Depression.

However, this debate is not helped by an equivalent psychological state of denial on the part of the Liberal Left. Liberal orthodoxy will not accept that the weakening of nuclear family structures has any ill effects, let alone that it might contribute to rising crime. Lampooned by Norman Dennis as the 'not deteriorating, only changing' school, one piece of evidence ought to be enough to stop it in its tracks – the fact that one in three of all male prisoners has spent time as a child in care.[24]

This polarisation of alternative causes of crime is futile and misleading. Where, after all, do we find the highest rates of divorce and illegitimacy? In Charles Murray's Middlesbrough, in Liverpool, on Tyneside and in the black ghettos of London, where unemployment is being passed down through generations. The collapse of the traditional family and the collapse of the traditional economy are conterminous. Nothing corrodes the institutions of civil society like poverty and the long-term absence of work. As to which came first, no one ever shut a factory because its workers were producing illegitimate children.

Superimposed on the economic background, moral and ideological factors do, however, exert an influence of their own. As Robert Reiner puts it, hundreds of thousands of young men 'face lifetimes without the incentives and disciplines conducive to conformity which regular employment (and the marriages and families it made possible) provided in the past'.[25] It is a complex, many-layered relationship. To admit to its existence is not to demand a return to the days when to bear an illegitimate baby was to become a social outcast, and the inaccessibility of divorce trapped women in violent, abusive marriages.

There are also independent, cultural factors in play. While hammering home a relentless tirade against criminals and 'thugs', the tabloid newspapers report without the merest hint of stigma examples of damaging behaviour: fathers who run off with their sisters-in-law because they are better in bed; teachers who set up happy love-nests with their pupils. Personal, sexual fulfilment has become elevated to the status of a fundamental human right.

'Permissiveness' and individualism are not sufficient causes of crime. But the Left's refusal to recognise that they may have had their criminogenic downside is its own version of the Right's selective blindness towards the economy.

★ ★ ★

'I suppose you already know,' the cynical sergeant said, 'I'm sure everyone's already told you: the job is fucked. Criminal justice has become a joke.' Not every street police officer would use such language. But at every level of the service, variations on the theme are being volubly expressed. There is a loss of faith in the criminal process, and a lack of confidence in the service's own ability to deliver results. These sentiments are not mere speculation, as crime statistics prove.

There are two main types of criminal statistics. The first, and most commonly quoted, comes from Home Office computations of the offences reported to, and recorded by the police. This is a deeply imperfect system, subject to many extraneous influences. The second method, usually held to be more accurate, is the crime survey: conclusions drawn from very large, representative samples, interviewed by researchers armed with a questionnaire. The most authoritative is the British Crime Survey, commissioned at regular intervals by the Home Office since 1982.

However, in the fat yellow volumes of annual Home Office figures, there is one class of statistic which *is* generally reliable: the number of convictions. For some reason, this gets very little attention from politicians or the media, although publication of the dubious 'headline figure' totals of recorded crime usually occasions a beanfeast. But it is in the conviction figures that the most startling changes in criminal justice are clearly visible. Since 1980, the first full year of Conservative government, convictions have tumbled drastically, for many types of offence. Here the extent of the old regime's collapse is laid bare.[26]

Some of the clearest evidence comes from the case of burglary. Like other kinds of property crime, burglary soared in the 1980s and early 90s. According to the British Crime Survey, the period 1982–92 saw a rise of about 88 per cent, to a projected annual total of about 612,000 burglaries which were successful, in that items were actually stolen. Small wonder that the public profile of burglary has altered beyond recognition. At the start of the period, the police would often 'screen out' burglaries: elect not to mount full investigations, because of the shortage of resources and difficulty in catching the perpetrators. A visit from a CID officer to the scene of the burglary was a rare event. That would now be seen as unthinkable. There is widespread recognition that for many victims, burglary is far from a 'trivial' offence. Several constabularies have adopted the Metropolitan Police's 'Operation Bumblebee' initiative, designed both to convince the public something is being done and to capture burglars. In 1994, when the new Police and Magistrates' Court Act allowed the Government to set national police priorities for the first time, burglary was one of them.

Despite the rise in the incidence of burglary, and the police effort now directed against it, the same period has seen a massive drop in the number of burglary convictions: from 65,700 in 1980 to 40,300 in 1993, the last year for which statistics are available. This is a real decline of more than a third.

With some types of offence, falls in conviction rates can be explained very simply: throughout the 1980s, the police used the practice of 'cautioning' offenders with growing frequency. A caution need not, despite the regular criticisms of the tabloid press, be a 'soft option': it requires an admission of guilt, and a record is kept on the Police National Computer which can be used when sentencing if the offender appears in court at a later date. More than 60 per cent of people cautioned do not, in fact, reoffend. But in 1983, the police cautioned almost as many people for burglary as they did in 1993: 11,700 against 12,821. If we add the number of convictions and the number of cautions together, the figures are no more encouraging. In 1983, 81,315 were either convicted or cautioned for burglary. Ten years later, the total was only 53,093.

One of the most terrifying of all crimes is aggravated burglary, when a burglar confronts, threatens or attacks the victim in their own home or place of work. It can attract very long prison sentences: notoriously, the judge in the Ealing vicarage rape case awarded five years for the rape of Jill Saward, and twelve years for aggravated burglary. In some areas of the country, it has become a 'fashionable' offence, and police have recorded a very large increase: from 642 cases in 1980 to 3,065 in 1993. In general, the more serious the offence, the more likely it is to show up in the police statistics. The rise in recorded aggravated burglary is unlikely to be the product of bogus statistics: it really has become more frequent.

One reason may be the considerably greater chance the perpetrator has of getting away with it. In 1980, there were 233 convictions, more than a third of cases reported. The 343 convictions in 1993 represented just 11 per cent of cases reported to the police.

Another type of crime which arouses intense public concern is sexual offences. Like burglary, the 1980s saw a great rise in public awareness. There was a steady rise in the number of cases reported to the police: from 21,107 in 1980 to 31,284 in 1993. But here too, the rate of conviction dropped. In 1980, 8,000 people were convicted of crimes including rape, buggery, child abuse and indecent assault. By 1993, this had fallen by almost half to 4,300.

Rape is a good example of a crime where an increase in the number of offences reported to the police cannot be advanced as evidence that the crime is getting more common. The number of reported rapes rose from 1,200 in 1980 to 4,600 in 1993, but much of the increase, possibly even all of it, was due to the change in the way police treated rape victims. At the start of the period, Roger Graef's fly-on-the-wall television series *Police* depicted a woman being badgered and interrogated as if she were at fault. It unleashed a public outcry, forcing the service to transform its approach. Now, most constabularies have a cadre of officers trained specially to deal with rape victims, working from 'rape suites' designed to look as little like a police station as possible.

In 1980, nearly half of those who did report a rape saw their assailant convicted in court: there were 457 convictions. For a while, the number of convictions increased, although it did not keep pace with the increase in the number of complaints. By 1989, there were 3,305 rapes recorded and 623 convictions – representing only 19 per cent of cases where the victim went to the police. Since then, despite the continued rise in recorded offences, convictions have fallen, both proportionately and in absolute terms. Only 482 men were convicted of rape in 1993, just 10.5 per cent of those accused.

Police figures suggest a doubling of assault cases in the period

1980–93. There is evidence that much of this may have been the result of better recording or more widespread reporting at the minor end of the scale; cases without heavy bleeding or broken bones, which at worst would be classed as common assault. In 1992, the more accurate British Crime Survey found a rise of only 21 per cent in assaults overall. However, the increase in serious assaults, where police figures are less likely to be subject to statistical vagaries, was much more dramatic.

In 1980, the police recorded 155 cases of attempted murder, and 4,390 of wounding endangering life. By 1993, these totals had increased to 585 and 8,153 respectively. Guns were used in just 274 cases of attempted murder and serious wounding in 1980. There was an astonishing increase of nearly 400 per cent, to 1,047 by 1993. In the same period, armed robbers threatened or fired at their victims nearly five times more often – on 1,140 occasions in 1980, 5,918 times in 1993. The use of knives also became much more frequent.

Convictions simply did not keep pace. If attempted murder went up fourfold, convictions only doubled to 62 in 1993 – representing less than a fifth of reported offences. The failure to convict the attackers of Mukhta Ahmed and Quddus Ali of this crime was therefore not an isolated phenomenon. In 1980, 1,277 people were convicted of woundings endangering life. In 1993, this had risen to 1,774. But given the rise in serious attacks, the proportion of reported offences which resulted in conviction fell from 29 to 21 per cent.

The conclusion seems inescapable. Judged purely as a crime control mechanism, criminal justice was falling apart. Its record in dealing with arson was no better. There were 13,600 cases reported in 1980: a figure which rose nearly 250 per cent to 32,300 in 1993. Arson convictions plus cautions fell in the same period from 3,265 to 2,598.

As with other property offences, there was a boom in fraud and forgery: up from 105,000 in the police figures in 1980 to 162,936 in 1993. This covers a broad spectrum, from the Guinness case to the use of chequebooks and credit cards stolen in muggings. In any event, convictions were down 30 per cent at 17,500. Taking cautions into account, there was still a small drop, from 26,336 to

25,577. Forgers and fraudsters were two-thirds less likely to be called to account.

Criminal offences are divided into two categories. First there are 'indictable' crimes, those in the more serious category which either must or, at the behest of the defendant, can be tried by jury in the Crown Court. Then come 'summary' offences, which are tried only by magistrates. In 1988, one of the many Criminal Justice Acts split up several classes of indictable offences, reducing less serious versions to summary status. This happened to some of the big boom crimes of the past fifteen years, including stealing cars, general theft (such as shoplifting), and some classifications of handling stolen goods. This makes comparisons with the early 1980s difficult.

Nevertheless, if we consider only the period up to the change at the end of 1988, both the conviction rate and the total of convictions plus cautions were already registering some impressive falls. In 1980, 43,831 people were cautioned or convicted for the theft of motor vehicles. By 1988, this was down to 30,388. The incidence of car theft had meanwhile risen from 324,354 to 366,174; the start of an increase which was to see a near-doubling by 1993. The British Crime Survey shows that police figures for vehicle theft are among their most accurate: because of the demands of car insurance, the 'dark figure' of unreported offences is only 7 per cent of the total. Between 1980 and 1988, the overall total of recorded theft and handling stolen goods offences increased from 1.4 million to 1.9 million. Convictions plus cautions fell from 310,000 to 256,000.

Robbery, a category which includes both armed bank raids and street muggings, was a class of crime where convictions and cautions did show a rise: from 3,600 in 1980 to 5,800 in 1993. However, at the start of the period, convictions plus cautions represented about a third of the 15,800 robberies reported to the police. By 1993 they were running at just over 10 per cent of the 57,845 recorded crimes.

Overall, there were 429,700 convictions for indictable offences in 1980. In 1993, this had fallen by 31 per cent, to 296,800. The total of convictions for every kind of offence, at both Magistrates' and Crown Courts, fell from 2.2 million in 1983 to 1.4 million in 1993. The total of convictions plus cautions for indictable offences has also fallen, albeit less dramatically. In 1983, 575,900 were either convicted or cautioned for indictable offences. By 1993, this had fallen to 517,100. If this had happened at a time when the crime rate had been steady, it might not seem so significant. But as we have seen, it did not. Rising crime; falling convictions. Here lies the true measure of the collapse in criminal justice.

★ ★ ★

When politicians and journalists discuss each new set of recorded crime figures, the caveats attached to their interpretation are gaily cast aside. The small fall in the overall total recorded in 1993 as against 1992 allowed Michael Howard to claim a political triumph. In the autumn of 1994, the Home Office issued a veritable spate of press releases which shared a common feature: an introductory paragraph claiming that this or that detail of Government policy was, in an utterly ludicrous phrase, about to 'crack crime'.

When the crime figures come out, a further element always creeps into public debate – police 'clear-ups', which are published in the same yellow volumes. There are no more discreditable statistics anywhere in criminal justice. When examined in the light of the above analysis, these clear-up figures seem completely absurd.

The amazing fact is that according to the statistics, in many offence categories the percentage of offences cleared up has not changed *at all*. For example, in 1980, the police claimed to have cleared up 74 per cent of sexual offences. In 1993, they recorded the slightly higher clear-up rate of 75 per cent. Of the nearly 50 per cent drop in convictions and 50 per cent rise in reported sexual crimes, there was not the merest sign. A similar happy story is told by the violence clear-ups – 75 per cent in 1980, and 1 per cent higher in 1993. In this period, the police recorded an increase of more than 100 per cent in the number of assaults, from 97,000 to 205,000. Convictions plus cautions only crept up from 57,000 to 63,000.

Burglary clear-ups did decline, from 31 per cent in 1980 to 19 per cent in 1993. Yet even this did not begin to reflect the doubling of offences, coupled, as we have seen, with the slump in cautions and convictions.

For some years, reforming police officers have stressed the negative aspects of the 'numbers culture', the drive to improve the figures, whatever the real quality of the work thereby represented.

At its crudest, under the old regime, the numbers culture was reflected in pressure on individual officers to make the requisite number of arrests and get convictions – PCs knew they had to feel more collars than their colleagues to get into the CID; detectives knew they had to get results to achieve promotion. As such, the culture was an engine of malpractice, a direct incentive to manufacture the vital 'cough'.

Malcolm Young, a retired Northumbria and West Mercia superintendent turned anthropologist, has written engagingly of the way he saw police figures of all kinds manipulated during his police career. At times in the 1960s, chief officers wished to demonstrate they had crime in their area under control: this gave rise to the practice of 'cuffing', a system by which real crimes would be made to disappear. The CID controlled the crime books in which offences were recorded and locked them up at night: if they fiddled them, no one else would know.[27]

In the seventies, says Young, the police were demanding more resources, and needed to demonstrate crime was on the increase: cuffing 'all but disappeared'. Then – as now – the need was to demonstrate effectiveness, above all through clear-ups, to show that 'the rising tide of disorder was valiantly, but only just, being held back'. The Home Office official 'counting rules' assist this goal. They state explicitly that conviction and caution are irrelevant: 'An offence has been cleared up when a person has been charged or summoned for the offence *irrespective of any subsequent acquittal*' [author's italics].

The rules add that if an offender dies before being charged; if the offence has been 'taken into account'; if an offender confesses while in prison for something else; if the offender is too ill to be charged; if witnesses disappear or die; or if the offence was committed by a child under the age of ten; then in all these circumstances, the crime will have been cleared up. There are two more categories which provide the police with yet more latitude: 'The guilt of the offender is clear but the victim refuses, or is unable, to give evidence', and 'there is sufficient evidence to charge the offender but the Crown Prosecution Service or a senior police officer decides that no useful purpose would be served by the charge'.

Crimes in this last category, Young writes, were put down as 'detected NFA (no further action)'. In the mid-80s, he suddenly realised he was recording 15 per cent of all offences under this heading. In 1986, his subdivision 'cleared up' nearly 13,000 crimes. Only 5,000 had gone anywhere near a court.

Even without the least hint of malpractice or abuse, it is clear that clear-up figures are of almost no value, although the pressure to produce them can waste other valuable resources. In 1992, John Stevens, the new Chief Constable of Northumbria, the force which covers Tyneside, disbanded a squad of forty-seven trained detectives whose job was to do nothing other than to visit men in prison and persuade them to own up to other crimes – none of which would ever lead to court proceedings.

However, there is also scope for overt corruption. In 1986, the *Observer* published the story of PC Ron Hill of Kent, who revealed how one division had improved its clear-ups from 25 per cent to 69 per cent in a single year. Its methods included writing down the numbers of cars spotted at random, identifying their owners from the Police National Computer, and then inducing criminals to 'admit' to having stolen them. The furore caused by this story did not end suspect clear-ups. In November 1991, the Police Complaints Authority launched an inquiry into the case of Anthony Everett, a psychotic depressive, who during seventeen days at Brentwood police station in Essex confessed to 391 burglaries and thefts. He was charged with only seven. Later it emerged that he had been in gaol for other offences when at least thirty-five of the burglaries 'taken into account' had been committed.[28]

Despite the efforts of the reformers, clear-up rates remain the principal standard by which the service is judged externally. The numbers culture has not been demolished: indeed, the developments of the early 1990s, with the setting of national objectives and emphasis on published 'performance indicators', have given it new life.

In London, launching his annual report for 1993–4, Commissioner Condon proudly revealed an increase in burglary clear-ups, from 23,000 to 26,000, from 13 per cent to 16 per cent. This, he said, was the result of Operation Bumblebee, which was 'transferring the fear of crime from the victim to the offender'. However, primary clear-ups – that is to say, actual arrests – for burglary had fallen by 5.6

per cent. The whole of the improvement and more was due to heavier use of prison visits and offences taken into account. In such cases, known as 'secondary clear-ups', no one is charged, and no property recovered. Nevertheless, Condon claimed, it was helpful for victims to know who had done it.[29]

The same process has been taking place on a larger scale nationally, and for many types of offence. The maintenance of clear-up rates has been achieved only by their dilution. Meanwhile, the debate about crime requires awareness of its salient characteristic: the fact that in important, often violent, categories, it is now more likely a crime will be committed, but less likely the offender will be brought to justice.

★ ★ ★

This is not an attempt to create a 'moral panic' over rising crime. In 1983, Geoffrey Pearson showed in his book *Hooligan: A History of Respectable Fears*, how lamenting the rise in violent crime and harking back to a mythical golden age had been recurrent themes since at least the Victorian period.

Glancing through the book, there are numerous precursors to John Major's reference to a 'rising tide of crime'. In 1979, HRH Prince Philip described 'this avalanche of lawlessness threatening to engulf our civilisation'; in 1975 the report of the Chief Inspector of Constabulary spoke of 'the trend of increased violence in our society . . . this menace to our way of life'. Meeting at Blackpool in 1958, the Conservative Party Conference heard delegates lament 'this sudden increase in crime and brutality which is so foreign to our nature and country'. Back in 1940 George Orwell wrote of the new, casual violence engendered by 'the anonymous life of dance-halls and the false values of the American film', while after a surge in bag snatches and shop raids in the 1920s, a briefing to youth workers in east London in 1931 warned they would be working 'on the edge of the volcano'.[30]

It is certainly true that perceptions, transmitted through the media, sometimes matter more in criminal justice than reality. In Newfoundland, the annual homicide rate is 1.3 per 100,000, exactly the same as in Britain. Here, where the annual murder total has hovered around 650 throughout the period covered by this book, we fear being swamped by violent lawlessness, but Newfoundlanders think they live in a peaceful, rural backwater. There is evidence to suggest the risk of being murdered in Britain has halved every century since the thirteenth century. Canada as a whole thinks it is a very safe country, because it compares itself to the United States, yet Canada's homicide rate is 2.6 per 100,000, about the same as Britain in the mid-nineteenth century.

Also true is the fact that those most at risk from violent street crime of all kinds come from the same group as most of its perpetrators, men under the age of twenty-nine. At 3.8 per cent, their annual risk of attack was nineteen times the risk for people over sixty, according to the 1992 British Crime Survey. Young men were five times more likely to be mugged than elderly women.

Discussion of the increase in crime usually takes place on the basis of a straightforward, linear graph. This shows little increase throughout the twentieth century, until a sudden, accelerating lift-off in the 1960s. If, however, we plot not crime totals but annual percentage increases, the rise appears to go back throughout the century, with an annual average rise of about five per cent. There have been earlier temporary steepenings in the gradient such as that recorded in the last fifteen years – in 1944, commentators were expressing alarm that boys aged eight to seventeen were committing 70 per cent more crimes than they had in 1938, and girls 130 per cent more.[31]

However, the fact that crime was considered a problem in the past does not justify complacency in the present. Some things really have changed. The increase in attempted murder and woundings endangering life is not a statistical chimera but real – the product of assaults in which knives and guns were used more widely than ever before. If not for the enhanced skill of the staff of hospital accident and emergency units, the homicide rate would also have gone up, as it did during the 1993 London ambulance drivers' strike.

This is not the place to enter the debate about legalisation or decriminalisation of drugs. But the fact remains that heroin and crack cocaine addicts steal to feed their habits, while crack dealers occasionally shoot each other or the police. Increases in property crime may partly arise because there is more to steal. There were no

video recorders in the 1930s. The present spate of computer theft –
whose value is said to be running at 20 per cent of burglary – is
another example. But the wide distribution of consumer goods does
not in itself cause crime.

Some Liberals do not want to believe any kind of crisis exists. It is
simply too disturbing. It may require new crime control measures,
which cannot be accepted. Those whom Jock Young terms 'Left
idealists', meanwhile, cling to the notion that crime waves 'merely
show that more state resources are at the disposal of the police and
the judiciary', thanks to the media's crime panics. If there is a crisis, it
is only one of 'the police getting out of hand'.[32]

If, however, to disregard the echoes of past jeremiads, something
different, something historically important is happening, then it lies
at the confluence of three distinct but related currents. The first is
economic: the deepening of relative deprivation in the islands of
long-term unemployment; the removal, as the Kilburn PC put it, of
hope. The second is moral: the weakening of altruism and self-
restraint.

The product of these two currents is the enlargement of a class
which has always existed: lawless, sometimes violent men in the
fifteen to thirty age group which has always committed most crime.
Lacking social reference points, they embark on a quest for
alternative means to self-validation. The third current is the
ineffectiveness of criminal justice. If all the social institutions which
might lead an individual to restrain his own, deviant impulses are in a
debilitated state, so too is the external check; the prospect of getting
caught.

Beatrix Campbell described a manifestation of this confluence in
her account of the riots on Tyneside in September 1991, largely
provoked by 'joyriding' car thieves: 'For young men whose self-
esteem was already in crisis, whose joyriding was perhaps fearless to
the point of being suicidal, the criminal justice system offered little or
no challenge or threat . . . at best, court became part of the young
men's social life, part of the circuit of visibility where what mattered
to them was not that their behaviour was perceived as *wrong* but that
it was seen as *important*.' She quoted a probation officer, who told her
the young men saw court as a place 'to meet their mates'.[33]

At the time of the riots, Northumbria had the largest number of crimes per police officer in the country: 63.2, against a national average of 39. It was also one of the most poorly-funded forces and could afford overtime payments averaging only 0.9 per cent of each officer's salary, against a national mean of 8.1 per cent.

The sanction of possible punishment had so lost effect that police officers were being followed home from court by criminals or their friends and being threatened, or worse. A fortnight before the riots, an officer who worked on a stolen vehicle squad returned home to find his house under siege by armed youths with petrol bombs, and his wife and children trapped inside. The trigger for the start of the riots on the Meadow Well estate was the death of a car thief in a police car chase: his parents indignantly told reporters that he was no mere joyrider, but a fully-fledged 'ram-raider', who drove stolen cars into shops in order to loot their contents.

Out on the streets, the night the rioting moved to Newcastle's West End, I witnessed Campbell's 'circuit of visibility' in action. 'I've always wanted to be harder than my dad, and now I am,' one youth exclaimed jubilantly, 'I'm out on bail for GBH.' Another sauntered over to a parked saloon car and nonchalantly jemmied it open with an iron bar – yards from a police panda car, whose occupants were powerless to intervene. Within seconds the stolen vehicle was delighting the crowd with high speed passes and screeching handbrake turns. 'Handbrakes!' yelled the man next to me, 'Love it, love it!'

A gang of youths had set fire to some cars on the main road; then they slipped into a backstreet. They were carrying the tools for arson: rags and cans of petrol. I watched them break into an empty house, chattering excitedly about setting it on fire. One of their friends lived opposite. Suddenly he burst out of his home, yelling at the others: 'Hey, come on, leave that now! Come and see, we're all on Sky TV!'

CHAPTER FOUR

The Retreat from Prosecution

ON 27 MAY 1995, the *Spectator* magazine published a remarkable article by John Ware, the BBC journalist and presenter of the *Rough Justice* programme. Under the heading 'Unjustly Not Imprisoned', Ware confessed he was feeling uncomfortable that his own and similar programmes dealt only with wrongful convictions – 'despite the fact that, because the accused now have greater safeguards, numbers in this category of victim are probably falling, compared with the soaring rise in victims of crime'.

The time had come to devote some of television's investigative resources in a new series which would secure evidence against local criminal 'untouchables', Ware said. 'Getting people out of gaol is held as the quintessential example of public service broadcasting. Why shouldn't gathering evidence on muggers and thieves be just as valid?'

As the article continued, it became clear that this notable *volte face* was based on Ware's personal experiences both of crime and the criminal justice system's apparent inability to contain it. 'Mo', a Moroccan said to hang about Ladbroke Grove in west London, had allegedly robbed him of his wallet and £200. Although the police took Ware on a frenetic drive around a local estate, they failed to locate his assailant. 'Mo is a full-time mugger,' Ware commented. 'He comes out to play at night. He's good, he's fast, he's a pro. I don't believe any self-respecting television researcher couldn't find him. But it seems Notting Hill CID can't.'

A little while later, the article went on, a man had tried to steal Ware's daughter's bicycle. The police took a long time to come to his aid, and although they contemplated holding an identity parade, eventually took no action. 'There was clearly enough evidence to justify a charge,' Ware expostulated. 'People can no longer be bothered to report crimes to the police. After my experience, I can't say that I blame them.'[1]

The frustrations felt by the Deols in Abbey Hulton and by the burgeoning groups of vigilantes had reached the liberal metropolis. Here was a pre-eminent exposer of injustice arguing for more vigorous crime control – six years earlier, when the Guildford Four were released, this would have been quite unthinkable. The symbolic significance of this change in opinion was underlined a few days later, when Ware's article was republished, accompanied by a harrowing photograph of a battered old lady, in the *News of the World*.

The national debate on crime and criminal justice had undergone a profound change. Its protagonists remained largely unaware of the fact that the statistics showed falling rates of convictions. But there was no shortage of people with unhappy personal experience, or knowledge of others who had suffered. Suspects' rights and miscarriages of justice had receded from public discourse. The emphasis had shifted towards the needs of victims, protection for the citizen, and what police officers have always called 'results'.

Often, as in Ware's article, the first port of call for complaint was the police. It comes as no surprise to discover that within the service itself, officers of all ranks share a corrosive loss of faith in the component parts of English criminal justice. From PC to Chief Constable, the same bitter themes recurred like a mantra. Trials had become a 'game' in which truth was often the loser, sacrificed to the ploys of cynical lawyers. Anachronistic, unnecessary safeguards designed to protect the innocent were allowing the guilty to go free.

It would be difficult to find a more extreme exponent of this disillusioned view than David Phillips, Chief Constable of Kent.[2] He says:

Our justice system has been Americanised, permeated with concern for criminal civil rights. As for the famous miscarriages of justice, they represented a tiny percentage of criminal cases, smaller than a measurable percentage.

We have put all our resources into protecting defendants. We have produced a system which is so concerned with protecting criminals, it works against the notion of justice. Instead of asking,

'How can we get to the truth of cases?' we ask, 'How can we protect people against the police?' If we were interested in the truth, instead of being bound by rules and silly restrictions, juries could make their decisions on the basis of common sense. Often the best or most important evidence is concealed. We have created a judicial system which sits in splendid isolation, and is about as popular as chocolate teapots.

Phillips consciously advocates the crime control model of criminal justice and contemptuously rejects the values of its due process opposite.[3] 'The whole concept of due process is foreign to us: it comes from the US Constitution. The primary purpose of the criminal justice system isn't to protect the rights of defendants: it's to protect society from crime, and ordinary people from criminals. If it doesn't give that protection, it is flawed.'

For most of his career, Phillips was a detective in the North-west. 'I have heard stories about wrong-doing by London detectives in the sixties and seventies,' he says.

Where I was, that is not how things worked. There was certainly more room for manoeuvre. But as for police officers telling lies or making up confessions: of the many hundreds of cases with confessions which I've been involved in, barely one confession was ever challenged. I've never known any allegation against me or the officers I worked with that we forged documents or made things up. As for 'noble cause corruption', it's a bloody nonsense. It's corruption. I would put officers away for noble cause corruption.

As we saw in Chapter One, Keith Hellawell, Chief Constable of West Yorkshire, another former detective from the North of England turned chief officer, is less sanguine. With due respect to Mr Phillips, the evidence of the Birmingham Six and the Guildford Four cases rather weakens the suggestion that malpractice was confined to the Metropolitan Police.

Charles Pollard, Chief Constable of Thames Valley, has a justifiable reputation as a police reformer, with a notably enlightened approach to community punishments and police accountability. But his disillusion with the criminal process is intense. 'The single most important thing in stopping people committing crime is to confront them with what they've done. The system allows them to account for nothing, to avoid all responsibility, because the trial is a game and it mirrors what they see they've been doing in offending – playing a game.'[4]

He is scathing about lawyers and the judiciary: 'The fear among judges that the wrong person might be convicted is now so great they want to leave a huge margin between them and the possibility of that happening. They are terrified the verdict of their court may be overturned on appeal.' Definably 'bent' lawyers, in the sense that their actions might make them liable to criminal conviction or professional disciplinary action, are a rare phenomenon, Pollard avers. However, 'there is a big middle area of lawyers who go way beyond their instructions, who will go to almost any lengths to get their clients off. Their tactics are driven by money: delay equals more cash, as well as increasing the chances of an acquittal. Barristers in the trial process take no account of the welfare of the community.'[5]

Commander Tom Williamson of the Metropolitan Police compares the strict rules governing the handling of suspects and witnesses in the police station with their distinct absence when it comes to lawyers' cross-examination in court:

> The criminal Bar subjects witnesses and victims to intimidation and the judiciary does nothing to protect them. The most vulnerable and powerless people are regularly being brutalised. Every witness finds giving evidence an ordeal. Yet lawyers browbeat, intimidate and attempt to confuse them. They are actually guilty of behaviour which if it happened during an interview at a police station, would have to be condemned by the judge and any evidence excluded on the basis that it would not be reliable.[6]

Williamson has a doctorate in psychology, and as an expert in cognitive processes has been the architect of new police interviewing methods. He adds:

Lawyers' training does not recognise how people process information. They appear to believe the eye is like a video camera, the ear like a tape-recorder: recording everything said and done. Memory does not work like this. It reconstructs events.

Lawyers require verbatim accounts, and instead of saying what they know, officers give in to temptation and try to supply them. Only now is there a generation who have been trained not to do this, but to supply, for example, the gist of conversations, not their supposed full text. Yet witnesses are still being rubbished when they say they can't answer questions because they are not sure. A degree of uncertainty ought to be taken as evidence that a witness may be trying to tell the truth. It is actually used to destroy their credibility.

In Williamson's view, these defects flow from the fundamentals of the adversarial system of justice. 'It is beginning to register publicly that it is a search not for the truth, but for points for the jury to tot up in reaching a verdict. Lawyers encourage the suggestion that the courts determine whether someone committed an offence or did not. They do no such thing. The Scots' not proven verdict does at least recognise that the courts in an adversarial system can't determine the truth.'

Down at street level, similar perceptions are evident. In the back of Kilburn squad cars and in the police canteen, I heard them time and again. For a minority of officers their disillusion has reached the level where they see little point in continuing to do their own jobs. 'If I were burgled as a private citizen, I wouldn't give prosecution evidence,' a PC told me on patrol one quiet night.

It wouldn't be worth the delays and harassment. Defence counsel paint this picture for juries of us sitting around sipping tea in a fog of smoke in the canteen deciding what lies to tell. I used to believe in all the old clichés: in the long arm of the law, and that the police always got their man; that crime doesn't pay and honesty is the best policy. Now I know crime does pay. I come to work because I've got a wife, a baby and a mortgage. If I could find another job that pays as well, I'd leave tomorrow.

According to a detective sergeant of twenty years' service, if police officers become cynical, it is an attitude they learn from appearing at court.

> Last week I was cross-examined for the third time in a single case: rather unusually, it was a second retrial. By this time the whole business had become boring and familiar to everyone concerned except the jury, who obviously were hearing it all for the first time. And then in his closing speech, defence counsel said: 'Look at Detective Sergeant R. He didn't seem at all surprised when I accused him of lying, did he? Is that because that's the sort of allegation which is rightly put to him all the time?'

Has the criminal process really become so ineffective? Have we reached the point, as David Phillips believes, where 'criminals can beat the rap most times'?

★   ★   ★

Certainly, the system has changed. It is important to realise that the case of the Guildford Four destroyed *what was left* of the old regime in criminal justice. Its effect on public and judicial attitudes was electrifying, but the regime had already been terminally undermined by two pieces of legislation. The first, the 1984 Police and Criminal Evidence Act, imposed the biggest changes to basic police practice since the foundation of the service in 1829. The following year, the Prosecution of Offences Act removed all police responsibility for bringing cases to court. It invented a new agency, the Crown Prosecution Service (CPS), whose staff were to prosecute all magistrates' cases themselves, and to do all the preparatory work for more serious Crown Court cases.

The two Acts did not, despite the fears of David Phillips, create a fully-functioning due process criminal justice system. But they had emerged from the ferment produced by the Confait case and the other polarising *causes célèbres* of the 1970s; amid the increasing realisation that justice might miscarry and that the police can seriously err. The real importance of the Acts is that they introduced an element of due process values into regions where crime control and police discretion had enjoyed free rein.

The 1984 Act, referred to hereafter by its acronym PACE, did not achieve this immediately, on coming into force at the beginning of 1986. Some of its most important provisions needed test case judgments by the Court of Appeal before their impact was properly felt. Nevertheless, PACE provided unprecedented protection for suspects in custody. It set strict time limits on detention: twenty-four hours in most cases, thirty-six hours when dealing with 'serious arrestable offences'. The days of making an arrest on a Friday afternoon, leaving the suspect 'banged up' over the weekend and returning to collect the 'cough' on Monday morning had gone.

PACE also regulated the conditions in which suspects could be detained, creating a new post of 'custody sergeant', responsible for all prisoners. The sergeant was to keep a detailed record of everything which transpired: the times of meal breaks, interviews, visits from lawyers or the police surgeon. He was also to ensure suspects understood their right to free legal advice in the police station, and to call a solicitor if required. A new 'duty solicitor' scheme with lawyers on 24-hour call was established at the same time.

Another provision in the Act was still more important. All interrogations in the police station were to be recorded contemporaneously – at first in handwritten notes, but soon, and by now universally, on tape.

The due process values which informed these parts of the Act were made explicit in sections 76 and 78. Section 76 of PACE says the courts must rule as inadmissible any confession obtained through violence or oppression, or through any other means which may 'render it unreliable' – even if it is true. The police must not offer inducements, such as a promise of bail in return for a confession. Moreover, it is for the prosecution to prove beyond reasonable doubt that a confession was not made in conditions which might call its reliability into question.

Section 78 says the courts may throw out any evidence which might reflect adversely on the 'fairness' of a trial. This was potentially the most radical provision of all: it gave the courts explicit powers to prohibit police methods of which they disapproved by excluding all evidence obtained as a result. A judgment by Lord Diplock in 1979 contrasts sharply with the PACE due process ethic. 'It is not part of the judge's function to exercise disciplinary powers over the police or prosecution as respects the way in which evidence to be used at the trial is obtained by them.' A clearer statement of crime control principles would be difficult to find.

There is a body of academic research focusing on the limitations of PACE.[7] As PCs will often admit, the Act's attempt to regulate policing on the streets with a new 'code of practice' has not made much headway. For example, PACE laid down criteria as to what might constitute 'reasonable suspicion' before an officer could do a stop and search. It is widely ignored: as in the old days, officers rely on their 'gut feelings'. In an area such as Kilburn where there are black offenders, the inevitable result is the stopping of disproportionate numbers of innocent black citizens. Stop and search remains an inexact science: 'You can't put your finger on it, but sometimes you just *know* someone's at it,' said a Kilburn PC.

Another PC said: 'You have to learn to get round the rules – it's just practical policing.' If he found himself under scrutiny after carrying out a fruitless stop, 'I would have to make up a story. I might say, "An old lady told me she had seen him buying drugs." ' Notes of an incident were supposed to be made in the car on the way to the police station, he added, 'but nobody does that: have you tried writing proper notes in a moving car? If anyone asked why you hadn't, you would think on your feet and come up with an answer, say it was "the prisoner's security". It's really just a question of having an answer for everything and covering your back.'

PACE says custody sergeants are supposed to authorise detention only if they judge it necessary after hearing the full facts of the case. In practice, detention is rarely refused. Sometimes, custody sergeants use a variety of 'ploys' in the hope that suspects will waive their right to a solicitor, such as rushing over the details of entitlements when suspects are booked in.

On the other hand, another PC insisted:

If an officer wants to do the wrong thing, it makes it much more difficult. Take the custody officers. At first, they were officers from your own shift: they knew you well, and perhaps they might be prepared to grant a bit of leeway. Now they're on their own roster and they do nothing else. You may hardly know them. Why should they trust you? They have to worry about their own jobs.

If you bring in someone with just a light cut, the first thing the custody officer does is call a doctor. If he lets something go, his own career may be on the line. If you've been in a fight and a colleague has been injured, the temptation might be to give the suspect a pasting. But if the prisoner has a broken arm and the officers are OK, someone is going to lose their job. If you started hitting someone in the custody suite now, it would cause mayhem.

In up to three-quarters of cases, suspects do not ask for solicitors. But for those facing questioning about serious offences, the provision of legal advice has become routine. In 1987 the Court of Appeal established that legal advice could be denied in only the most exceptional circumstances: if the police had proof beyond reasonable doubt that a named solicitor planned to conspire with the suspect to destroy evidence or pressurise witnesses.

The consequence of all these measures is that allegations of fabricated or coerced admissions, once such a common feature in contested trials, have almost vanished. The West Midlands Serious Crimes Squad scandal saw the collapse of several cases where the scientific Esda test revealed the interpolation of incriminating pages in 'contemporaneous' interview notes. The affair also prevented the use of 'confessions' supposedly made in the squad car on the way to the station after an arrest. 'Sometimes people really do make admissions in the car,' a Kilburn detective said. 'It frankly isn't worth writing any of it down. The courts just won't accept it as evidence.'

Some kinds of evidence may still occasionally be 'improved', especially the recording of outbreaks of disorder. 'If you know the law, there are certain phrases to write up,' another PC said.

It still sometimes happens: the most senior person present writes up their notes first, and then everyone else bases their notes on his. You might do that when you had all been to an emergency call, where you've taken action, jumped in with both feet and arrested somebody. It's just a little bit of creative writing: not out of villainy, but enough to justify an arrest, and hopefully get a conviction.

But he insisted:

Outright stitch-ups of defendants are much harder to arrange. One day I was watching the American TV series *NYPD Blue* with some police friends. They showed an interview where the cops threatened to beat up the suspect. And we all agreed, 'Couldn't we get some amazing results if we could do that here.' Because with a tape running, even if you wanted to, you can't.

The statistical evidence bears him out. Baldwin and McConville's 1980 research study found only a quarter of Crown Court defendants were said to have made no admissions at all. No fewer than 25 per cent of convictions essentially depended on a confession: without the confession there would have been no prima-facie case at all, or only one of the most threadbare quality, which would not have produced a conviction. In the case of the Guildford Four it was precisely the *absence* of other evidence which made the police work all the harder for a confession.

The contrast with more recent surveys is striking. The equation has been reversed. Post-PACE, the weaker the other evidence, the less likely there is to be an admission. Suspects who confess tend to be suspects who would be convicted anyway. Another study by McConville, this time carried out for the 1993 Royal Commission on Criminal Justice, found that 60 per cent of a sample of 524 suspects interviewed by the police did make admissions. However, there was already strong supporting evidence from another source against 87 per cent of those who admitted their offence. In most of the other cases where suspects confessed, the police would 'probably' have been able to find corroboration.[8]

A variety of other research into confessions and the use of a suspect's right to silence since PACE came into force in 1986 has reached differing numerical conclusions. But two important trends emerge from the different studies. The more serious the crime of which a suspect is accused, the more likely he is to call for legal advice during interrogation, and the less likely he is to answer questions or make admissions. As for 'unsigned verbal admissions' – present in 40 per cent of London cases in 1980 – they did not figure at all in the post-PACE research.[9]

On the basis of the Baldwin and McConville 1980 study, we may draw a simple but crucial conclusion. If, at that time, a quarter of convictions would not have been recorded without the defendant's confession, most of the equivalent cases now are not being prosecuted at all. Police investigators are often faced with the starkest of choices: to find other ways of doing business, or to abandon any prospect of conviction.

The period since PACE has seen an explosion in the use of 'police bail', where suspects are questioned and released on the condition that they reappear at the station at a later date. Individuals released in this manner are suspected of having committed a crime, but have made no admissions. PACE means they cannot easily be coaxed, induced, threatened or beaten into making them; nor can a taped confession easily be fabricated. Some of these people are innocent. Some will be charged at a later date when other evidence is discovered. Some of them, both guilty and innocent, will never now be charged, although in 1980 and earlier, they would have been facing almost certain prosecution.

PACE turned policing upside down. In many areas, the training for officers before its introduction was inadequate. There were months, sometimes years of chaos, and cases were thrown out by judges unnecessarily because police had inadvertently failed to observe the new regulations. For years PACE was regularly denounced by the Police Federation and many senior officers. As late as 1992, John Evans, Chief Constable of Devon and Cornwall, was able to make a speech at the annual Bar conference demanding the restoration of the 'right to interrogate'.

With the passage of years, however, the Act has become familiar. The controversy has faded, and in the light of the Judith Ward or Kizsko cases, police officers have become less enthusiastic about uncorroborated confessions. When uncorroborated admissions rarely produce even a charge, it becomes easier not to dwell on the might-have-been convictions lost as a result of PACE.

Cases lost through the other milestone legislation of the eighties, the Prosecution of Offences Act, are, on the other hand, a very different matter.

★   ★   ★

The first strange thing that Ethel Rolton noticed was that her neighbour Lillian's front door was open, and the lights were on. Ethel called out, but there was no sound. Puzzled and a little frightened, she eased her way into the first floor flat. Lillian Hedgecock was sitting in the rocking chair she always used in the living room. The cupboard where she kept her valuables and papers had been opened, and they were strewn across the floor. There was blood everywhere, and Lillian was dead. As she waited for an ambulance, Mrs Rolton noticed that Lillian's purse, normally kept in a drawer in the kitchen, lay open and empty on a sitting room chair.[10]

Lillian Hedgecock was eighty-two and lived alone on the Wyvil estate in Clapham, south London. The Wyvil is a cosy little estate of houses and low-rise flats, and Mrs Hedgecock, for many years a widow, was popular with her neighbours. The children knew her as the 'cat lady', because of her pets. She was murdered not long before 5 p.m. on Saturday 26 January 1991.

Less than an hour after the body was discovered, a full scale inquiry was underway, led by Detective Superintendent John Jones – one of the most experienced murder investigators in the country. In his 34-year career, which ended with his retirement in 1994, he was involved with inquiries into more than 100 killings, and he lost count of those he actually led – 'probably thirty or forty', he says. He was an expert on drug-related violence, and in the early 1990s, as head of 'Operation Dalehouse', a huge investigation into a spate of shootings and murders by London crack cocaine dealers, he achieved spectacular success, with twenty-five separate prosecutions for murder and attempted murder. He enjoyed an unblemished reputation for integrity and accuracy.

It seemed likely to Jones and his colleagues that Lillian had been killed by someone she knew. There was no sign of forced entry, and like many elderly people, she was very conscious of her own security – a year earlier, she had been reluctant to open the door to a uniformed community policeman, simply because she had not met him before. There were gaping knife wounds to her face and throat, blood on the chair and carpet, and underneath her slippers. It appeared she had been attacked from behind, as she sat facing the fireplace in her chair, but had risen to her feet and made for the front door, where there were more bloodstains. Finally, her attacker had thrown her violently back into the chair.

Laid out in the mortuary next day, she was seen to have been stabbed thirteen times. She had twelve wounds to her neck and mouth, probably inflicted with a small kitchen knife. One had severed her vocal chords, preventing her from crying out. A last terrible blow to her chest had been dealt by a much larger weapon. The detectives surmised that after stabbing her in the sitting room, the killer had left her for dead while he went to the kitchen to look for her money. There she had surprised him by getting up; and he had thrown her back as he stabbed her with the larger knife. She had probably died a little after 5 p.m.

By 9.30 p.m. on the evening of the murder, uniformed officers began house-to-house inquiries, to discover if anyone had seen something which might provide a clue. Two PCs called at the flat of one of Mrs Hedgecock's male neighbours. For the purposes of this account, we will call him Dennis Smith: it is not his real name. The aim of the author is not to disturb Mr Smith's present anonymity by making him the subject of a witchhunt, but to reveal a systematic failing in English criminal justice.

Mr Smith took some time in coming to the door. At first, the police had to talk to him through his letter-box. Smith said he had 'heard nothing', although he had been in most of the day. He said he hadn't seen Lillian Hedgecock for a week, and had never been inside her flat. Twice, he volunteered the suggestion she 'often' kept her front door open, even in January. This immediately struck the police officers as strange: they had not told him Lillian had been killed inside her flat, let alone that the door had been open when her body was found. When they later compared notes with their colleagues, it emerged that all Mrs Hedgecock's other neighbours said she always kept her door firmly locked.

The police saw Smith again next day. They were still only making routine inquiries, and as they did with many of Lillian's neighbours, they asked him about his movements on the day she died. He said he had been in a local pub, the Prince of Wales, at midday, and had then gone home at 12.30, stopping at a betting shop on the way. He had gone out again at about 5 p.m., to visit a tobacconists' in the South Lambeth Road. If true, that meant he was away from the estate at the time Lillian was killed. He was asked again when he last visited Lillian's flat. This time he replied he hadn't been there for at least two months.

By now, the police were becoming suspicious of Dennis Smith. He had contradicted himself, saying on the first evening he had never been to Lillian's flat, but next day saying he had, albeit not for two months. They decided to research his background.

In his mid-fifties by 1991, he had been convicted of many thefts and acts of violence over the period 1953–74. His last conviction, for which he was gaoled for three-and-a-half years, was for a series of violent robberies on elderly people in the West Country. He was unemployed, but did a variety of casual odd jobs. He was also an addicted gambler, and according to his neighbours, was 'constantly' borrowing small sums from old people on the estate in order to finance his debts. In this capacity, they said, he had been a regular visitor to Lillian Hedgecock.

It was most unlikely he had not been to her flat for two months. Several residents told the police that a few weeks before Lillian's murder, her brother-in-law confronted Dennis Smith, and warned him to stop sponging off his sister-in-law.

On 2 February, Smith was arrested and interviewed by two detectives. He admitted he had been an addicted gambler, but he said he now 'had it under control'. He said he had got to know Lillian through their mutual interest in cats. He accepted he had often borrowed money from her, but tried to resolve the contradiction between his two earlier stories by saying he had never been inside her flat, although he had been in the habit of visiting it; she would bring the money out to him while he waited on the landing.

It emerged that Smith had spent time in the army, including two years in the SAS. He told the police he was sacked, for 'being a nuisance and mucking about'. Later, they discovered he was discharged for a violent attack on an officer.

As for the day of the murder, Smith gave further details, saying he had arrived home at about 2.40 p.m. after his visit to the pub and betting shop. He had a nap for two hours, and got up again about 5 p.m. He had some tea, then decided to go to the tobacconists' in the South Lambeth Road, a brisk ten minutes' walk away. He said he went straight home again from the shop, and knew nothing of the murder until his first visit from the police. Smith was released on police bail, and asked to return to the police station a fortnight later.

The police used the interim to dig deeper into his background. Smith spent much of his youth in approved school and borstal. He had been dismissed from several jobs for violence. He had been married twice, and the detectives traced both his wives. He married his first wife in 1963. She said he beat her within a week of the wedding, claiming he was 'the sort of man who would use violence against women without provocation'. Most of their arguments concerned his gambling. At one stage he got a job as a bus conductor, but was sacked when he stole the day's takings to put on a horse. The couple had a daughter, but the beatings continued. He went to prison for burglary, but begged his wife to forgive him. At last she left him because she was too frightened to stay.

Smith married again in 1969. His second wife also told the police of regular beatings. Once, she said, he had ripped out her earrings, splitting her earlobes. The first wife had described an identical attack. The second wife still had the affidavit she dictated to her lawyer on divorcing Smith in 1977. It said: 'Many times he would threaten her with a knife and threatened to kill her. She was quite convinced that one day, he would.' Smith's second mother-in-law had to obtain a court injunction because she too became a victim of his violence. In 1971, Smith came to London and got a job as a trainee pub manager. He was sacked when he hit a customer.

The investigating officers also found a man who had been Smith's best friend and a criminal associate: they had carried out numerous burglaries together. The man said he ended the friendship because of Smith's temper, and because he too was frightened. One day, Smith had pulled a knife on him during an argument in the street.

Further evidence of Smith's propensity to violence emerged from his neighbours on the estate. A Mr Quinlan described how Smith threatened him with a knife: on this occasion, the police were called. The licensee of the Prince of Wales, a nearby pub, said she had barred him for two years after he threatened a customer, once again with a knife. She said he told her he was always armed, as 'protection against muggers', and had bragged about his time in the SAS, saying: 'Once you've killed once, it's easy to do it again.' A customer from another pub, the Gladstone, said Smith got violent when he was on a losing streak. Once he had tried to borrow money from people in the pub, and had drawn a knife with a six inch blade when he was refused.

None of this was evidence he killed Mrs Hedgecock, and some of it would not been admissible at trial. But meanwhile, evidence which linked him more directly to the killing was also starting to emerge.

Other people on the estate said he had been desperately short of cash and had been trying to borrow money in the days before the murder. Nell Palmer, who lived below Mrs Hedgecock, said he asked her for money frequently. On occasions when she refused, he had become highly agitated, swearing at her. Mrs Palmer's husband died only a week before Lillian: Smith knew this, because he had given her £1 for a wreath. But the day before the murder, he visited her three times, asking successively for loans of £10, £4 and £1.

Eugenia Roche, Lillian's closest friend, said Smith came to her door at about 5.15 p.m. on the day of the killing – when he had claimed he was in the South Lambeth Road. He had asked her for £5, but she declined. She said she saw him again at 8 p.m., walking towards Lillian's block. He told her: 'I think Ethel's been mugged. There's coppers up there.' This was more than an hour before his first visit from the police – which, he had told detectives, was the first he knew of any attack. Mrs Roche said he was carrying a plastic bag which appeared to contain clothing. Another man on the estate also said he saw Smith carrying a bag of this kind. Mrs Roche added that the following evening, she came across Smith standing on the landing outside Lillian's flat. He was wearing only boxer shorts and he was weeping. Seeing Mrs Roche, he told her how terrible the murder had been.

Jacqueline McAvoy said she, her mother and her sister had many rows with Smith over his constant attempts to borrow money. On one occasion, he had picked up a long kitchen knife and threatened her. Two days after the murder, she met Smith on the estate while the police were knocking on doors, making their house-to-house inquiries. She said he told her: 'I was really upset when I heard about the murder. I haven't been able to sleep since. I hope they catch them. They weren't satisfied with stabbing her once: she was stabbed thirteen times.' At the time Smith was alleged to have said this, the number of Lillian's wounds was a secret known only to the detectives and the pathologist.

Another neighbour, Jeremiah Lynch, made a further important disclosure. Three days after the killing, he said, Smith asked him into his flat. At this stage, the police had seen Smith only to make routine inquiries. He was not yet a suspect. But according to Mr Lynch, Smith asked him: 'Should I take legal advice in case the police stick me up for the murder of the old lady?' He said Smith had showed him a flick knife, saying he always carried it for his own protection.

A final piece of evidence came from Ahmad Dadd, who ran the tobacconists' on the South Lambeth Road. If Smith were telling the truth about his visit there late on the afternoon of the killing, Dadd would be his alibi. Lillian died on Dadd's birthday, so he remembered the day well. He told the police he knew Smith, and it was true he had been there that day. However, it was not in the late afternoon, as Smith insisted, but between noon and 1 p.m. Dadd was certain he made no visit later in the day.

Dadd said that a few days after his first arrest and interrogation, Smith came into the shop and asked to go into the back room for a private talk. There Smith asked him if the police had been round asking questions: certainly they had, Dadd replied, but as yet he had not made a statement, because he had been out each time they called. Then, Dadd went on, Smith told him: 'They are probably going to come here and ask you, did I come here or not? You remember I came here on the Saturday.'

Smith was arrested again and interviewed on 11 April. He was held in the police station for two days, and the transcripts of the tapes of his interrogation fill 426 pages of foolscap. Searching his flat after he was taken into custody, the police found a pair of training shoes. There were recent traces of blood on their uppers and soles. There was not enough to carry out a DNA test to establish if the blood came from Lillian Hedgecock, but it was human blood of a consistent type. Smith admitted he had been wearing the shoes on the day of the murder, but could not account for the blood.

He denied visiting the other neighbours who said he had tried to borrow money: they were all lying, he insisted. He repeated the claim that he had been to Dadd's shop in the evening: Dadd too was lying, Smith said. He denied he had ever threatened anyone with a knife, while all the allegations about violence at work and to his former wives were also complete lies. He said he had never carried a knife or other weapon. He claimed Jacqui McAvoy was lying when she said he had told her Lillian was stabbed thirteen times, as was Mr Lynch. At the end of this interrogation, Smith was charged with the murder.

In the ensuing weeks, the police found further evidence – a man whom Smith had recently beaten up and threatened with a knife after an argument in a pub, and yet another woman whom he threatened with a knife. In Smith's flat they found a knife of exactly the type the pathologist said had been used to inflict the wounds to Lillian's face and neck. Several witnesses identified it as the knife she used to cut up meat for her cats, or an identical model. Lillian's own knife was missing from her kitchen. Chicken ready for cutting was found in a pan when her body was discovered.

It was not the strongest murder case in history. Some of the evidence was circumstantial. Yet taken in its totality, it made a convincing indictment, unless, as Smith had told the police, each and every one of the witnesses who made statements against him was lying. The Crown Prosecution Service took over the case, and instructed an experienced barrister, Brian Barker QC. On 21 May, he held a conference with the police and CPS and gave advice that in his opinion, there was a strong case against Dennis Smith. It would be difficult for him to avoid going into the witness box to explain himself, which meant exposing himself to cross-examination about the many twists and turns in the stories he had told the police. Barker considered that the prosecution easily met the standard laid down by the CPS rulebook, the Code for Crown Prosecutors, that there must be a 'realistic prospect of conviction'.

An 'old style' committal – a hearing in which the main Crown witnesses give evidence to establish the existence of a prima-facie case – was scheduled to begin at Thames Magistrates' Court on 21 October. Barker had planned to conduct the committal himself. However, with some weeks to spare, he realised he would be engaged elsewhere. The police and CPS agreed that his junior, Warwick McKinnon, who had been involved with the case since its outset, would do the job instead.

Then, with less than three weeks to go, the CPS decided it would not engage a barrister for the committal at all, in order to save money. It would be done by one of its in-house prosecuting lawyers. The police assumed he would be a solicitor called Martin White-house, who had worked on the case since Smith was charged, and had been to several meetings with both counsel and police. But on 17 October, four days before the proceedings were due to start, the CPS changed its mind again. A prosecutor named Sampson sent a memo to the police saying he was going to present the committal, not Whitehouse. In the time available, he did not have an opportunity to meet the officers to discuss the case. Mr Sampson found himself in an impossible position. The purpose of this account is not to question his commitment or ability. But it seems self-evident that a system which could ask him to undertake this brief under these circumstances was seriously at fault.

As the committal got underway, Detective Superintendent Jones was away at the Old Bailey, involved in another case. He left a junior detective at the Magistrates' Court to monitor progress. Before the proceedings started, Mr Sampson told the court he planned to call only six of the witnesses, plus the pathologist. On the second morning, without having called the evidence of Smith's police interviews or his contradictory stories, the blood on his shoes or the knife, Sampson held a brief discussion with the stipendiary magistrate. Then he announced the Crown was dropping the case. After six months in prison awaiting trial, Smith was free to go.

Before making this decision, Sampson consulted neither the police nor Brian Barker QC. What had prompted it? In early February 1995, I contacted the CPS press office in London and requested an explanation, or preferably, a meeting with Mr Sampson. Why had it been decided not to have counsel conduct the committal, I asked and why had the case been allocated to a lawyer unfamiliar with it, with so little time until the committal? The weeks went by, and no replies were forthcoming. Every so often, I made a call to check progress, and each time the reply was the same: 'We're working on it.' Finally, towards the end of April, the press office said it could make no comment other than to say that Mr Sampson had acted in accordance with the Code for Crown Prosecutors, while the magistrate had not objected to his dropping the case. An interview about a matter of this kind was out of the question.

Eleven months after the abortive committal, in September 1993, Sir Montague Levine, the Southwark coroner, heard an inquest into Lillian Hedgecock's death. The same witnesses gave the same evidence. Smith was present, represented by counsel. He refused to answer any of the coroner's questions. In early 1994, Smith launched a civil action for damages against the Metropolitan Police, alleging wrongful arrest, malicious prosecution and false imprisonment for the months he had spent on remand. The police contacted the CPS and asked for all their papers. They were told that in the period since the inquest, the CPS had thrown them away.

Dennis Smith may have killed Lillian Hedgecock. Equally he may not. In any event, a jury never had the opportunity to decide.

What were those criteria in the CPS Code which supposedly justified the withdrawal of the case against him? One thing is clear: they provide remarkable latitude for interpretation by the individuals involved in each case. As the Code itself puts it, 'Crown prosecutors at every level in the service will have great scope for the exercise of discretion at various stages of the prosecution process . . . the judicious exercise of discretion, based on clear principles, can better serve the interests of justice, the interests of the public and the interests of the offender than the rigid application of the letter of the law.'

That 'discretion' whether to mount, continue or drop a prosecution is to be derived from two principles, the Code adds. First is the 'evidential sufficiency' test. Before the CPS was founded, the law allowed the police to prosecute if there was a prima-facie case. This was a low threshold: there had simply to be evidence which meant there was a case to answer. The advent of the CPS brought a revision of enormous importance to the working of the law in this area. The CPS will only bring a case to trial if it considers there is 'a realistic prospect of conviction'. This is a much higher threshold. Inevitably, assessing any case in these terms is a subjective judgment, which requires the prosecutor to predict the future reaction of a jury or magistrate. The Code lists a series of factors which the prosecutor should take into account, but many of these merely involve further subjective judgments. 'Does it appear that a witness is exaggerating, or that his memory is faulty, or that he is either hostile or friendly to the accused, or may be otherwise unreliable?' the Code asks. 'What sort of impression is the witness likely to make? How is he likely to stand up to cross examination?'

The real answer to these questions is that it is simply impossible to know how a witness will react before he gets into the box and gives evidence. Juries are not homogenous: their reactions to witnesses will differ widely. The performance any witness may give is also likely to vary according to many factors beyond the prosecutor's control. It may be simply a question of health or general well-being. Some witnesses may behave very differently according to whether a defendant is in custody, or has been given bail.

Meanwhile, in almost every case, the prosecutor will never have met the witnesses he is supposed to assess, but will merely have read their statements, taken by the police. It is difficult to see how anyone could meaningfully evaluate 'the impression a witness is likely to make' on this basis. The police are supposed to supply a form to the CPS setting out their own predictions of the witnesses' resilience. Inevitably, the contents are extremely unreliable and based on guesswork.

Other elements which should, according to the Code, influence the judgment of whether a realistic prospect of conviction exists are equally subjective. Taken together, two of them are farcical: 'If there is a conflict between eyewitnesses, does it go beyond what one would expect and hence materially weaken the case?' and 'If there is a lack of conflict between eyewitnesses, is there anything which causes suspicion that a false story may have been concocted?' In the CPS, you *can* have it both ways.

It is reasonable to ask if a witness 'has a motive for telling less than the whole truth'. But the Code's next question, 'Are there matters which might be properly put to a witness by the defence to attack his credibility?' amounts in practice to an invitation to abandon cases because a witness happens to have a criminal record. In rape and sex assault prosecutions, it opens the way to drop cases because the victim is a prostitute, was promiscuous, or had a previous relation-ship with her assailant. The CPS wants its crime victims and witnesses to be middle-class and squeaky clean.

This section of the Code concludes: 'The Crown Prosecutor must be prepared to look beneath the surface of the statements. He must also draw, so far as is possible, on his own experience of how evidence of the type under consideration is likely to "stand up" in court before reaching a conclusion as to the likelihood of a conviction.' One could put this another way: having read the case file, the prosecutor should act on a hunch.

In 1994, the CPS 'discontinued' 160,000 cases, about 11 per cent of the total. This represented an increase of about 50 per cent since the year of its foundation in 1986. Of the prosecutions dropped, 43 per cent were abandoned because there was thought to be insufficient evidence.[11]

The second principal criterion set out in the Code requires an even bolder judgment than the prediction of how witnesses will react in giving evidence. Having been satisfied that there *is* a realistic prospect of conviction, the prosecutor must decide if proceeding is 'in the public interest'. Cases which failed to cross this hurdle amounted to 28 per cent of the total in 1994.

What is public interest? The Code adopts the definition of this somewhat elusive concept given by Lord Shawcross when he was Attorney-General in 1951. It had never been the practice in Britain that criminal offences would be prosecuted automatically, he said. One had to take into account 'the effect which the prosecution, successful or unsuccessful as the case may be, would have upon public morale and order, and with any other considerations affecting public policy'.

It is difficult to believe that the 2,000 salaried solicitors and barristers who make up the ranks of the CPS spend much time dwelling on lofty notions of 'public morale and order'. The pre-eminent public interest here is not justice, but cost.

The commonest type of 'public interest' discontinuance is when the CPS decides to handle a minor offence through a 'formal caution', administered by the police. This saves the expense of an appearance in court. The CPS can order a caution if the offender is very young, very old, or mentally ill. They may do so if a victim or complainant no longer wishes to pursue a case, or if there are other, more serious charges pending. But in over half the cases dropped by the CPS on public interest grounds, the reason for replacing prosecution with a caution is that a court would be likely to impose only a 'nominal' penalty.[12]

Cautions have their place, especially with first-time minor offenders. Less than twenty per cent of those cautioned for a first offence ever come to the notice of police again. Indeed, the police know this very well: in these circumstances, it is likely that they, not the CPS, will decide to caution instead of charge, and the file will never get as far as the CPS at all.

Nevertheless, the effect of cautioning is a further cession of power from the courts to an executive bureaucracy. Discontinuances on public interest grounds involve another kind of quasi-judicial decision. Here, however, the CPS rules not on the merits of the witnesses but the appropriate punishment, its absolute lack of direct contact with the accused and victim notwithstanding. Magistrates' courts are public. There, justice can be seen to be done. The CPS and police are private and inaccessible.

There is a further cost-driven factor which exerts a powerful influence on prosecutors' decisions. Under pressure from the Treasury, the CPS has, since 1992, set its staff annual 'performance indicator' targets aimed at getting the cases which are to be dropped thrown out at the earliest possible stage. By 1994, this had achieved a situation where 46 per cent of dropped cases were discontinued before the first hearing in the Magistrates' Court. According to the 1993–4 annual report, the aim was to increase this figure by 5 per cent a year for the foreseeable future. The quicker Crown Prosecutors make their decisions, the better, and cheaper for all concerned.

Sometimes, however, they make them *too* quickly: before the police have finished important inquiries, which might, with a little more patience, have produced a conviction. The CPS insists that its relationship with the police has improved immeasurably since its admittedly disastrous start in 1986. In November 1994, it conducted a survey of 'discontinued' cases, finding prosecutors consulted the police about decisions to drop charges 91 per cent of the time; and of these cases, the police protested in only 4 per cent of the total.[13]

My impression is that the conclusions drawn by the CPS from

these figures are far too complacent. Often, the police do not bother to complain because they have become weary of doing so, and see little point. 'After a while, when cases get returned or dropped, experience tells you it isn't worth all the paperwork making a fuss,' said a Kilburn detective sergeant. 'The majority of cases do go smoothly. With those that don't: well, over the years, you become accustomed to the process. The passion dies out of it, and you accept that things have gone wrong. Apart from anything else, getting steamed up with the CPS usually achieves precisely nothing.'

In being asked to make impossible judgments about the course of trials which have not taken place, Crown Prosecutors are being asked to usurp the function of the court. Every day they make quasi-judicial decisions. A service which places such a high premium on cost and value for money is asking its staff to interpret 'realistic prospect of conviction' in the most conservative way: so that 'realistic' becomes 'virtually certain'. In the words of a London CPS case-worker: 'We don't like committing cases which contain flaws, and we won't do so. There's trial readiness and there's trial readiness. I prefer it watertight.'

A jury of twelve which has heard all the evidence tested by cross-examination is far from infallible. It is hardly surprising that the CPS lawyer who merely reads the papers sometimes gets it wrong.

★ ★ ★

When the police first got to Patricia Freely she was bruised, bloodied and sobbing hysterically. In the early hours of 2 October 1994, she had staggered from her bedsit in Willesden, north-west London, to the home of a friend. A man she knew and trusted had tried to rape her, beaten her, and slashed her hand with a knife.[14]

The police took her to a special 'rape suite' at Kilburn police station, a set of rooms designed to be as little like a police office as possible, fitted out like a domestic sitting room with sofas and a television. There she was seen by a police surgeon and made her harrowing statement.

Patricia, a clerical assistant of twenty-three, said her attacker was Aidan Donaghue, a barman in a local public house. Weeks earlier, she had been out with him a few times, and they had slept together.

But although she still saw him from time to time in the pub, they were now 'just good friends', she insisted, and there was no question of resuming a sexual relationship. On the night of 1 October, he asked her to go to the Galtymore Ballroom, a popular Irish dance-hall on Cricklewood Broadway. She readily agreed. When the evening came to an end, he offered to walk her home. She accepted because she thought she would be safer. In the autumn of 1994, the Willesden and Kilburn areas saw a spate of late-night 'stranger rapes'.

When they arrived at her bedsit, Aidan asked – 'aggressively', she said – to come in. She agreed on one condition: they were not to have sex. Apart from considering that phase of their relationship to be over, Patricia had a medical reason for not wishing to sleep with him that night: as the police surgeon later confirmed, she was suffering from a bout of the fungal infection, thrush.

No sooner were they inside than Aidan attacked her, forcing her on to the bed. He bit her breast, and then, she told the police, 'he drew his right hand right back and punched me with his clenched fist straight on to my left eye. At the same time he had his other hand around my throat. Then there was a second, harder blow to my jaw. I thought he had broken my jaw because the pain was so severe. My ear was ringing.'

He tried to force her legs open in order to have sex. But despite his ferocious attack, she resisted. Finally he brandished a knife. Patricia screamed, 'Oh my God, you have got a blade' and he slashed her. For a short time she passed out. When she came to, Donaghue had gone, fearful perhaps that the noise would wake a neighbour. Distraught and still in pain, she ran out into the street.

Patricia was able to describe the knife in some detail: it was a rather unusual, curved model, which Donaghue kept on a bulky keyring. After taking her statement, the police went to his house and arrested him. A knife which fitted her description was still in his possession, and the blade bore traces of blood. He was no stranger to the inside of police stations. Since 1990, when he was sixteen, he had notched up convictions for thirty-two separate offences, including stealing cars, possession of a knife, theft, burglary, aggravated burglary, arson and assault causing actual bodily harm. He had served one short gaol sentence, everything else having been dealt with by fines or community service orders.

Interviewed by detectives, Donaghue confirmed he had been to Patricia's bedsit. He said they had got into bed together, and he had assumed she was consenting to sex, as she had done before. On the three previous occasions they had slept together, he had used a condom, he said, but this time, he had none with him. He claimed that as they began to make love she realised he was using no protection, and 'went berserk'. He denied using his knife. Donaghue claimed he had been unable to calm her and ran from the flat in fear for his own safety. At the end of the interview, he was charged with attempted rape.

Yet this was not simply a case of one person's word against another: there was evidence to corroborate Patricia's allegations. Donaghue had no explanation for her injuries. The police surgeon's report found these to be extensive. She had severe bruising around her eyes consistent with the striking of repeated blows, he said, and further bruising to her breasts and groin. Her left breast had been bitten, hard, and her left hand bore a deep cut, caused by a small blade. (The police also found some of her blood on the sheets on her bed.) The surgeon concluded: 'These findings are consistent with the described events.'

There was also the knife, with its apparent film of blood. This, the police thought, might provide the evidence to clinch the case, and it was sent for forensic science analysis.

The Metropolitan Police laboratories were a little slow in coming up with the results. There was a delay of several weeks. This was too long for the CPS. In early November, they informed the police they intended to discontinue the prosecution on three grounds: that Patricia and Donaghue had had a previous sexual relationship; that they had drunk alcohol at the ballroom; and that she had fainted during the alleged attack, and so could not say with certainty whether intercourse took place.

'The hardest part was telling Patricia,' the detective said. 'She was still in a traumatised state: now this man was going to be hanging about the area without having faced trial. We had assigned a woman officer to help her and befriend her and she was determined to see it through. And then we had to tell her the CPS didn't want to proceed.'

A few days after the case was dropped, the laboratory completed its report. It found 'small stains of human blood on both keyring fobs, and the belt-clip, and a light smear of blood on the blade'. The laboratory uses a six-point scale to state whether there was support for the suggestion that blood might belong to a particular victim. It runs from 'no support' through 'weak support', 'moderate support', 'good support', 'strong support' and 'very strong support'. The report said there was 'strong support' – more than a ninety per cent chance – the blood on Donaghue's knife was Patricia's.

The detective said: 'I can't say for certain whether there was a miscarriage of justice. But I can say that this was a decision which should have been left to a jury, not made by the CPS. Patricia would have had a hard time in the witness box. But inviting someone in is not the same as inviting them to have sex. The CPS seems to think that legally, it is.'

The record of the CPS in sex attack and rape cases appears particularly erratic. In the early 1990s it proceeded to trial with several highly publicised prosecutions in which the evidence *did*, unlike the case of Patricia Freely, boil down to a conflict between the stories told by victim and alleged perpetrator. Austin Donellan, a student at London University, was acquitted of the 'date rape' of a woman with whom he had attended a party. Both, it emerged, were intoxicated, and the only issue was consent. Later another student was acquitted of rape at Brighton, after his alleged victim accepted they indulged in bondage and naked massage, but insisted she had not consented to penetrative intercourse – which he then forced upon her. Finally there was the Surrey police section house case, where a woman officer alleged she was raped by one of her colleagues. She did not report the incident for three months, during which she socialised happily with her alleged assailant, and sent him postcards when on holiday.

At the same time, however, the CPS was discontinuing other rape cases where there *was* corroborative evidence. In May 1995 the women's organisations Women Against Rape and Legal Action for Women published a dossier of further rapes – many of which had violent, 'aggravating features' such as the use of weapons – which the CPS had discontinued because the victims were prostitutes. A few days later, Christopher Davies was convicted and gaoled at Maidstone Crown Court for raping two prostitutes. The CPS having discontinued the case, the two women had fought it as the first private criminal prosecution for rape in English legal history.[15]

There are particular difficulties in convicting men of rape, as the statistics cited in Chapter Three suggest – a five-fold rise in the number of reported attacks since 1990, but no increase in conviction. But the problem, as far as the CPS is concerned, is the manifest inconsistency of its decisions.

Why was Austin Donellan prosecuted, and Aidan Donaghue not? The answer lies partly in the Code for Crown Prosecutors, and its web of subjective, value-laden criteria. Donellan's alleged victim was a middle-class, English student. Donaghue's was a much less educated, working-class Irishwoman who had already experienced a casual relationship with her attacker. Under the terms of the criteria, the CPS was inherently more likely to drop the case against Donaghue. Meanwhile, reaching the 'speedy discontinuance' performance target took precedence over waiting for a vital forensic test.

A Reading case from October 1994 reveals another phenomenon for which there can be no excuse: the dropping of a prosecution because of a mistaken interpretation of the law by the CPS. Ranjit Gill and Caroline Chalkley were returning home after an evening out when they recognised two men, whom they knew as persistent burglars, getting into a car near their flat. They knew one of them by name, while the other had a large, distinctive birthmark on his face. When Chalkley and Gill opened their front door they saw immediately that the place had been ransacked. A stereo system, jewellery, a video recorder and other items were missing.

They telephoned the police, but meanwhile went out to see if there was any sign of the men they had seen earlier. They found them in a car park. Chalkley and Gill blocked in the men's car, and a furious row, which began to turn violent, ensued. Neighbours heard the noise and called the police. When they arrived, the two men were asked to open the boot of their car. Inside was all the stolen property.

All the evidence needed to prosecute the men for burglary was in place. But the CPS insisted – wrongly – that the fact Chalkley and Gill already knew the men by name and by sight would not be admissible. They would not be able to say to the court that the two men they had found in possession of their property were the two men in the dock. A CPS memorandum to the police stated: 'The only evidence the court will be entitled to hear is along the lines of, "I recovered the proceeds of a burglary from someone I know very well as Safaz." What the witness will not be able to say is that "the person I am referring to as Safaz is the person standing in the dock".'

Nor could an identity parade be held to put this right – because this would be unfair to the suspect with the birthmark, while Gill knew the suspect Safaz too well! On 21 October 1994, the case was discontinued on the grounds that there was no identification evidence, and therefore no realistic prospect of conviction.

It was always inevitable that the establishment of the CPS would cause some cases to be dropped. Before the CPS came into being, the standard of evidence was sometimes appalling. 'Years ago you used to say, "let's give it a run",' a Kilburn sergeant said. 'Actually you were prosecuting on a wing and a prayer. And when the people came to court, they pleaded guilty! But the fact was, there was very little supervision, and often the evidence was incredibly weak.'

Before the CPS, said the Metropolitan Police's Commander Michael Briggs, 'if you were the arresting officer in a Magistrates' Court case, you literally went to court the next morning with the details scrawled on a fag packet'. A CPS lawyer, who transferred to the new service from the Metropolitan Police solicitors' department, added: 'The Met was very bad in years gone by. It wasn't just Magistrates' Court offences: it was committals for Crown Court trial. I knew of many examples where police officers would go for committal on the basis of one or two sheets of paper. And meanwhile, the defendant was in gaol on remand.'

Yet it is not as if the CPS is much good at weeding out the weak cases which really ought to be dropped. In 1993, the verdicts on well over half the 14,800 defendants acquitted in the Crown Court were not brought in by the jury at all, but by the judge: either 'ordered' before the start of the trial, or 'directed' at the close of the prosecution case. Juries were responsible for just 42 per cent of all acquittals. The test the judge has to apply in such circumstances was summarised in the case known as 'Galbraith' by the former Lord Chief Justice, Lord Lane: 'Where the judge comes to the conclusion that the prosecution evidence, taken at its highest, is such that a jury properly directed could not convict upon it, it is his duty, upon a submission being made, to stop the case.'

Research for the 1993 Royal Commission on Criminal Justice concluded that 45 per cent of these directed and ordered acquittals were 'unforeseeable'.[16] The Crown could not proceed because witnesses had disappeared or refused to give evidence, or changing circumstances had weakened the case unexpectedly in other ways.

However, a majority, 55 per cent, were 'certainly or possibly foreseeable', meaning there were weaknesses in the evidence which ought to have been spotted. On the basis of this study, had CPS staff really possessed the soothsaying abilities implied by the Code for Crown Prosecutors, they would have halted another 5,000 serious cases each year before incurring the cost of a Crown Court hearing. The study described its findings as 'an indictment of the CPS'.

Moreover, as the study observed, directed and ordered acquittals have been rising steadily since 1983. The advent of the CPS in 1986 did nothing to slow their rapid increase. A second Royal Commission research report, an opinion survey of almost everyone concerned in the Crown Court trial process, found that defence and prosecution barristers and judges considered the prosecution evidence was 'weak' in a fifth of all contested cases. More than 90 per cent of these ended in acquittal.[17]

The CPS seems to be operating in an almost haphazard fashion: throwing out cases with utmost expedition where conviction might have been possible, while pressing ahead with others where it seems most improbable. What on earth is going on?

The answer is partly constitutional. Charles Pollard of Thames Valley makes an important point about the CPS which I have heard many times from police officers of less senior rank. It is a commonplace to note the weakness in the constitutional accountability of the police. But imperfect as police accountability may be, it operates as a model of democratic control and access when compared to the CPS. Pollard says:

As a chief constable, I have to make decisions which are subject to scrutiny. But the CPS can act with effective autonomy, despite its enormous authority in deciding who should be prosecuted and who should not. It claims to act in the public interest, but it has absolutely no contact with the public. There needs to be a means of creating a dialogue to make the CPS accountable. Meanwhile, when the CPS makes decisions which force us to discontinue, it is us, the police, who have to tell the victim.

The position has been exacerbated by the almost continuous reorganisations undergone by the CPS since its foundation. When it was founded in 1986, it was based on regions coterminous with the police constabulary areas it served. These have been reduced to thirteen areas, none of them coinciding with either police or local authority boundaries.

'We are extremely accountable,' a senior Crown Prosecutor insisted. 'Every time we discontinue a case, we have to justify our decision in our management reports.' It was a revealing remark: the accountability of the CPS is internal, and managerial – not public or democratic. Those management reports will never be published. Instead, the public must content itself with the glossy CPS annual report, with its coloured pie charts recording a story of unending improvement and success, and its cheerful message from the head of the service, Director of Public Prosecutions, Barbara Mills. Her 1994 report betrayed no trace of the fact that the preceding twelve months had seen intense public criticism of the CPS. Instead, she boasted of 'providing the public with a high quality and efficient prosecution service throughout England and Wales'. The service looked forward to 'building on our achievements', she concluded.[18]

But in its dealings with the media, the service reveals its official mind: secretive, sensitive, and painfully slow at providing information or help. I had hoped to complement my time with the Kilburn police with a few days as a 'fly-on-the-wall' in the CPS office which handles all their cases, Harrow. It took three months for the CPS to say 'no'. Instead, I was granted a briefing with some senior officials – on condition they must not be named. 'I suppose we are part of the civil service which grew up in a secrecy mode,' one of them said a little sheepishly. 'But I think I'm accountable.'

In a theoretical sense, he was right. Ultimately, the CPS is answerable to the Attorney-General, and so indirectly to Parliament. It will answer MPs' letters about a particular case, if not journalists' inquiries, although in practice, little information will be divulged.

Case law suggests that a policy not to pursue a whole category of prosecutions – for example all thefts worth less than £100 – would be liable to challenge through High Court judicial review. But the courts have also made clear that 'public policy' would not permit them to reverse CPS decisions in individual cases, however unjust the decisions might seem.[19]

Meanwhile, although the slim Code for Crown Prosecutors is publicly available, the CPS makes most of its day-to-day operational decisions on the basis of its voluminous 'manuals', which are said to contain much more detailed guidance about what, for example, might constitute enough evidence for proceeding in a rape trial. These remain entirely secret. Why not publish them, I asked the senior CPS man at my 'unattributable' briefing. That, he said, would be out of the question: 'If we published our manuals, that might well give the criminal opposition the opportunity to avoid prosecution by knowing how we work.'

One man who remains disappointed with the way the CPS has turned out is David Faulkner, who as Deputy Secretary at the Home Office 1982–92 played a greater part than anybody in setting it up. 'It started disastrously because the costing was all wrong,' he says, 'and it has struggled to catch up ever since.'[20] CPS funding was initially determined by the management consultants, Arthur Andersen, who conducted a study of police prosecution work to calculate how much money the new service would need. According to Faulkner, 'they got it wrong by a factor of almost fifty per cent'.

The 1981 Royal Commission on Criminal Procedure recommended a locally-based, decentralised prosecution agency. But the then Home Secretary, Leon Brittan, was determined to create a national body, Faulkner recalls. As a Minister in the most centralising government in recent British history, Brittan had little interest in creating devolved local structures: 'He wanted it to become an instrument of government policy.' In retrospect, Faulkner adds grimly, 'that may have been a mistake'.

There are also structural reasons for the failings of the CPS. It allocates the very biggest cases to a 'special casework' department. The rest, from the traffic cases, low value criminal damage and minor thefts to the burglaries, muggings, serious assaults and rapes, join an endless production line. The CPS has 2,000 lawyers to deal with more than 1.5 million cases a year. With this sort of workload, the due process values on which the CPS was founded remain an unrealised ideal. It is difficult to scrutinise the quality of police investigations and predict the performance of witnesses when you are dealing with an average of three separate cases every working day.

The very first CPS annual report, describing the new service's first year of operation, 1986–7, noted the effect of this deluge in plaintive terms: 'Many thousands of minor process cases now fell to be prosecuted by the CPS instead of the police . . . The need to review such cases absorbed a great deal of time of lawyers who would have been better employed on more exacting and interesting levels of case work.'[21]

In the early years, the problem was exacerbated by understaffing. In the heady days of the Thatcher-Lawson boom, the CPS rates of pay were not competitive enough to attract private sector lawyers who could easily earn more elsewhere. The inadequacies of the Arthur Andersen report notwithstanding, the CPS began life with barely two-thirds of its complement of lawyers. Inevitably, not all those it managed to entice represented the *crème de la crème*. Many of the less able remain.

Since the start of the 1990s recession, the CPS has operated at full strength, and has been able to recruit more selectively. But the case production line remains a heavy burden, on both the CPS and the police. Instead of Commander Briggs's 'fag packet', the CPS requires a file containing full documentary details of each and every case. Its demands are such that the Metropolitan Police estimate that after making an arrest and charge – any arrest and charge – an officer will be off the streets doing paperwork for an average of four hours: half an eight hour shift.

Often the observance of this bureaucratic semblance of due process takes much, much more time than the eventual court appearance. One May morning in 1995, I accompanied a senior Crown prosecutor from a CPS office in east London to the local Magistrates' Court. (The usual CPS rules applied: I cannot say exactly where it was.) She staggered to her seat in front of the stipendiary magistrate under a pile of case files several feet thick. Business got started at 10 a.m. sharp. In less than three hours, prosecutor and magistrate between them dispatched no fewer than twenty-four separate cases, of bewildering diversity. Some were routine remand appearances for serious matters – armed robberies, firearms offences and a sexual assault. Others were final hearings of lesser charges dealt with on the spot.

The first was a criminal damage charge against a man who had got drunk and broken one of his ex-wife's windows with a stone. The defendant, an unemployed builder, had no convictions, and was contrite: he wanted only to plead guilty and get out of the courtroom as speedily as possible. His case file was about half an inch thick. Besides the police report summarising the incident, it contained twenty pages of photocopied police pocket notebooks, and a detailed formal statement from the ex-wife. The police had been required to fill in ten separate forms. Each of them repeated much of the same information – the name of the defendant, charge, date and so on.

The forms in the file were as follows: form MG1, the 'front sheet', containing the basic details of the defendant; form 67a, the charge record; form MG17, a list of previous formal cautions, of which the defendant had none; form MG16, his previous criminal record, also blank; form MG3, with information about the defendant's employment situation and income; form MG5, a summary of evidence; form MG6, the 'confidential information form', the place to put comments about the strength of the case, possible problems with witnesses or whether there might have been an accomplice; form MG7, the initial remand application form, used as a summary in the case of a court appearance before the main hearing (in this case it merely repeated what was in form MG5); form MG9, the witness list; form MG10, a calendar on which dates when witnesses would not be available should be blocked out; and finally, form MG12, the list of (in this case non-existent) exhibits.

It took less than three minutes for the prosecutor to read the police summary of facts and for the magistrate to decide to award £80 compensation and £32 costs, plus a conditional discharge – meaning that if the defendant appeared before the court again within the next twelve months, he might be sentenced more severely for this offence.

As the cases proceeded through the courtroom, the prosecutor juggled the files from pile to pile. The faces in the dock behind her changed with bewildering rapidity, but she and the magistrate were an efficient double act; standing no nonsense, they were there to get the job done by lunchtime. 'With a lay bench, we might have had only a third of the throughput,' she said as the twenty-fourth case was dispatched. 'But the stipe [stipendiary] knows the issues. He doesn't need to mess about.' On her desk next to the files was a little plastic card: a table setting out how much the prosecution should ask for costs in each type of case – £32 for a plea of guilty to a summary Magistrates' Court charge, rising to £404 in respect of an unsuccessful not guilty plea in the Crown Court.

Some of the defendants facing minor charges had no lawyers at all. The morning closed with nine 'overnight' cases of people arrested the previous day. All of them were represented by a 'duty solicitor'. Dressed in a frayed, check suit, his grasp of the details of his clients' affairs was visibly less sure than the prosecutor's and at times he just seemed to ramble.

Blink, and one might have missed it. But suddenly, amid the remands and adjournments, the fines and conditional discharges, the magistrate sent a man represented by the same solicitor to prison for six months. His crime, committed three weeks earlier, was to be seen by police driving his car while already disqualified. The file was incomplete: it lacked a print-out of his driving record from the Driver and Vehicle Authority computer, and a police summary of facts. Forced to rely entirely on a policeman's written statement, the prosecutor uncharacteristically stumbled.

The defendant was a middle-aged Ugandan refugee, and his English was poor. But in the view of the magistrate, it was good enough to enter a plea of guilty. The duty solicitor told the court the man had sold the car now, and lamely suggested there was a 'cultural aspect' to his offence: 'What he is used to back in Uganda in respect of the authorities is completely different to the authorities here.' The magistrate told the man he had defied the law. He would learn not to do so again the hard way. His day in court lasted barely ten minutes. The privatised guards took him down to the cells. Then on with the next case. At the start of the 1980s, Doreen McBarnet criticised the 'ideology of triviality' surrounding Magistrates' Courts.[22] Their proceedings may sometimes seem perfunctory, but they send more than 20,000 people to prison every year.

They also absorb most of the CPS lawyer's working day. Their service's qualified staff spend most mornings on their feet in court, and sometimes afternoons as well. Much of their office time is spent studying the appropriate files. In the Crown Court, the CPS must instruct counsel, because its staff have no right of audience. The result is that while the lawyers are absorbed in the vandalism, pub brawls and shop theft cases, most of the work on the bigger Crown Court prosecutions is handled by unqualified clerks or 'case-workers'. It is they, not the lawyers, who prepare the prosecution briefs for counsel; and it is they who decide which barristers to brief. In 1995, a new CPS 'teamwork' system came into operation, aimed at bringing Crown Court cases under closer legal supervision. However, the sheer pressure of work meant it made only a marginal difference.

The standard police view was summed up by a detective inspector. 'The CPS just doesn't prosecute aggressively,' he said. 'Much of the time, they aren't acting as prosecutors at all.' But CPS error is not individual but systemic. It is only a manifestation of deeper currents: the retreat from prosecution, and the bureaucratisation of justice.

★ ★ ★

The adversarial trial remains the abiding popular image of English criminal justice. Most people assume that most criminal convictions emerge from the courtroom battlefield, with the evidence tempered by the heat of cross-examination.

Nothing could be further from the truth. In Magistrates' Courts, where nine-tenths of the annual million or so non-motoring charges are heard, well over 80 per cent of defendants plead guilty. A CPS survey of all cases heard by magistrates in March 1992–April 1993 found a staggering 97.6 per cent ended in conviction. The minority that do enter a not guilty plea still have a more than a 70 per cent chance of being convicted.

In the Crown Court, the proportion of those prepared to fight their case by pleading not guilty to all charges is much higher: just over a third of defendants whose cases proceed to a hearing. It is this group of 26,000 people, about two per cent of all defendants, who experience what most people would recognise as a trial.[23] For the rest, criminal justice has become a process, its staple product, guilty pleas.

Defendants are encouraged to plead guilty through a variety of institutionalised pressures. Sentence 'discounts' of one third off the normal tariff in return for guilty pleas are now formalised in both Magistrates' and Crown Courts. They have spawned a whole legal vocabulary of pseudo-contrition, to be heard from the mouths of advocates every working day. Defendants *may* plead guilty because they feel remorse. More often, they do so out of what they perceive to be a rational choice. But the reason for giving a defendant a discounted sentence has nothing to do with whether he regrets his crime or not. He gets it because even in a serious case, a guilty plea may be dealt with in less than a morning, whereas a contested trial may drag on for days or weeks, so a saving of thousands of pounds is made.

Formalised sentence discounts involve an inevitable risk: that some innocent defendants who are inadequately represented or who lack confidence in their chances will adopt the line of least resistance. According to the 1993 Royal Commission's Crown Court Study, prosecuting barristers thought 9 per cent of those who pleaded guilty would have been acquitted had they decided to fight.[24] But at least sentence discounts are out in the open. The second means by which the high rate of guilty pleas is maintained is more insidious. This is the widespread practice of charge bargaining and charge reduction – the dropping of the most serious charge against a defendant in return for a plea of guilty to a lesser offence.

The negation of justice which these techniques represent is usually described from the point of view of the defence, notably in *Standing Accused*, a study published in 1994.[25] Based on 'fly-on-the-wall' observation of solicitors' practices and files, the book describes the routine neglect of clients' interests. In most offices dealing with all but the most serious criminal defence work, defendants rarely met their solicitors. They were generally interviewed by unqualified clerks, whose almost automatic assumption was that they must be guilty, and that their interests would best be served by a guilty plea.

As a result, clients were often deprived of any opportunity of putting their case to their own advisers, or of relating their side of the story. Prosecution evidence was usually assumed to be overwhelming and unchallengeable, and, the book concludes, numerous defendants who at first intended to contest their guilt at trial, ended up pleading guilty, even when the case against them was evidentially weak. The ethical restraint which ought to prevent a solicitor from allowing a client who protests his innocence to plead guilty did not appear to be effective. The authors write: 'Either the solicitor simply relies on the guilty pleas produced by his subordinates in their office encounters with clients, or the solicitor himself directly shares in and operates the system's underlying belief in the guilt of most criminal clients. In short, ethical constraints are displaced by the adviser's belief that irrespective of what they say, clients *are* guilty.'

Like their CPS counterparts, qualified defence solicitors spent most of their time on their feet as advocates in the Magistrates' Court. Often, their first real encounter with the client was outside the court, waiting for the hearing. There, 'the idea that the prosecution should be "put to the proof" – required to establish a case against the defendant – is not accepted as "valid" or "realistic" by defence solicitors', the book goes on. The researchers observed a daily process of haggling over charges outside the courtroom between defence and CPS, and recorded them verbatim. Often, they suggest, the object was to obtain a 'sweetener' for the defendant, in order to induce a guilty plea. The following exchange, from a case where the client faced several charges of theft and one of criminal damage, was typical:

SOLICITOR: Will you drop the criminal damage?
PROSECUTOR: But he's a pain in the arse.
SOLICITOR: I know, but go on, he's pleading guilty to all the other stuff.
PROSECUTOR: (Good humouredly) Oh, all right!

In the Crown Court, the pressures on defendants to change potential not guilty pleas to guilty intensified. Again, there was a parallel between defence and prosecution. Just as the CPS lawyers left most Crown Court file work to the case-workers, so the book found that defence solicitors left their Crown Court preparation to their unqualified clerks.

The 1993 Royal Commission expressed its concern at the large number of 'cracked trials', the thousands of cases where defendants elect jury trial instead of being dealt with at the Magistrates' Court, only to change their plea to guilty on the morning of the case. Its solution – rejected by the Government – was to remove the right to jury trial for all but the most serious offences. But according to *Standing Accused*, the most common reason for cracked trials was not the fickle nature of criminal defendants, or the weakening of their resolve once they saw the prosecution witnesses, but the blandishments offered them by defence counsel at the door of the court.

In Crown Court cases, at pre-trial conferences on the day the case was due to start, counsel 'softened up the defendant for a plea, giving reassurance of their loyalty to the *defendant* but not to *the defendant's case*'. Barristers emphasised that a plea was the only hope of avoiding prison, airily citing their familiarity with the judge and Crown counsel. Often, the book reveals, they poured scorn on a client's story, making comments more appropriate to a police interrogation: 'The chances of a jury believing you are very slim'; 'If you contest this and are convicted you'll definitely go to prison and it's just a question of the length of time.' Sometimes, they had a hidden reason for exerting pressure of this kind: the rudimentary work necessary to construct a defence case had not been done. Possible witnesses had not been interviewed by the solicitors, much less warned to be at court.

At the Crown Court, the pace of the deals between prosecution and defence became more frenetic. The book reports the case of a juvenile girl charged with wounding with intent (Section 18 of the Offences Against the Person Act – a very serious charge with a maximum life sentence). Her solicitor had already described her to counsel as 'thick as pigshit, I never speak to her'. Before she was persuaded to change her plea from not guilty to guilty to the less serious charge of ordinary wounding ('Section 20'), counsel addressed her as follows:

'I've had a word with the prosecution and I think it will be appropriate to plead guilty to simple wounding and they will drop the Section 18, which is much more serious. However there is a problem at the moment. He is instructed by the CPS and he said 'no can do' so it looks as if it will have to go off [be adjourned] today; but if we *can* get it reduced to a Section 20 my advice still stands. In front of the right judge, I'm sure this *can* be disposed of by way of a Section 20 – but this judge is not particularly strong; so if he can't drop the Section 18 today, I still think there's a good chance of it in front of the right judge. It will still have to be adjourned because we want a social inquiry report.

In court, there was no hint of this browbeating, which left the client bemused:

DEFENCE COUNSEL: A young lady of under twenty-one, with no previous convictions. *My instructions* are that she would plead not guilty to Section 18 but guilty to Section 20 [authors' italics].
JUDGE: I have a report.
DEFENCE COUNSEL: Oh, maybe we *can* dispose of it today.

The authors conclude:

Barristers evince little interest in scrutinising the evidence or in attempting to convince a defendant of its weight and probative value. Rather, conferences are treated as 'disclosure interviews', the purpose of which is to extract a plea of guilty from the client . . . In place of forensic testing, 'the evidence' is reified, set up as a totality, and invested with a force which irresistibly points to guilt. In place of evidence, a whole gamut of persuasive tactics is deployed against clients enabling barristers to take control of cases and to prevent most clients from becoming, in any real sense, defendants.

However, while these various processes are obviously deeply inimical to the interests of defendants, they also represent the betrayal of the victims of crime. Time and again, the CPS reduces charges likely to require a Crown Court trial to the status of offences which can be dealt with cheaply in the Magistrates' Court. When a

Crown Court trial is unavoidable, the worst charge may be dropped in return for a plea of guilty to a lesser offence. Here is the other side of the story described in *Standing Accused*. Needless to say, the Code for Crown Prosecutors studiously avoids giving charge bargaining its proper name, preferring the anodyne term, 'the acceptance of pleas'.

There will always be scope for 'judicious discretion' of this kind, the Code says. Sometimes, for example, a person charged with burglary will admit to ordinary theft: 'Where the court is able to deal adequately with an offender on the basis of a plea which represents a criminal involvement not inconsistent with the alleged facts, the *resource advantages both to the Service and the courts generally* will be an important consideration' [author's italics].

The Code says this should not lead to charging suspects with offences likely to attract a disproportionately lenient sentence. But even without the promise of a guilty plea, this is exactly what is happening. There is now a nationally imposed set of 'charging standards' for assaults, the result of which is that an attack which would once have attracted a charge of causing actual bodily harm (ABH), will now be reduced to the much less serious offence of common assault – for which the usual penalty is a bind-over to keep the peace or a trivial fine.

This saves a great deal of money: defendants accused of ABH can choose to be tried in the Crown Court, but common assault is a 'summary', Magistrates-only offence. In 1995, the CPS ready-reckoner apportioned an average of £80 total prosecution costs for a Magistrates' Court hearing, which rose to £600 if the same case went to the Crown Court.

Common assault will now be the charge for an attack which causes 'grazes, scratches, abrasions, minor bruisings, swellings, cuts or a black eye'. However, the new charging standards also mean that many attacks which would once have been classified as causing grievous bodily harm (GBH), which can only be tried in the Crown Court, now rate only as actual bodily harm – a Magistrates-Crown Court 'either way' offence. Under the new standards, ABH includes attacks which cause 'injuries resulting in loss of, or broken, teeth, temporary loss of sensory functions (including loss of consciousness),

extensive/multiple bruising, displaced/broken nose, minor frac-
tures, cuts requiring medical attention e.g. stitching, psychological
injury (more than fear, distress or panic) supported by medical
evidence'.[26]

A guilty plea to ABH in the Magistrates' Court usually attracts a
fine. Meanwhile, in some ABH cases, defendants threaten to plead
not guilty and elect Crown Court trial, prompting the CPS to
reduce the charge to common assault. To be charged with GBH,
you now have to carry out a very serious assault indeed, one which
causes an 'injury resulting in permanent disability, permanent visual
disfigurement (not minor), permanent loss of sensory function –
broken/displaced bones/limbs etc., substantial blood loss', requiring
'lengthy treatment or incapacity'.

Charge bargaining even affects more serious cases involving
professional criminals. In the summer of 1994, two Kilburn officers
stopped a known drug dealer. As they asked to search him, he made a
move with his hand towards the waistband of his trousers, saying,
'I'm going to fucking kill you.' The police jumped on him and
handcuffed him. He was found to be carrying a loaded Smith and
Wesson revolver and spare bullets.

The police wanted to have him tried for possessing a firearm with
intent to endanger life. This carries a maximum life sentence.
However, at the behest of the CPS, the charge was reduced to simple
possession, to which he pleaded guilty. By this time, it had been
established that the man was prepared to admit to possessing the gun,
and to saying 'I'm going to fucking kill you'. But if the more serious
charge had been followed through, he planned to plead not guilty,
claiming that the remark had been addressed to an 'unnamed third
party', from whom he claimed to have borrowed the gun. He
claimed his remark was meant not as a serious threat to kill a police
officer, but as an expression of exasperation at the friend for getting
him into trouble. In the absence of the 'friend' as a defence witness,
most juries, one suspects, would not have believed his story. But it
was never heard in open court: the deal was done in private.

At present, this dismal vista of bureaucratised, cost-determined
justice is getting worse, not better. Since 1993, legal aid has been
paying defence solicitors and barristers on a 'fixed fee' basis in all but
the most serious of cases. Under this system, the biggest payment is

made for taking on the case, regardless of the plea. Therefore the defence's interests lie in rapid turnover, not in dragging things out in court. Prosecutors are paid on the same basis, although they do have to check charge bargains with the CPS office which instructs them – in practice this is a very weak restraint. For the prosecution, a plea of guilty, even to a charge which does not really measure up to the true seriousness of the offence, saves time and money for all concerned: the police, the courts and counsel.

One final parallel between defence and prosecution is the appalling fact that in over half of Crown Court cases, both defence and prosecution barristers receive their brief only on the eve or morning of the trial. Even in contested cases, where a not guilty plea is sustained, more than 50 per cent of defendants meet their barrister for the first time on the day of the trial. According to the Royal Commission Crown Court study, a third of subsequent conferences between client and lawyer last less than fifteen minutes, and 70 per cent less than half an hour.[27]

Sometimes this may not matter. Indeed, the study found barristers themselves eminently satisfied with the position. More than nine-tenths of them thought they had enough time to prepare, even when they read their instructions for the first time on the day of the trial. Four-fifths of defendants, and three-quarters of those found guilty, rated their counsel's work as 'good'.

However there are too many exceptions, and the results of poor preparation can be seen in Crown Courts every day. Prosecutors who barely know the facts of the case will open a trial with a wooden reading from the file of documents. Each side will miss obvious points in cross-examination, often failing to ask the crucial question which will make or break a case.

I witnessed an extraordinary example one day at a London Crown Court, where I went behind the scenes with a judge. A man charged with possessing an offensive weapon, after police found a metal kung-fu flail in the van he was driving, told a convoluted story about borrowing the vehicle from one of those 'unnamed third parties'. Had the flail been fingerprinted, it might have ended the matter, but budget curbs meant the police had not had this test performed. The judge showed me the case papers during an adjournment and a vital fact caught my attention: when the defendant was arrested, his house keys were on the same keyring as those for the van. The prosecutor failed to notice this, and never put it to the defendant. He was acquitted.

Here was a case which did go to the jury. Inadequate preparation is another reason why defence and prosecution counsel will go to some lengths to avoid such an outcome by obtaining a guilty plea.

How can this state of affairs have arisen? How can the hours of preparation by the police, the CPS and sometimes the defence, be jeopardised by half-baked presentation in court? As long as the practice of criminal law remains a two-tier profession, this feature of the system will not be eliminated, and reducing the extent of its consequences will not be easy.

The situation is made even worse because barristers wield disproportionate power and so can get away with inadequate preparation. Their convenience and continued income is put above the interests of victims, defendants and justice. If a barrister suddenly has time on his hands, he will try to cram in another case, rather than spend more time on the preparation of a later trial.

A detective sergeant said:

> You have to go to court to see the way the police are treated. The prosecutors think they're so high and mighty: the way they look down their noses when they speak to you, you feel like spanking them. Yet half the time they bugger up the case because they haven't prepared it properly. The courts are run for the benefit of the Bar old boy network: you see them at lunchtime, defence and prosecution in the Bar mess, having a glass of wine together, looking after themselves as usual.

In an effort to improve matters, in May 1995 the CPS set a series of targets for barristers. They should have read the case papers and offered advice at least seven days before the trial in cases likely to last up to three days, rising to three weeks for those cases liable to go on for more than ten days. But at the same time, the CPS recognised the targets were likely to be breached. Its memo to its area offices states: 'It is acknowledged there will always be exceptional cases in which the above target dates cannot be met . . . if counsel is unable to meet the target date set out in the above time scale, the CPS must be notified so a revised date can be agreed.' This is not the language of tough sanctions.

★ ★ ★

The bureaucratisation of justice and the retreat from prosecution go hand in hand. It is this retreat which is, above all, responsible for the declining conviction figures set out in Chapter Three.

Nevertheless, the prospects of acquittal for the minority of defendants pleading not guilty at the Crown Court *have* increased. By 1994, 60 per cent of them were being acquitted of all charges – more than 15,000 people. In 1983, before the foundation of the CPS and PACE, that proportion was exactly half. In 1975, at the height of the unreconstructed old regime, 55 per cent of those who pleaded not guilty were convicted.

The distribution of these acquittals is not even across all offence groups. Unfortunately, the full picture is obscured by a baffling and irritating omission in the official statistics. It is easy to discover how many people are charged with each kind of offence, and also the total number of defendants convicted or cleared. But the conviction figures are not broken down according to plea. Therefore it is impossible to find out how many people end up being convicted or acquitted of particular offences *after pleading not guilty*.

There is, however, one set of tables which offers some highly suggestive clues: the supplementary volume of Crown Court tables, published each year by the Home Office to complement its annual book of criminal statistics. Although this does not break down convictions according to plea, it does show the numbers acquitted and convicted of each different type of offence. In dealing with certain types of the most serious offence, the tables reveal a startling fact – the rate of acquittal in these categories is far in excess of the overall average.

In 1993, the last year for which figures were available at the time of writing, nearly half the 873 rape trials (411 cases), ended in acquittal. Yet in the same year, 80 per cent of the total number of all Crown Court defendants were convicted (most of them, of course, after pleading guilty). In other words, the rape acquittal was about two-and-a-half times the average.

In March 1994, *Getting Away With Rape*, a Channel 4 documentary by the TV producer Lynn Ferguson, demonstrated that in the majority of rape cases where the victim knew her alleged assailant, the position was even worse. She monitored all acquaintance rape trials at the Old Bailey over a three month period, finding that only 32 per cent ended in conviction. In some of these trials, the victim had met her assailant only shortly before the attack: the extent of the acquaintance was having shared a single drink. One man featured on the programme had been tried for rape *seven* times, and on each occasion, he was acquitted. Another was acquitted on five occasions.

David Lederman QC successfully defended the same man three times. On each occasion, the man was accused of raping his victim after meeting her at a bar or nightclub, offering to drive her home, and then taking her to remote country lanes where he carried out his attacks. Each time, the man's defence was that this was not rape but consensual casual sex. Lederman betrayed no ethical qualms, telling the programme:

> What eighteen to twenty year old girl who's gone to a discotheque and within five minutes is going for a drive with a man she's never met before, what has she got in the back of her mind? I mean, is she really going for a drive in order to discuss the Liberal Democrat next election manifesto in relation to local government elections, or is she going in the car with, in the back of her mind, the thought that she quite fancies him, he quite fancies her, and something exciting might happen?

Another offence with an overall high rate of acquittal is assault or wounding endangering life: 40 per cent (991) of the 2,500 tried were acquitted – double the overall average of acquittals. More than a third of those tried in the Crown Court for less serious assaults (some of which would nonetheless have rated as grievous bodily harm) also walked free.

Thirty per cent of the ninety-one people who were tried for attempted murder were acquitted. 40 per cent (121 defendants) of those tried for threatening or conspiring to murder were also cleared in court. Surprisingly enough, nearly one third of the 297 people tried for murder were acquitted by a judge or jury – a fact

conveniently forgotten when politicians and police officers talk, as
frequently they do, of murder's 90 per cent clear-up rate.

All these offences share a common characteristic: they are offences
against the person, in which the victim (with the exception of
murder, of course) must inevitably become the principal witness. In
very many cases, a case of this kind will turn on the word of the
victim against that of the alleged perpetrator. An alleged rapist will
say the woman consented to sex; a person accused of wounding
endangering life, that he acted in self-defence against the victim.
Already confused and vulnerable, the victim of rape or violence
undergoes a second assault by adversarial cross-examination, in
which there will be little that is off-limits.

Moreover, the proportion of convictions for serious violence and
rape has declined over time. In 1980, less than a third of the 406 men
tried for rape were acquitted, although at this time, the law had not
changed to prevent cross-examination about the victim's sexual
history. (Ferguson's documentary found that this rule, introduced in
1986, was usually honoured in the breach, with only rare interven-
tions to prevent such lines of questioning by prosecuting counsel or
the judge.) The acquittal rate in trials for wounding endangering life
was also lower, at 30 per cent.

In trials of crimes of property, the results are very different. More
than 12,000 people were convicted of burglary in the Crown Court
in 1993, and only 1,100 were acquitted – a proportion less than half
the overall 20 per cent acquittal rate. Less than 20 per cent of robbers
succeeded in not guilty pleas. In crimes of this type, it need hardly be
said, there is more likely to be independent evidence: stolen
property, finger prints, and so on.

The evidence from rape and violence cases points clearly to a
different kind of failing – a failing in the rules and procedures of
adversarial justice. There clearly seem to be various categories of
offence where the trial process seems to find it difficult to cope.

In numerical terms, however, the most significant fall is not in
convictions after contested trials, but in the number of cases actually
committed to the Crown Court. This decline appears particularly
remarkable when viewed against a background of rapidly rising
crime.

In 1977, when recorded crime totals were less than half their present level, 57,000 cases were committed to the Crown Court. As the crime figures rose, committals at first more than kept pace. In 1982, there were 68,000 committals; in 1984, 75,000; in 1985, 83,000; in 1987 nearly 99,000; and in 1988, 106,500 cases. In this period, Crown Court committals were actually increasing more rapidly than recorded crime.

However, as the crime figures began the steepest increase in history in 1989, committals faltered, then began to decline. There were 98,000 committals in 1989; 103,000 in 1990; 104,000 in 1991, 101,000 in 1992 and just 87,000 in 1993 – about the same as in 1986. Over the period 1986–93, recorded crime soared from a total of 3.8 million to 5.5 million offences.[28]

Concealed within these figures is a further phenomenon: the reclassification of offences. Just as charge bargaining can reduce an assault from GBH to, in some circumstances, the summary offence of common assault, so the 1988 Criminal Justice Act took whole groups of offence out of the Crown Court figures altogether. Car theft, for example, was reclassified as 'TWOC', taking without owner's consent, to be heard only by magistrates.

We have seen the mechanisms of retreat: charge bargaining, cautioning, and discontinuances. But why, ultimately, has it taken place?

The first reason for the retreat from prosecution is that the police, in many areas, have simply been overwhelmed. Rising crime, increasing bureaucracy, and curbs on overtime and forensic science budgets has forced a prioritisation. The vastly increased time which must be spent on the least serious offences means fewer of them can be dealt with. Meanwhile, in the words of a divisional chief inspector, 'I should be able to tell you I've got so many sergeants, so many detective constables, and so many trainees. The reality is that more than half of my squad have been abstracted to deal with murders and other major crimes.'

Similar pressures operate within the CPS. The lead comes not from the requirements of justice, but from the Treasury. Everything, says the retired Law Lord, Lord Ackner, has come to be judged by the yardstick of finance, 'but you cannot use that yardstick when you come to measure justice'. Doing so means justice, inevitably, must suffer.

On 1 January 1995, the retreat from prosecution reached
something of an apotheosis, in the shape of a new manual and
accompanying form, to be used when considering what action to
take against each and every suspect – the police Case Disposal
Manual.[29] It ranks every offence, motoring, criminal and alcohol-
related, on a scale of points from one to five. Five-point offences –
such as murder – would always be prosecuted. Four-point crimes
had, what the manual terms, 'a high probability of prosecution', so
that an officer needed to be able to justify a decision not to charge.
This category includes GBH, forgery, arson, perjury, burglary and
perverting the course of justice.

Then come the huge group of three-point crimes. These are
'pivotal', in that a decision to charge will depend entirely on the
circumstances. In this category are many offences where cautioning
– the normal alternative to prosecution – would once have been
unthinkable: indecent assault, theft, handling stolen goods, buggery,
prostitution offences, resisting arrest, criminal damage and assault
occasioning actual bodily harm.

The decision to charge, says the manual, it to be made by listing
the 'aggravating' and 'mitigating' factors. Enough mitigating factors,
and even a four-point crime might lead only to a caution – a case of
GBH, for example, which arose from 'a single blow, an impulsive
action under provocation'.

There are general factors, such as the impact on the victim, if
applicable, the offender's history, the likelihood of penalty if the case
is brought to court, and whether the crime involved is a 'prevalent
offence' arousing local concern. There are also specific factors for
each offence type. An indecent assault might only be cautioned if it
was a 'single offence of a trivial nature', or if there was a 'genuine
mistake as to the identity of the victim'. Possession of drugs – not
only cannabis but 'Class A' substances such as cocaine, crack and
heroin – will usually be cautioned if only 'small amounts, for
personal use' are involved.

The possessor of an offensive weapon will not be prosecuted
under the manual's guidelines if there was 'no risk, weapon not on
display, mistaken belief that there would be no offence if carried for
protection only'. The unlicensed owner of a shotgun or firearm may
no longer expect to go to court if his licence had merely lapsed.

Deception offences will go unprosecuted if they were 'committed over a short period, low value', or 'driven by poverty/personal need'. As for causing actual bodily harm; there will be no prosecution if it was a single blow causing only superficial injury.

Still less serious, two-point, offences will never be prosecuted at all unless there are serious aggravating factors. In this class are charges of being drunk and incapable in a public place – once the daily mainstay of 'fag packet' Magistrates' Court prosecutions. A charge will be laid now only if the same offender is arrested four times for the same offence within a four-week period.

Meanwhile, if a person refuses to accept a caution – which does, after all, require an admission of guilt, and of which a central record is kept which can be cited in court at a later date – the manual's recommended alternative is not, surprisingly enough, to charge. It invents a whole new 'case disposal' – the 'formal warning'. No central record is kept of such warnings and they cannot be mentioned in court if the offender is later charged with another offence. Warnings also require an admission of guilt, however. In some circumstances, a refusal to accept a warning may lead to a further new disposal – the 'not proceeded with'. This means, essentially, that nothing has happened at all. But it differs crucially from its predecessor, the 'no further action': it counts as a statistical crime clear-up.

The Case Disposal Manual – introduced at first in London and several counties, with others rapidly following suit – enlarges police discretion on an unprecedented scale. It requires that officers of junior rank take fundamental decisions with massive implications for the lives of those they arrest, without reference to any court or outside authority. The judgments it demands are even more subjective than some of those required by the Code for Crown Prosecutors. How, for example, do you measure whether a sexual assault is 'trivial'? It is inescapable that many of those judgments will be shaped by factors which have nothing to do with the true merits of the case: the officer's workload; his opinion of the suspect; and the possibility that he may, in return for non-prosecution, become a useful informant in future. Some of the latitude for private deals over bail in police interview rooms, which PACE tried to remove, has been restored.

The Manual – drawn up after consultation between the Metropolitan Police, the Association of Chief Police and the CPS – alters institutionalised police practice significantly, but its introduction took place without any trace of public or parliamentary debate. Then again, it is but a symptom, albeit of an extreme kind. The retreat from prosecution was underway long before it was ever conceived.

CHAPTER FIVE

The Problem of Organised Crime

NEW YEAR'S EVE, 1993 is not a date which the Kano family of Wimbledon will easily forget. This was the night three men burst into their house, threatened to kill them at gunpoint and made off with jewellery, cash and credit cards worth £30,000.[1]

Zein Kano, his wife Lina, and his two eldest sons, Nael, aged sixteen, and Bassel, thirteen, were getting ready to celebrate at a hotel in the West End of London. They had ordered a home delivery pizza for their younger offspring – Khaled, eleven, and Amer, aged five. Baby Karim was to be looked after by their two servants, Maya Lama and Mariam Youssef. Mr Kano, a Nigerian businessman, was rich.

Chris Webb, the pizza delivery man, reached the house at 8.45 p.m. He announced his presence on an entry phone outside the security gates guarding their drive, and the Kanos let him in. Webb knelt down to sort out the pizzas outside the front door, which was opened by Bassel. As he did so, a man dressed in a black boiler suit and a balaclava covering everything except his eyes pushed past him into the house. He dragged Webb in after him, and pushed him into the sitting room. Webb was then trussed up with wire. As he lay on the floor, he watched another man in a balaclava beating Mr Kano. The struggle ended when the man produced a gun, coshed Mr Kano on the head and pressed the weapon to his temple. 'Shut up,' he shouted, 'or I'll kill you.'

There were three intruders altogether, two of them armed. Most of the family was rounded up in the kitchen. As Mr Kano was led through from the sitting room, he saw young Khaled being dragged down the stairs. The leader of the gang pointed his gun at the children and told Mr Kano: 'Take me to your safe or your family will be dead.' Two of the men followed him up the stairs into one of the bedrooms. There Mr Kano opened the safe. The robbers took a pillowcase from the bed and eagerly scooped bracelets, rings and other valuables into it.

They were not satisfied: now they demanded cash. In the master bedroom, the Kanos had £500. Mr Kano was terrified: Lina had not been brought downstairs and he suspected she was in the bedroom. In the event he had no choice: the robbers pushed past him into the room. They took her watch, handbag and the cash. As they told her to join the rest of the family, they asked her if she had called the police. They marched her downstairs at gunpoint, repeating the question insistently. In the kitchen they forced her into a chair, and tied her hands behind it.

The gang realised Nael, the oldest boy, was missing. 'Where is he, where is he, is he calling the police?', one of them asked. Mr Kano replied: 'No, no, he doesn't know what's going on, he's having a shower, please leave him alone.' Two of the men took him upstairs again, promising to kill him if the boy was not produced. 'Having taken all our jewellery and money, I was petrified they were going to shoot one of my family,' Mr Kano said later. Outside the door to Nael's bedroom they stopped. In English, Mr Kano shouted: 'Open the door, open the door.' But immediately afterwards he added in Arabic: 'You are not here, you are not here.' The gang leader shouted: 'Open the door or we will shoot your dad.'

Suddenly the attack came to an end. Through the landing window the men saw the blue lights of police cars. Hearing the commotion downstairs, Lina had pressed a security 'panic button' in the bedroom, and Nael *had* called the police, as the men had feared. All three intruders ran out of the house.

They were soon arrested. Keith Bramble, their leader, had emerged from a six-year sentence for the same offence, aggravated burglary, less than three months earlier. He had been under intermittent police surveillance ever since. He was chased by uniformed officers into a dead-end alley, where he tried to hide in some bushes. At 9 p.m., just fifteen minutes after pushing the pizza man through the door, he surrendered, still wearing his mask, gloves and boiler suit. Under the bushes the officers found the pillowcase from the Kanos' home, packed with valuables.

Simon Whyte climbed over the garden wall after running out of the house and hid by the shed at the bottom of the garden. Still carrying some of Lina Kano's jewellery, he gave himself up after being bitten by a police Alsatian. In a nearby dustbin the police found his gun. The last of the attackers, Hiram Braithwaite, remained at liberty until 10.10 p.m., when he was found hiding on the flat roof of a neighbouring house.

The three men were tried at the Old Bailey over two weeks in July 1994. There were forty-six prosecution witnesses. In addition to the evidence gathered immediately after the attack, some of the Kanos had been able to identify their assailants. All three men pleaded not guilty. Both police and civilian witnesses were accused of lying about every aspect of the case, with the result that Judge Richardson allowed the jury to hear the formidable list of previous convictions notched up by each defendant. (The law allows juries to hear about the previous character of defendants if they base their defence on attacking the character of witnesses who testify against them.)

Bramble claimed that instead of being arrested yards from the Kanos' house with most of the stolen goods beside him, he had in fact been lifted off the street in another part of London. He said all the stolen items were planted by the police.

Whyte's defence was even more far-fetched: that he had been 'kidnapped' miles away in Kennington, beaten up by police officers and planted with Lina Kano's jewellery at Tooting police station. A robber had indeed been arrested outside the shed that night, he claimed, but this was someone else, who had deliberately been allowed to go free. He had, of course, to explain the medical evidence of dog bites noted by a doctor called by the police after his arrest. This, his lawyers suggested, had been fabricated for financial reasons, because the doctor was paid for his call-out, and wished to earn similar fees in future. Whyte did not impress the judge, who in summing up described his story as 'so unbelievable as to insult your intelligence'.

As for Braithwaite, he too claimed he had been arrested elsewhere and 'fitted up' with the Kano aggravated burglary. He said he had been selling cannabis on a nearby main road and panicked when he saw the police, who thereby fitted him to the Kano burglary frame.

The jury retired to consider its verdict at 11.12 a.m. on 18 July. It returned at 2.10 p.m. The youngest juror, a woman in her early twenties, was chosen as foreman. When the jury returned, she interrupted the clerk as he asked whether they had reached a verdict, saying: 'We want to acquit them all.' There was a roar from the public gallery. Four of the jurors waved at the men in the dock and gave them the thumbs-up sign, shouting above the hubbub 'good luck, well done'.

Later, the police learnt the three defendants had been in unusually high spirits as they left Belmarsh prison for court that morning. Yet there was no evidence any of the jurors had been 'nobbled': indeed, nobbling an entire jury is an almost impossible feat. If there had been interference, a hung jury, not a unanimous not guilty verdict, might have been expected. As for the Kanos, they and the children have not got over their experience.

Here, with the tiny minority of cases where defendants enter a Crown Court fight, due process ideology has real meaning; the real power of the legal protections for suspects can be painfully evident. This is the upper tier of a *de facto* two-tier system, and it includes the worst crimes, those which arouse the strongest public fears: serious violence, murder, rape and the work of organised, professional gangs. It is on this tier that virtually all public debate about criminal justice is located, and it overwhelmingly preoccupied the 1993 Royal Commission.

For their part, the police have few doubts. Anticipating the comments of David Phillips, Charles Pollard and Tom Williamson quoted at the start of Chapter Four is a long history of lobbying by the most senior officers, dating back to Sir Robert Mark, Metropolitan Commissioner in the 1970s, and beyond. A quintessential statement was contained in Sir Peter Imbert's valedictory address as Commissioner in October 1992. Sir Peter said:

> It is many years now since I read the book *The Famous Trials of Marshall Hall*, a great advocate, but I remember thinking even then that the tales of how he managed to acquit his clients by a skilful blend of charm, eloquence and thespian trickery, when many of them were manifestly guilty, did not leave the criminal justice system with a great deal of credit. Neither did it leave the victims with a great deal of justice . . . the current system has

become a confrontational process, where that process itself and the rules of evidence deny the opportunity fully to examine the truth. What is aired is then attacked in combat so that the truth is sometimes made to appear fiction, and fiction is portrayed as fact.[2]

As a description of the trial of Keith Bramble, these comments do not seem inappropriate. There *was* important testimony excluded because of the rules of evidence criticised by Sir Peter. The police had tapes of all their radio communications, in which the officers who made the arrests described what was happening as it took place. The tapes contained the voices of both Bramble and Whyte, juxtaposed with officers telling their control room where they had found their suspects.

The defence argued successfully that to include the tapes would breach the technical legal rules prohibiting 'hearsay' evidence, which accord absolute primacy to oral testimony in court. The tapes, they said, contained material in which police officers described the actions of defendants, and this should only be done in the witness box, when allegations could be subject to cross-examination. Perhaps they would have made no difference: here was a jury which seemed determined to disbelieve the police. The decision was unchallengeable in law. It is not, however, difficult to sympathise with the opinion of police officers involved in the case that the judge's decision to exclude the tapes ran counter to both justice and common sense.

Was this case representative of a deeper, systemic malaise, of an adversarial trial system which no longer serves the public interest? Or was it a freak example, to be mainly blamed on the perversity of the jury?

This is a difficult question to answer, as there is a complete absence of research in this area. There is no systematic study of cases in which it might reasonably be said that 'factually guilty' defendants were discharged or acquitted. As a result, the debate is conducted at the level of anecdote and assertion: the data for definitive conclusions does not exist. However, there is evidence that criminal justice seems close to breaking down in certain areas. One salient example is the system's dealings with professional criminals and organised crime.

★ ★ ★

The public perception of organised crime in Britain remains filtered through a bizarre nostalgia. Their deeds still endlessly disinterred by the media, the professional criminals of the 1960s have passed into legend, been reinvented as stock characters in an Ealing comedy with menace: the Great Train Robber, Ronnie Biggs; the under-world enforcer 'Mad' Frankie Fraser; and above all the Kray twins, flamboyant society gangsters who knew how to achieve 'respect'.

On the day Ronnie Kray died in Broadmoor, I spoke to Commander Roy Penrose, the national co-ordinator of Regional Crime Squads – the chief of the principal police units deployed against organised crime. 'He was a music-hall turn, a cartoon character,' Penrose said. 'The real people making the real money laugh at the way the Krays did things thirty years ago.'

Organised crime has not penetrated our political, social and law enforcement institutions as it has in Italy or Russia, or to a lesser extent in the United States. But the Kray image has become a distant anachronism.

NCIS, the National Criminal Intelligence Service, defines the phenomenon as follows 'Organised crime constitutes any enterprise or group of persons, engaged in continuing illegal activity, which has as its primary purpose the generation of profits, irrespective of national boundaries.'

One representative was Francesco di Carlo, a Sicilian mafioso who until he was gaoled for twenty-five years in 1987, lived in splendour amid the 'stockbroker belt' in Woking, Surrey. His wife was active in local charities, and his neighbours believed that the dapper individual who left for London on the commuter trains each morning worked in the hotel business. Di Carlo did indeed own hotels, and other 'straight' commercial interests, but his main business was the import of heroin and cannabis.

His neighbours were also unaware that he was wanted in Italy for helping to plan the 1983 murder of General Dalla Chiesa, an anti-terrorist expert sent by Rome to fight the Mafia. In fact, di Carlo and other fugitives from Italian justice had set up a special Mafia cell in Surrey. An even more senior *Cosa Nostra* figure, Alfonso Caruana, lived a few miles away from di Carlo near Charterhouse School, in a

£450,000 mansion, and his brother, Pasquale, occupied a house worth £350,000 on the other side of Woking. Both men fled once di Carlo was arrested. Their money-laundering operation stretched from Hong Kong to East Africa, taking in banks in the Bahamas, Tokyo, Vienna, New York, London and small High Street branches in the West Country.[3]

Di Carlo may have originated abroad, but in his international connections and in his invisibility he typified the emerging new order of organised crime. According to Commander Roy Clark, head of the South-east Regional Crime Squad, 'The clever ones now are absolutely anonymous. Journalists don't know their names and sometimes police officers don't know them either.' The most serious players lived in almost complete obscurity, enjoying millionaire lifestyles, Clark said, funding all manner of other criminal operations and wherever possible, getting other people to take the risk.[4]

The routes into this group are many and varied. There are some who have never been convicted of a single criminal offence; others who have graduated from the little league. Clark says:

In the mid-eighties, we became aware at Scotland Yard of a group of tearaways in the East End. They were outrageous, bold as brass, ramraider types; they would jemmy open a warehouse and load up a lorry in broad daylight, that sort of thing. A few of them fell by the wayside. Some went away for a long time. Some got respectable and settled down. One or two ascended the ladder of criminality. They are living as millionaires, beyond conventional criminality.

Organised crime in Britain has reached the point where for those lower down the scale, it has taken on many of the characteristics of ordinary employment, whose vocabulary it shares. Police and criminals alike describe a planned offence as 'a job'. Offenders released from gaol, for whom conventional paid occupations are not easy to acquire, speak of the deadly temptation of 'a bit of work' coming their way. In some cases, if offers a regular wage, and often a service flat. Yet most of this activity takes place at a rarefied level, far from the routine concerns of everyday policing and criminal justice.

When the Government set the first national police performance targets in 1994, they focused on the local divisional crimes which most visibly affect ordinary citizens: burglary, robbery and car crime. 'Out on division, people don't give two tosses that there are people making millions of pounds a year,' Clark said. Chief constables sometimes express reluctance at having to part with their annual precepts to fund the Regional Crime Squads: they could easily use the money in other ways. Organised crime's direct connection with the everyday is not always appreciated: the fact that car thefts may be being organised by a ring, whose success will influence insurance premiums; and above all the direct connection between the organised import of drugs with the petty muggings and burglaries carried out by addicts feeding a habit.

The investigation into the attack on the Kanos by Bramble and his associates was highly unusual among professional crime inquiries, because it began with a rapid response to emergency calls, and was witnessed by many people. Usually, law enforcement is not so lucky. More commonly, investigations of this kind depend fundamentally on the detective's most basic tool: the use of criminal informants. Moreover, in recent years, informant handling has undergone a distinct shift. In inquiry after inquiry, they have provided intelligence not about crimes already committed, but before they actually take place. Often, the source of the intelligence will be personally involved, as a 'participating informant'.

The origins of this change can be traced back to the 1970s. Then, the archetypal professional crime was the bank raid or security van heist. In a series of controversial and highly-publicised trials, armed robbers from the 'firms' and families of London and other big cities were regularly arraigned on the evidence of 'supergrasses', informers turned prosecution witnesses. The grasses themselves pleaded guilty, sometimes to long strings of the most serious offences, and then went into the witness box to accuse their former associates. In return, while others were getting sentences of twenty years or more, they would receive the 'supergrass tariff' of just five years. In reality, most went nowhere near a prison, but spent their sentences in 'protective custody' – in conditions which amounted to nothing more stringent than a pampered form of house arrest, guarded by police officers.

This arrangement led to the imprisonment of many notorious and violent robbers. But it carried within it the seeds of its own destruction. Its employment as the principal means of fighting organised crime was more than the courts could stomach. In 1975, as he ruled on cases which had been put up by the first and most successful supergrass, Bertie Smalls, Lord Justice Lawton called him a 'craven villain'. Smalls, who had been an extremely active criminal and confessed to thirty robberies, had not even received the supergrass tariff, but was given absolute immunity from prosecution at the behest of the then Director of Public Prosecutions, Sir Norman Skellhorn. This, Lawton said, was a 'distasteful spectacle' which must never happen again.

In later cases, other judges were equally critical. Sentencing men convicted in 1979 on the evidence of the supergrasses David Smith and George Williams, Judge Michael Argyle sounded the system's death-knell. The Crown witnesses were 'two of the most dangerous criminals in British history', he said. He found it 'nauseating to hear these hypocrites and to reflect that as a matter of policy they have been sentenced to five years each'.[5]

In the 1980s, armed robbery lost its allure for professional criminals. Video surveillance, automatic bullet-proof screens and other technological changes made bank hold-ups a dangerous and difficult business. Meanwhile, the police were demonstrating their readiness to use the ultimate deterrent. The proliferation of firearms among criminals – some of them very far from professional – led to the formation of armed response teams, on permanent patrol. There was a steady trickle of incidents in which would-be robbers were shot dead. One of the most controversial cases occurred at an abattoir in Plumstead, south-east London, in July 1987. The police had prior intelligence that a gang planned to hold up a wages van, and decided to 'let the job run'. Scotland Yard's specialist firearms team, PT17, lay in wait, and in the ensuing confrontation two men were killed, Nicholas Payne and Michael Flynn, although they had not fired at police or the wages van staff.

Armed robbery has become a haphazard, disorganised crime, often driven by addiction to crack cocaine. Serious professional criminals for the most part now invest elsewhere: in drugs, fraud, and forgery. Often, there is no visible, public, criminal event. Without informants, the only way crime of this type is ever likely to come to light is through sheer chance.

A tip-off from an informant may be by far the most common way of making the first detection of a professional organised crime, but the reluctance displayed by the courts in accepting the evidence of supergrasses means hard evidence has to be provided by other means. The solution which has been widely adopted by the Regional Crime Squads lies with the growing use of undercover police officers. Acting on informants' intelligence, the undercover teams pose as criminals, trying to arrange a 'buy' for the drugs or counterfeit notes. Sometimes, to allay suspicions, they may part with thousands of pounds in hard cash to acquire a sample. The undercover agent secretly tapes whatever transpires, and arrests swiftly follow. When it comes to trial, the undercover officers may well give evidence under *noms de guerre*, or even behind a screen.

The problem is that almost inevitably, the informant behind an operation of this type is bound to be involved in the crime, if only on its fringes. In some cases, the informant's role is truly peripheral: he might, for example, have been asked if he wished to buy some drugs, but declined. But on other occasions, he may be closer to the heart of a conspiracy. Only the finest of lines separates the participating informant from the *agent provocateur*. Therefore sometimes there is another danger: that by providing minor titbits, the informant will buy himself an 'insurance policy', granting effective immunity from prosecution for really serious crime.

★   ★   ★

As Brian Charrington landed from Spain at Teesside in one of his two private aircraft, Customs and Excise were waiting. They had tracked his wanderings in South America, bugged his telephones and observed his secret meetings with the Colombian cocaine cartels. Now, on the morning of 26 June 1992, they had his plane surrounded before it could taxi to a halt. 'Operation Singer', one of the biggest law enforcement operations in British history, was about to reach its climax.[6]

Charrington was many times a millionaire. Besides his planes – paid for with carrier bags of cash – he had a specialist diving vessel, a yacht, and a fleet of expensive cars including a Rolls Royce and a Bentley. The only visible legitimate business behind this wealth was Longland's Car Sales, a scruffy second-hand motor showroom on the outskirts of Middlesbrough. His real money came from the very top of the drugs market, from large-scale importation.

By the end of that June day, Charrington was in custody, and the officers, a special squad based in Leeds, were jubilant. Searching his home, a lavish detached bungalow in Nunthorpe, they discovered £2.4 million in cash. The banknotes were contaminated with cocaine, amphetamines, cannabis and heroin, although some had been issued only a fortnight earlier from cash machines in south-east England. In that time, they had passed up the drugs economy foodchain from the fingers of users at street level to the drugs business apex. Among Charrington's papers were records of a £4.5m down-payment made weeks earlier for cocaine.

Customs' triumph was to turn to dust. On 28 January 1993, shortly before Charrington and ten others were due to face committal proceedings on charges of importing a tonne and a half of cocaine, Crown counsel withdrew all charges against him. After two long trials over the following eighteen months, all but one of the remaining defendants were acquitted. Customs were left with just one conviction: that of Ghanaian businessman Joseph Kassar, who was gaoled for twenty-four years. Amid the debris of this fiasco, the British taxpayer was left with a bill for £40 million.

Aged thirty-five at the time of his arrest, Charrington was born and raised on Teesside, on a bleak estate in Hemlington. He was an early convert to the criminal life, and by the early 1980s, had acquired numerous convictions for burglary, theft and handling stolen goods. He was typical, it might have seemed, of the disorganised petty criminals of the dispossessed North-east. But around 1984, he began to learn from his mistakes, and to move from stealing to drugs. Within months, he was Teesside's main cannabis wholesaler. He soon graduated to organising his own cannabis shipments. He bought Longland's Motors, but it was an increasingly unconvincing 'front'. 'Out on the forecourt, there were junk cars on sale for £1,300 a piece,' says one witness who prefers to stay anonymous. 'Round the back were his own vehicles: big BMWs and a Merc.'

His lifestyle, apparently supported on exiguous means, made him a natural object of interest for Customs and the police. In 1989, Customs busted one of his regular cannabis supply lines. They seized drugs worth £500,000 from the day-trippers' minibus which was carrying it (unbeknown to the day-trippers) to England from Calais. But seizing drugs and amassing intelligence are not the same as gathering evidence which will meet the necessary standard of proof in court. Charrington remained at large. It was a natural progression from cannabis to cocaine.

In the spring of 1991, Customs became aware the Charrington was doing business with a network of drug importers which had already aroused the interest of police. They began to work with officers from the number two and number four Regional Crime Squads, respectively covering the Midlands and the North-east, who had poured many months of effort into gathering intelligence about a drugs supply line from Holland to Merseyside. Among the line's protagonists was Curtis Warren, a mixed-race Liverpudlian with connections in the international big league of crime. Also included were the Colombians, Mario Halley and Camillo Jesús Ortiz, sobre-suited hardmen whose origins lay in the slums of Medellin.

Ortiz and Halley sold cocaine for export. Their entrepôt was Venezuela, and in its capital, Caracas, they devised an audacious method for smuggling cocaine in bulk. In 1990, they set up the Conar Corporation, ostensibly to send scrap metal and ingots to Europe and North America. Their flash of genius was to hide the drugs inside 28-tonne lumps of lead so thick that unless you knew where to drill, you would be most unlikely to find what lay within each ingot – an aluminium box containing cocaine. The lead was, of course, impervious to X-rays. They sent several shipments of this kind to the USA. In 1991, Charrington and Warren began to discuss the possibility of organising a series of vast cargoes for Britain and the rest of Europe.

Brian Charrington had one little secret he was very keen to keep. At the start of his career, when he was still carrying out burglaries and thefts, he had been arrested by a Detective Constable Ian Weedon of the Cleveland police. Charrington agreed to turn informer. Weedon became his registered handler, a position he was to keep. In the late 1980s, Weedon rose to detective sergeant, and worked at the

Middlesbrough office of the number two Regional Crime Squad. This brush with the big time did not last, and in 1990 he was moved back to routine CID work.

When a criminal player who acquires Charrington's status becomes a registered informant, it poses serious ethical and legal dilemmas. In the 1980s, they crystallised in London around the case of Detective Chief Superintendent Tony Lundy, said by his admirers to have been 'the most successful detective in the history of the Metropolitan Police'.

However, his chief source, Roy Garner, was also one of London's leading gangsters, involved in massive VAT fraud, armed robbery, extortion and drugs. Garner helped Lundy convict several top robbers, but as Garner continually evaded arrest, while also receiving huge rewards for solving robberies from insurance companies, he became known among some officers as 'The Untouchable'. Eventually, when Garner was gaoled for sixteen years for cocaine smuggling in 1988, Lundy gave evidence in his defence. We know not what he said: before Lundy went into the witness-box, the press and public were excluded, with the court sitting in camera.[7]

Lundy himself became the subject of a series of ultimately inconclusive investigations. Finally, he took early retirement on medical grounds a few days before facing a disciplinary tribunal. In any event, Scotland Yard instituted new procedures, designed to ensure that in future, the relationship between informants and their handlers would be rigorously monitored. Every handler was to have a 'superviser', to whom each and every meeting and telephone conversation had to be reported. All conversations were also to be set down on paper. These rules extend from the top of the CID to PCs dealing with everyday local crime, embracing sources in the league of Charrington or Garner to small-time handlers and thieves.

In Cleveland, the rules appear to have been less strenuously applied. It has not been possible to inspect Weedon's informant 'logs' of his dealings with Brian Charrington: when defence lawyers tried to acquire them, the police succeeded in suppressing their disclosure on grounds of Public Interest Immunity. But sources who have seen them say that in view of what later transpired, they contained surprisingly few details. There was no evidence that his value as an informant was commensurate with his magnitude as a criminal.

In the gaols of the North of England there is a select band of criminals who are convinced they were 'grassed up' by Charrington. What they all have in common is that their convictions are not for drug offences but for relatively small-scale robberies and burglaries. They include Kevin D., once Charrington's driver and bodyguard, at the time of writing, a resident of HMP Frankland, Co. Durham. D. admits that in 1987 and 1988, he travelled widely on Charrington's behalf to pick up and deliver drugs. He was convicted, he claims unfairly, of a robbery, which was committed, he says, when he and Charrington were enjoying an evening out together with their wives. D. insists he was part of Charrington's insurance policy: a sacrificial victim offered up to keep the police away from his drugs business.

A senior member of the Leeds Customs squad who tracked Charrington raises further doubt about his value as an informant: 'Whatever else he may have said, it is inconceivable that Charrington could have supplied any information about drugs importations without our knowing about it.' Any information of this kind obtained by the police would have been passed on to Customs, and logged in to a joint intelligence computer. Moreover, Charrington was not just any criminal. In 1991, Customs began to co-operate actively with the number two Regional Crime Squad in an operation to target Charrington. No one bothered to mention that the man both law enforcement agencies now dubbed 'Target One' was not only a criminal, but in police eyes, also a valuable informant.

By the late summer of 1991, Charrington's negotiations with the Conar Corporation had reached an advanced stage. On 16 September, he and Curtis Warren crossed the Channel from Dover to Calais. They told immigration staff they were going to Europe. They drove to Brussels where they parked their car, then flew to Malaga in Spain. From Malaga they went to Madrid, thence finally to Caracas. On the way back, they flew from Caracas to Amsterdam, and then travelled on to Brussels. On 28 September, they reappeared off the ferry at Dover in their car, and presented British Visitors' Passports. They said they were now returning from a trip to Europe.

Their full passports with the Venezuelan entry stamps were posted back to them later from Holland.

Ivonne Cruzatty, the Conar Corporation secretary, later testified that Charrington had made several visits to the firm's Caracas office. On 25 September, the penultimate day of their visit, the MV Sierra Express left Caracas bound for Felixstowe, laden with lead ingots – and a staggering 1.5 tonnes of 95 per cent pure Colombian cocaine, with a street value of £250 million.

The front for the import of lead was a company in England which did regular business with Joseph Kassar, the man later gaoled for twenty-four years. One of his friends and business colleagues, Joey Nana-Asare, was later to become a key prosecution witness. Now, as the drugs made their way to England, he tipped off Customs about his suspicions. Surveillance of Warren and Charrington was redoubled.

On 4 October, dizzy with impending success, Charrington held a birthday party at the Tall Trees Hotel, just outside Middlesbrough. That night, possibly a little drunk, and unaware how closely Customs were tracking him, he let his guard drop. He spoke on an open telephone line to a contact in Venezuela and discussed a lucrative side deal to the main import. It was to be a 'rip-off' – a 13 kilogramme suitcase full of cocaine to be shipped into Heathrow, where a baggage handler in on the conspiracy was to snatch it from the conveyer belt.

His phone was being tapped. The shipment – worth £3 million – was intercepted. It was only a fraction of the size of the cargo inside the ingots. But it was still a substantial seizure: to get that amount of the drug into the country using 'body-packers', couriers who swallow cocaine wrapped in condoms, would need more than thirty trips.

Yet even this breakthrough was useless in building a case against Charrington. Under British law, tapes made from bugging devices left in cars or buildings can be played to juries, and they have been used to convict both professional criminals and terrorists. However, phone tap evidence is inadmissible in court. This is an extraordinary anomaly, and if it did not exist, Charrington would now be in prison.

In America, phone-taps have been the cornerstone of numerous successful prosecutions of the Mafia. In Britain, the police and Customs officers involved in an investigation cannot even see phone-tap transcripts. Phone-taps remain subject to arcane and cumbersome rules, under which any intelligence product can be viewed only by a specialist group of 'readers'.

It is left to the readers to visit the special British Telecom unit which carries out the taps, go through the transcripts and make summaries. Photocopying is strictly forbidden, and all 'GC' – non-incriminating general conversation – expunged from the record. This places a heavy responsibility on the readers, who may simply fail to spot items of significance. In the words of one detective superintendent, 'You're totally dependent on the reader, and some are better than others. If you're dealing with Jamaicans, they may be speaking patois. Officers who aren't familiar with it may ignore really important remarks.'

In Charrington's case, the consequences went further than preventing his prosecution for the Heathrow airport rip-off. The seizure of his cocaine at Heathrow made him realise that the authorities were on to him.

After the shipment landed in October, it stayed in a Felixstowe warehouse for several weeks, but when Customs inspected the ingots, they found nothing. With hindsight, they wish they had simply sawed one of the ingots in half. Unfortunately they did not do so. An abortive attempt was made to drill into them, but the drill bit broke. Ortiz and Halley arrived in Britain, to supervise the removal of the drug. By the middle of November, 500 kilos had been distributed to Charrington, Warren and their associates. The rest went on by sea to Greece and Holland.

Millions of pounds to the good, and aware how close the authorities had got to busting this first shipment, Charrington looked to his insurance policy. A second massive shipment was being planned for December. He asked to see his old acquaintance, Detective Sergeant Weedon. This time, however, the detective found he was being fed information not about local robberies, but massive imports of cocaine.

Weedon passed on Charrington's disclosures to his former boss, Detective Inspector Harry Knaggs of the number two Regional Crime Squad. As he was bound to do, Knaggs told Customs, and in the ensuing weeks, Customs officers met Charrington directly. He was, of course, able to provide full details of the impending second shipment: this time, there would be no mistakes when it came to opening the ingots. But as far as Customs were concerned, nothing he might say about the second shipment would deflect them, if they had the evidence, from charging him with the first.

The second shipment of cocaine landed in England at the end of January 1992. Over the next ten weeks, Customs watched as the lead was moved three times: to Stoke-on-Trent, and then on to different warehouses in Liverpool. At Stoke, they had broken into a shed at night and drilled into the ingots, removing the drug and resealing the metal. The size of the haul dwarfed all previous seizures – more than 900 kilos, worth £140 million.

In March, most of Charrington's alleged co-conspirators were arrested. Ortiz and Halley were intercepted in Holland, supervising the removal of yet another shipment. They are now serving long sentences in Dutch gaols. Charrington had taken care to be out of the country. But as they reviewed the mounting pile of evidence, Customs and their in-house prosecution department (unlike the police, Customs and Exise do not employ the CPS), decided to move against him. He could not be charged with the second importation, about which he had supplied information in advance. But they believed they could prove he had organised and profited from the first drugs cargo. Customs held a top-level meeting with officers from the Cleveland police, at which it was agreed that Charrington should be arrested. So to June and Teesside airport, and what looked like a significant 'result' in the fight against organised crime.

Now events took a very strange turn indeed. Detective Sergeant Weedon and Detective Inspector Knaggs began to protest about the way their informant was being treated. Customs had the evidence to send Charrington to gaol for thirty years, but the detectives wanted the charges against him dropped. They chose an extraordinary means of applying pressure – through Ministers of the Crown, and a young Conservative MP.

Tim Devlin is the Tory member for Stockton South. None of the key players in this story live in his constituency, so the rules of parliamentary etiquette would normally have ruled out any involvement. But Weedon's father, Geoff, was a prominent member of Devlin's local Tory association. Until July 1994, when he was unceremoniously sacked for his 'poor voting record', Devlin also occupied a post of some significance in the criminal justice system. He was Parliamentary Private Secretary to the Attorney-General, Sir Nicholas Lyell – the Government's chief law officer, the Minister with ultimate authority over all prosecutions.

Weedon *père* made the first approach to Devlin by telephone, asking if his son could visit him to talk about something 'really sensitive'. One Sunday morning in November 1992, Detective Sergeant Weedon turned up at the door of Devlin's Stockton terraced house, while he and his wife were having breakfast. According to Devlin:

> Weedon said that I was one of the Government's law officers and I could sort it out. I told him it was improper, and probably a breach of police discipline, that he'd come to see me at all. Weedon replied that his boss, Knaggs, had been to see his senior officers and told to sit tight. He was bloody frightened, and said the Colombians were coming over here with guns. So I told him, 'Leave it to me, and I'll try to sort it out.'[8]

Within a week of Weedon's visit, Devlin lobbied Keith Hellawell, then Cleveland Chief Constable, and, more important, Sir John Cope, the Paymaster General, the Minister with overall responsibility for Customs. Weedon kept up the pressure, making regular telephone calls. One day he called to say that Charrington had been moved to Strangeways prison in Manchester, where he had been beaten up. Devlin pulled strings with the police and prison authorities and had him moved back to a safer prison on Teesside.

Devlin agreed to meet Charrington's wife: 'She was covered in these amazing gold chains with links half an inch thick,' he said. She told the MP she wanted safe passage for herself and her husband out of the country, the dropping of the charges and the return of the drug-impregnated £2 million confiscated by Customs. At her behest, Devlin visited Charrington in prison: 'He told me he felt he'd done his part of the deal, and the authorities weren't doing theirs.'

Meanwhile, further pressure was being applied by Charrington's lawyers. Finally, on 19 December 1992, three weeks after Devlin met Charrington, Devlin's ministerial boss, Sir Nicholas Lyell, chaired a truly remarkable meeting. Present were Charrington's barrister, Gilbert Gray QC, senior members of the Customs legal department, and a second Ministerial law officer, Sir Derek Spencer, the Solicitor-General.

That a lobbying campaign can have led to a meeting between the two senior government law officers and defence counsel in order to discuss whether a pending criminal trial should take place or not was an event unprecedented in English criminal justice history. It represented an ultimate blurring between the political and the judicial arms of the State. One expects such things to happen in the more corrupt jurisdictions of the Third World, but not in Great Britain. Here was the triumph of expediency over justice, and an overtly political usurpation of the role of the court.

Charrington's representatives could always have tried to make submissions to his trial judge that the proceedings should be stayed. Instead, they were canvassing his defence with two elected politicians.

At the secret December meeting, Gray distributed two incredible documents: thirty-page statements by Knaggs and Weedon, in which they not only attested to his value as an informant, but announced that if the case went ahead, they would give evidence in his defence. Lyell was urged to use his power of *nolle prosequi* – so ordering Customs to halt the case against Charrington in its tracks.

Lyell was already under strong pressure as a result of the recent collapse of the Matrix Churchill 'arms-to-Iraq' case, when he tried and failed to suppress evidence that the defendants were working as agents for MI6, by signing certificates of Public Interest Immunity.

He declined personally to halt the prosecution of Charrington. But the Customs Board of Management had been given the clearest possible hint how seriously he viewed the position, and feared that the revelation of Charrington as an informer would send the entire case up in flames. As the board deliberated, Lyell's office was kept closely informed of developments. Finally, at the end of January

1993, the Customs lawyers appeared in Manchester Magistrates' Court and announced they would be offering no evidence against Charrington. He was free to go.

After telling local reporters he was delighted to be free and felt 'totally vindicated', the master criminal-turned informer vanished, leaving his home, motor cars and business. Meanwhile, as Lyell had attempted to do in the Matrix Churchill case, the Cleveland police succeeded in concealing all documents concerning Charrington's relationship with their detectives under the cloak of Public Interest Immunity.

There the matter might have rested. But on the weekend after Charrington's release, the regional paper *Yorkshire on Sunday* published an article suggesting there had been something of a clash between Customs and the Regional Crime Squad. Its author was John Merry, a tenacious Darlington freelance reporter. A few days later, Devlin telephoned Merry at home, and urged him not to pursue the story any further.

Devlin, who was taped by Merry, hinted that the dropping of charges against Charrington had arisen not because of a cock-up but a calculated, official conspiracy. Charrington, he claimed, was 'one of the best helps we have had in the drugs world for some time', and could have 'closed down half the Colombian cartels'. By arresting him, 'jolly old Customs who think they know best' had 'screwed it up'. Because of Charrington's arrest, there had been a change of plan, he said: 'The whole idea was to collapse the case and say, "bastard's walking free", then let him go back to his original lifestyle and arrangements in Middlesbrough and wait for the time in due course for his friends to turn up and say, "right, how about another load?" '

His role in the war against drugs could still be invaluable, if only Merry would not publicise the case too much, Devlin said: 'Obviously, the less you do would be appreciated by the law enforcement authorities.'

There was no truth in Devlin's claims. In a disastrous misjudgment of Merry, he seems to have believed he could protect Charrington by appealing to Merry's higher instincts. 'I puffed it up a bit to make it sound more interesting,' he admitted months later. 'Local journalists like to be told they're doing important national work.' Unfortunately for Devlin, his words achieved the opposite of what he had intended. After taking legal advice that the public interest outweighed his assurance that the conversation had been 'off the record', Merry chose to plaster it across the *News of the World*.

'I got a first class bollocking from the Attorney-General's office,' Devlin told me, 'the police went spare, the Customs went spare.' His intervention could not have been more disastrous for the case against the remaining ten defendants. The tapes were played in court, and allowed defence lawyers to suggest that the jury was being bamboozled. As one barrister put it, 'government law officers appear to have been involved in some very shady dealings, which need to be explained fully and frankly if our judiciary is not to be brought into disrepute'.

After the end of the Operation Singer trials, the Police Complaints Authority was asked to launch a major inquiry into the behaviour of the Cleveland police and the Regional Crime Squad, to be carried out by police from Thames Valley. Its terms of reference did not, however, include the actions of Government law officers. At the time of writing, its prospects of reaching a firm conclusion appear to have been diminished. The two senior officers leading it have retired.

Thames Valley's main job was to decide whether this was merely a case of two law enforcement agencies colliding like tankers at night, or if there had been identifiable malpractice. One curious incident certainly figured in their investigations. In the summer of 1993, Customs officers logged a 'target' vehicle leaving the country on the ferry to Spain. It was a £70,000 BMW owned by Brian Charrington. Driving the car was none other than the newly-retired Detective Inspector Harry Knaggs, accompanied by his wife, Delia, still a serving Cleveland PC.

The dropping of the charges against Charrington was a gift to the lawyers acting for the remaining ten defendants. It allowed them to argue in court that this was a murky case in which important truths were being withheld. One beneficiary was Charrington's travelling companion Curtis Warren, who at one stage – preposterously – suggested he was working for MI5. Warren was to be freed not by the jury but the judge, Mr Justice May, after a series of legal rulings in which all the important evidence against him was declared inadmissible.

The case against Warren had seemed formidable. There was copious surveillance evidence of meetings between him and the Colombian Mario Halley, coupled with computer print-outs of the numbers dialled when Warren called Halley and others on his mobile telephone. There was the circuitous trip to Caracas when the first shipment was leaving. Finally there were details of clandestine meetings with Joseph Kassar, who did regular business with the 'front' company for the import of the ingots.

There was no dispute that Warren met Halley in both England and Holland and spoke to him repeatedly by telephone. But Mr Justice May said this could not be adduced as evidence of Warren's involvement in the conspiracy. The reason, the judge said, was that there was 'no clear evidence' that Halley himself was part of it.

Customs found his decision baffling. Both Halley and the other Colombian, Camillo Ortiz, had been caught and gaoled in Holland – when Ortiz was arrested, he was actually drilling into ingots full of cocaine, identical to those shipped to England, using the specially made tool which he had earlier employed to empty the ingots in Liverpool. As he drilled, Ortiz was speaking to Halley on his mobile phone. Halley was in England at the same time as Ortiz, and for some of the time the two men stayed together in the same hotel.

In November 1991, Customs searched Halley's London hotel room. He had no drugs, and was not charged with any offence, but as the Customs men burst in, Halley tried to flush a piece of paper down the lavatory with the name 'Camillo Ortiz' written on it, together with the name and telephone number of another hotel where Ortiz was at that time resident. He had a second piece of paper bearing the name and fax number of a Venezuelan company, Venimporex, of which he was a director. It shared the same address and fax as Conar, the firm which exported the ingots. But the judge ruled there was 'no clear evidence' that Ortiz and Halley were accomplices.

The court had heard how Halley went to Liverpool with Warren while the first shipment of ingots was being stored there and the drugs taken out; how Halley then met Charrington, Warren and others in London when the cocaine was being sold and distributed;

and how Halley spent the next few days buying expensive motor cars for export in Park Lane showrooms, paying with bundles of cash. Yet Mr Justice May concluded: 'Whereas it might be possible to suspect and perhaps infer that Halley was concerned with drugs generally . . . there is, in my judgement, no possible evidential basis for inferring that Halley was concerned with the particular importations which are the subject of this case.' To admit evidence of Warren's contact with Halley would, under section 78 of PACE, adversely affect the fairness of the trial. All the evidence of meetings and telephone contact between Halley and Warren was discarded.

In a further ruling, the judge dealt equally briskly with Warren's trip to Venezuela. Ignoring his bizarre route, his use of two passports and his highly misleading statement on his return to Dover that he had been 'to Europe', Mr Justice May said this did not 'support an inference that Curtis Warren's trip abroad was clandestine'. There-fore that had to be excluded as well.

Finally came the evidence of his meetings with Kassar. These had taken place after Warren was observed flying into Manchester airport from Holland. A Customs man had checked Warren's name from his passport, and while Warren was leaving the Customs area, the officer turned to a colleague and pointed him out. The second officer then began the surveillance operation, following Warren out of the airport building to the car park, where Warren got into a Rover car which was registered and insured in his name.

Yet Mr Justice May excluded all the evidence of subsequent clandestine meetings on the grounds that the airport identification amounted to 'hearsay'. Because the second customs man had not actually checked Warren against his passport, he could not be sure the man he and his colleagues had under surveillance was Warren. All they could say was that they saw meetings involving 'a person who was five foot, eight inches tall, stocky, thick-necked and dark-skinned'. That description, the judge added, would be consistent with Warren. But it also 'fits thousands of other people'.

There was no case left, and the judge directed the jury to acquit. Warren got up and left the dock. He went down to the ground floor of the big, modern courthouse by the side of the Tyne, as if to go; then had second thoughts. He took the lift back to the third floor, where the trial had resumed, and marched up to a little group of Customs officers, who were disconsolately discussing his release.

His reappearance took them by surprise. Curtis Warren told them: 'I'm just off to spend my £87 million from the first shipment, and you can't fucking touch me.'

★ ★ ★

Law enforcement operations involving informants have another inbuilt drawback: the vulnerability of the informant. In the early 1990s this was substantially increased by changes to the law on the disclosure of evidence to the defence.

Until 1991, this rested on guidelines laid down by the Attorney-General in 1981. These stated that the Crown ought to supply the defence with any 'unused material' gathered by a criminal inquiry which had 'some bearing on the offences charged and the surrounding circumstances of the case'. But the guidelines also allowed the prosecution to withhold material, if they believed that its disclosure might lead to intimidation or attacks on a witness or informant.

In 1991, a ruling by Mr Justice Henry, who was trying Ernest Saunders and the other defendants in the Guinness fraud case, greatly extended the definition of what constituted 'unused material'. From then on, it included not only the statements of witnesses who were not called to give evidence but virtually all the working papers, drafts, tapes, and computer records generated by an investigation. The following year, the law changed again. In its judgment on the successful appeal of Judith Ward against her conviction seventeen years earlier for killing ten people with the M62 coach bomb, the Court of Appeal said the Crown had no power whatsoever to suppress sensitive material. If the prosecution wished to keep anything secret, it would have to give notice to the defence, and then argue the point in front of a judge in a pre-trial hearing.

From the point of view of organised crime control, this was a disaster. In some cases, merely the announcement that sensitive material existed placed informants in danger. Organised crime cases began to be dropped altogether on a regular basis, because the police and Customs could not take the risk.

In 1993, the position was modified once again, this time in the Crown's favour. Sitting on a murder appeal, Lord Taylor, the Lord Chief Justice, said the prosecution could now apply to the judge *ex parte*, that is to say, without the defence being present, and make their arguments as to why evidence ought to be withheld in private. In 'highly exceptional' cases, they might do so without even telling the defence such a hearing had ever been held. But this did not solve the problem, or end the controversy over disclosure. In every major inquiry, one or two police officers would be assigned at an early stage to go through all the paperwork and computer records to decide what, if anything, ought to be withheld, in order to safeguard important witnesses and informants.

They did not always get their way, and cases continued to be dropped. According to Roy Clark of the South-east Regional Crime Squad, in 1994 and 1995 his unit was withdrawing an average of one-and-a-half cases a month, representing about a tenth of its output. At Scotland Yard, a national survey suggested at least 100 major charges were withdrawn in 1994.

Reading the confidential police summaries of some of these cases, it is easy to understand the frustration which officers volubly expressed. A notorious example was the prosecution at Reading Crown Court in 1993 of Edward Shephard, Marianne MacDonald and Sam Remington, three members of the Animal Liberation Front, for conspiracy to commit criminal damage. They had been arrested in possession of Molotov cocktails, balaclavas and a rope ladder, and were accused of planning an arson attack on a lorry containg live animals.

Before the trial started, their defence counsel argued that the entire police intelligence database on the ALF, known as the Animal Rights National Index, ought to be disclosed if they were to have a fair trial. Disregarding all the other evidence against them, they had to know on what basis they had orginally been suspected. Judge Spence ruled in their favour, ignoring prosecution claims that all future inquiries into animal rights terrorism would be compromised. The Crown was forced to offer no evidence, and the judge directed their acquittal. After their release, Remington stood on the steps of the court and read a candid statement to the local media, saying: 'It was our intention to remove the animals from this vehicle and then damage it. The only reason this trial collapsed was because the prosecution refused to reveal to our defence lawyers material held about us on computer by the police.'

In the summer of 1994, police in the south of England were given information that amphetamines worth £500,000 were for sale. An undercover officer met the manufacturer, but failed to make a deal, leaving his pager number in case the putative drugs salesman changed his mind. Many weeks later, the officer was contacted again: this time, of course, the informant had no idea this had happened, and was not even in the country. 'We thought this one was a stone bonker,' said the detective who led the inquiry, 'we had incredible surveillance evidence, showing the defendants struggling through the undergrowth carrying huge barrels of chemicals to a shed where they had set up a drugs factory; we even had pictures of them stirring the mixture up.'

When the case came to trial, the judge initially refused to grant defence submissions that the police reveal the informant's name. But after further argument, he made another ruling which amounted to the same thing, ordering the Crown to reveal full details as to how the main defendant had got hold of the detective's pager number. According to the inquiry chief, 'the logic of that judgment is we can't use undercover officers or informants *at all*'.

In some cases, defence counsel give every appearance of manipulating the system, using the possibility of disclosure of an informant's identity as a means of obtaining 'technical' acquittals which in other circumstances would be most unlikely. In May 1992, a man appeared at Humberside Crown Court, charged with two vicious robberies in which people had been tied up and clubbed with the butt of a sawn-off shotgun, wielded by a man wearing a police uniform. An informant gave the police the address of the gang's leader. He was arrested after a raid which recovered two sawn-offs, the uniform, much of the stolen property and the tax disc from the (stolen) getaway car.

The trial collapsed after the defence argued that notwithstanding all this evidence, the defendant could not have a fair trial unless his lawyers had the opportunity to interview the informant. They said their client did not own the guns and knew nothing about the stolen property. Questioning the informant would enable the defence to ask whether he might originally have told the police that some unknown third party had committed the robberies. This was never more than a hypothetical possibility, and in fact, the informant had been quite certain that the robber was the defendant. But Judge Herod QC acquiesced, saying that if this 'led to the discovery of the identity of the informer, so be it'. The internal police summary of the case comments: 'The informant took no active part in the offence. This appears to be a straightforward case of the most serious nature which led to the acquittal of a professional criminal.'

The most common argument made by the defence for the disclosure of informants' identity is the claim that the 'grass' did not merely inform, but actually organised the crime. With participating informants, claims of this kind are virtually inevitable. An example, taken from police summaries, occurred with a series of two armed robberies in Kent in 1993, in which the getaway driver turned informer – because, he claimed, he had been threatened by one of the others with a gun. As evidence of his *bona fides*, he gave the police his share of the proceeds from the first robbery.

When the trial started, the defence alleged that a 'major crack dealer' had forced the defendants to commit the robberies and had then tipped off the police. They called no evidence to support this proposition. But the judge ordered full disclosure, forcing the Crown to drop the case. The police summary comments: 'It now seems that the Prosecution have no answer to any defence of duress by an informant, participating or non-participating, no matter how absurd, frivolous or lacking in credibility. It is therefore hardly surprising that Flying Squad sources indicate that a number of prisoners currently awaiting trial are considering using this ploy.'

The crux of the problem is that sometimes, allegations of this kind have been shown to be true. The factually guilty *have* sometimes walked free by exploiting the early 1990s disclosure rules. But at the same time, unscrupulous law-enforcement officers have shown themselves ready to use the cloak of secrecy to act unethically against the innocent. The knowledge that this has happened, however rarely, taints the entire debate.

★　★　★

It is axiomatic that in order to be effective, informants will not be model citizens. But citizens do not come much less model than John Banks: dishonourably discharged British army private and self-styled South Vietnamese major; mercenary; convicted blackmailer; and supposed contract killer. Time and again, Banks has supplied information for money and given evidence for a variety of law-enforcement agencies. He has sometimes caused them deep embarrassment by telling blatant lies in court. He has also sent many people to prison, and received many thousands of pounds for his services. If there were ever a case for striking an informant off the official register altogether, it would seem to apply to Banks. However, at the time of writing, an informant Banks remains. His police codename is 'Dave Lea'.

Banks's mercenary campaigns began in the summer of 1975, six years after he left the army, with an advertisement in the *Daily Telegraph* appealing for former paratroopers and SAS men to fight for the African cause in what was then Rhodesia. The affair soon degenerated into farce, when some of the dogs of war were sacked for getting drunk at a London hotel. But six months later, at the beginning of 1976, he was back, this time recruiting for the anti-Marxist side in Angola. Of about 180 who went, fourteen were murdered by a Greek fighting on their own side. Two were executed by the victorious MPLA, and others killed in action. Many were never paid.

Allegations that Banks was an *agent provocateur* surfaced as early as 1977, with a sensational seven-week Old Bailey IRA arms trial. Three men, who were said to have negotiated a deal to buy guns worth £25,000 from Banks, received long prison sentences. Defence counsel Rock Tansey claimed Banks had been the prime-mover behind the abortive deal from start to finish, inciting the defendants to buy weapons they had not wanted. In 1977, this was not a claim which juries were ready to believe.

In 1980, Banks was convicted and gaoled for two years for blackmail and threats to commit murder. (He already had several theft convictions.) The blackmail involved a claim by Banks that he had information about a 'Cuban plot' to assassinate the then Nicaraguan President, Antonio Somoza. He sent two heavies to collect $250,000 from the London Embassy, and claimed he represented professional killers who had already dispatched two African heads of state. When he came to trial, his defence included extravagant claims about his previous services to the British State: an alleged sponsored attempt to kill the terrorist Carlos the Jackal and assassinations in Yemen.

In April 1981, six months after sentence, Banks absconded from Coldingley open prison. He was on the run for eight months. His punishment was extraordinarily light: twenty-eight days' loss of remission and fourteen days' loss of privileges. The prison Governor, Jim Anderson, commented at the time: 'I don't yet know why John Banks got the sort of award you usually get for a late return from home leave, rather than eight months on the run.'

After his release, Banks slipped into relative obscurity. But he prospered. Variously describing himself as a 'military adviser', a 'security consultant' and as a dealer in goods such as brandy, he moved to a sumptuous home at Gainsborough, Lincolnshire, filled with priceless antiques. His business methods were sometimes unorthodox. They were not notably characterised by loyalty.

In 1989, Terry Castles, a former mercenary who had worked with Banks before, was paid by him to go to Zaire as a courier for what he was told were mineral rights documents. In fact, as he discovered just in time to burn the papers in his Kinshasha hotel, they were plans for organising a *coup d'état*. Banks, he later said in evidence at a trial in London, had set him up, and tipped off the Zairean authorities. Castles was arrested, tortured, held for six months in appalling conditions, and told he was going to be killed. Eventually, he was released on the orders of General Mbuto. But on his return to his Aldershot home, Castles was arrested by British police. They told him he was wanted in connection with a murder on the basis of a statement by Banks, which claimed he had been involved. Fortunately for Castles, Banks had miscalculated the date of his return from Africa. On the day when he was supposed to be committing a murder in England, he had the unshakeable alibi that he had been in a Kinshasha dungeon.

Another individual betrayed by Banks was Douglas Bailey, a businessman. He met Banks in May 1992, when he needed help in collecting a bad debt. Banks told him at length about his Government connections, his work for the police and for foreign heads of state, and Bailey gave him £5,000 'upfront', Banks promising to return the following week with the money owed. Mr Bailey never saw him again. He eventually issued civil proceedings, but when he sought a possession order on Banks's home, it transpired it was in the name of his wife, Maggie, and mortgage arrears owed to Barclays Bank amounted to £224,000 – £44,000 more than the property was worth.

It was as a result of this writ that Banks swore an affidavit stating he owned neither his house nor the furniture. But he added: 'HM Government owes me £25,000 for work done for them.' When Bailey threatened to expose him, Banks telephoned him and made a series of threats, which Bailey taped. Referring to a former partner in his debt-collecting work he said: 'Mr R. is extremely good at breaking legs. I am extremely good at breaking legs, so we work together occasionally: to break legs. Whenever mutual situations occurred where somebody had to be hurt we worked together because he had extremely large muscles which are very good at cracking kneecaps which occasionally we need in our business. OK?'

In April 1993, this tape was played in court during a drugs trial in which Banks was the star prosecution witness. That very evening. Banks telephoned Bailey again, while the trial was still in progress. He said that if Bailey gave evidence against his reliability as a witness, his 'health would not be good', but if he did not attend, he would get paid. Bailey drew this to the attention of police, who took no action.

These powers of persuasion and intimidation make Banks a dangerous informant. The total of those he has helped to put away is unknown, because sometimes the authorities have managed to conceal his role, even where defendants have reason to believe they were tricked or coerced by him into committing offences. What is clear is that since the 1977 IRA trial, most of the cases in which he gave live evidence ended in acquittal. When he and his record are on display, juries do not believe him.

In 1991, for example, he claimed at the Old Bailey that a woman had offered him money to assassinate her husband. She was cleared of soliciting murder. Later the same year, a 'sting' operation organised on information received from Banks led the Scotland Yard Art and Antiques Squad to an Ulster Defence Association member who offered paintings worth £2 million – part of the legendary Alfred Beit collection stolen in Ireland several years earlier – to a detective posing as a buyer at the Heathrow airport Penta Hotel. The Crown dropped all charges on the morning the trial was due to begin, when it became clear there was no way to avoid calling Banks as a witness.

But in 1992, when Customs and Excise prosecuted Martin Poole and James Collis at Winchester Crown Court for trying to buy 75 kilos of cannabis, Banks stayed in the background. The two men were arrested at Fleet Services on the M3 with £30,000 cash, in the company of Senior Investigating Officer Michael Stephenson who, most unusually for a sting operation of this kind, was trying to sell them the drugs, not buy them.

Their defence was that Banks, through a mixture of threats and intimidation, had coerced them into purchasing the cannabis which was, in any event, worth more than £100,000: the £30,000 cash was, somewhat improbably, to be accepted as a deposit. Collis and Poole claimed Banks had threatened them repeatedly, telling them they had to buy the drugs as 'compensation' for the failure of another deal Banks had made with one of their associates. Stephenson admitted he had gone undercover to a meeting with Banks and Collis and Poole. But they had no chance to cross-examine Banks himself. Customs claimed they had no idea of his whereabouts, making it impossible to serve a subpoena. He remained a phantom presence at the trial, lending only implausibility to the defence.

It was only months later, at another drugs hearing, that it emerged that at the time of the trial of Collis and Poole, Stephenson was in regular contact with Banks. Stephenson explained this extraordinary lapse by saying: 'Mr Banks was an informant whose identity we were trying to protect.' Later he added that had he really tried, he could have contacted Banks, allowing Poole and Collis to put him on the stand. No disciplinary action was taken against him.

Entrapment is not a recognised defence in English law. But Home Office guidelines state:

'No public informant should counsel, incite or procure the commission of a crime ... The informant should always be instructed that he must on no account act as an *agent provocateur*, whether by suggesting to others that they should commit offences or encouraging them to do so.' The police must never commit themselves to a course which, whether to protect an informant or otherwise, will 'constrain them to mislead a court in any subsequent proceedings'.

One of the hallmarks of Banks's career is his readiness to betray his own friends and associates. One of the most shocking examples occurred in the case of Raymond Okudzeto, who was tried and acquitted of importing heroin.[9]

Okudzeto, a man in his mid-fifties with no previous convictions, made an unlikely drug dealer. He had been a Ghanaian minister, and in earlier stages of his business career, had been a millionaire. By the time of his entanglement with Banks, Raymond, now engaged in a variety of import and export trades, had been forced to cope with more modest means. But he remained a man of obvious cultivation, and his wife was a distinguished American academic. They lived in a mansion flat in the expensive London St John's Wood district.

Okudzeto first came across Banks in the mid-eighties. From the first days of their friendship, Banks made much of his contacts with the authorities, and told Raymond that if his business interests ever brought him information of possible interest to law enforcement agencies, he should let him know. Banks said he would contact the appropriate agency, and in due course both men would share any payments or rewards. Okudzeto passed on intelligence in this way no fewer than ten times to Banks. It was Okudzeto who was the source of what was probably Banks's biggest coup – the information leading to the recovery of the Alfred Beit paintings from the UDA man at Heathrow. By the time of the events discussed below, Okudzeto had not been paid for this tip, and he later said in evidence that Banks owed him thousands of pounds.

If John Banks had not been forced against his will and against the advice of the police officers who were protecting him to give evidence against Raymond Okudzeto, Okudzeto too would have gone the way of Collis and Poole. The basic facts, heard first in September 1992 and then at a retrial in April 1993, appeared simple. Okudzeto had put up a woman over from Kenya in his London flat. He had offered a sample of heroin to an undercover Customs man;

and then, a few days later, after the woman had vanished, a search discovered £40,000 worth of the drug in the flat.

In the early autumn of 1991, as Okudzeto languished on remand in Brixton prison, the story he told his solicitor, David Bray, sounded preposterous. Far from trying to import heroin, Okudzeto said, he had thought he was working with the authorities all along, as part of a sting operation organised by his close friend Banks. Banks, he said, had told him what to do from the moment he first received a telephone call from a casual contact in Kenya, Evans Anyona, who offered him drugs. He had had no hesitation in telling Banks, and assumed he would inform the authorities as he had done in similar circumstances before.

It was Banks, Okudzeto insisted, who had told him to invite Anyona's courier, Mary Wambui, to his home, and Banks who suggested he take a sample of the heroin which Mary had brought to a meeting with a prospective purchaser. Banks, Okudzeto went on, had told him to expect the purchaser to call at his flat to collect the rest of the shipment, which Wambui had hidden in his bathroom, saying that when the buyer was there, Customs men would arrive to arrest both the buyer and the courier.

The last thing Okudzeto ever expected was that he was the victim, not a participant in the law enforcement sting. When the 'purchaser' turned out to be an undercover Customs man come to arrest only Raymond Okudzeto, he found himself not only betrayed but bewildered.

Bray believed his client. Within three weeks of Okudzeto's arrest on 31 October 1991, he wrote to Customs, in the shape of case officer Sue Robinson, who was handling her very first file. Bray asked for the disclosure of all witness statements, and 'memoranda and attendance notes made by officers of HM Customs of any conversations with witnesses including John Banks', and wanted confirmation that he was the informant. From this very early stage, Bray made it plain that the basis of Okudzeto's defence was that he was the victim of an entrapment organised by Banks acting as an *agent provocateur*.

However, for many months, Customs kept Banks and his murky role concealed. Bray's letter asking for disclosure was simply never answered. At committal proceedings shortly afterwards, they made no mention of Banks and stonewalled all questions relating to his involvement. Worse still, the officers made what looked like an attempt to mislead Okudzeto's defence. At the committal, Officer Stephenson gave evidence under a false name as an undercover man. At the same time, a separate, written statement from him, in which he was named as Michael Stephenson, the man in charge of the case, was put before the court. Neither Customs not their in-house lawyers made any attempt to point out that these two different sources of evidence were one and the same man.

Later, when the case came for its full hearing at Southwark Crown Court, it emerged that only Stephenson, and his superior Philip Connelly, knew what was going on. The other officers were told none of the details of Banks's role; some did not know of his involvement at all.

Finally, after further fruitless requests for disclosure, Bray tracked Banks down to his home in Lincolnshire. An inquiry agent braved his dogs and security system and knocked on his door in an attempt to serve a subpoena. Banks replied that nothing would induce him to appear in court, and that the subpoena was not worth the paper it was written on, because 'I will have my people in London quash it'. For once, however, Banks had overestimated his value and influence. His people could not quash it. When the court convened in May 1992 for what should have been the trial's opening day, Banks was listed as a witness bound to appear.

There were still further delays. Abruptly, the Crown tried, and failed, to have Banks's evidence heard in camera; this took several days of legal argument, and the case was postponed until September. And then, as the case of the Crown and Raymond Okudzeto finally got underway, the prosecution at last disclosed a vital document which should have been produced months earlier – the Customs official log of conversations between Stephenson and Banks. More than any other piece of evidence, it proved that Okudzeto, who had now spent nearly a year in the Victorian hell of Brixton prison, had always told the truth. Yet Stephenson admitted that he had even then produced it only because he thought it might 'support Banks's evidence'.

It did nothing of the kind. It showed that for ten days after Okudzeto passed on the tip about the heroin to Banks, Banks made no mention of him in his conversations with Stephenson. Instead, Banks told the Customs man only that he had acquired information which might enable them to arrest a drug courier from Kenya. Only at a very late stage did he make the claim that 'Evans's man in London' was 'a Ghanaian whose name began with an "O" ' – a deliberately vague reference to a man Banks had actually known for years.

Telephone computer records of the numbers called from Banks's telephones proved that he was in almost constant contact with Okudzeto, just as the defendant had alleged, persuading him, against his better judgment, into playing an active role in the sting. Giving evidence, Banks had claimed he spoke to Okudzeto only two or three times. On this and other points, skilful cross-examination reduced him to snarling, incoherent rage.

The atmosphere in court was extraordinary. For each of the five days Banks gave evidence, armed policemen searched everyone entering and leaving court. Almost every day, Assistant Chief Investigation Officer Philip Connelly, in charge of all UK anti-heroin operations, was present, week after week. It seemed to be a strange use of his time, given the relatively small quantity of drugs involved.

After the not guilty verdict, Judge Fingret praised the tenacity displayed by David Bray and Okudzeto's counsel, Stuart Stevens. Without it, he said, vital documents, and probably Banks himself, would have remained concealed, and an innocent man would have gone to prison. Bray later summed up the lessons of the affair for debate on criminal justice policy: 'This case suggests that in secrecy may lie abuse. We must accept that informers may not be savoury characters and may have convictions. But as long as the authorities are prepared to countenance the activities of *agents provocateurs* such as John Banks, then there must be full disclosure.'

Yet the Okudzeto case was not the end of the career of John Banks, informer. In 1995, information he supplied to police led to the gaoling of five men for terms of up to seven years on charges of trying to buy arms for supply to ex-Yugoslavia. They claimed that they too had been set up, with Banks acting as *agent provocateur*. One of them, Reginald Walker, a former soldier, had actually been paid by Banks to travel to Croatia to gather 'intelligence' – this, Banks had told him, was as part of a freelance operation on behalf of MI6.

The secret intelligence logs made by Banks's police handler in this case, Detective Inspector Peter Shepperdson of the Metropolitan Police, indicate the moral ambivalence entailed in dealing with a man such as Banks. In the summer of 1992, before the gun dealing operation – codenamed Mensa – got underway, Shepperdson recorded deep misgivings at the prospect that Banks might have to give evidence in the Okudzeto case. Was he one of the 'people in London' who Banks thought would quash his subpoena?[10]

Shepperdson's log states:

I spoke to Mike Stephenson and stated that Lea (Banks's pseudonym) was very active at the moment and any publicity at this trial was likely to seriously impede major police operations that are current. Stephenson stated that he would be applying for his evidence to be given in camera. I stated that that would be preferable. I did however point out that we had stopped prosecution on a more serious case in which it was proposed to expose his identity. I would be in favour of this happening in this case rather than to expose him to danger *and to place his future usefulness in jeopardy* [author's italics].

On 7 December 1992, weeks after Banks had been displayed to ill effect in Okudzeto's first trial, Shepperdson was worried only about his informant's 'cash flow problems' and recorded a series of approaches to senior officers which he had made to get rewards paid to Banks. Among those he lobbied was Deputy Assistant Commissioner (now promoted to Assistant Commissioner) David Veness of the Scotland Yard specialist operations department, 'who considered that Lea was entitled to a substantial payment'.

However, Shepperdson went on, Veness had told him that 'there were strong reasons why this should not be paid prior to the [Operation Mensa] case being tried. He may have to give evidence and *it would be better for the jury to hear that he had not been paid*. He was also under close scrutiny from the media and it would be better for everyone if decision on reward be delayed until after the results . . .' [author's italics]. Nevertheless, Banks was still calling the shots: 'I stated that I realised the reasons for the delay in paying Lea, but asked that if Lea's finances became seriously in deficit could this be reconsidered.'

Two months later, Banks was worrying his police handlers with reports of strange callers who had impersonated police officers at his home, while 'an ex-terrorist who still has contacts with the IRA' had warned him his life was in danger. However, after checking out these claims, Shepperdson found the callers were not fake policemen after all, but 'private investigators trying to recover proceeds of fraud civilly'. Nevertheless, Shepperdson made the suggestion that 'Lea' be given a 'package deal to go abroad for a time' and then public funds be found to 'relocate him after the Okudzeto trial'. In the end, Banks did relocate, of his own volition, finding employment as a special investigator for Winnie Mandela, the estranged wife of the President of South Africa. No doubt she remained unaware of his background.

The reason given in Shepperdson's memoranda for not paying Banks a reward until after the end of the Mensa trial – that payment in advance would not play well with the jury – was ethically dubious. But at least the police discussed the matter. In another set of cases mounted by the Midlands (number four) Regional Crime Squad, the issue does not seem to have arisen at all.

At the heart of this affair, which came to a head at the end of 1994, was a Detective Constable Alan Ledbrook, the handler for an informant turned *agent provocateur* called Graham Titley. In at least three cases, Titley instigated forgeries of American Express travellers' cheques. None of them resulted in convictions, and separate judges condemned the police operations in coruscating terms. But by the time the cases came to trial, Titley had been paid more than £100,000 in rewards, with the police repeatedly negotiating with Amex to provide bigger payments. The proceeds of Titley's deceit enabled him to open a beach bar in Corfu.[11]

Titley's involvement with the Midlands Regional Crime Squad began in August 1990, when he was arrested in possession of £10,000 in counterfeit currency. Within a few days, he was providing information to Ledbrook, in the hope that he would receive a lighter sentence. He came up for trial in February 1991. He had a long criminal record, starting in 1970 with an indecent assault on a four-year-old girl. His many convictions thereafter were for relatively minor offences, involving cars, burglary and handling stolen goods. In no sense was he a major player in organised crime.

In view of Titley's lowly criminal status, the 'text' composed for the benefit of his trial judge on 6 February, by Detective Superintendent R. Beards, then the Regional Crime Squad's second-in-command, was utterly extraordinary. Pleading for leniency, Beards insisted that Titley could help to smash 'major criminals throughout the UK and Europe . . . who are engaged in the large-scale distribution of drugs and counterfeit currency'. Even more far-fetched was Beards's claim that he might also expose 'paramilitary organisations in Northern Ireland who are using the proceeds of drugs sales to fund their terrorist activities'. Titley had never been to Ulster in his life.

In the face of such a commendation, however, the judge had little choice but to impose a relatively light sentence, gaoling Titley for eighteen months. He was released after only seven, and throughout his time in gaol, continued to meet Detective Constable Ledbrook. After release, he went to live in Staffordshire.

Towards the end of 1991, the police used Titley to target a man called David Docker. A grandfather in his early sixties, Docker lived in a modest bungalow in Stoke-on-Trent. By his own admission, in the fifties and sixties he had been an active criminal. But he insists: 'I've not been at the villainy game for twenty years. My business – until it was wrecked by Titley – was factoring: buying and selling ends of lines, overproduction, and so on.'

On the other hand, according to Ledbrook's superior, Detective Chief Inspector Trevor Lowbridge, who also developed a close relationship with Titley, Docker was a big-time criminal. Lowbridge needed authorisation to run an undercover operation from the Crown Prosecution Service, to protect officers from possible prosecution, and to allow them to put up money to make them look convincing to their criminal targets. He told the CPS in a letter that Docker's far from opulent lifestyle was merely a clever cover. He was in the 'upper league criminal fraternity', he claimed.

Like Beards, he added the spice of national security: 'A more sinister element is that there are terrorist associations.' No evidence to support this assertion was ever produced. Lowbridge added that the proposed operation had been discussed at 'senior management level' and 'authorised in writing by an assistant chief constable' from the West Midlands police.

Titley and the police set up an operation of labyrinthine complexity to trap Docker and some of his business associates. With Titley acting as the link between Docker and a team of undercover officers whose identity remains secret, they tried to induce Docker to arrange the importation of a huge container lorry-load of cannabis from Holland, saying they wanted to buy it. Docker at first went along with the scheme – but only in an attempt to get the undercover police 'buyers', who struck him as curiously naïve, to pay him 'up-front'. He had in mind only a lucrative con-trick, but his scheme came to nothing.

The drugs angle having failed, in March 1992, the operation switched its emphasis to American Express. A top CPS official, C.W.P. Newall, the director of headquarters case-work in London, gave permission for the police first to obtain and then to attempt to supply Docker and his friends with fake Amex cheques. He promised that if Titley and the undercover officer known as 'Mickey' had to commit offences to trap Docker, they would be given immunity from prosecution. Newall made no attempt to verify any of the police claims being made about the value of this operation. With the customary 'hands off' CPS approach, he took what he was told at face value.

After numerous vicissitudes, Docker and six others were lured to a hotel on the M1 where fake cheques worth £4 million were being stored in a car boot. They never handed over any money for them, and at the point when they were suddenly arrested, they had become suspicious, and had resolved to drive away. They had never actually set eyes on the false cheques. But the police claimed they were conspiring to handle them.

As they waited for trial, without further ado, Titley was paid £37,500 by Amex. The bank's chief UK and Ireland special agent, Sue Simpson, had to forward police submissions made on behalf of Titley to the bank's global security chief, based in America. She wrote: 'We do rely heavily on the Regional Crime Squad who are equipped for the extensive surveillance etc. necessary to bring about a successful result. Our goodwill may be affected in a good future [sic] if we disregard their requests entirely.'

Docker spent the next fifteen months in custody, with disastrous effects on his livelihood and health. At last, the case came to trial at Wolverhampton Crown Court in September 1993.

The trial was a fiasco. First, it had to be delayed because Titley had disappeared. For many months, defence lawyers had tried unsuccessfully to get the Crown to disclose documents to which their entitlement was not in doubt. They included details of other rewards from Amex to Titley. Even after Judge Richard Gibbs ordered this disclosure in a pre-trial review, it was not made.

Then it came to Detective Constable Ledbrook's turn to give evidence. He failed to appear, with the police claiming he had had a nervous breakdown. One officer explained his absence in court by saying Ledbrook was drinking a bottle of vodka a day, but his detective partner, who had even been on holiday with him, told the court he did not drink. Ledbrook later took early retirement on the grounds of his ill-health.

Finally, the Crown came up with the disclosure which had been missing for so long. To the astonishment of the defence, it transpired Titley had been paid several other rewards by American Express, most recently just weeks before the trial. Suddenly there were far too many unanswered questions. Judge Gibbs dismissed the charges as an abuse of process, delivering a ruling of unusual vehemence. There had been 'bad faith in deliberate concealment or failure to disclose material evidence', he said. He had an 'open mind' as to why Ledbrook was unable to appear. But without him, there could be no fair trial.

After the collapse of the Docker case, the Police Complaints Authority began an investigation. Yet despite this, and the comments made by Judge Gibbs, the CPS remained determined to press ahead with two further pending prosecutions – both of them involving Titley, forged Amex cheques, Detective Constable Ledbrook and the Midlands Regional Crime Squad. Moreover, months before these cases came to court, the Police Complaints Authority declared its inquiry had a 'possible criminal dimension'. No fewer than thirteen police officers had been interviewed under caution.

The first case was against a man from the Manchester area called Graham Redford. It bore striking resemblances to the Docker imbroglio, and was dismissed without a jury being sworn in by a judge at Leeds Crown Court in November 1994. The second case was more serious: it was Titley's biggest prosecution. It concerned not merely a supposed attempt to purchase forgeries, but an operation to print counterfeit cheques with a face value of £20 million. Unfortunately, this was an offence which, without Titley and his police handlers, would never have taken place.

After Docker's arrest, Ledbrook and his colleagues helped Titley to leave the Midlands altogether, and he relocated in South Wales. There, in the autumn of 1992, he inveigled himself into the acquaintance of Bernard Wilson, a self-employed Cardiff print salesman facing bankruptcy, as a result of bad debts caused by the recession. Wilson, a thin, nervous man who had always taken pride in supporting himself and his family, had no convictions or any other kind of history of involvement with the police or criminals. A less likely master forger would be hard to conceive.

Titley offered him a 'partnership', making exaggerated claims about his own business expertise, and lent him £2,000 over several weeks in an attempt to keep him afloat. Only then did he first suggest forgery. Wilson admits he agreed to fake innocuous items such as Equity cards, but is adamant that from the outset, he refused to have anything to do with counterfeit money or anything which might cause others harm – such as vehicle MOT certificates. But having taken this bait, he was doomed.

Titley introduced him to undercover police officers working with the Midlands Regional Crime Squad – despite the fact that Wales did not form part of its territory. They, of course, posed as criminals. Within a few weeks, Wilson found himself the object of escalating threats: if he did not co-operate, Titley told him, he and his family would be harmed. 'I thought I was dealing with the Mafia,' Wilson said later. One night, Titley and two other men drove him to the middle of the Severn suspension bridge. They said that if he did not agree to organise the printing of fake Amex cheques, they would throw him off.

Meanwhile, Regional Crime Squad officers, including Led-brook, were once again negotiating personally with American

Express to obtain a 'reward'. Yet they also deliberately misled the bank. They had intelligence about a huge counterfeit conspiracy, they claimed, saying cheques worth $30 million had already been printed – although none were yet in existence. The police told Amex to provide an 'upfront' payment of £10,000, saying they needed this to show 'good faith' to Wilson and his 'co-conspirators'. In fact, as the officers knew, Wilson and the seven other hard-up printers he recruited to manufacture the cheques needed this money to buy the specialised colour printing equipment they needed before any counterfeiting could begin. Amex duly coughed up.

It was not until April 1993, by which time the entrapment scheme had been running for several months, that the Midlands Squad informed its South Wales counterpart of the 'crime' about to take place. The Welsh officers, led by Detective Chief Inspector Albert Reakes, met Ledbrook and one of Amex's top security men, Special Agent John White. To their credit, they insisted no reward should be paid until after the end of any trial, when the true worth of the Midlands officers' informant could be properly assessed. According to a statement Reakes made later to the PCA investigators, White 'promised faithfully that no payment would be made until we had authorised it'.

On the weekend of 14 May, the printing operation began. The South Wales officers swooped on the workshop the same day and arrested Wilson and all his colleagues. However, White did not keep his promise. He paid the first instalment of a £50,000 reward within a week of the arrests, with the rest following shortly. A few weeks later Reakes phoned him and asked if any reward had been paid. White's own statement to the PCA said: 'I said we hadn't. That was not true. The issue of the reward payment was, as I saw it, a matter for our company and the Regional Crime Squad who had Titley registered as an informant.'

By his own account, when he learnt what had happened two months later as a result of the disclosure at the trial of Docker in Wolverhampton, Reakes was 'astounded'. He added: 'John White apologised profusely. I can recall him saying, "I'm sorry I lied but I was told not to tell you." '

Unaware of the full picture until a late stage, Wilson and his associates pleaded guilty at a pre-trial hearing in the summer of 1994.

They could have expected to be gaoled for ten years, despite the fact that for all of them, this was a first offence. Later, when the full trial began at Swansea Crown Court in September, they tried to change their pleas to not guilty. However, Judge Hugh Williams refused to allow this, saying it would serve no purpose, because he was not minded to send any of them to prison at all.

His comments on Titley and the Midlands Regional Crime Squad were still more outspoken than those made by Judge Gibbs in Wolverhampton the previous year. He said: 'This was a scandalous, corrupt incitement which led to the defendants being fitted up to commit crimes none of them would have dreamed of committing otherwise. At least one serving police officer from the Midlands Regional Crime Squad knew or believed that the informer was acting as an *agent provocateur*. The informer was not only acting as *agent provocateur*, but was doing so when he was being handled by a serving police officer from the Midlands.' At a further sentencing hearing in December, he added that the police operation amounted to 'skulduggery and an abuse of power'. He gave all eight defendants short suspended sentences.

★   ★   ★

The inescapable preliminary conclusion to be drawn from the cases of Charrington, Banks and Titley is that the lurid tones in which the debate over organised crime is usually conducted oversimplifies and trivialises a profound legal-ethical dilemma. Law enforcement agencies cite the example of organised crime, and especially the problems created by the disclosure of evidence, to justify policy shifts away from due process, and towards crime control.

At the same time, local, divisional CID officers are being urged to adopt the methods developed against big-time organised crime in dealing with ordinary burglars, low-level drug dealers and thieves. In 1993, the Audit Commission, with warm encouragement from the Home Office, published a highly influential report, announcing that the way to deal with ordinary crime was through the use of informants, by developing local intelligence and by 'targeting' known offenders. Instead of investigating crimes, the police should be mounting 'pro-active' operations designed to trap the 'players' on their ground.

To some extent, this amounted to no more than an edict ordering detectives to re-invent the wheel: successful divisional CID operators have, like their colleagues in the Regional Crime Squads, always relied on informants. To get anywhere, drug dealers and thieves have to plug into an underground market economy which is always vulnerable to security leaks. Most local informants – like Charrington and Titley – begin their careers after being arrested, when future information is their only chip to bargain with. In Kilburn, the highlight of a dull week was always a raid (a job) at a suspected drug dealer's premises.

Yet using informants to target known offenders can, as we have seen, be a dangerous business for the integrity of criminal justice. It also raises the awkward possibility that the police may spend most of the time chasing criminals whom they happen to know about, while an entirely different set of 'players' runs rampant with impunity.

Meanwhile, a last example serves to demonstrate just how unsatisfactory things have become. It concerns the wrongful acquittal of two men charged with arguably the most serious of all crimes: contract assassination.[12]

In the rarefied police units which deal with organised crime, a piece of verbal shorthand describes a ploy used on several occasions by defence lawyers in the late 1980s: the 'Norris defence'. David Norris was a registered police informant with numerous convictions for burglary and other crimes, and his cover had been blown. In the 'Norris defence', defence lawyers took advantage of the fact that his role had become widely known, and alleged that he had been the informant in cases where he had in fact played no role at all. When police or other Crown witnesses denied his involvement, they were accused of lying to protect Norris in order to cast doubt on their reliability. In the resulting confusion, juries recorded acquittals.

On 28 April 1991, the Norris defence ceased to be available. That evening, two men arrived at his house in Belvedere, Kent, on a motorbike and shot him dead. The murder bore all the hallmarks of a professional contract killing. Murders of this kind are extremely difficult to investigate. But soon after the shooting, the police received a windfall. The South-east Regional Crime Squad had been running a large operation against a group of drugs importers, known as 'Operation Bohemian'. Within weeks of the shooting, they arrested two men, Stuart Warne and Renwick Dennison. To the officers' astonishment, Warne and Dennison began to confess not only to involvement in drugs, but to helping to organise Norris's murder.

Over many months, held in protective custody, Warne and Dennison made statements of meticulous detail, describing each and every aspect of the killing. They were able to supply hundreds of factual details which the police were able to corroborate, down to the level of where they encountered roadworks while travelling with the men who actually did the killing.

Warne said he became involved early in 1991, when he was offered a contract to kill a rival London criminal, John Dale, who was shot – but not killed – on 1 April. Warne was part of a network which supplied cannabis to Northern Ireland. Working with Dennison and others, he arranged for John Green and Terence McCrory, both active members of the proscribed Ulster Defence Association, to visit England. Then the name of Norris was added to the list, for a fee of £35,000.

Dennison admitted driving McCrory and Green to the area where Norris lived, where they picked up the motorbike. Later, Warne and Dennison took them both to a hotel on the Kent coast, whence they returned to Northern Ireland.

Both men were willing to give prosecution evidence. But if this was an attempt to return to the discredited supergrass system, there was an important difference. On 1 November, Warne and Dennison pleaded guilty to importing drugs and conspiracy to murder. They were sentenced not to five years but life. Any incentive they might have had to lie was distinctly weak.

Green and McCrory were arrested the following March. Twelve months later, their trial began at the Old Bailey. After six weeks, the defence made a legal submission. After due deliberation, Judge Lawrence Verney, the Recorder of London, ruled all the evidence given by Warne and Dennison inadmissible, and the prosecution collapsed. The reason was a single discrepancy between the statement made by Dennison and another witness, a Margate hotelier called Bernard Baldwin. He owned the premises where

Warne and Dennison took Green and McCrory after the killing. Baldwin said he thought they checked in at a time when the murder was being committed. He was contradicted by other witnesses, including his wife – who said she booked Green and McCrory in – and the hotel staff. When the police initially interviewed him, he said he had a poor memory, and could not recollect the men at all.

But the judge accepted arguments that this discrepancy could not be left in the evidence to the jury. It was, he said in his ruling, a 'fundamental inconsistency'. It rendered the whole of Dennison's evidence unreliable, and if Dennison could not be trusted, nor could Warne. It would be 'unsafe to proceed'. One recalls Commander Williamson's remarks about lawyers and their limited understanding of human memory, quoted in the previous chapter.[13] Judge Verney, it would seem, expects witnesses always to be word perfect.

Green and McCrory returned to Northern Ireland, and quietly resumed life in the UDA.

CHAPTER SIX

The Culture of Policing

If you visit a chain restaurant or transport cafe and see a young person, especially if unkempt or haggard looking, possibly with patchy face or acne, taking inordinately large helpings of sugar in his tea or coffee, this may indicate an addict. Such young people who fold their arms across their chests and scratch their upper arms, and the sides of their chests, are going through the classic behaviour of the beginning of withdrawal symptoms of the heroin addict. Frequent yawning is also a sign. If these signs are combined with a runny nose and red eyes, you are almost certainly looking at an addict, and, by natural inference, a thief.

Watch for the possession of 'these are your rights' cards or pamphlets by loiterers. Obviously, they will be carried by persons who consider it at least possible that they will break the law and be interrogated by police. Thus they are carried by male homosexuals, by industrial and other agitators, by Angry Brigade (British Urban Guerilla) inadequates and similar amateur criminals.

David Powis, *The Signs of Crime: A Field Manual for Police*, 1977

LURKING beneath every discussion about policing and criminal justice is a pervasive concept: 'police culture'. Academics and journalists reach their conclusions by different routes. But they tend to agree that the culture of British policing is intolerant, reactionary, macho, sexist, racist, and above all, astonishingly resistant to change.

Diagnosis of cop culture is central to the debate about criminal justice. As Robert Reiner writes, the 'rules, recipes and rites' of police culture shape much of what happens on the streets, because the law 'does not even purport to determine practical policing'. It leaves big gaps to be filled by police 'discretion': whether to stop, whether to arrest, whether to charge, whether to employ the relative concept of 'reasonable force'. Each generation of police officers becomes socialised into this culture, Reiner adds: 'The culture survives because of its "elective affinity", its psychological fit, with the demands of the rank-and-file cop condition.'[1]

Reiner is far too acute an observer to suggest that every aspect of this culture is unchanging, and indeed immutable: the outlooks of police forces differ, he says, and can alter over time. But in the view of other commentators, both journalists and academics, police culture is set as in stone. Attempts to reform it are doomed to failure. Police culture, moreover, is blamed as the source of most things that go wrong with the criminal justice system: one of its indelible elements is a tendency to break the rules.

A version of this analysis can be found in the memoir of the retired West Mercia superintendent, Malcolm Young. According to Young, policing is 'a social construction geared to the maintenance of élitist power, and is primarily concerned to keep control over a materially disadvantaged underclass.' Coercive, authoritarian, at times even totalitarian, the only function for police officers is as a 'socio-political tool of the state and government'.

Young writes that throughout his career, his colleagues had exhibited a 'fear and suspicion of liberal views and an almost generalised hatred of active socialists'; merely to be seen with the *Guardian* newspaper was to draw down ridicule and contempt. Even a 'supposed élite group of police intellectuals', a 1984 reunion dinner of scholars at the Bramshill police staff college, displayed 'transparent bigotry'. Young said that they threatened to boycott the following year's dinner if the Labour leader Neil Kinnock were invited as guest speaker.

As for 'liberal' police reformers, their only purpose is public relations. In fact, he says, they are merely 'licensed court jesters', adding: 'Attempts at radical change will always fail, for as a researcher I have recognised that the place of the analytic jester in the police is still one charged with potential for disaster, for he disturbs the hegemonic mode by which the society is sustained.'[2]

Less than twenty years ago, the culture described by Young was being handed down explicitly from the summit of policing. Sir Robert Mark, who purged much of the corruption from the CID, is remembered as a great reforming Commissioner of the Metropolitan Police. Everything is relative. The book which contains the quotations at the start of this chapter was written by one of Mark's most senior colleagues, Assistant Commissioner David 'Crazy Horse' Powis, who shortly after its publication became Scotland Yard's top CID man.

The Signs of Crime: A Field Manual for Police was published in 1977, and Mark wrote the foreword, saying: 'I have often complained during a long police career that of all the mountains of printed matter about the police, almost all consist of fiction, and there is virtually nothing that contains anything of merit. This book is a noteworthy exception.' He commended it to all 'serving and future' officers.[3]

In Powis's field manual, the idea that police were 'tools of the state and government' became an acknowledged virtue:

Watch for criminals using vehicles who may, owing to extreme political views, intend to harm the community you have sworn to protect. This will show in their ordinary conversation, where almost unconsciously they will use the jargon and phrases of their beliefs. This intense and extremist gabble, if spoken with a cultured voice, particularly if the speaker is a woman, should make you pause and think through the likelihood you have stumbled on an important matter.

Sometimes the book is hilarious, as in this advice on searching derelict buildings:

Give commands to an imaginary dog handler, implying in these commands that the dog is quite a savage example of his species. Use a name like 'Viceroy' or 'Khan'. It may bring about the surrender of nervous thieves. Do not be prejudiced against the use of dogs. Of course they have failures and mistakes and can embarrass you in good-quality premises, but are infinitely worthwhile.

Even at the time it was published, younger officers regarded Powis's manual as something of an embarrassment. It in no sense represented emerging new strands in police thinking which were already beginning to become influential; and as a record of traditional police attitudes, it ought to be treated as a somewhat eccentric caricature. Nevertheless, it does unintentionally provide a window into a state of mind in which the populace can be neatly separated into deviants and the rest: 'Watch for the "athlete" dressed in a tracksuit, running about residential streets, either at dusk or early morning. While one must not become morbidly suspicious, experience does indicate that there seems to be a correlation between such persons and homosexual nuisances.' In the world of David Powis, heterosexual joggers stuck to broad daylight.

All through the work there is a bizarre prurience:

The smell of semen is very distinctive. If you are trying to make up your mind whether the persons you are interrogating are motor-wandering thieves, fugitive escapees living and sleeping in their clothes or merely honest travellers, this smell in the vehicle, especially if stale, can be a pointer to a depraved style of living consistent with a life of thieving, prostitution or political 'drop out' activity. It goes without saying that no females need to be present for such an odour to be detected.

Dealing with prostitution, Powis observed: 'Whether my experience is statistically significant or not, you must decide for yourselves, but of all the really skilled inside sneakthief ponces I have known, every one was homosexual.'

In public at least, senior police officers no longer use the language of David Powis. His disdain for homosexuals and suspicion of ethnic minorities – at one point, the book contains a rousing endorsement of the now-discredited 'sus' (suspected persons) laws – have become officially taboo. Yet the fact remains that less than twenty years ago, a Metropolitan Police Commissioner recommended this book to every new recruit. Many of them remain in service. Was this strange text a reflection of 'natural' or 'authentic' police culture? Did it stem from a set of attitudes which beneath the surface, are never likely to change?

The mainstream of liberal media and academic opinion would reply to these questions with an emphatic 'yes'. In a recent critical legal textbook, Andrew Sanders and Richard Young summarised an important research tradition. The police, they write, are imbued with 'an impending sense of chaos and the importance of the thin blue line holding it at bay. Only the police know what it is really like "out there". If the naive, well-meaning, respectable majority knew what it was like, they would not make the police work with one hand tied behind their backs.' The police, they add, reinforce their intolerant view of the world through their social isolation: 'A considerable body of research has tried to ascertain whether the intolerance and authoritarianism characteristic of the police is a product of socialisation after joining the service, or a characteristic of the type of people who become police officers.'

According to Sanders and Young, miscarriages of justice and evidential malpractice flow directly from police officers' cultural intolerance. Cop culture, Sanders and Young go on, leads to 'a very particular view of what constitutes "suspicious" behaviour and impatience with any rules which get in the way of the "fight against crime". Legality is often sacrificed for efficiency. Thus, cop culture acts as a powerful crime control engine at the heart of the machinery of criminal justice.'[4]

As legal academics, Sanders and Young are principally concerned with cop culture's consequences for due process and the rule of law. Journalists' interests have tended to focus on broader, attitudinal themes. An influential example came with the lengthy fly-on-the-wall observations made by Robert Chesshyre, a former *Observer* Washington correspondent. He spent several months observing police in Streatham, south London, in the late 1980s, and if he did not coin it, he popularised a term which has since become an increasingly meaningless cliché – the 'canteen culture'.[5]

Explaining the culture's resistance to change, Chesshyre stressed the anti-education attitudes held by influential 'canteen cowboys', who could nullify any attempts at reform by enlightened senior officers. He added: 'The Metropolitan Police is like a giant school with too many pupils in the D-stream. The bright kids do okay, but they are rapidly removed to the sixth form, where their impact on the school culture is minimal. The lads set their own priorities, which have little to do with those being promulgated by the headmaster.' Chesshyre claimed:

The papers read by the police are almost exclusively tabloid. Many of the brighter officers are, in any case, studying for promotion exams, leaving little time for intellectual refreshment. The ground is fertile for the lowest common denominator to flourish. It makes for a quiet life to succumb to this collective embrace, and to banish disturbing thoughts and private misgivings: the office of constable can be performed almost entirely on reflex actions.

Six years after Chesshyre's book was published, the canteen culture concept has become the media explanation for every conceivable kind of police failing or malpractice. When a Surrey officer was accused and acquitted of raping a female colleague in February 1995, the Old Bailey heard lurid details of high jinks in the section houses used by the youngest recruits. In the view of the *Daily Telegraph*, the canteen culture was to blame. In the following month, canteen culture was variously held responsible for awards of civil damages against the police, racial discrimination within the service, miscarriages of justice, and excessive force against protesters demonstrating against the export of veal calves.

It would be extremely naïve to claim that this gloomy picture of intolerance, authoritarianism and rule-bending has no basis in reality. There are too many documented examples of its persistence. Each new case of an innocent, too often black, man collecting thousands of pounds in damages, after alleging assault or false imprisonment, serves to reinforce the analysis that nothing much has changed.

Recent research on the Hampshire police by Dr Jennifer Brown suggests a majority of policewomen have endured sexual harassment, while 6 per cent have been seriously assaulted.[6] In 1993, the Metropolitan Police paid £30,000 damages to an officer of Turkish origin, Sarah Locker, who became the target of grotesque sexist and racist comments when she tried to join the CID. She was given her cheque by a CID commander in a public presentation: it looked like a happy ending, but within a few months, she was off work suffering from stress. She lodged a fresh discrimination action, alleging her life had been made a misery by colleagues who could not accept her previous victory.

Chesshyre's canteen culture has not been eliminated. Yet there is evidence to suggest that it is not pre-determined or inevitable, and

that for some years it has been in retreat. Side by side with the old
police culture, an internal police 'progressive tendency' has been
gathering strength. It has not achieved the critical mass necessary to
effect a wholesale transformation in the character of British policing,
and recent Government policy has placed its future in jeopardy. But
it is not yet defeated.

To understand how police culture can change, it is necessary to
examine the elements which go into its formation. First comes the
experience of officers on the streets: the acts and situations which
make policing unique. The second is the law: legislation may not
shape every aspect of practical policing, but as we have seen, PACE
wrought many changes. The third element is pay and conditions of
service, which play a large part in determining who joins the service
in the first place. Next comes conscious police policy, and attempts
at reform from above.

The last element is the hardest to grasp, but perhaps the most
important of all. It is best addressed by asking the question which has
been asked since Sir Robert Peel's foundation of the 'new police' in
1829 – whom do the police serve? In as far as policing has a primary
purpose, it lies in the response: and in the individual answer each
officer carries around in his head.

★   ★   ★

The first factor, street experience, is the least susceptible to change. It
may not be true that 'only the police know what it is like out there'.
But other groups of people do not acquire their knowledge in quite
the same way. As Reiner writes, other jobs are dangerous: deep sea
diving or coal mining. But the risks run by police officers are
different: 'The police officer has to confront the threat of sudden
attack from another person, not the more calculable risks of physical
or environmental hazards. It is undoubtedly less in Newbury than
New York. But the police officer faces, behind every corner he turns
or doorbell he rings, some danger, if not of firearms at least of fists.'[7]

Mere words cannot easily convey what that sense of danger
means, or how its constant presence acts as an inexorable bonding
force between members of the service. It came home to me on my

first outing with officers from Kilburn: a routine raid for stolen property, at a flat in a low-rise block a few hundred yards from my home. In the end, it turned out to be somewhat embarrassing. The information supplied to the police, on the strength of which they had obtained a search-warrant from a magistrate, was totally inaccurate, or at least out of date. The occupant was a polite and innocent African student, who was trying to pay his way through art college by turning out watercolours of the Buddha, all of which bore the motif 'Peace and Healing'.

However, as the police tiptoed up the stairs of the block, led by the 'special events team' – civilian police employees who do nothing all day but open doors with hydraulic jacks – a thought lodged powerfully in my mind: 'What on earth am I doing here? This guy could be anyone! And why am I near the front?' Suddenly, I was scared.

In Harlesden, the danger can be even more tangible. Seasoned local officers say that since a three-week surveillance operation led to the successful prosecution of a number of local crack dealers, policing the Stonebridge estate is easier than it was. In the old days, at the start of the 1990s, any police officer who set foot there was at risk of attack. One of the worst incidents came when two PCs were cornered by gangs of youths who approached them from opposite ends of the footbridge across the main road through the estate. They were beaten, but managed to escape: the youths had been planning to drop them thirty feet on to the carriageway beneath.

I walked through the Stonebridge with a young PC, Norman Jones. PC Jones seemed palpably nervous: on return to Harlesden police station, his story came tumbling out.

Months earlier, he had answered a 999 call from a man called Francis Coyle. He was worried because the woman in the flat next door was screaming in what sounded like sheer terror. Coyle joined PC Jones at the neighbour's front door. PC Jones said: 'I knew it wasn't exactly an ordinary domestic because of the screaming. I'll never forget it. But I thought it would just be a guy in there going bananas.'

In fact, the woman's boyfriend, Gregor Hobbins, a private soldier, had stolen a high-velocity assault rifle from Chelsea barracks, and was threatening to kill her in a jealous rage. When PC Jones knocked, Hobbins opened fire through the door. Coyle was killed outright; Jones sustained a terrible wound to his left arm. Hobbins was convicted of manslaughter and wounding with intent, and gaoled for ten years. PC Jones said:

> I nearly lost the arm. I was off sick for eighteen months. For four months, the doctors couldn't tell me if they were going to be able to save it or not. I still have only 70 per cent movement. It wasn't just the pain, it was the stress. I lost my marriage to the shooting, I lost my head for a while. They know my name on the Stonebridge, and sometimes they try to wind me up; they say 'next time we fucking shoot you, we'll fucking shoot you dead'.
>
> The time I really think of the danger is when there's a burglar alarm on an industrial estate in the middle of the night, and you've got to open doors and go in. Realistically speaking, I suppose I shouldn't have gone back to work. But I did, because I wanted to prove to myself I could, and work somewhere like the Stonebridge. It took me eight months to really work properly again; then I bust my wrist chasing a suspect. Now I'm easing myself back in a second time.

Even unarmed, the police have an awesome weapon to counter danger: power, the use of legal authority. Senior officers are fond of repeating the notion that they strive for the ideal of 'policing by consent'. But the daily experience of police officers is coercion, imposing their will where consent is notably absent. Like danger, this marks them out from the rest of society. Once police power starts to be exercised, its legal boundaries confer vast latitude and discretion. They also impose a fearful responsibility.

To see this authority in action is very different from listening to later desiccated and dissected accounts in court. It was visible during that first raid on the art student, as the police prodded his tubes of paint and poked his bag of modelling clay in the bathroom. He telephoned his girlfriend while the search was in progress, but he had to ask. The officers were polite and apologetic. But unbidden, the thought formed in my head: in circumstances like this, these people can do almost *anything*.

Sometimes power and danger meet, in the lawful exercise of

'reasonable force' – controlled violence. To exercise authority effectively requires confidence and action. It demands swift decision making which may later come under the most intense scrutiny. Most people, living ordinary middle-England lives, rarely see or use violence. For police officers, who must spend the rest of their time behaving like everyone else, the sudden, controlled and legitimate use of violence is a requisite for survival.

Very late one freezing night, a man crawled into Kilburn police station bleeding from two stab wounds. He had got into a fight with a friend at a flat on the South Kilburn estate and the friend had attacked him with scissors. He believed the friend was still in his flat and he had a machete. When we arrived at 1 a.m., music was booming through the letter-box. The flat was on the first floor of a small block, with an open landing. Seven Kilburn officers congregated nervously outside: the entire complement available that night. The police knocked. As soon as the door opened they rushed in, wrestled the occupant to the floor and handcuffed him. He was a powerful man in his early twenties, dressed in T-shirt and shorts. On this occasion, there were few niceties.

On another early morning three days before Christmas, I accompanied an inspector on a routine tour of local nightclubs. For the first hour it was a soporific experience, as we sat and drank tea with proprietors, talking aimlessly about football and the state of business. Our third visit was to a discothèque in Neasden, just off the North Circular Road.

As we arrived, a tousled youth staggered towards the panda car, complaining bitterly about a bouncer who had thrown him out. He disappeared and we went inside. It was 2.30 a.m., but the club was packed. Suddenly there was a deep boom from outside. We rushed downstairs from the first floor bar. Through the closed circuit TV monitor at the front entrance, we watched as the same youth swung a huge club – a heavy wooden fencepost – again and again at the door, screaming in blind fury. The manager was keeping people back from opening the door but the crowd at the bottom of the stairs was building up fast.

The inspector used his radio to call for help. On the screen we saw it arrive while the youth carried on swinging, unaware of the presence of a squad car and police van, until the handcuffs were almost upon him. His arrest was the signal for a mini riot, as his girlfriend and twenty or thirty male friends burst out of the club. They waded into the police, yelling and lashing out. Two of the women dived into the back of the van in an attempt to rescue the prisoner. 'In these situations you go in, get your man, and get out quick,' the inspector said. 'If we stay here, we're all going to get attacked.'

Ten minutes later, as he sat on the bench in the Kilburn 'custody suite' being processed, all violence had drained from the fencepost assailant. 'What am I doing here, please let me explain myself,' he wailed, 'let me go now, please, I can't be late for work in the morning.' He held his head in his hands. 'Oh God. Look, please, it was my twenty-first birthday!'

The responsibility of authority also means knowing when not to use it. One spring day a Kilburn PC went to a local school to ask for volunteers to stand on an identity parade. According to the rules decreed by PACE, they ought to share the basic characteristics of the suspect: he needed nine strapping mixed-race teenagers. 'We were offering them ten pounds each' the officer said, 'and transport to and from the school. So I stood outside as they came out and one kid came up to me and spat at my feet. Then they all started, twenty or thirty of them, walking past me and gobbing. I was covered in it. It was disgusting, and there was nothing I could do.'

There is a final, unique aspect to routine police work: regular contact with victims of crime. Even incidents which do not appear serious may produce heartrending trauma.

Jane, aged twenty and profoundly deaf, had been about to enter Harlesden Post Office; she was carrying an envelope with her motoring documents, planning to buy a tax disc. A man had run from behind her and snatched it from her hand. Now, two hours later, in her mother's sitting room, she was inconsolable. 'I didn't hear him behind me. It happened so quickly.' She could not stop weeping: 'I'm so scared. The documents have got my address.' The police searched the alley near her home, a notorious spot where a hefty detective was robbed a few weeks later, but there was no sign of the valueless papers. 'Bastards, the bastards,' the PC muttered. 'It's the bloody shittiness of the area.'

It is impossible to shut off entirely the emotional impact of incidents such as these, let alone the reactions of victims of really serious crime. Malcolm Young is right to identify the 'Manichaean', binary division of the world made by many officers, between 'decent people' and, according to the vagaries of localised police slang, 'slags', 'scrotes', 'bad guys' or (in Young's first area of service, Northumbria) 'prigs'. This view is evident in almost every conversation with an officer, although it may well be coupled with a sympathetic understanding of the socio-economic roots of crime. A PC said: 'I walk round the South Kilburn estate thinking as I see people: "victim, perpetrator, victim, perpetrator". It's almost as if they've got great big signs flashing on their heads. There's just a few big Irishmen who know how to look after themselves who are neither one nor the other.'

Surely it is false to claim that the origins of this world-view lie in notions of serving the élite. In Kilburn, I heard one sentence repeated many times, often to explain an officer's opinions of other aspects of criminal justice. 'We see the victims.'

In big cities at least, few police officers live in the area where they work: as one PC put it, 'you don't want to come across someone you've nicked when you're shopping with the family in Sainsbury's'. I once spent six months as a porter in a hospital operating theatre. Working there, on unsociable shifts, began to change my perception of reality: it became difficult to remember most people are not suffering life-threatening illness. Police work also deals with a kind of pathology, and it can have a similar distorting effect on officers' outlook. Several times I found myself trying to convince sceptical Kilburn officers that my own street 200 yards from the police station was a convenient and congenial place to live, with all kinds of advantages to which they were oblivious.

It is on these foundations that the standard account of police culture has built the idea that police see themselves as the 'thin blue line' holding chaos at bay; as the last, perhaps the only, barrier between order and anarchy. In the old regime days of David Powis, this may well have been true. As his manual put it, 'remember, you have a professional duty to make yourself as experienced as possible in all criminal matters, the better to protect the public'.

However, the passing of the old regime in criminal justice has had its cultural side-effects. With the encroachment of due process and the takeover of prosecutions by the CPS, police officers know that at a certain stage, their role in a case will cease, other than as a possible witness. Most realise that to cling to their old self-image would be to subscribe to delusion. Retreat has brought an awareness of limitations. A Kilburn PC said:

> We used to have enormous powers, and yes, perhaps we abused them. You made your arrest and you prosecuted the case. What you did could get someone put away. Now you haven't got that power. You get used to people not being charged, or getting off at court. So people don't care in the same way. You just do your job, and what will be, will be. Attitudes are nothing like as hard as they used to be.

In contrast to the situations pre-PACE, officers involved in a case will usually not be allowed in court, except while giving their own evidence. 'Nowadays, you won't bother to stay for the result,' the PC went on. 'Sometimes you'll get to hear of it later: obviously you will if it's a serious case. But for routine stuff at the Magistrates' Court, maybe not.'

A Detective Inspector made similar comments:

> If someone gets convicted for something they've done, that's a good result nowadays. It's not a measure of police performance whether someone gets discharged by the courts, or the CPS discontinues. It's such an effort to get someone before the court now, sometimes it hardly seems worthwhile.
>
> The old, back-to-the-wall culture has gone because of PACE. There's less pressure on suspects, but equally, there's less pressure on the police. If you arrested someone in the old days and you didn't get a charge, the sergeant would want to know why. Your guvnors assessed you by the collars you felt and the number who went down. Now, you get on with the job, it's out of your hands. There isn't the pressure bearing down on you from above.

Another detective said: 'If you look at the crime figures and the conviction rates, the pessimistic view is that we've lost. The realistic view is to accept the figures, and just do the best you can. That is what you're paid for.'

On an afternoon drugs raid at a flat on the South Kilburn estate, I saw how far the 'thin blue line' mentality had receded. The flat's location high in a tower block meant surveillance was impossible: the raid's success or failure would be down to luck. In the event, everyone was out, and the police found only a bag of what might have been herbal cannabis. An earnest discussion took place among the officers as to whether it was even worth taking it back for analysis. 'I've already got paperwork up to here,' one of the drugs specialists said, 'and even if it is grass, it'll only be a fine or caution.' They were evenly split, with some arguing they should put everything back, get the door fixed and leave. In the end, the decision was made to confiscate it – but only because this would make the raid easier to justify.

A further element of this aspect of cultural change is summed up in a piece of Kilburn division slang – the 'THJ', meaning 'typical Harlesden job'. A THJ is a serious crime of violence where the victim refuses to make a statement, or where every potential witness refuses to co-operate. In the six months I spent with officers from the division, there were at least two dramatic examples. One was a double shooting in a nightclub at 5 a.m. one Saturday morning. One man took two bullets in the neck, the other a wound to the head: both miraculously survived. Apparently no one saw it happen. The second was a 'domestic' that 'went seriously pear-shaped'. A man who had abandoned the mother of his baby and set up home with another woman received a visit from his ex and her mother. One of the women went to his kitchen and stabbed him in the body and thigh, cutting the major artery in his leg. He could have died; in the words of an officer who went to the scene, 'it looked like a butcher's shop'. He was taken to the Central Middlesex Hospital, survived, and refused to make a statement.

However, changes in police culture are not all the product of changes in the law and criminal justice. Police officers with impeccable crime-busting credentials are beginning to say unexpected things. 'I've become much more liberal-minded since I became a police officer,' a detective inspector said. He had just spent

months on a dark, dreadful case, which had resulted in the charging
of a serial rapist. He added:

> I know there are no single solutions to these problems. When I
> was eighteen, it all looked much easier. There was right, and there
> was wrong. The reason why people commit crime are very
> complex. I still get angry at people's behaviour, but not with them
> as individuals. And I don't want to be part of a society where
> people don't have rights. I would rather see the guilty acquitted
> than the innocent convicted. It's very important the police are
> kept in check by society. There are those who would otherwise
> abuse their power.

★　★　★

Robert Chesshyre claimed the job of policing could be done 'almost
entirely on reflex actions', and that the service was characterised by
outright hostility to education. True as this might once have been, of
all the canteen culture clichés, this one bears the least resemblance to
the present reality.

In 1968, there were just 168 graduates throughout the entire
police force of England and Wales: they made up a tiny 0.1 per cent
of the serving establishment. More than half of all police recruits
lacked a single 'O' level pass. Less than 2 per cent had attained a
standard of two 'A' levels or more.

In the space of twenty years, the position has been transformed
completely. In 1988, fewer than one in eight new recruits had no 'O'
levels or GCSEs. More than a quarter had at least two 'A' levels, and
in some constabularies, the proportion of new recruits who were
graduates stood at twelve per cent. In London and elsewhere, the
police were turning away more graduates than any other class of
applicant, wary of recruiting too many ambitious people for whom
promotion might not be available. Nationally, there were 6,625
graduates already in service, who made up 5.4 per cent of the
establishment. Since 1988, the proportion has continued to rise.

A 1989 survey by researchers at Manchester University found the
police had not only improved the educational standard of its own
intake, it had 'appreciably improved its competitiveness *vis-à-vis*

other employers'.[8] From the late 1970s, the standard of police recruits has been well above the school leaving average: 'It would seem that the police service is increasingly being accepted as a career for the better educated.' Moreover, the more recent the group of recruits, the better their education.

It seems difficult to believe that this could have had no effect on police culture. Some of the graduates identified by the Manchester survey had obtained their degrees by a variety of in-service schemes, which from the early 1960s, were set up to boost policing's intellectual profile. When interviewed by the researchers, they said their view of the world had changed markedly. 'I was getting blinkered. My perceptions of the outside community were very much police-geared. Getting away from the police for three years opened my mind,' a chief inspector told the Manchester team. A superintendent said he had learnt to 'reject stereotypes', an inspector that he had 'learnt to consider possibilities, to see contrary views', and when 'unfortunate people' were brought into the station, he was 'much more able to accept and understand them'.

These were middle-ranking or senior officers: Chesshyre was railing at the canteen 'D-stream'. But there has to come a point where the numbers of educated officers become so large that anti-intellectualism no longer looks so 'fashionable'. On some shifts, in some police stations, I believe this stage has already been reached. I can only state what I have seen and heard: this is impressionistic evidence. But in Kilburn and Harlesden police stations, a degree is not regarded as a liability, nor as an impediment to 'real police work', even by officers of many years' service. Broadsheet newspapers are widely read: the *Guardian*, the *Financial Times*. Moreover, several junior officers are reading for the part-time degree in police studies which Portsmouth University began to offer in 1992. This closes a little circle: the course involves studying the very criminologists who have made studying policing their lifetime's work. At the time of writing there were 1,200 students on the Portsmouth course. In its first crop of graduates in 1994, many scored first and upper second class honours.

There is no mystery over why this improvement has taken place. Conscious policy initiatives – in-service grants, the special graduate entry scheme and so on – had an impact. But the most important factor was money. In 1979, the new Conservative Government ended years of simmering police industrial militancy, by implementing an index-linked pay award recommended before the election by Lord Edmund-Davies. At a stroke, the pay of junior police officers leapt up by 40 per cent – from the level of manual workers to above the graduate average. The police salary on appointment rose from £3,189 in 1978 to £4,956 by the start of 1980. The average annual pay for people leaving university at the time was £3,922. Of course, for less qualified school leavers, the new police salary was even more attractive.[9]

Improving pay did not only affect recruits: it had major cultural implications for officers already in the service. David Buss, who spent fifteen years as a London PC in 1973–88 recalled the policeman's lot before Edmund-Davies:

> I remember being absolutely skint, standing on the North End Road in Fulham, waiting for the pubs to shut at 10.30, and so for the chance to arrest a man for being drunk and disorderly. That meant you could take him to court the next morning: four hours overtime. I found it demeaning. You would be offered all sorts of freebies by publicans, even greengrocers, and you'd take them, because you were so badly paid.[10]

A still-serving PC said: 'Overtime was everything. Once I went five months without a day off. Your guvnors would require you for two days off of the eight you were owed each month as a matter of course. But the opportunities to build on that were legion, and you bloody needed them.'

Spending so much time at work, it need hardly be said, increased the isolation of police officers from the rest of society. It also had a disastrous effect on their marriages.

In the CID, the absorption in policing was even more complete. 'You lived, ate, slept, drank the job,' said a detective sergeant. 'It was no place for a married man. I'm proud I was part of the tail end of that culture, in a way: there were real characters. You don't get that now. But it wasn't a healthy way to live. At the weekend now, there will be one detective rostered on. Then there would have been five or six

of us; and we'd spend most of our overtime in the pub.' A detective
inspector said:

> It used to be a thirteen hour day in the CID. Inevitably, every
> single evening was spent in the pub. There was no way you could
> order something like a diet Coke: the response would have been,
> 'are you sure you want to work in the CID?' Drink and that
> macho culture went together. I'm not saying it has disappeared.
> But if I go for a drink after work, it'll usually be just a quick one;
> then I'll be going home to my family. And if I want Perrier or
> Coke, Perrier or Coke I will drink.

The police force of the 1960s and 70s was heavily populated by
ex-military, and it was easy to impose military-style discipline.
'There used to be a cliché: "The job wants". Whatever that was, it
got done,' the detective continued. 'You cannot recruit more
intelligent and educated people and treat them like squaddies. It
means middle management have to work much harder. As you get
older, you find young people joining the job are changing faster than
the senior officers, who often can't understand those changes; who
find their decisions are being questioned.'

Financial corruption has not been wholly eliminated from
policing: it probably never could be. But it has become much rarer –
as experienced criminals agree. 'I used to buy my way out,' said a
man in his fifties serving six years for commercial burglary at
Latchmere House prison, 'now you can more or less forget it.' Better
pay has underlined the reforming drive begun by Robert Mark. An
acting detective inspector said: 'Hand on heart, I did see evidence of
low-level corruption for the first five years of my service: tenners and
twenty-fives, that sort of thing. I've seen nothing of that nature for
the last fifteen years.'

Money also acted as a brake against the fabrication of evidence, he
said: 'People say to themselves, "I've got £35,000 a year, a wife and
two kids. Why should I give a fuck whether this bloke goes down or
not?" The public expect us to be whiter than white; they also expect
us to get results. Well, sometimes they won't get those results, is the
way I look at it.'

Improving pay has made it possible to increase the average age at which recruits join the service. The old joke that 'you know when you're getting older because the police are getting younger' is no longer true. In the 1970s, twenty-one was old to be joining the police in many forces, and the minimum of eighteen years six months was the norm. Thousands of people entrusted with the awesome powers and responsibilities of a constable were still in their teens. In 1994, the mean recruiting age in London had risen to twenty-six years, eleven months, and there were many recruits taken on in their mid and late thirties. This change has had significant effects elsewhere.

New police officers have now had experience of adult life outside policing, and the influence in the canteen is palpable. The newer officers in Kilburn include former motor company executives, teachers and engineers. One night, I went out patrolling with two PCs in their thirties. One had been in the job for eighteen years; the other, driven south from the Chesterfield area by unemployment, for five. The conversation turned to the 1984 miners' strike. To their mutual amazement, the two PCs discovered they had both spent weeks on the picket line at Markham Main colliery – one as a striking miner, the other as a policeman.

Different cultures can exist within policing simultaneously. Some police stations develop a notoriety stretching back years: a reputation for brutality or corruption which seems almost impossible to shake off. Stoke Newington in north London, beset by controversy from the death by shooting of Colin Roach inside the station foyer in 1983, to allegations that officers were 'recycling' crack cocaine ten years later, is an obvious example.

Even within the same police station, there may be striking differences of outlook between shifts. Chief Inspector Euan Read of Thames Valley related the alarm at the constabulary's headquarters when it was discovered in early 1994 that all the male members of a 'relief' at Reading had had skinhead haircuts: 'That did seem to send out a worrying signal about their attitude to the public.' The shift was swiftly broken up.

It is relatively unusual for officers to spend more than ten years on street patrol work. Here cultural change may be more noticeable than in specialist public order units or parts of the CID. As in any organisation, cliques of friends of like mind develop in policing. It is inescapable that policing rural areas is a less confrontational business than dealing with the inner city, and officers' shared culture will develop to match the demands placed upon them.

It is not possible to be categoric. But on the evidence of my own eyes, I do not believe that the usual bleak descriptions of police or canteen culture deserve their current blanket status. They are becoming an anachronism.

I caught one straw in the wind, appropriately enough, on an early visit to the Kilburn police canteen. There, in easy earshot of her colleagues, a PC of five years' service told me: 'I've been "out" as a lesbian since I joined the job, and it's not been a problem. My team come to the house I share with my partner. Even the older ones just accept it.' She was not the only 'out' lesbian in the division. Later, when another female constable began a relationship with an officer from another station, it became an item of interested gossip – but in such unpejorative terms that I did not realise for some time that the object of her affections was also a woman. Until his promotion a few months earlier, the division had also included an 'out' gay man: he was recalled by his colleagues as a 'good copper'.

Some of this tolerance is down to good management. Euan Read of Thames Valley said: 'If you make clear as a shift inspector what standards you expect, and what you will tolerate, they will follow you. If two of your officers beat someone up, and you do nothing, then the rest will follow that lead. I had a gay woman on a shift and she had had a bad time from my predecessor. She ended up inviting me and some of her colleagues to her gay wedding.'

There is already a Gay and Lesbian Police Association, which mounted a recruitment stand at the 1994 Gay Pride conference. I compared notes with Mariecca Coulson, who joined the Metropolitan Police in the late 1970s, and now works as a lawyer. 'Fifteen years ago, all this would have been unthinkable,' she said. 'There was once a girl who happened to be gay who made the mistake of confiding in her skipper one night when she was drunk. It went round the station overnight and her life was made a misery.'[11]

The persistence of racism within the police service is so well-documented that any optimism must be tempered with strong caution. Chief Inspector Ron Hope, chairman of the Black Police Association, launched at Scotland Yard in September 1994, has written of the 'justifiable perception that those who join will be subjected to racism within the service, as well as possible opposition or hostility from friends, relatives and black members of the public'. Despite years of ethnic minority recruitment campaigns, and avowed internal equal opportunity policies, it was 'difficult to see any real improvement in working conditions. We may have had new policies, but many of the long-standing practices continued.'[12]

Until 1967, there was an effective colour bar. Norwell Roberts, the first black recruit, for years used to deny he met with hostility because of his colour. 'He will tell you a different story today,' Hope writes. In the mid-80s, Hope conducted a survey of black officers, who described a total lack of understanding of racism by senior and junior colleagues, and widespread racist language, jokes and abuse. A similar picture emerged from the Policy Studies Institute report based on two years of observational work published in 1983. It told of the general, unquestioned use of terms such as 'nigger', 'coon', 'spook', 'Paki' and 'spade', together with the astonishing insensitivity of white officers towards black colleagues. One of many incidents in the PSI study described an inspector speaking of 'fucking niggers' while a black PC stood next to him.[13]

In 1990, Assistant Commissioner Wyn Jones of the Metropolitan Police organised a seminar in Bristol for black officers. More than 300 attended, and spoke of the fear of victimisation if a complaint were made, the failure by managers to tackle racist language, the perception that career opportunities were limited and feelings of isolation and lack of support.

It has to be said that the leadership of the service has, in the most recent period, shown an impressive determination to confront internal racism. Within weeks of becoming Metropolitan Commissioner, Sir Paul Condon publicly rejected the notion that there was bound to be racism in policing because it existed in society outside. His endorsement of the Black Police Association – whose formation was, arguably, a sign of growing confidence – sent a further unmistakable signal to the force. Meanwhile, the police nationally have developed equal opportunity and grievance procedures which, at least on paper, far outstrip those of virtually any other employer.

With all due caveats, and bearing in mind the continuing stream of cases making their way through industrial tribunals, there are nevertheless signs of progress. The number of black officers, which

in the years following the appointment of Norwell Roberts crept up
so very slowly, has begun to grow more quickly. In 1990, at the time
of the seminars, there were barely 400 black officers in the
Metropolitan Police; by April 1995, the number had reached 724.
This is still less than 3 per cent. But it means that in every division,
there will be on average more than ten black officers. For that reason
alone, racist behaviour must become harder to sustain. What had
once seemed a distant goal, the day when two black officers would
be out on patrol together in a squad car, is beginning to happen.
Premature wastage rates among black officers, for many years much
higher than among their white counterparts, have begun to decline.

On the ground in Kilburn, there are other signs of change.
Officers sometimes snorted at equal opportunities policies, raising
the chimera of 'positive discrimination'. Yet in six months, I did not
hear a single racist joke; not once a racist term of abuse, and this in an
area in which black people were being arrested with depressing
regularity. This was not down only to my presence: on occasion,
officers vouchsafed extraordinary confidences and disclosed things
which might jeopardise their careers if published.

'There are still people who think in a racist manner,' a black PC
said, 'but it is much more difficult to get away with it. Police culture
has changed: it's much less knee-jerk right-wing. It's true you don't
hear racist jokes.' He related an incident five years earlier, when he
used the grievance procedure over an attempt to transfer him: the
senior officer who dealt with the case displayed intense relief he only
alleged he had been treated unfairly, not racial discrimination. 'After
that, some people snubbed me. One day there was a guy who'd been
getting quite aggressive and I heard him talking about "fucking
blacks". He hadn't realised I was there. The next day, he came up
and started being really friendly: he seemed to realise he'd made a
mistake.'

Nevertheless, the vital thing remained to 'fit in'. He added:

It's not really the PCs who bother me. Most PCs will take you for
who you are. The advice I give probationers, whatever their
colour, is, get on with the most macho person on your team. If
they say jump, ask, how high? That way, you've got no problems.
You can be a totally useless worker, but if you get on with the

team, the sergeant will write you up well. As you get more experienced, you get more confident. If you're not desperate for promotion, you don't have to toe the party line.

Some white Kilburn officers disclosed an awareness of racism which also marked a departure from the account provided by the PSI report. A sergeant of more than twenty-five years' experience described a period as a drugs intelligence officer in Harlesden. 'I realised I was having to fight my own prejudice, because doing drugs work in Harlesden, you can get to the stage where you see all the blacks as villains. Blacks control the crack trade and you can find yourself thinking they're all at it. That is the point to ask for a move.'

I do not want to sound too starry-eyed. In the spring of 1995, the Metropolitan Police disclosed statistics showing that black people were much more likely than whites to be stopped on the street. Only one tenth of stops produced a criminal charge, and some of these were not for substantive crimes which might have justified the stop, such as possessing drugs, a weapon or stolen property, but for minor public order offences arising from the stop itself.

At the end of June, Sir Paul Condon appeared to play to the more reactionary elements within his own force when the media were leaked a letter he wrote to black 'community leaders', inviting them to a meeting to discuss the fact that a high proportion – in some areas, more than three-quarters – of street robbery victims claimed their assailants were black. The basis for the figures in the leaked letter was never properly explained, and for several weeks, as controversy raged around him, Sir Paul said nothing in public to clarify his intentions. Meanwhile, Home Secretary Michael Howard capitalised on the furore with enthusiasm, allowing the *Daily Express* to lead its front page with the headline: 'Black Crime: I back Commissioner – Howard.'

A few weeks earlier, Granada TV's *World in Action* filmed a group of police officers from North-west England stamping and cheering at a performance by the racist comedian Bernard Manning. The evidence for the persistence of police racism is pervasive. Nevertheless, it is my belief that it *is* possible to reduce, and even eliminate it, and that in some inner city and county divisions, this is being achieved.

The PSI study argued that even officers who used extreme racist language, often treated black people fairly and politely in the streets. New research by Carolyn Hoyle at the Oxford Centre for Criminological Research draws analogous conclusions in the field of domestic violence.[14]

Canteen culture traditionally classes domestic violence as among the category of 'rubbish jobs', where the sole aim is to leave the scene as quickly as possible in order to be able to get on with some 'real policing'. According to the standard feminist critique, officers are unsympathetic, fail to make proper inquiries and are reluctant to prosecute.[15]

Hoyle was given access to the incident computer of a large county constabulary and so was able to investigate several hundred domestic violence cases over a seven month period. She traced and interviewed the officers involved, and in each case began by asking for comments on domestic violence in general. Here the replies fitted the cynical 'canteen' pattern. However, when asked the second question, 'what happened', the officers displayed a remarkable appreciation of the social circumstances of the couples involved.

For example, one officer began by saying he detested 'being a social worker when I'm out there doing a busy shift', because we 'haven't got time to try and find out what's gone wrong in these people's lives . . . I don't see why I should try to understand their marital problems when I've got enough of my own.' But asked about the particular incident which led Hoyle to him from the computer, he said: 'Her husband had been arrested on a previous occasion for actual bodily harm but she had withdrawn at a later date . . . They had only been married for one year. She's at the end of her tether. He drinks, doesn't have a job or help around the house. He just slobs around. He's very possessive. He drinks a lot and spends her money. He's been intimidating towards her and her two children.'

Another officer spoke of 'bloody domestics', complaining 'we just haven't got time to sit there and drink cups of tea while they talk about their problems'. At the incident in question, he seemed to have done just that, saying:

The history behind this relationship is very complicated. The man has been in and out of mental institutions for years. In one stay at a mental hospital he met his present girlfriend and occasionally he stays with her and then returns to his wife. His wife has experienced a lot of tragic incidents recently, including one child's cot death. One child of hers is mentally retarded and one baby with a heart complaint. As well as having to deal with the mental problems of the husband, who is a paranoid schizophrenic.

Yet most studies of police culture rely on police officer's own subjective accounts, and draw direct conclusions about their practice. Hoyle comments: 'They ask questions about how officers feel about the expectations of their performance; how they feel they respond and how they should respond.' By focusing on what actually happened, her work 'challenges the idea that behaviours are consistent with attitudes'.

I cannot suggest Kilburn division is typical. In 1994, its relatively enlightened atmosphere was fostered by the arrival of a new divisional chief, Chief Superintendent Paul Green. Policing is a job in which grumbling about superiors is normally endemic: Green was universally well-regarded both as a manager and police officer.

Some of its officers fully appreciated Kilburn's differences from other parts of London. A female officer said:

I began at a central London division where the old culture flourished. You treated new people like shit, as an initiation; and it was very macho, even among the women – hard drinking after every shift, even night duty, in the pubs at Smithfield market. They used to say I couldn't enforce the law: the truth was, I didn't like sticking people on for things I do myself all the time, like driving without a seatbelt. After that, this was a breath of fresh air.

These signs of progress, in an inner city area with high levels of serious crime, must be taken as signs of hope. Better practice and more tolerant attitudes are not impossible. They already exist.

★ ★ ★

The necessary conditions for changing police culture from below are external: the law, and the incentive of cash. But the fourth element outlined above cannot be neglected: top level policy, which since the early 1980s has fostered an ideology of reform. In sharp contrast to the thinking of earlier decades, this ideology has been largely self-generated. Senior police progressives have been influenced by external stimuli: hostile media campaigns, and as we shall see, the trauma of inner city riots. Yet their responses have developed within the service, not been imposed from without, and it is within the service that the progressives have had to fight and win important battles for their colleagues' hearts and minds.

This has not always been easy. To officers schooled in the police culture of the 1950s and 60s, the idea of dialogue with police critics was anathema. Chester Sterne, crime correspondent for the *Mail on Sunday*, joined the Metropolitan Police as one of its first civilian press officers in 1966. 'People simply didn't think about the place of the police in society and their relationship to it,' he says, 'their attitude was, "we're police officers, for God's sake!". The senior officers were ex-military and they drank gin and tonic. The PCs were artisans, who kept Britain in line.'

The response the organisation had to the criticism which began to burgeon from the end of the 1960s was to dig itself more deeply into the bunker. Sterne says: 'You work for the *Observer*. At that time, you would have been regarded with the most intense suspicion – virtually a Marxist.'

As he purged the CID, Sir Robert Mark consciously tried to enlist the help of the media, and adopted a policy of unprecedented access to the press. But in most of the service, fundamental attitudes remained unchanged. When Sir David McNee took over as Metropolitan Commissioner in 1977, access to the press decreased again and the link between the police and the outside world was broken. The police were attracting escalating criticism: for fabricating verbals, financial corruption, overreacting to demonstrations, and for criminalising black youths through the 'sus' law. In much of the country during this period, there was a stock response: the lawyers, newspapers and community groups who questioned what the police were doing were 'unrepresentative'.

Rather than seeking dialogue, both leadership and rank-and-file reacted to their critics with head-on confrontation. In the late 1970s and early 1980s, the Police Federation, representing ranks up to chief inspector, intervened repeatedly in the runs-up to elections with high-profile 'law and order' media campaigns, using language deliberately modelled on Tory political rhetoric.

The apotheosis of the polarisation between the Left and the police came in 1982, in a speech by James Anderton, the former Greater Manchester Chief Constable. He accused critics of the service of being the masterminds of a 'quiet revolution taking place around us', its goal 'political power to be wielded against the most cherished elements of the establishment, including the monarchy'. According to Anderton, 'it is as much the duty of the police to guard against this as it is to guard against crime. I sense and see in our midst an enemy more dangerous, insidious and ruthless than any faced since the Second World War.'

Looking back at the late 1970s, the progressive senior officers of the 1990s shudder. 'It was the decade of death in police thinking,' says Commander Michael Briggs of the Metropolitan Police. 'There was a sense of security which was utterly false. It was partly the fault of the Tory media, which was generally boosting us with constant "thin blue line" headlines. The idea of strategic thinking about policing, crime and disorder was totally absent.'

Then came the climacteric: the inner city riots of 1981, and the following year's inquiry report by the great liberal jurist, Lord Scarman.

At the core of Scarman's report were two crucial principles: that police should consult the communities they policed, and be accountable to them for their actions. Accountability, Scarman said, 'renders the police answerable for what they do. Thereby it prevents them from slipping into an enclosed fortress of inward thinking and social isolation which would, in the long term, result in a siege mentality – the police in their fortress (happy as long as it is secure) and the rest of us outside, unhappy, uncertain and insecure (for we do not know what they will know, or how they will do it).'[16]

Scarman did not coin the term 'community policing'. It was the main theme of one of his most impressive witnesses, John Alderson, Chief Constable of Devon and Cornwall. But his report insisted that the principles applied by Alderson in the lanes and villages of the rural South-west were equally important for the future successful policing of Brixton, Toxteth and Mosside. According to Paul Whitehouse, now Chief Constable of Sussex after a career spent mainly in the North of England, 'some of us had been applying Scarman's principles before he stated them for a long time'.[17] In a sense, community policing was no more than a restatement of the vanishing Dixon ideal.

In the big cities, Scarman commented, senior officers had been wont to claim that 'the demand for community policing ignores the harsh realities of crime'. He went on: 'Policing is, however, too complex a job to be viewed in terms of a simple dichotomy between "hard" and "soft" policing styles. Community policing – which I understand to mean policing with the active consent and support of the community – is too important a concept to be treated as a slogan.' Policing by consent could not be put into a separate box marked 'community relations'.

In the space of a few paragraphs, Lord Scarman launched the policing equivalent of the hunt for the holy grail. The search for viable means of establishing community policing came to dominate national debate both inside and outside the service for years to come.

Concealed within this quest, two distinct approaches can be discerned, mirroring Scarman's two principles of consent and accountability. The first is technical: the attempt through techniques of management to develop a closer relationship between the police and public – to form a 'partnership'. The second is a more fundamental change, and requires more than a shift in attitudes: ultimately, it needs alterations to the constitutional position of the police. It boils down to the *democratic* reworking of those old and basic questions: what is the service ultimately for, and whom is it supposed to serve?

It is beyond the compass of this book to chart the many twists and turns involved in the technical side of this search. The future historian who attempts to write a definitive account will need a thorough grasp of management theory and jargon. In the 1980s, the police fell in love with 'systems analysis', and the primary sources, their tomes and policy papers, are characterised by bewildering diagrams and impenetrable prose. The seminal volume was a doctoral thesis by Ian Beckett and James Hart, two inspectors in the Metropolitan and Surrey forces, which was completed in the summer of 1981, at the same time as the riots took place. With its references to 'ideographic and nomothetic methodological approaches', and octopus-like flow diagrams of 'inputs to and outputs from activity of resource appraisals', much of it surpasses the present writer's understanding.[18]

There was no greater enthusiast for such work than Kenneth Newman, who became Metropolitan Police Commissioner in 1982. A former head of the Bramshill staff college, his national influence was immense. He enjoyed a warm relationship with Margaret Thatcher.

His aims, set out in his annual reports, were to restore public confidence by insisting that officers observe due process, and to achieve public consent by making the police 'professional'. Consent, he said, depended on 'the legitimacy – both actual and perceived – of the methods used by the police to discharge their mandate'. The style of policing had to be 'consonant with the demands of an energetic and vigorous democracy'.[19] He cited Scarman with approval on many occasions, and in an attempt to gain the support of the force, effected a radical organisational shake-up. Big areas of inefficiency were eliminated, and lines of command shortened. He introduced a new, formal system of 'planning by objectives'.

Newman believed his ideas would permeate police culture through 'cascading' – a trickle-down of ideas from the Scotland Yard experts to the canteen. He also issued a code of ethics to every officer, the Handbook of Guidance for Professional Behaviour. Unfortunately, it contained all-too-typical examples of deadening management jargon, and as Tom Williamson writes, ended up by reinforcing a sense of alienation between 'street cops' and 'management cops'.[20] Among his more prominent strictures was an attempt to eradicate freemasonry, which had for decades wielded a vast and secret influence, especially in the CID. Within weeks of his edict being issued, the Metropolitan masons formed a special new lodge, whose members included some of the cream of Scotland Yard.

Meanwhile, Newman's staff, who were struggling to implement the 'community policing' ideal, were experiencing difficulty. The 1986 Metropolitan Police internal appraisal document commented plaintively that the word 'community' had acquired 'halo status', adding: 'There are difficulties in forming policy around a term that begs definition. For the vast majority, irrespective of their racial, social or economic status, it represents little more than a collective attempt to lead a private life.'

It went on to cite a MORI opinion poll, which found that most people left their communities well alone. Only 5 per cent had attended a tenants' or residents' meeting in the previous twelve months, 3 per cent a council meeting, and 13 per cent a community centre or social club. Even these figures were inflated by the greater community participation of higher income groups: the 'involved' people were mainly 'middle-aged, middle-class, working full time, owner occupiers'.[21]

A key element in the Newman strategy became known as the 'multi-agency' approach, in which the community was to be encouraged to 'police itself'. One vital building block was the establishment of the Neighbourhood Watch schemes, which began to mushroom in this period. Another was the setting-up of community-police consultative groups, consisting of police, councils and local voluntary groups. In 1984, these were legally enshrined by PACE.

It was no accident that both Neighbourhood Watch and the consultative groups had most significance among precisely the same higher income groups who were already, as the MORI poll showed, most likely to have some 'community' involvement. It did not help that the groups were boycotted for several years by hard-Left Labour councils. Nevertheless, Newman's pseudo-democracy rapidly became most effective where it was arguably least needed – in the affluent middle-class suburbs. To this day, consultative group meetings tend to be dominated by established local organisations, and rarely reflect the views of those most affected by the rough end of the policing – the young, disadvantaged and ethnic minorities.

If the local police chiefs who attend the groups have an enlightened attitude and are prepared to listen to their critics, they can be a valuable way of taking soundings, and of letting grievances be aired. But as a means of achieving police accountability, their scope is extremely limited. They can be ignored, and they do not involve any transfer of power.[22]

At the heart of the technical approach to the community policing ideal has been a series of attempts to alter the priorities of patrol officers by reorganising their shifts. This dates back to Beckett and Hart, and has become known as 'sector policing'.

Various local experiments were tried throughout the 1980s; here and there, when enough personnel and money were behind them, they enjoyed a measure of success. The idea is that within every division, officers should develop a relationship with the people of small 'sectors' of the community, allowing them to shift the emphasis of their work away from so-called 'fire brigade' policing, which merely reacts to events. Unfortunately, it is impossible to do away with the latter: there will always be emergency calls – burglaries, murders, fights and road traffic accidents.

The experience of the Kilburn division illustrates the extent to which these demands can frustrate the most sophisticated managerial intentions. Along with the rest of the Metropolitan Police, it was for years organised on the basis of four rotating 'reliefs' (shifts) plus a cadre of specialist 'home beat officers'. The latter had no need to answer emergency calls, and were supposed to get to know the community in the widest sense – in roles ranging from the gathering of criminal intelligence to giving lectures in schools.

In 1992, the whole of the Metropolitan Police tried to move to sector policing at once. The old reliefs were split into much smaller teams, each of which was given responsibility (or in management jargon, 'ownership') for a sector of the ground. The home beat officers were abolished: the new teams would fulfil their former role, by spending much of their time rostered on to day shifts. Instead of the former handful of home beat constables, everyone in uniform would spend a large part of their time as a community police officer.

Eighteen months after it started, the experiment was largely abandoned in Kilburn. The new teams were so small that in the evenings and at night, always the busiest time for emergencies, there might only be five or six officers available to respond to calls. In an area such as Harlesden, with its large, dangerous council estates, frequent street robberies and drug-related violence, this was dangerously thin. Instead of spending their extra day shifts on community work, officers found themselves catching up on the endless mountains of paperwork. In the words of one sergeant, 'by redeploying the old home beat officers, we actually lost eighteen months of community contact, and the priceless intelligence that could provide'.

At the start of 1994 the number of Kilburn sectors was reduced from four to three, allowing for the formation of bigger teams, and the shift pattern changed again. The home beat officers were effectively reconstituted, in the shape of specialist 'community action teams'. In some divisions, the scrapping of sector policing went further, with a return to the old relief system, in exactly the same mould as before.

It would be wrong to suggest that the changes of the Newman era failed absolutely to move towards the Scarman ideal of policing by consent. In some more specialised areas, police practice was transformed. After Roger Graef's pathbreaking TV documentary series, *Police*, showed the harsh treatment of a Thames Valley rape victim, police in most regions devised new and more sensitive methods to deal with the victims of sexual offences. One field in which the 'multi-agency' approach was notably effective was in the formation of child protection teams to deal with violent and sexual abuse. They worked closely with local authorities and other agencies. Less dramatic but still measurable progress was achieved with various crime-prevention initiatives, and also against racial violence, again with multi-agency support.

Nevertheless, leaving aside their unintelligible vocabulary, the Newman reforms were hampered by a deeper flaw. On the night of 6 October 1985, they met their Waterloo: the riot at Broadwater Farm in Tottenham, and the savage, bloody killing of PC Keith Blakelock. Tottenham came less than a month after rioting in Handsworth in Birmingham, which saw an entire shopping street reduced to smoking rubble and two men burnt alive; and the murder of a photographer in another riot in Brixton after officers shot an innocent black woman by mistake. The failure to realise Scarman's vision had been underlined in the most dramatic way: by the renewal in still more violent form of the same inner city violence which had inspired it.

PC Blakelock, a popular home beat officer who worked in the middle-class suburb of Muswell Hill, was hacked and stabbed fifty-four times. He and a handful of similarly ill-prepared colleagues were chased and attacked by a mob, when they went into the Broadwater

Farm estate at the height of the riot to protect firemen. His death triggered an unprecedented crisis of police morale. Senior officers found themselves under attack on two fronts, external and internal, for catastrophic operational failures on the night, and for their support for allegedly 'soft' community policing following Scarman's report.

Rank-and-file opinion was summarised by an editorial in the Police Federation journal, *Police*. It was headed 'Scarmanised!' and claimed: 'Compromise and the avoidance of confrontation only leads to disaster. This is the time to reassert the primacy of the rule of law. Senior officers must, from now on, do that which is right, rather than which is expedient.' A few days after the riot, Newman faced the wounding humiliation of being booed and heckled at a Federation meeting.

An article in *Police Review* magazine suggested that the political polarisation expressed by James Anderton three years earlier had not diminished. Headed 'Gradually Losing the War with the Left,' it said the police had lost a propaganda battle being fought against them by 'vacillating politicians, indifferent legislators, naïve senior police officers, and ably assisted by judges and magistrates'. It had produced 'the new fad, the latest in-word – racism – and the blanket catch-all smear which goes with it'. Its author hoped he would never again see 'weakness displayed towards the criminals within the ethnic community', and that senior officers would restore their ebbing grip on 'those renegade sections of society'.[23]

A few months later, in his 1985 report, Newman tried to tackle these critics. He warned against the 'war' analogy, saying it would lead the police to identify parts of the community as an 'enemy sub-culture, with all the mutual antipathy, convenient stereotypes and recrimination of a war setting. The alienation of a "war" footing will reduce public support.' He added: 'The long term danger will lie in our becoming hardened and brutalised, thus encouraging both selective recruitment and training policies to intensify that drift.'[24]

Belatedly, he was right. But Newman had sowed the wind and reaped the whirlwind. His vision of community policing by consent had always contained fatal limitations. It was, by definition, exclusive and authoritarian.

Newman had been Chief Constable of the Royal Ulster

Constabulary, and when he took over as the mainland's most senior policeman, he made the grave error of equating the fight against terrorism with the fight against crime in the inner city. In an address to the European Atlantic Group in 1983 he said: 'There are two particular problems in the Western societies which have the potential to affect the balance between order and freedom. The first problem is concerned with the growth of multi-ethnic communities. The second is related to indigenous terrorist movements engaging in terrorism to promote separatism or an extreme ideology.'

Both might require sacrifices to due process and civil liberties: 'Individual liberties are important, but we must not become so obsessed by them that we overlook the importance of communal freedom and security.'

The challenge to order presented by the multi-ethnic inner city was concentrated around a number of 'symbolic locations', he said – places such as Broadwater Farm and Railton Road in Brixton, the so-called 'front line'. In these types of areas, he stated that 'unemployed youths, often black youths congregate', and 'the sale and purchase of drugs, the exchange of stolen property and illegal drinking and gaming is not unknown. The youths regard these locations as their territory. Police are viewed as intruders, the symbol of authority . . . they equate closely with the Dickensian rookeries of Victorian London.'

The facts of this account were broadly accurate. But this analysis of them was a strange way of implementing Scarman's prescription that to police such places effectively required accountability to local people. In this speech, which in the years before Broadwater Farm he echoed repeatedly elsewhere, Newman's approach was redolent of precisely the 'convenient stereotypes' of an 'enemy subculture' which he later came to condemn.

In another revealing passage from the same speech, he suggested the 'multi-agency' approach was little more than a means of extending the range and number of coercive agencies in play, with the police retaining the leading role. It was implicitly anti-democratic: 'It is not sufficient to think only in terms of crime control. We need to lift the problems to a higher level of generality, encompassed by the expression "social control" in a benign sense, in order to provide a unifying concept within which the activities of police and other agencies can be co-ordinated.'

Critics of police in the fraught inner city could not be taken at face value, Newman suggested, for it was there that 'political agitators exploit civil liberties issues, play down the issue of general communal security and make it difficult to promote that sense of security and confidence that is the precondition for economic investment'. He called for obligatory identity cards, a requirement that everyone inform the government of their place of residence, and the keeping of government files on individuals' employment, income, education, hospital treatment and mental health. These draconian measures would not, he claimed, affect the 'core freedoms' of parliamentary democracy.

Possibly Newman modified his opinions in the light of Broadwater Farm. These earlier comments do not sit easily with his later rejection of the 'war' model. They do, however, conform very closely with the description of policing proposed by Malcolm Young – as a 'social construction geared to the maintenance of élitist power', and as a 'socio-political tool of the state and government'.

The extent to which the political ideology of senior police officers influences activity on the streets is a subject which needs research. Most of the PCs who stopped black motorists on the flimsiest of pretexts in the early 1980s would not have read Newman's speeches. But they gave a dismal lead, which would have been picked up enthusiastically by senior and middle-ranking officers who found in them messages they wanted to hear. Paul Condon's leaked letter about black street robbers in the summer of 1995 may have had similar effects.

They also contained an element of self-fulfilling prophecy. The idea of 'symbolic locations' was an extraordinary inflation of the binary world-view of traditional police culture: slags and victims, them and us; whole areas within and outside the norms of a democratic polity. It was an invitation to police these locations as if engaged in some low intensity warfare, and ran the deadly risk that the people of the 'rookeries' might retaliate in kind.

Newman, however, was a man of his time. If he did not challenge the characterisation of the police force as the tool of state and élitist power, many others shared the exact same view. Conservative politicians were normally too cautious to state such a view openly. But the memoirs of Sir Ian MacGregor, who led the National Coal Board against the bitter 1984–5 miners' strike, are a different matter.

Soon after the beginning of the strike, he says, he had to go and see Margaret Thatcher to complain about the police, and told her: 'I never thought I would be sitting here in the UK, wishing I had a bunch of good untidy American cops out there. Because, whatever you say about them, if someone points out a law is being broken, then they go and do something about it. Unhappily, I must tell you that our British police don't seem to have the same conviction about their job.'

In Derbyshire and Nottinghamshire, 'the police seemed unable or unwilling to intervene'. This was not a struggle between the National Coal Board and the union but between 'men who want to work and a bunch of thugs'. MacGregor goes on: 'After that session in the Prime Minister's study – and very quickly indeed – the National Reporting Centre at Scotland Yard was brought to life.' (This was a mechanism for deploying thousands of police officers to mining areas from other parts of the country.) 'The national organisation of squads of riot-trained police had never been required on this scale before and there were many predictable left-wing expressions of alarm about it. But all their protests begged the question: what was the country supposed to do? Lie down and let Scargill walk all over it?'

Here was a massive usurpation of local police accountability by a government which had to defeat the miners at any cost. Anyone who travelled to Nottinghamshire during the strike will not forget the consequences. The sheer numbers of police deployed in the area presented an awesome spectacle. They did not confine themselves to maintaining order at each picketed pithead, but mounted vast pre-emptive operations which pushed at the frontiers of legality. Pickets were stopped from taking part in perfectly lawful activity by roadblocks at every major junction, on the dubious grounds that this would prevent a breach of the peace.

The police were not the only local criminal justice agency which appeared to cede all normal local mechanisms of control to the central state. In Magistrates' Courts, where sometimes hundreds of minor public order charges would be heard in a single day, the Bail

Act's stipulation that each case must be considered on its own merits was totally ignored. In case after case, defendants were granted bail on the basis of stringent, identical conditions which had been typed and duplicated in advance. They amounted to a ban on the accused taking any future active part in picketing or the strike, on pain of summary imprisonment.

Even this was not enough for MacGregor: he complains of a 'pattern of leniency' in magistrates' punishment of pickets, and a 'sinister lack of will'. He also had to remain vigilant against police backsliding: 'After that meeting with the Prime Minister, the general attitude of the police changed . . . we only heard of isolated incidents of forces not wishing to be involved in such duties.' Nevertheless, 'from time to time I would pass on what you might call complaints about soft spots in the police coverage to the Department of Energy'. He was in little doubt why some police lacked backbone – 'politically-orientated police committees'.[25]

Those committees, the police authorities of councillors and magistrates who controlled budgets and chose constables, in fact found themselves virtually powerless to resist, as the government juggernaut rolled on. In the so-called tripartite relationship of Home Office, chief constable and police authority, they were the junior partner. The extreme difficulty experienced by local police authority chairs, such as Merseyside's Margaret Simey, in trying to modify the actions of chiefs such as Kenneth Oxford was now writ large on the national stage. Any progress towards Scarman's vision of local accountability could be simply overridden.

In mining areas, the police themselves had deep misgivings, as they found themselves required to confront, in some cases, their own friends and families. They were rapidly outnumbered. The thousands of officers working far from their constabularies were in a position not unlike the *Guardia Civil* under General Franco, who laid down as a matter of policy that officers should work at the other end of the country from their homes, so their actions would not be influenced by their community roots.

There was another hidden hand behind police operations in the miners' strike and other contemporary political conflicts besides that of Ian MacGregor. Throughout the 1980s, a body known as the

'Tiger Committee' met regularly in the Cabinet Office, its task, the monitoring of and reaction to 'domestic subversion'.

The committee, whose existence is revealed here for the first time, is chaired by a senior Home Office civil servant – normally the deputy secretary. Usually there would be about thirty people present: members of the Security Service MI5, the Secret Intelligence Service MI6, of the Metropolitan Police Special Branch, and a few 'ordinary' senior police officers from other parts of the country. Sometimes, when particular political crises loomed, officers might be called in on an *ad hoc* basis. However, before being allowed to attend, an officer would have to be 'brainwashed' – the highest level of positive vetting, involving an exhaustive trawl through his private and public life.

The general agenda in the eighties was the peace movement, industrial militancy and political activism. The row over the 1983 GCHQ trade union ban was a particular concern: the Government was petrified it might be forced to default on the international responsibilities stemming from its signals intelligence treaty with the United States, known as the UKUSA pact. Often the transcripts of phone-taps were produced and discussed. According to one officer who attended regularly: 'There was no doubt as far as the police on the committee were concerned that others present were far better informed about many things than we were. Our role was subordinate. But the committee's discussions often had direct operational consequences.' In London, its deliberations were relayed to the Metropolitan Police's own Internal Security Committee, which met every Friday in the Assistant Commissioner's office.

All electronic communications discussing Tiger were scrambled and documents went by personal courier. Meetings would typically be held with very little notice. There was 'almost a paranoia about the activities of the hard Left,' the officer said, 'an obsessive quest to discover if it was a conspiracy, or if events occurred without being brought together by any particular organisation'. Tiger endlessly picked over the personal details of the peace movement's leadership: Rebecca Johnson from the Greenham Common airbase peace-camp, and Joan Ruddock and Bruce Kent from the Campaign for Nuclear Disarmament.

As for MI5 in this period, the officer commented: 'I thought they

were barking mad. They were neo-fascist in their views. They were
sold: and viewed anyone who challenged the authority of the state in
any way at all as subversive. They saw that as their patriotic duty.'

The Tiger Committee still exists. Its more recent meetings have
been preoccupied with animal rights extremism; protests against the
export of veal calves; and direct-action campaigns to prevent
the building of new roads, as at Twyford Down in Hampshire and the
M11 extension in London. In 1992, MI5 was given the 'lead role' in
intelligence gathering against Ulster terrorism, creating a day-to-day
relationship with the police which was closer than ever before. Aside
from this, at any one time two officers from Scotland Yard are on
attachment to MI5 as a permanent point of liaison.

★   ★   ★

While the miners' strike revealed the feeble nature of police
accountability in the face of a Prime Minister such as Margaret
Thatcher, it had a galvanising effect among a rising cadre of liberal
senior police officers. According to Commander Michael Briggs of
the Metropolitan Police:

> An awful lot of work had gone into convincing the troops that
> community policing was the way forward, and that this depended
> on the stability of teams. Suddenly officers were being told:
> 'Report for the coach on Sunday morning for picket duty at
> Manvers Main.' The Government, through our own senior
> people, was saying the strike reigns supreme, even if that means
> you've only got three people left for late turn.
>
> It had to be policed, and policed effectively. But I knew at the
> time it would be an aberration, the negation of a great deal of
> progress which had been made. Suddenly we were right back to
> fire brigade policing, to civil defence policing. And there were
> psychological factors. Our people were living in Nissan huts, in
> buildings unfit for habitation, facing strange and hostile situations,
> where the only strength they had was each other.

After the miners' strike came the equally violent year of
confrontation, 1986–7, with pickets outside Rupert Murdoch's

News International plant. Commander Alex Marnoch, who recently retired after a career which embraced both the controversial Special Patrol Group and heading the Brixton force, said:

> After the miners' strike, Wapping and the 1985 riots I had a feeling we were spinning out of control. When officers came back from the mining areas, some of us tried to get them time off, give them counselling. They had been in a barrack room environment: up at three or four in the morning, fighting with ordinary working people. If we let them come straight back to work in London, their immediate tendency was to go out and crack a few heads.[26]

With the policing bit between its teeth, the Government was reluctant to let go. In 1986, the City of London Anti-Apartheid Group stepped up its regular protests outside the South African Embassy in Trafalgar Square. Marnoch and the demonstrators made an agreement about the location and organisation of the picket, but the Ambassador protested to the Foreign Office, arguing it gave them too much space and latitude. Marnoch said:

> I was summoned to a meeting with senior civil servants from the Foreign Office and the Home Office, and told the agreement had to be scrapped. I refused, saying this was an unconstitutional attempt to interfere with a police operation. I was not going to ban demonstrators. When I was at Brixton before 1985, as Commander of L District, a senior Home Office official tried to tell me, 'Speak to me, not the Commissioner.' There was an increasing tendency from the early eighties on to bring pressure to bear.

Other significant figures found themselves instinctively recoiling from this attempted politicisation. Richard Wells, now Chief Constable of West Yorkshire, said: 'In the miners' strike, we presented ourselves as holding the ring between equal and opposing forces, and trying to distance ourselves from each. But when the chief constables made arrests to stop pickets on their way to, as they saw it, scenes or crime, I don't think they had thought through what the other view of that might have been.'[27]

Just as the Edmund-Davies award brought great changes in the nature and culture of police recruits, the progressive tendency among the leadership of the service was also beginning to emerge. After the Second World War, both provincial chief constables and the Metropolitan Police's senior echelon were mostly representatives of an 'officer class' who had been groomed, Sandhurst-style, at a special training college abolished in 1939. Primacy of service to the social élite and government was an instinctive reaction.

However, by the 1970s, in both London and the provinces, a new generation was working its way through the system. Its members had all started 'on the beat', and many of them had acquired a university education along the way – Marnoch at the London School of Economics, Briggs at Oxford. They found they could hold their own both academically and socially. Briggs recalled: 'I went to Oxford with great trepidation. I was in my mid-thirties, the first policeman ever to attend my college. I ended up running the college disco; they wanted me to run the junior common room. The discipline side used to ask me for advice – how should they deal with mindless criminal damage? I advised them to patrol the college on Friday nights: and the first one caught should be kicked out.'

A few had entered the service as graduates. Richard Wells joined the Metropolitan Police in 1962, with a First in Modern Languages from Oxford. Paul Whitehouse, Chief Constable of Sussex, joined the Durham force in 1967 – the first Cambridge graduate to join the police since 1948.

Whitehouse made clear his reluctance to accept the old shibboleths of policing from the beginning of his career. Within a year of joining the service, he demonstrated that a degree was not a bar to acceptance by his colleagues when he was elected as his local Police Federation representative. Not long afterwards, after getting married, he challenged one of the many extraordinary rules which typified the old style of police management, which said that officers of the Durham constabulary could not buy a house until they had completed twenty-five years of service: 'I was told I couldn't live in my house because we had bought it. I was hauled up before the assistant chief constable and then the deputy: I said, my wife intends to live there, and are you going to stop me living with her? They changed the rules.'

Rising educational standards among police officers at all levels has a distinct effect on their own perceived social status. Commander Briggs said:

> In the sixties, the management was astonished that anyone with A levels would want to do constabulary duty. People saw policing as a social status move, in the sense that they hoped their children would not have to do police work. By the seventies, officers whose kids weren't hacking it academically were beginning to put them through the old cadet system. In the eighties, senior officers' children, who had excellent educations, were joining as recruits. This was a big shift, accelerated by Edmund-Davies: from seeing policing as a working-class, low status job to the point where they would be proud for their kids to be constables. There is a whole story here about growing confidence and economic power.

This story has a cultural subtext which has nothing directly to do with policing. The TV drama character Inspector Morse is interesting because he confounds the common stereotype of the artisan Mr Plod: his house is filled with books, and he listens to opera. In general, however, police officers' leisure time is supposed to be taken up with nothing more taxing than drinking or football, or at a certain level of seniority, golf. The reality is different: I whiled away one quiet Kilburn nightshift discussing aspects of two personal passions, mountaineering and modern jazz.

Disquiet at the use the government made of the service in the 1980s is one route to emerging police radicalism. Class awareness is another.

A Kilburn sergeant, a reader not of the *Sun* but the *Financial Times*, said:

> I was in a pub in Harpenden the other day and a solicitor was holding court about a friend of his, an accountant, who'd been arrested for fraud at five o'clock in the morning. He wanted to know why we couldn't have simply made an appointment to see him. To stop him shredding the bloody evidence, that's why. As far as he was concerned it was totally outrageous: what made us

think we could treat his chum as a common criminal, even when
he may have committed criminal offences?

In the summer of 1992, the then Home Secretary Kenneth Clarke
invited reporters for drinks. Earlier that week, Robert Maxwell's son
Kevin had been arrested. Clarke, a criminal barrister turned
politician, could not contain his anger. It was 'disgraceful', he said,
that 'someone like that' should have had to be woken at 6 a.m. by
police; warming to his theme, he recalled the equally dreadful
spectacle of the convicted Guinness fraudster Gerard Ronson being
forced to wear handcuffs. The police, he said, no longer knew their
proper place. A few weeks later, he went public with this theme,
complaining about officers' lack of respect for the decent folk of
'middle-England'.

His comments drew a furious response from Sir Peter Imbert,
Commissioner of the Metropolitan Police. Addressing the London
International Police Exhibition and Conference, he accused Clarke
and his middle-Englanders as being totally out of touch with the
realities of policing and criminal justice. Their wealth and privilege
allowed tham to 'live, shop, and socialise in relatively comfortable
surroundings . . . an existence mostly, but not wholly, sanitised from
the impact of crime'. Such people wanted guarantees of safety, but
were unprepared to recognise the escalating demands on the police.
They had no interest beyond the statistical clear-up rate, because
they had 'prospered under a political credo where quantitative
outputs are all'.

Imbert went on to deliver a stinging rebuke. 'It has been observed
that these middle-Englanders have a role to play in making the laws
of the land, yet they may also be content to break them when
convenient: perhaps ignoring a motorway speed limit; walking the
narrow line between tax evasion and avoidance; or "neglecting" to
pay a fare if the opportunity arises.' It was all very well for middle-
England to bemoan mounting crime figures and police ineffectiveness. But it failed to link them to 'a society and criminal justice
system' which were the ultimate cause of both.[28]

From a Metropolitan Police Commissioner, these were radical
words. The police, he was saying, are not there to serve the state or
the social élite: but the entire citizenry. To underline the due process

principle of equality before the law, he was prepared to tackle a Conservative Home Secretary directly.

By the time he made this speech, after five years as Commissioner, Imbert was near retirement. The legal, constitutional frameworks to police accountability had not changed. But the period saw a certain coming-of-age among police progressives, and the expression of fresh, democratic attitudes which were the antithesis of most of what had gone before. The idea that the basic job of the police was to serve the élite and state was coming under attack from the most surprising of sources: the leadership of the service.

As Robert Storch put it in relation to the arrival of the 'new police' to the industrial North in the 1840s, 'the implantation of a modern police . . . resulted from a new consensus among the propertied classes that it was necessary to create a professional, bureaucratically organised lever of urban discipline and permanently introduce it into the heart of working class communities'. Their role, as seen by Storch and the substantial research tradition which he represents, was as much political as legal: 'The coming of the new police represented a significant extension . . . of both the moral and political authority of the state.'[29]

Applied to David Powis's field manual, with its ravings about left-wing 'drop-outs', or to the events of the miners' strike, the conclusions Storch drew about mid-Victorian England seem just as appropriate to the late twentieth century. But by 1987, as Imbert took over at Scotland Yard, he and some senior colleagues in London and the counties believed the police had reached an impasse, from which the only way out was a root-and-branch reinterpretation of their purpose. Imbert says:

The police had gone through an incredibly difficult period and the service was in danger of losing its whole identity. The caricature of the police officer was no longer the bucolic bobby on his bicycle but the riot-trained officer in his NATO helmet. We needed to reaffirm what we were in business for. The Conservative view is that we were there to defend the rich against the poor. In my own mind, I think we should be policing for and on behalf of the public, not against them. We are not a political tool, and we shouldn't be used as one.[30]

On his appointment, Imbert was seen as a safe pair of hands. He had been Sir Kenneth Newman's deputy for the latter part of his tenure, and maintained a low profile. Much of his early career had been spent in the Special Branch, Britain's political police. Later, in 1975, as a bomb squad superintendent, he talked the Balcombe Street IRA gang out of their week-long hostage siege. There was just one sign of his incipient radicalism – his decision as Chief Constable of Thames Valley to give Roger Graef's camera team untrammelled access to policing on the streets, in the cells and interview rooms.

One of Imbert's first acts as Commissioner was to engage Wolff Ollins, a consultancy firm, to produce a study of the Metropolitan Police. Its report, which with typical openness Imbert had published in August 1988, was filled with criticism. There was 'no corporate identity', it said. The Metropolitan Police was an organisation characterised by splits – between junior and senior officers, and police and civilian staff; between the uniform branch and CID. Patrol officers, who came into most frequent contact with the public, were regarded with widespread contempt – in the words of one of the study's anonymous interviewees, 'what's on the streets tends to be the residue'. Many senior officers were 'struggling to manage', and spent little time talking to their staff. Their subordinates were 'wary' and often needlessly aggressive, both with each other and the public.[31]

The result was the 'Plus Programme', a vast and disparate attempt to change not only the philosophy of policing but many of its technical details. Its heart was a new 'mission statement', known as the Statement of Common Purpose and Values. Its most radical signal was contained in a dozen words in its final paragraph: 'We must strive to reduce the fears of the public and, so far as we can, to reflect their priorities in the action we take. We must respond to well-founded criticism with a willingness to change.' Here was explicit recognition that the public ought to be the determinants of policing, not merely its passive objects. At the same time, Imbert imposed a symbolic semantic shift. Henceforth, his organisation was not to be described as a police 'force'. In new logos on cars, letterheads, posters, badges and buildings, it officially became the Metropolitan Police *Service*.

The ambitions of Plus were too great. It was an attempt to

revolutionise not only cultural attitudes but priorities and working methods. An organisation which had always been focused on measurable, quantitive outputs – arrest figures, crime clear-ups – was now being urged to put quality before quantity. A coercive 'force' was now to become a service in which the 'quality' which mattered most of all was that of its own relationship with the public. Sometimes, the finer points of this approach got lost in the transmission and it could boil down to little more than a vague exhortation to be polite, to be nice to people. Every officer and civilian worker attended a day-long seminar at which the philosoph-ical side of Plus was discussed. But while this was an impressive organisational feat, the skill of the seminar facilitators was bound to vary. Some of the officers who attended were already in sympathy with Plus's aims; it is questionable whether a day at a talking shop was likely to do much to erode internal opposition.

Moreover, aside from the philosophical statement, Plus had another eleven 'components', which were supposed to reform everything from police uniforms (with the replacement of the old serge tunics with pullovers and Gore-tex anoraks) to the labyrinth of official forms. Launched with a fanfare of trumpets in the internal Metropolitan Police newsletter, *The Job*, this side of Plus raised expectations that all police officers' material problems were about to be solved at once. Many never were: when Plus came to an end, the Metropolitan Police was still, for example, using an ancient radio system which has sometimes broken down in highly dangerous situations – most notably, at Broadwater Farm. Paul Whitehouse raises another objection: 'Why did they call it a programme? Programmes are finite. You want something that will last forever.'

Nevertheless, there were measurable advances. Imbert set up a special Plus unit to implement its principles, led by Alex Marnoch. A lifelong supporter of the Labour Party, he was in instinctive sympathy with Plus's democratic impulse. Through Marnoch, Imbert put out feelers to the leaders of London's Labour councils. As their leaders began to visit Imbert at the Yard for regular beer and sandwiches, the Newman years of boycott and hostility gave way to a new *rapprochement*.

Some of the Metropolitan Police's most implacable political opponents were won over by this burgeoning charm offensive. In

1985, after PC Blakelock's murder, Bernie Grant, MP for Tottenham, notoriously commented the police had got a 'bloody good
hiding'. For years afterwards, he used to hold regular press
conferences, at which he would disclose details of horrendous local
abuses of police power. In 1993, in the week Imbert headed for
retirement, he appeared on a platform with Commander Perry
Nove, and appealed for witnesses to help the new investigation into
Blakelock's death set up after the Tottenham Three appeal. Later he
told me: 'We do not get the number of complaints about the police
we used to get in the past. They have become a lot more sensitive.
They are not perfect, but they are doing better. There is a different
approach, a degree of respect.'[32]

The mission statement's commitment to 'respond to well-
founded criticism' from the public was mirrored internally. Imbert
established a 'Commissioner's user group,' consisting of about thirty
officers at all ranks and civilian staff. Its monthly meetings – one of
which I attended – were characterised by an extraordinarily frank
exchange of views about the way the service was being run. At
divisional level, there were similar changes: at Kilburn, the
'divisional working party' was widely praised as a vehicle for
communicating grievances and problems from the 'ground floor'.
Plus also set in motion a series of changes to the system of promotion
and assessment. The patronage of local and area barons, who might
in some cases have been swayed by the influence of freemasonry, was
reduced.

The service ethic of Plus was eventually taken up by the
Association of Chief Police Officers, which adopted the mission
statement at national level. In some constabularies, its principles
remained no more than unrealised rhetoric. In others, reforming
chief constables developed their own, local variants with enthusiasm.

In South Yorkshire, Richard Wells sent out a powerful signal at
his first management meeting, when he stopped a chief superintendent from interrupting an officer junior – in the disciplined hierarchy
of South Yorkshire, this had been unheard of. South Yorkshire has
its own mission statement, which includes the exhortation:
'Remember that although the office of constable carries power and
authority, respect must be earned.'

'There was always a danger that Plus would be paid only lip service,' Imbert admits. In some areas and divisions, reactionary local chiefs did very little to translate its ethic into practice on the streets. But he adds: 'If you listen to what police officers say, you would think that it didn't work at all. Yet if you watch them over time, you will see that its values have got across, and that people can articulate things which once would have been considered cissy. If you probe a little, people will admit: "Yes, that has changed a bit, and so has this." And there will be something else, and something else.'

'The Plus seminar was a waste of a day,' a Kilburn sergeant said. In the next breath he added: 'But Plus did erode the "them and us" divisions in policing. It made us more ready to listen.' A PC made equally contradictory comments: 'To be honest, Plus was a load of rubbish. But it did make people stop and think. It made people realise that we couldn't carry on as a police force the way we were. We had to have consent, or at least the overwhelming majority's consent.'

In trying to achieve a cultural revolution from above, Plus overreached itself. It is doubtful whether such revolution would be possible without the kind of structural, external factors described above. Meanwhile, the constitutional limits to a redefinition of policing remain in place: Plus's essentially qualitative interpretation of public service depended on goodwill from the Government. In the early 1990s, this benevolence was abruptly withdrawn. But Plus gave progressive attitudes an official imprimatur, and it put the older 'canteen cowboys' on notice. With Plus and its provincial counterparts, the traditional police culture found itself squeezed from two directions: from the new breed of entrants, and from the reforming ideology of progressives at the top.

One day I was talking to a PC in Harlesden. At twenty-nine, he had two years' service: he had spent his early twenties as a manager for Ford. Like so many officers, he was expressing his frustration at the CPS, complaining that when minor problems needed ironing out in trivial magistrates' cases, he might waste hours of his time: 'These people won't take messages or return your calls,' he said, 'if you don't get straight through to the guy dealing with the case you may as well forget it. It's so bloody unprofessional – where is their quality of service?' He had never heard of Plus, but his words would warm Peter Imbert's heart.

By the mid-1980s, in some parts of the country, the police had taken on some of the characteristics of an occupying army. Few officers would now see that as a model to be espoused. Confrontation has come to be regarded as a sign not of virtue, but of failure. A Kilburn PC said:

When I started here ten years ago, we would go to the big Irish dance-halls on Kilburn High Road every Saturday and Sunday night and line up on the pavement – us on one side of the road, and the lads from West Hampstead division on the other. We were there to intimidate. The first drunk would come out and we'd arrest him, and then it would start: a scrap, a free-for-all. You could be as rude and aggressive as you liked. That has all changed. We go to the High Road if there is an emergency. Otherwise, we live and let live.

CHAPTER SEVEN

Policing the Police

AT THE end of July 1994, Mr Justice McKinnon gave judgment in the matter of Derek John Treadaway versus the Chief Constable of the West Midlands. This was an old case, dating back to Treadaway's arrest on Maundy Thursday, 1982, but the police had tried to prevent it being heard at all, and years of preliminary argument had taken the proceedings up to the Court of Appeal and back again.[1]

Throughout the entire period, Treadaway had been telling an extraordinary story. He said that five police officers came to his cell at Bromford Lane police station in Birmingham, cuffed his hands behind his back so that he was helpless, then drove him to the brink of suffocation by placing sealed plastic bags over his head. He said he had blacked out, and then, fearful for his life, agreed to sign a confession to four armed robberies he did not commit. At his trial at Leicester Crown Court in 1983, the jury did not believe him. Mr Treadaway was convicted, and gaoled for fifteen years.

At the time he first made these allegations, Treadaway was twenty-seven. He had numerous previous convictions, mainly for thefts and other forms of dishonesty, but also two for assaults on policemen who had been trying to arrest him. But after being released from his last prison sentence in January 1978, he tried to reform. On several occasions thereafter, he was arrested by members of the West Midlands Serious Crime Squad, but he was never charged with an offence. Six days before his arrest in 1982, he and his wife, Susan, and their two children moved into a new house in the Hodge Hill area of Birmingham.

The Serious Crime Squad came for him again at 5.15 a.m. on 8 April 1982, as part of 'Operation Cat', an investigation into a number of robberies committed in 1979. Several suspects were arrested on

the same day, after being named in statements to police by Keith
Morgan, a professional criminal turned supergrass.

The officers who came to Treadaway's home were led by
Detective Inspector John Brown, accompanied by Detective
Constable Alan Pickering and Detective Sergeant Timothy Russell.
Treadaway was in bed with Susan when they arrived, and he put up
no resistance. The police let him get dressed. Treadaway told his
wife to call his solicitors, Glaisyers, a well-known local firm. As he
followed the officers down the stairs to a waiting squad car, he
shouted out their telephone number.

Treadaway and the detectives reached Bromford Lane police
station at 5.30 a.m. This was still four years before the Police and
Criminal Evidence Act came into force: there was no custody
sergeant to take responsibility for his detention and welfare, and no
statutory requirement to ensure his request for legal advice was met.
Treadaway was swiftly booked in and his details entered by a
uniformed officer on a 'persons in custody' sheet. His interrogation
began almost immediately, at 5.38 a.m. Messrs Brown, Pickering
and Russell were all present. According to Treadaway, the
atmosphere was 'friendly', although he denied all allegations put to
him. He asked when he was going to see his lawyer: Mr Brown said
'the Boss' had left instructions he could not do so. This first session
ended at five minutes to six.

Treadaway was interviewed again three times during the morning, the last session ending at midday. He made no admissions. Then,
for the next five hours, he was left alone in his cell.

In his evidence to Mr Justice McKinnon in 1994, Treadaway
described what followed. 'At about 5 p.m., Mr Pickering and
another man came to my cell,' he said. 'I was told I was going for a
ride and would need the handcuffs on. I put my hands out in front of
me. I was told, "no, behind your back". I co-operated. My hands
were handcuffed behind my back.'

He was led out of the cell and into a corridor. One of the officers
told him: 'The boss wants a word with you.' He went up some steps,
to an interview room. Brown and Russell were in the doorway, he
said, and Pickering and another officer were on either side. Brown
shoved a statement towards him, saying it contained claims by
another suspect arrested in Operation Cat, John Louis Brown (no

relation), who had told the police he met Treadaway before a robbery in Erdington. 'I told him I'd had enough,' Treadaway said. He turned and began to walk back towards the cells. His account continued:

Mr Brown told me to calm down. He said, 'Come in son, and sit down.' Mr Brown and Mr Russell were in front of me. Mr [Detective Constable John] Price was to my right, leaning against a wall. Mr Pickering was at my side and a fifth man, whose identity I do not know, was behind the door. I sat down. I never had a chance to see if the door was closed. As I sat down, Mr Brown pulled up a chair in front of me as if to talk to me. Mr Brown made a nod or looked up at whoever was behind me just before a bag went over me. Without warning, a bag went over my head from behind. I couldn't work out what was happening. I tried to get to my feet. I was restrained by the handcuffs being held down and by others holding me.

I could see through the fabric of the bag. I was told to stamp my foot when I had enough. Mr Brown said that. The bag was being bunched up behind the back of my neck. I had my chin held down and I managed to bite a hole in the bag. Hands were all over my face, Mr Price's hands mainly. Mr Price said: 'He's bitten a hole in it!' Mr Brown told someone to go out and get another bag. I believe Mr Pickering went out to get it. There was a short exchange that I would sign eventually. I said that I wouldn't.

The second bag was placed over his head and there was a similar struggle, Treadaway said. One of the officers noticed the bag was not airtight, because it already had a hole in it, and Detective Inspector Brown said: 'Get some more bags. Surely we've got some more bags in the car.' Pickering went out again and returned with the third bag. Treadaway went on:

I couldn't see who put the bag over my head. My back was to the door. I struggled and passed out, I don't know for how long. When I came to, I found myself in a heap on the floor. I felt a burning sensation, as if my chest was on fire or going to burst . . . I was told to take a deep breath. Before I could do so, there was another bag, a fourth, over my head. There was a struggle for a short time and I stamped my feet. The bag was pulled off my head. Everyone vanished except for Mr Russell and Mr Pickering. Mr Pickering took the handcuffs off me then. I was shoved into a chair which had been brought up from the desk. A statement was shoved in front of me. A pen was thrust into my hand and I was told to sign at the bottom.

Treadaway, who is right-handed, said he signed the statement with his left hand. But the officers compared it with the signature he had already left on the persons in custody sheet, and realised he had not made his normal mark. Russell wrote out a second statement, and made sure that this time, Treadaway signed it with his right hand. He told Mr Justice McKinnon: 'I didn't say any of the things written in that statement. I signed it because I didn't want to go through what I had just been through.'

Later that evening, two visitors were allowed in to see Treadaway in his cell. His wife was given twenty minutes with him at 7.50 p.m., and at 8.35, he saw Ewan Smith, a solicitor from Glaisyers. Susan Treadaway had contacted the firm's emergency number shortly after her husband's arrest, and Smith had been trying to see his client all day. He had been fobbed off by a series of officers who had told him Treadaway did not want legal advice. Throughout this affair's long history, Treadaway continued to insist he *had* asked for a lawyer, but the police had refused.

That very night, in a long statement to Smith, Treadaway made his allegations about the police officers and the plastic bags for the first time. He described being handcuffed in his cell, and as Smith recorded in his notes, showed where the cuffs had abraded the skin of his wrists during the subsequent struggles. The story he told was in most respects identical to the account he gave in the High Court witness-box twelve years later. He denied involvement in any of the four robberies to which he had 'confessed', saying: 'I was petrified when I signed it because I thought I was going to be killed.'

At Smith's behest, the police agreed to call a doctor to examine the injuries to Treadaway's wrists. At 10.25 p.m., he was seen by a police surgeon of more than twenty years' experience, a Dr Chitnis.

Treadaway repeated his story, and Dr Chitnis wrote it down in his notes.

As for his injuries, Dr Chitnis confirmed there were wrist abrasions, which he said were 'common' when a suspect had struggled wearing handcuffs. However, sometimes people sustained injuries of this type from handcuffs even when there was no violence. He also found 'petechial haemorrhages', tiny amounts of bleeding beneath the skin, at the front of Treadaway's right shoulder, and others on his upper chest. There were 'two minute abrasions' inside the right corner of his mouth. There were no petechial haemorrhages to his face, eyes or neck. Dr Chitnis certified Treadaway as fit to be detained. Next day, he appeared before the local magistrates and was remanded in custody.

He repeated his story at his trial a year later, where he pleaded not guilty to all charges. 'They nearly killed me,' he told the jury, 'on four separate occasions a bag was put over my head. On each occasion it was forced on me. You do not think I would let them do it? I struggled as hard as I could against five men.' However, the Crown called a Dr Davis, an independent medical expert, who drew attention to the fact that there was no evidence of petechial haemorrhages around Treadaway's face, eyes or neck. He would have expected to see such marks if Treadaway were telling the truth. Two of the jurors believed Treadaway none the less. It was not enough: he was convicted with a majority verdict.

In prison, he continued to protest his innocence. Three years after his trial, PACE came into force. Under its provisions, Treadaway's 'confession', made in the absence of a lawyer or any form of contemporaneous interrogation record, would probably not have been allowed as evidence. Post-PACE, it is likely that he would not have been tried at all, much less convicted. But legislation of this kind does not have a retrospective effect. Treadaway stayed in prison.

The West Midlands police force tried hard to ensure that the civil action Treadaway launched in 1985 would never come to trial. Before serving a formal defence in response to his detailed allegations, they applied to the court to have the action 'struck out', on the grounds that Treadaway's allegations were preposterous, and did not deserve the court's attention. This first attempt failed, and in

1987, the case advanced an important stage when it was 'set down' for hearing. But in 1989, the police lodged another application to strike it out, this time on the basis that too much time had elapsed to make a fair trial possible. In July 1990, a junior Birmingham judge, a Deputy District Registrar, granted their request.

Nevertheless Treadaway stuck to his guns. His first, unsuccessful appeal against the striking out was heard by a West Midlands circuit judge in May 1991. Finally, on 26 February 1992, the Court of Appeal in London ruled in his favour. There were further delays, but in June 1994, the legal prevarication came to an end.

The trial of Treadaway's civil action against the West Midlands chief constable lasted seven working days. Mr Justice McKinnon heard from Treadaway, his ex-wife, his former solicitor Ewan Smith, all the police officers and several expert medical witnesses. Three of the experts, Professor Knight, Dr Barrowcliff and Dr West, were called by Treadaway. Dr Davis gave evidence for the police, repeating the conclusions he had drawn eleven years earlier at Treadaway's trial for the robberies.

By now, Detective Inspector John Brown had risen two ranks, to detective superintendent. He was, as he told the court, the most prominent survivor of the scandal which engulfed the West Midlands Serious Crime Squad when the former Chief Constable, Geoffrey Dear, disbanded it in 1989 amid numerous allegations of malpractice and fabricated confessions. Then, as the Police Complaints Authority and the West Yorkshire police began their huge, two-year investigation into the squad's activities, he had to endure the indignity of transfer to a 'non-operational' post with the Policy Review Department. But he had not been sacked. Before his transfer, he had been in an extremely powerful position, as deputy chief of the number four (Midlands) Regional Crime Squad, the unit which was later to become embroiled with Graham Titley and American Express.[2]

Detective Sergeant Russell had become a detective inspector. As for Derek Treadaway, with the usual one-third remission for good behaviour, he had been released from prison in August 1991. His wife had ended their marriage in 1987, and his children had grown up without him.

Establishing the veracity of a story such as that told by Derek

Treadaway twelve years after the alleged event was never going to be easy. The standard of proof in civil cases is lower than in criminal matters: the court has to decide the issue on the balance of probability, rather than beyond reasonable doubt. But as Jeremy Gompertz QC, counsel for the police, reminded the court, 'In a civil action where fraud or other matter which is or may be a crime is alleged . . . there is no great gulf between proof in criminal and civil matters.' He cited a 1957 judgment by Lord Denning: 'The more serious the allegation, the higher the degree of probability that is required.'[3] In a case such as this, where serious criminal offences – assault and conspiracy to pervert the course of justice – were being alleged against serving senior policemen, the standard of proof would have to be high.

The medical evidence did not appear to be conclusive either way. The haemorrhages Dr Chitnis found on Treadaway's chest and shoulder could have arisen for a variety of reasons, even from passive pressure, such as lying on a hard surface for a long period. Equally, the experts agreed, they might have been caused during a struggle such as that described by Treadaway. One of the experts, Dr Barrowcliff, was more positive: in his view, the haemorrhages were 'exactly' where he would expect to find them if a plastic bag had been held over the plaintiff's head. The judge concluded that the haemorrhages provided 'slight support' for Treadaway.

As for the abrasions inside his mouth, Dr Barrowcliff, Dr West and Professor Knight all said they were consistent with 'pressure upon the face of moderate to substantial degree'. Dr Davis, the expert called by the police, disagreed. But the judge did not find Dr Davis a 'satisfactory witness', and at the close of the trial, Gompertz elected not to place any weight on his evidence.

Mr Justice McKinnon commented in his judgment: 'Dr Davis did not strike me as a truly independent expert. He gave every appearance of fighting a cause. It was clear that, as he admitted to me, he had exaggerated his evidence to a substantial degree at a time when he was purporting to give evidence as an independent expert called on behalf of the prosecution in a criminal trial, namely that of the Plaintiff in this action in 1983.' In the judge's view, the mouth abrasions gave further 'slight support' to Treadaway's allegations.

Finally, there was the *absence* of haemorrhaging to Treadaway's face and neck. In sharp contrast to Dr Davis's claims in 1983, the other three experts concluded that 'a plastic bag over the head almost never causes signs of so-called asphyxia, that is petechiae in the eyelids or face'. Cross-examined before Mr Justice McKinnon, Dr Davis was forced to admit that his evidence which helped convict Treadaway eleven years earlier had been mistaken. 'His persistent reluctance to accept what I find must have been plain to him contributed to my assessment of him as an unreliable witness,' the judge said. The absence of facial haemorrhaging did not weaken Treadaway's account.

However, while the medical evidence supported his story, it certainly did not prove it to a high probability. This corroboration was to come from an unexpected source: from the accounts given by the police officers themselves.

The first important controversy related to the handcuff abrasions on Treadaway's wrists. Treadaway and his ex-wife both insisted he was so docile that the police did not use their handcuffs when they came to arrest him. If that was true, it corroborated his allegations. The police all agreed that once Treadaway reached the police station, there were no cuffs on him at all. If he was not cuffed when he was arrested, he must have got the abrasions later, during his interview, as he had always claimed.

At the robbery trial in 1983, a potentially vital conflict had arisen between the evidence of the then Detective Inspector Brown and Detective Constable Pickering. Brown gave evidence that Treadaway and Pickering had been handcuffed together after the arrest. Pickering denied he had been cuffed to the defendant: Treadaway's hands had been cuffed together. Brown changed his evidence to fit in with Pickering. Asked to explain this change of story in 1994, Brown said he had 'deferred to Pickering's memory'.

The next conflict arose over Ewan Smith's failure to gain access to his client until after he had signed his 'confession'. With what Mr Justice McKinnon described as his 'usual efficiency', Smith had kept detailed notes of his dealings with the police that day. He had made his first telephone call to Bromford Lane at 9.30 a.m., to be told by a Chief Inspector Speake – the Serious Crime Squad officer in overall charge of Operation Cat – that Treadaway had not requested a lawyer. Should he do so, Speake said, Smith would be informed.

Mr Smith knew from experience that the police at that time frequently refused requests by suspects to see their solicitors. He was also aware that Mrs Treadaway had been on to his firm's emergency number long before the office opened, asking for a lawyer to visit her husband. He expressed his surprise to Chief Inspector Speake, who told him he should not 'prejudge' the matter.

Over the next half hour, Smith made three further telephone calls. Other officers he spoke to repeatedly assured him that Treadaway had been asked if he wanted a lawyer, but had declined. By 10.16 a.m., Smith was so concerned he dictated a letter of protest to the third most senior officer in the West Midlands, Assistant Chief Constable David Gerty, who was responsible for all CID investigations. Shortly after eleven o'clock – still six hours before Treadaway's last, crucial interrogation – Smith personally delivered it to the force headquarters in central Birmingham.

At 11.45 a.m., Gerty telephoned Smith in his office. He said he was not prepared to 'go over the head' of Detective Chief Inspector Speake: the decision as to whether Smith could see his client would be left to him. Smith suggested that Gerty allow him personally to ask Treadaway whether he wanted a solicitor present: this could be done in the presence of Gerty, Speake or any officer of his choice. Gerty replied that the police had 'an inquiry to complete and a duty to do so'. Smith inquired how his proposal could possibly impair the course of justice. Gerty said: 'Now come on Mr Smith, I'm not going to be pushed into that one.' The conversation came to an end.

Twenty minutes later, Gerty telephoned again. He said Treadaway had stated 'quite categorically' he did not want a solicitor. Once again, Gerty refused to countenance Smith's suggestion that he might ask him personally. Shortly afterwards an agitated Mrs Treadaway rang to ask Smith if he had managed to get into Bromford Lane. With a heavy heart, he told her there seemed to be nothing more he could do.

In their evidence to Mr Justice McKinnon, Brown, Pickering and Russell maintained Treadaway at no time asked for a solicitor. They claimed they did not hear him tell his wife to contact Ewan Smith at Glaisyers at the time of his arrest. However, they were also forced to accept they had not ever asked him if he wanted a lawyer. Moreover, they were not the source of Assistant Chief Constable Gerty's claim that Treadaway had 'categorically' refused legal advice. Perhaps, they suggested, this had come from the uniformed custody officers. Patrick O'Connor QC, Treadaway's barrister, suggested there was a much simpler explanation: it had come from Brown.

Cross-examined by O'Connor, Brown made an important admission. Asked whether there was a 'policy decision' to refuse lawyers to suspects detained in Operation Cat, he said: 'It would seem so, yes . . . that has to be so, yes.' The reason for this policy, he said, was that letting solicitors into the interrogations 'might have hindered inquiries'. Did deciding whether a suspect could see a solicitor have anything to do with whether he had confessed, O'Connor asked. 'That is a very difficult question to answer,' Brown replied.

Another Birmingham solicitor, George Jonas, also spent 8 April 1982 vainly attempting to see clients arrested in Operation Cat. Like Smith, he was told they did not wish to see him, and managed to gain access only after they had confessed. One of them, John Pender, was later to allege he had been savagely assaulted. When Jonas got in to see him, he noticed his hands were black. The reason, Pender told him, was that he had been trying to protect his genitals, and had been kicked so many times that polish from the officers' boots had come off on his skin.

In his evidence in 1994, Detective Superintendent Brown insisted that his last involvement with Derek Treadaway was at his third interview, which finished at 9.55 a.m. He had attended neither the insignificant fourth interrogation session, nor the fifth when Treadaway 'confessed'.

Treadaway's last interview, when he was allegedly asphyxiated, took place between 4.55 and 5.25 p.m. Brown said that at 5.10 p.m., he and the then Detective Constable Price began an interview in another part of the police station with John Pender. By this time, Pender had already confessed: its purpose was apparently to see if he was prepared to supply information which might lead to new inquiries. Alone of all the officers in the case, Brown had lost the pocketbook notes he had taken in 1982, which might have contained a record of this meeting. There was no mention of the Pender interview at 5.10 in any of Brown's official statements.

The officer who actually conducted it, the now Detective

Inspector Price, did record Brown's presence in his own notes – the only written record that it ever took place. But as Patrick O'Connor pointed out to Mr Justice McKinnon, Treadaway claimed both Brown and Price had taken part in the plastic bag attack, but then left the room. Only Russell and Pickering had been present when he signed the first and second 'confessions'. There was plenty of time for Price and Brown to have spoken to Pender *after* the attack on Treadaway.

O'Connor made a further compelling point. Brown, as leader of the Serious Crime Squad 'crew' which arrested Derek Treadaway, was personally responsible for investigating the offences of which he was accused. It seemed 'inconceivable' that he should elect to play no part in the interview which produced his confession, in favour of going to see another suspect for whom he was not responsible and who had already confessed.

There was another hole in the police officers' story about the crucial last interview with Treadaway. From the time he finally got to see Ewan Smith three hours after signing his 'confession', Treadaway had been consistent in saying that before the detectives brought out the plastic bags, Brown had shown him the statement made by John Louis Brown, 'shoving it' in his face and describing its contents. As we have seen, John Louis Brown – who was being held at a different police station miles away – claimed to have met Treadaway in Erdington just before a robbery. When Treadaway first saw Ewan Smith, he gave him an accurate précis of what John Louis Brown had said.

Yet in their evidence, both at Treadaway's trial in 1983 and at the High Court in 1994, the police maintained they did not know the contents of Brown's confession when they were questioning Treadaway, much less shove it in his face. Cross-examined as to how he could have described it to Ewan Smith so accurately, Brown, Pickering and Russell had no adequate explanation. Even their own counsel, Jeremy Gompertz, admitted this was something of a 'bull point' for Treadaway. It cast serious doubt on the general credibility of their account.

There was more to come. Detective Superintendent Brown might have survived the investigation into the Serious Crime Squad, but he had not done so unscathed. In 1987, he had supervised the investigation into Paul Dandy, who was charged with shooting a security guard during a robbery at the Midlands Electricity offices in Erdington. By this time, PACE was law, which meant his interviews had to be contemporaneously recorded. However, the West Midlands Serious Crime Squad was not using tape-recorders, and Dandy's interrogation was written down. He refused to sign the notes.

Later, his defence lawyers had them tested by 'Esda', the scientific technique which can reveal whether documents such as police interview notebooks have been completed in consecutive order.[4] Dandy's lawyers were able to prove that the incriminating pages of his alleged confession had been added after the rest of the interview notes were written. The prosecution withdrew all charges. Dandy, who had spent eight months in solitary confinement, sued for wrongful arrest and malicious prosecution. In October 1993, he accepted £70,000 damages in an out of court settlement.

Detective Superintendent Brown was not among the officers who interrogated Dandy (none of whom was disciplined or sacked). But his conduct in the case was highly questionable, none the less. In 1992, Brown made a statement for the purposes of defending Dandy's action for damages. He claimed that two or three days after Dandy's bogus 'confession', the interrogating officers told him that *Dandy* had somehow managed to destroy some of the contemporaneous notes being made by the police, while the interview was still in progress. These pages had therefore been 'rewritten'. Brown said that even if the defence had not come up with the Esda results, he had always intended to raise this matter with prosecuting counsel before any of the officers gave evidence at Dandy's trial. However, it was inescapable that for ten months, he had not bothered to tell the CPS anything about this highly unusual 'rewriting'. In 1988, after an internal police inquiry, he pleaded guilty to the disciplinary charge of neglect of duty, and received a reprimand. His career was not impeded.

There was a further disciplinary conviction against John Brown: a 1992 finding that he had failed to keep track of payments from police funds to two informants, both prostitutes. He had fought this vigorously, but in the end, the Chief Constable had preferred the word of the two women to that of Detective Superintendent

Brown. He was only fined a month's salary, but the conviction rankled. He was so resentful, he told Mr Justice McKinnon, he had even considered withdrawing his co-operation from the West Midlands police legal department, and refusing to give evidence in the Treadaway case. This, as O'Connor remarked, was a remarkable threat from an experienced senior detective.

Mr Justice McKinnon heard all the evidence, then retired for a month to consider it. The court reconvened to hear his judgment on 28 July 1994. He began by saying he had no doubt that Treadaway was 'cynically denied access to a solicitor', and that Brown, as Treadaway always claimed, had denied his request. It was Brown, the judge said, who had given Assistant Chief Constable Gerty the 'false information' passed on to Ewan Smith.

Mr Justice McKinnon said he had 'no doubt' that Treadaway was not handcuffed at his home, while Brown's withdrawal of his story that Treadaway and Pickering had been handcuffed together was 'not just a mistake'. The judge went on: 'His explanation of changing his evidence to accord with Mr Pickering's recollection is not credible, and having seen Mr Brown, I do not believe it . . . the Plaintiff came docilely. There was no struggle and no possible reason for marks on both of his wrists.' He believed Treadaway's ex-wife Susan's evidence that no handcuffs were used: 'She is no gangster's moll but a decent woman, who was, as I believe, doing her best to tell the truth.' By the same token, she told the truth about telephoning Glaisyer's and Ewan Smith.

The judge had no doubt that as he had always said, Treadaway was shown John Louis Brown's statement about their alleged meeting in Erdington. There was a 'high degree of probability' that Brown did indeed 'shove it' in Treadaway's face. The real significance of this episode was not that it had happened, but that Russell, Pickering and Brown had spent the last twelve years lying about it.

Mr Justice McKinnon concluded this part of his ruling with some comments about Detective Superintendent Brown:

He was a most unsatisfactory witness. At times, prolonged in some instances, he seemed incapable of answering simple questions straightforwardly. His stock in trade, as Mr O'Connor submitted, does seem to be ambiguity – a leaving of his options open so that, later, any gaps can be plugged without his having appeared to have committed himself to any particular position. His track record confirmed that conclusion . . . I have no doubt that he simply did not tell the truth in a number of respects.

There had, the judge accepted, been discrepancies in some of the details of Treadaway's allegations over time. But in contrast to the detectives, he was not a practised witness, and he did not prevaricate. Mr Justice McKinnon went on: 'What I have found compelling is the "core consistency" of the Plaintiff's account. Not only did he complain within three hours of his alleged ordeal, but he did so giving chapter and verse.' He had added Brown to the complaint, although there was no written record of his being present during the last interview at all: 'What a risk,' the judge commented, 'he could have been at another police station or doing something else which would have provided him with a cast-iron alibi. As it was, even if he attended the Pender interview, Mr Brown was clearly available, something the Plaintiff could not have known at the time.'

Similarly, there was no reason to make up the involvement of Detective Inspector Price, who was never part of the arresting 'crew'. Again, Treadaway could not have known the timings made it possible for him to have been present at his last interrogation. Price did not give evidence at the 1983 trial, and he told Mr Justice McKinnon that the first he knew he was being accused of participating in a serious assault was when he was asked to come and give evidence while the 1994 hearing was already underway. The judge found this incredible: 'Lack of communication between police officers is one thing. An impenetrable Chinese wall around Mr Price, in the circumstances of this case, is quite another. I regret I have to say I simply do not believe Mr Price's denial.'

Then the judge came to the medical evidence. From the earliest stage, Treadaway had described his chest feeling as if it were going to burst when the bags were placed over his head. This was entirely consistent with the sensations the expert witnesses said were to be expected as asphyxia starved the muscles of his heart of oxygen. Was this just another piece of good fortune? The judge commented: 'If the Plaintiff is a fabricator, not only is he a most talented one, but his inventions have had a remarkable degree of good fortune poured upon them.'

The wrist abrasions were not explained by the police version of events, nor were the cuts inside Treadaway's mouth, nor the petechial haemorrhages to his chest and shoulder. However, 'all these injuries *are* explained by the Plaintiff's account'. While taken individually, each injury provided only slight support for his story, considered together, they provided 'rather more than slight support'.

Mr Justice McKinnon at last reached his conclusion. He was satisfied to a high degree of probability that Derek Treadaway was, as he had claimed for twelve years, assaulted by five members of the West Midlands Serious Crime Squad. The only issue in the case was credibility, and, the judge went on, 'I believe the Plaintiff.'

His judgment continued:

> I regret to have to say I do not believe the evidence of four long-serving police officers, namely, Mr Brown, Mr Pickering, Mr Russell and Mr Price. All four of them were present at the Plaintiff's fifth interview, and all four played their various parts in the serious assaults upon the Plaintiff . . . What happened to him amounted to nothing less than torture. The police officers concerned had shown contempt for the Plaintiff and thus for the rule of law.

This he went on, 'can only be regarded as a very serious abuse of authority by the police, which merits a substantial award. I have endeavoured to keep it within reasonable bounds, while remembering just how oppressive, cynical and unacceptable was the treatment meted out to the Plaintiff.' Mr Justice McKinnon ordered the police to pay damages of £50,000.

★ ★ ★

Shocking as it is, the case of Derek Treadaway has a significance beyond the violence and perjury described by the High Court judgment. It presents a serious indictment against the system of police discipline and complaints: against the way the police are policed.

Treadaway, as we have seen, complained of being assaulted as early as 1982. There was an inquiry by officers from the Lancashire police, which found 'no evidence' to substantiate what he said. At the time of this first investigation, the only external point of reference in cases of this kind was the old Police Complaints Board, established by the 1976 Police Act. The Board had no power to involve itself in an inquiry at all: it could only direct appropriate disciplinary action on being presented with a completed file.

The Board's limitations were widely recognised. In its own Triennial Review in 1980, the Board called on the Government to set up a specialist team of officers to investigate serious assault allegations, under the supervision of a judge. It dared to state the obvious: 'Assaults which are alleged to have occurred during arrest or while in custody are unlikely to be witnessed by civilians, and where there is a denial supported by one or more police colleagues and no corroborative evidence to support the allegation, neither criminal nor disciplinary action against a police officer is likely.'[5]

The 1981 Royal Commission was similarly critical, and argued the case for fully independent methods of both investigating and adjudicating complaints. The Police Federation supported the proposal, taking the view that an independent body would not only protect the public and command its support, but also it would protect police officers against malicious complaints. Officers cleared by an independent organisation would be seen to be convincingly vindicated.

The most devastating case against the system which existed before PACE was made by Lord Scarman in his Brixton report. His analysis has a lasting applicability.[6] No matter how effective police recruitment, training and leadership, Scarman said, complaints were inevitable. It was vital to establish methods of resolving them which commanded both police and public confidence. However, the system arising from the 1976 Act had failed:

I have received considerable evidence of a lack of confidence in the impartiality and fairness of the procedure, not only among members of the ethnic minority communities but among the public generally ... People, it is said, do not believe their complaint will be investigated or judged fairly, and they are worried that if they do complain they will subsequently be subjected to harassment and intimidation by the police. The chief criticisms centre on the fact that under the present system, the police investigate themselves.

Scarman concluded: 'The existing system lacks a sufficiently convincing independent element, particularly in the consideration of the more serious complaints ... It is clear to me that many will continue to criticise it so long as the investigation of complaints remains in police hands.'

Against this, he went on, the only cogent argument was cost. But the Government had to decide 'whether the gain in public confidence which would ensue outweighs the resource and financial costs involved'. For his own part, Scarman had no doubt: 'If public confidence in the complaints system is to be achieved, any solution falling short of a system of independent investigation available for all complaints (other than the frivolous) is unlikely to be successful.'

Cost and inertia won. The 1984 PACE Act did not create an independent system, but merely replaced the old Board with the Police Complaints Authority. This remains largely reliant on the police. In more than half of all complaints, the PCA takes no role at all: the police themselves make the decision that the complaint is not serious enough to warrant external supervision, and they deal with it alone. In another 40 per cent or so, the police will refer a case for possible supervision, only to be told this is unnecessary. The PCA is left with less than 1,000 of the most serious cases each year, well under 10 per cent of the total, where one of its lay members will 'supervise' police inquiries. They may veto the choice of chief investigating officer, or declare themselves unhappy with the quality of a finished inquiry. But they do not direct investigations in any meaningful way. With just eight members allocated to the authority's investigation wing, each with more than 100 inquiries to supervise each year, this would, in any event, be a physical impossibility.

Lord Scarman anticipated that the Government would not bring itself to create a fully independent body, and addressed himself to probable alternatives. If a solution along the lines of the PCA and its 'supervision' were to emerge, he said, its members must be treated as fully-fledged members of the inquiry team, not as an 'irrelevant fifth wheel to the investigation coach'. In reality, this is exactly what PCA supervisors have become.

Occasionally, members have tried to adopt a more 'hands-on' approach. Jeff Crawford, who sat on the PCA for six years until 1993 and supervised the investigation into the West Midlands Serious Crime Squad, used to attend interviews with officers in the most serious cases. However, most PCA supervision is essentially bureaucratic, consisting of no more than the hurried study of completed case papers. This lack of power has helped to shape an institutionalised acquiescence. The PCA displays little inclination for pushing at its limits. Sometimes, as in the case of Derek Treadaway, it reveals a marked distaste for dealing with difficult or controversial cases.

On 10 August 1994, within a fortnight of Treadaway's High Court judgment, Superintendent D.A. Jeavons wrote to Treadaway's solicitor, Raju Bhatt, saying he had been asked to investigate the case all over again, and asking Mr Bhatt to arrange an interview with his client.[7] Bhatt's response was to inquire what, if anything, the PCA was planning to do about the case, and what was the scope and purpose of Jeavons's proposed investigation.

There was every reason to believe that the PCA might wish to pursue the Treadaway case with the utmost vigour. Brown, Pickering, Russell and Price had all been members of the West Midlands Serious Crime Squad, the subject of the biggest inquiry in the PCA's brief history. They had been denounced as violent liars in the strongest possible terms: Mr Justice McKinnon's finding that serving detectives had inflicted physical torture was an unprecedented event.

Furthermore, Treadaway was not the only person convicted of serious offences, on the basis of a disputed confession, who had accused Squad members of extracting an admission by means of asphyxiation with a series of plastic bags. As the PCA must have been well aware, Keith Twitchell, gaoled for twenty years for robbery and manslaughter in 1981, alleged in a petition to Home Secretary Kenneth Baker ten years later that he was given the plastic bag treatment twice. After blacking out, he said, he signed a pre-prepared confession to involvement in an armed robbery in which a security guard was shot dead.

His account bore striking resemblances to that of Derek Tread-away: he described being handcuffed with his arms behind him, severe chest pains, and an officer saying: 'The bastard signs or he goes out feet first.' Like Treadaway, he was denied a lawyer until he had signed the statement.[8] Twitchell repeated his allegations while attached to a lie-detector machine supervised by Dr William Canning, a consultant forensic psychiatrist at Coleshill Hospital, Birmingham, who concluded his story was 'very convincing'. According to an independent inquiry into the Serious Crime Squad, another three men arrested before 1983 made allegations they were 'plastic-bagged'.[9]

Nevertheless, in his reply to Bhatt on 17 August, Superintendent Jeavons revealed that the PCA had decided to take no part in supervising the inquiry into the Treadaway case on 4 August – less than a week after Mr Justice McKinnon's ruling. Bhatt wrote to the PCA chairman, Sir Leonard Peach, asking for an explanation. Bhatt cited a passage in the authority's own published literature: 'The authority must supervise the investigation of all complainants related to a death or serious injury. Perjury, corruption or other serious offences must also be supervised.'[10]

The reply from John Cartwright, the PCA deputy chairman and former SDP MP, on 25 August, was surprising, to say the least. Notwithstanding the new High Court judgment, the authority had chosen not to take matters further because the old Police Complaints Board had 'reviewed the investigation into Mr Treadaway's original complaint'. It would also be difficult to supervise inquiries into an event which had taken place twelve years earlier.

A fortnight later Bhatt wrote again to Cartwright. He was amazed that a previous review by the Police Complaints Board might be thought to have any relevance, he said: Mr Justice McKinnon's ruling had clearly been based on 'evidence called before him which those responsible for the original investigation were unable or unwilling to unearth'. The Chief Constable would not, he pointed out, have ordered a fresh investigation, had he considered the original 1980s inquiry had been adequate. The PCA, Bhatt concluded, had 'chosen to abdicate its responsibility on the basis of spurious reasoning'. It appeared to be 'unwilling or unable to perform its functions' as the guardian of the public interest.

Cartwright's reply, in three short paragraphs, was a masterpiece of bureaucratic complacency. The PCA's decision not to get involved in the Treadaway case had been 'carefully considered', he said, and Bhatt's protests did not affect it because they did not 'raise any new issues'. As for Bhatt's 'sweeping and generalised criticisms', they were 'not borne out by the facts'. The previous year, the authority had supervised a record 954 investigations. 'If current trends continue', Cartwright added excitedly, 'the 1994 total will be even higher.'

Few of these cases, if any, will have approached the seriousness of Treadaway's. But presented with the ancient question, *quis custodiet ipsos custodes*, the PCA elected to duck the challenge. In the ensuing weeks, Bhatt continued his correspondence with the West Midlands police, seeking their opinion on the matter, and information about the scope and independence of their own investigation. Finally, on 2 November 1994, Assistant Chief Constable D.G. Ibbs confirmed that the police *had* asked for PCA supervision and that this was refused: 'I regret they chose not to do so . . . whilst it is unfortunate, I am not in a position to challenge that.' The police, he added, had made their 'disappointment' known to the authority.

Ibbs said Superintendent Jeavons was a 'most experienced investigator . . . academically qualified to Master level, and this will give you some idea of his analytical and research skills. The Force therefore have chosen the best possible candidate to undertake this important investigation.' In the absence of PCA supervision, this was an assertion which could only be taken on trust.

'Importantly [*sic*] time is of the essence' Ibbs told Bhatt. Indeed it was. On 1 January 1995, Detective Superintendent John Brown retired, having reached the end of the normal thirty-year police career. However diligent Jeavons's investigation, he was now beyond the reach of police disciplinary sanctions.

At the time of writing in July 1995, Messrs Russell, Pickering and Price remain serving police officers. Jeavons has reached the end of his inquiry and has, as a matter of routine, submitted a report to the Crown Prosecution Service, which will decide, according to its normal criteria, whether any criminal charges may be appropriate. The Home Secretary has referred Treadaway's robbery convictions to the Court of Appeal. Four years after Keith Twitchell's solicitors submitted a petition arguing his innocence, the Home Office has agreed to reopen his case in the light of the Treadaway judgment.

★ ★ ★

As we have seen, the argument against the police investigating themselves has been made before. However, this is not the only inadequacy of the existing system.

In some cases, police investigations *are* carried out in exemplary fashion, and sometimes they find compelling evidence of serious malpractice. But time after time, the ultimate outcome is no more satisfactory than the Lancashire inquiry into the case of Derek Treadaway during the 1980s. To investigate is only the first stage. In its failure to act, to produce a just 'result', the police complainants and disciplinary system reproduces the failings of the larger criminal process in microcosm. It too has become sluggish and bureaucratised. Like the CPS, it has retreated from prosecution. The result is that 'factually guilty' police officers may also escape retribution.

A 1991 Home Office research study suggests that the victims of deviant police officers, those responsible for making the annual 17–20,000 complaints, have already reached this conclusion.[11] Certainly, the researchers did not find high levels of satisfaction with the investigation of complaints. Of a sample of complainants whose cases were supervised by the PCA, only 26 per cent were very satisfied, or fairly satisfied with this stage of the system. Fifty-four per cent were very dissatisfied and 20 per cent fairly dissatisfied. The figures for the more than 90 per cent of cases in which the PCA did not supervise the investigation were even worse: 82 per cent were very or fairly dissatisfied.

However, these results look relatively good when compared to complainants' opinion not of the inquiry, but the eventual outcome. Here, only 4 per cent were very or fairly satisfied. Eighty-six per cent were very dissatisfied, a proportion which barely changed according to whether the PCA was involved or not.

There is a considerable research tradition which considers the police complaints system in somewhat relativistic terms. Its success or failure is judged by its effectiveness in regulating police culture and behaviour, and as a deterrent to future police deviance.[12] Robert Reiner has adopted these arguments and turned them on their head: 'For years it has been the refrain of the radical and liberal criminologists when arguing against the "hang 'em, flog 'em" brigade that policing and penal policy have a limited role in restraining deviance. This analysis should be extended to police deviance.' In other words, the fear of being caught is no more effective at restraining the bent policeman than the criminal. The disciplinary system will only be effective if it influences 'cultural understandings which are the immediate determinants of law-abidingness or deviation', Reiner adds – discipline only fulfils its purpose when it changes *attitudes*, because these are what determine individuals' actions.[13]

In fact, ineffective as it seems from the outside, inside the service the disciplinary system is widely feared. The description in the 1991 Home Office police complaints study of officers who revelled in complaints, and boasted of papering their walls with them, does not tally with my experience.

In Kilburn, I heard several stories from PCs with unblemished records who had been subjected to rigorous investigation on the basis of what appeared to have been malicious complaints. In each case, for the object of the complaint, it had been a traumatic experience. One officer had been attacked when he tried to arrest a rapist on the run from prison. The rapist had seized his hand and broken four fingers, snapping the bones like twigs. Later, as he recovered in hospital, he found his assailant had alleged he had stolen his watch. 'It was crazy, a mad thing to say,' he told me. 'But that didn't stop me getting the third degree from the area complaints team. How do I know that it isn't down on my file, even though unsubstantiated, and that one day it's not going to stop me getting promotion or a move to a better job?'

These were not groundless fears. Police personnel policy has changed to accommodate the system's failings: officers who attract numerous complaints will now find themselves at a serious disadvantage.

Valuable as Reiner's insights are, the ultimate yardstick by which the police complaints system needs to be judged is not relativistic, but absolute. Serious complaints often amount to nothing less than allegations of criminal offences in their own right. When law-enforcers are seen to get away with *criminal* acts, it inflicts heavy damage to society's shared notions of the rule of law.

The Home Office study backed its figures by reproducing individual replies to the question 'What, if anything, do you think you achieved by complaining?' The answers included: 'Only that the police could get away with manufacturing evidence in my case'; 'I achieved the knowledge that the police investigating the police is a farce'; and 'a wasted two years of heartache to myself and my family'.

Similar comments are often to be heard from the victims of crime. Disregarding the system's impact on police culture, we need to ask a simpler question: does it deliver justice?

★ ★ ★

Roy Hanney, a television engineer with no criminal convictions, got caught up in the Poll Tax riot of 1990 entirely by accident. He had taken part in the demonstration earlier in the day, when no violence took place. But he had to leave early to attend a job interview in the afternoon, and it was sheer coincidence that he happened to be on his way home when the streets of the West End of London suddenly filled with riot police. As violence flared between the police and people who had been on the march, Hanney began taking photographs.

Towards the end of the afternoon, the Territorial Support Group, the Metropolitan Police specialist public order squad, began an operation to clear the streets. Mr Hanney, then twenty-nine, had been standing in an alley near the cluster of second-hand bookshops on the Charing Cross Road. The next thing he knew, a TSG unit with shields, batons and NATO flame-proof uniforms was pushing a crowd of 500 people up the road towards him. He slipped and fell amid the crush, was seized in an armlock and bundled into a police van.[14]

The following November, he was tried at Southwark Crown Count for affray – an offence which carries a maximum three-year gaol sentence. After lunch on the third day of what was expected to be a five-day trial, all twelve jurors found themselves together in the lift. They held a brief discussion, and then, before the afternoon's proceedings began, the foreman sent a note to the judge. It said: 'We are unanimously convinced of the defendant's innocence. We hope this helps.' The judge stopped the trial, and Hanney was formally acquitted.

The main evidence against him had come from two TSG officers, PC Tony Egan and PC Richard Ramsay. Both officers committed perjury. Egan and Ramsay told the court they had written up their statements describing the incident quite independently, in different parts of London – Egan at Rochester Row police station near Victoria at 6.45 p.m., and Ramsay three hours later, miles away at the TSG's base in City Road. They vehemently denied collusion. But the structure of both statements, and much of the phraseology, suggested otherwise.

'We were deployed on a short shield cordon attempting to push a violent crowd of 500 plus north in Charing Cross Road, WC1,' PC Egan began. PC Ramsay's statement started: 'We were deployed as a short shield unit forming a cordon attempting to push a violent crowd of about 500 plus north in Charing Cross Road.'

'The order was given to charge into the extremely violent crowd,' PC Egan went on. 'As we moved forward I saw a man whom I now know to be Roy Hanney. He was wearing an army-type jacket which was zipped up, and he had closely shaven fair hair.' Back came the echo from PC Ramsay: 'The order was given to charge into the violent crowd. As we moved forward, I noticed a man I now know to be Roy Hanney. He had a close-cropped head and an army combat jacket on.'

Cross-examined by Hanney's counsel, Dexter Dias, PC Ramsay insisted the similarities – which ran to the end of the statements, and included an identical mistake about the day the riot took place – were 'coincidence'. He argued he could not possibly have copied his colleague's statement because he had described Hanney's hairstyle as 'close-cropped', whereas PC Egan had said it was 'shaven'.

It was an unfortunate example to choose as evidence of his originality. Dias asked him to look at his handwritten version, from which a typescript had been prepared. He had crossed out 'shaven' and substituted 'close-cropped'. At that moment, the credibility of

Ramsay's allegation that he saw Hanney 'draw back his right hand and throw what appeared to be a brick into the police cordon' was somehow diminished. Once again, Egan's language was virtually identical, although he said the alleged missile 'appeared to be a lump of concrete'.

Once inside the van, Hanney told the court, PC Egan attacked him, punching him repeatedly in the head. Later, the police surgeon found bruising on his forehead, eyebrows and back. In the tense months before his trial, Hanney had not expected there would be any evidence to corroborate the allegation that PC Egan had assaulted him. But on the morning the hearing was due to begin, the CPS supplied his lawyers with a statement which had not been previously disclosed. It was the account of a Ms Nicola Todd, aged nineteen, who was arrested at the same time – all charges against her being later withdrawn. She travelled in the van with Hanney, saw PC Egan punching him, and on arrival at the police station, she refused to be interviewed until she had seen a senior officer in order to make a complaint. Later that evening, she made a statement describing the attack to a chief inspector.

Todd said Egan held Hanney's head with his right hand while he punched him with his left. 'He hit him repeatedly,' she said, 'at some stages he changed to punching him with his right hand because the man was trying to cover his head. It went on for at least three minutes.' Hanney and Todd had never met: until the trial started, he was unaware of her existence. Giving evidence, she said she tried to stop the attack by holding Egan's arms, 'but my own arms were restrained by my own arresting officers'. She was frightened and horrified, and had 'never seen so much violence'.

At the police station, Hanney endured a final ordeal. As he stood in a long queue of anti-Poll Tax demonstrators waiting to be charged, PC Egan held him for several minutes in a vicious restraining wristlock. He was not struggling: even if he had been, there were many police officers present who could have swiftly overpowered him. It caused him excruciating pain: later medical examination showed he suffered a bruised nerve, with loss of sensation to two fingers.

Hanney had made a formal complaint on the day of his arrest. It was not until December 1991, nearly two years later, that Rosemary

Woolf of the PCA – which had, on this occasion, elected to use its powers of supervision – wrote to tell him of the outcome. She had seen the transcript of his trial, she said, and the officers had been interviewed. Here there was a conflict: 'The officers maintain that their accounts of your arrest were truthful and deny committing perjury.' It was true that 'the trial and this inquiry have cast doubt on the truthfulness of the officers' accounts'. However, 'there is unfortunately no conclusive evidence concerning the circumstances of your arrest which could prove that the officers' accounts were false'.

Although both Nicola Todd and another prisoner in the van had supported the allegation that PC Egan attacked Hanney there, Woolf went on, 'Some doubts have been raised.' This was because PC Egan had been wearing a gauntlet, and might not have been able to inflict Hanney's injuries thus clad. It had not apparently occurred to the PCA that the officer might have removed it.

The CPS had already decided that there was insufficient evidence to bring criminal charges against the police, Woolf added. Now the authority had to decide whether to press for a disciplinary hearing: 'In making such a decision, the authority must bear in mind that the standard of proof required is the same as that required to bring a criminal conviction: the case must be proved *beyond reasonable doubt* [Woolf's italics].

'That may not be possible if the facts complained of are denied by the officers and there is no way of establishing the truth of what happened, for example if there was no independent evidence or if the accounts of witnesses conflict . . . after carefully considering all the available material, the authority are [*sic*] not convinced that sufficient evidence exists to prove your case beyond reasonable doubt.' There would be no disciplinary charge over the performances given by PCs Egan and Ramsay in the witness-box at Southwark Crown Court, nor over the assault on Hanney in the van.

Here was the PCA behaving in a manner redolent of the CPS at its worst: a quasi-judicial decision, in which the authority had quietly usurped the function of a police disciplinary tribunal, based on the lack of absolute certainty that a charge against the officers could be made to stick.

There was one final matter: Egan's use of the wristlock. This, the

PCA concluded, was indeed 'unnecessary'. With commendable courage and honesty, another police officer present at the time had told the authority's investigators that Hanney, far from struggling, had been 'standing quietly in the queue'. This in itself might have been construed as an unlawful assault, especially given the lasting injury to Hanney's hand. But on the advice of a police deputy assistant commissioner, the PCA had decided the 'appropriate' punishment was for PC Egan to be 'strictly admonished by a senior officer'.

Roy Hanney did not consider this a just outcome to his complaint, and he promptly sued the police for assault, wrongful arrest, false imprisonment, and malicious prosecution.

Meanwhile, Raju Bhatt, who was acting for Hanney in his damages case, tried once again to get some sense out of the PCA. In a letter on 20 January 1994 to Rosemary Woolf, he pointed out that the jury at Hanney's trial had, in sending their unusual note to the judge, apparently been satisfied that the officers lied on oath. As for the alleged assault in the van, the existence of two independent witnesses suggested that here was a case which 'cries out for assessment by a tribunal'. The way the authority had exercised its judgment had done nothing to inspire public confidence in the police complaints procedure, Bhatt added.

This time, the reply came from Peter Moorhouse, the PCA deputy chairman. 'Such is Mrs Woolf's concern at the tone of your letter that she referred the file to me for a "second opinion",' he said. Not that there was any point in Bhatt's protest: the official notices informing the officers that they were under investigation had already been withdrawn – which meant that legally, there was nothing that could now be done.

There were some discrepancies between the different accounts of what occurred in the van, Moorhouse said, and possibly between the descriptions of PC Egan's assault and the medical reports of Hanney's injuries. 'You are, I know, aware that disciplinary charges must be proved beyond reasonable doubt, and before recommending or directing a charge against an officer the authority *must consider that the evidence available is sufficient to meet this standard*' [author's italics]. 'The authority cannot and will not recommend charges on the basis of "give it a run in front of a tribunal" which is the emotive basis [*sic*] implicit in your comments.'

Moorhouse was setting a bureaucratic standard that explicitly outstripped even the CPS 'realistic prospect of conviction' test. His principle seemed to be that unless *all* doubt had already been removed, police officers could not be charged with disciplinary offences. In his scheme, there was no point in having tribunals weigh the evidence at all. This was simply not their job. Under such a principle, it need hardly be said, there would be no prospect at all of a tribunal considering a case such as that of Derek Treadaway.

On 10 January 1995, the Metropolitan Police settled Roy Hanney's action by paying him £30,000 damages. A statement was read in open court. It described his arrest, the blows rained upon his head in the van and the painful wristlock. In response to Hanney's protests, the statement said that PC Egan told him: 'You think you are clever . . . this will teach you a lesson.' It added:

> The Plaintiff considers that the wrong that was done to him by the police officers concerned in this matter can never be repaired and never be forgotten by him. He brought these proceedings in order to vindicate his good name and reputation, and in order to achieve public recognition of what he regards as a grave wrong-doing on the part of the police officers who continue to serve in the police force.

The Hanney case helps to explain the exponential growth in civil damages actions against the police. Many of the plaintiffs in such actions have already sought satisfaction from the police complaints machinery, and failed. Police sources have frequently suggested to me that the growth is largely a function of media publicity for the possible rewards; according to one police lawyer, the number of actions rose during the early 1990s recession because solicitors realised there was good business to be had, financed by legal aid. But men such as Derek Treadaway and Roy Hanney are not gold-diggers. They issued proceedings because they wanted not cash, but vindication, and action against officers who had disgraced the service.

Paul Dandy made the point after receiving his £70,000 in

October 1993. As we have seen, he had been freed after eight months on remand when Esda showed his robbery confession had been fabricated. He said money could never make up for the time he had spent in prison – where he had been strip-searched every day, and was driven to attempt suicide. He added: 'The police got off scot-free. I would have preferred the police to have got the sack rather than them still being active members of the police force.'[15]

In 1985, the Metropolitan Police solicitors' department received 175 actions for damages from members of the public. Over the next decade, the total at first rose slowly: there were 211 actions in 1990. Then it began to speed up and by 1994, the total was 489.[16] The sums paid in damages rose steeply. In 1988, the Metropolitan Police paid £250,000 in out of court settlements, with a further £140,000 awarded by judges or juries after contested trials – a total of £354,000. By 1990, this had more than doubled, to £745,000. The 1993 total represented a further doubling, at £1,589,000.[17] Similar rates of growth were experienced by many provincial forces.

The Metropolitan Police estimates it settles a third of all actions by paying damages which may range from a few hundred pounds to tens of thousands. It will go to trial with one in fifty or less, usually losing around half of them. The rest may be struck out, or simply lapse. There is a prevalent police myth that most actions are settled for 'commercial' reasons, because of the potential costs in lawyers' fees in losing a finely balanced action. A senior Metropolitan solicitor denied this, admitting that 'when we settle a case, it is because there are weaknesses in our evidence. The majority of people who take these actions do have a genuine grievance, even if a few see it as a way of making money.'

In 1994, there were 194 settled actions against the police in London: a figure which amounts to only a tiny proportion of the total contacts of all kind between the police and the public. But in virtually all of these cases of avowed police misconduct, there was no substantive action taken against the officers concerned. The rotten apples remain in the barrel.

At the time of writing, the Police Federation, the Home Office and the PCA have been embroiled in negotiations for two years, in an attempt to restructure the complaints and discipline system. Their stated intention is to increase the proportion of complaints upheld by investigation – at present, less than 10 per cent. One proposal, favoured by the PCA, is to create a 'sliding scale' system, under which the most serious complaints would still need to be proven of beyond reasonable doubt, but less serious matters could be adjudicated on the balance of probabilities. Understandably, the Police Federation is reluctant to abandon the protection which the standard of beyond reasonable doubt provides for its members, although the PCA is optimistic agreement will be reached.

However, desirable as it is that more complaints be substantiated, present experience demonstrates that this will not be enough to remedy the existing system's defects. Sometimes, the facts of a complaint *are* substantiated, but the complainant's sense of grievance barely alleviated.

One example is the case of Malkjit Natt. In 1991, he was arrested by PC Craig Gande and PC Darren Bray for threatening to kill his wife during a domestic row at their home in Newham, east London. Unbeknown to the police, he was carrying a tape-recorder, which he turned on secretly in the back of the squad car carrying him to the police station.

On the tape, which Natt eventually played in open court, one of the officers was heard telling Natt that this was 'not his country'. His proper home was in India, he said. (Natt had lived in Britain for twelve years.) He would be dealt with more harshly on the subcontinent, one of the officers said: 'That's what we should do with you, fucking shoot you.' The other officer then called him a 'wanker'. Finally, Natt was advised to 'go home to India or Pakistan or wherever you fucking come from ... It's not your fucking country.'

Natt's allegation of racism by the two officers was not supervised by the PCA, nor even the central Scotland Yard complaints unit. Like the majority of complaints, it was handled internally at a local level, by a department of the east London area police management. The complaint was upheld. In January 1992, the two officers were fined a day's pay.

The following June, Natt's complaint briefly became a *cause célèbre* when the tape was broadcast by the BBC, during a programme about police attitudes to racial violence. The Metropolitan Police was forced to disclose the less than condign punishment meted out to the officers, and Commissioner Sir Peter Imbert took the unusual step of making a statement at a press conference. He said:

> This case could have been dealt with in other ways. It would have been better dealt with centrally. I make no bones about it, I think a harsher punishment could well have been appropriate. Those officers know that they were extremely fortunate to be fined only one day's pay . . . I say now that sort of behaviour is not acceptable within the Metropolitan Police Service.[18]

Gande and Bray were not convicted of the serious disciplinary offence of adopting what the police discipline code called 'racially discriminatory behaviour', for which they could have been sacked. The only charge against them was that they had been 'abusive to a member of the public'. How it is that telling a man to 'go back home to India or Pakistan or wherever you fucking come from' can be held to be not racist is beyond comprehension. But this was the conclusion which the police disciplinary tribunal reached in its charge and verdict.

Even in the rare cases where the disciplinary authorities do apply severe punishment, police officers have exceptional rights of appeal – first to their commissioner or chief constable, and then to a tribunal appointed by the Home Secretary.

In 1990, PC Rhys Trigg became involved in an argument with Daniel Goswell, who was sitting in a parked car in Plumstead, south-east London. Trigg claimed that Goswell had been driving dangerously, at high speed. He ignored Goswell's protests that the car had no battery and no ignition key, and declined his invitation to check that the bonnet was cold. When Goswell refused to get out of the car, he summoned assistance, and the incident ended with Trigg dealing him a vicious blow across the temples with his truncheon. Goswell, who is black, needed several stitches and even four years later, continued to suffer from blackouts and dizzy spells. He was convicted in the Magistrates' Court of common assault and threatening behaviour – charges arising solely from the incident with PC Trigg – but won an appeal to the Crown Court.

Goswell complained about his treatment, and the investigation was supervised by the PCA. In May 1992, a disciplinary tribunal ruled that PC Trigg should be sacked. He appealed to Commissioner Sir Paul Condon, but in March 1993, his dismissal was confirmed. Trigg appealed again to the Home Secretary, Michael Howard, who appointed an appeal panel chaired by James Anderton, the retired Chief Constable of Greater Manchester who used to boast of his personal link to God. Trigg was reinstated. At the time of writing, he has been transferred to Bromley, a more bourgeois and ethnically 'whiter' area than Plumstead.

Goswell decided to sue. The Metropolitan Police's own attitude to the case is clear from its formal defence to his action for assault: 'The striking of the Plaintiff by the said Trigg with the truncheon constituted the use of excessive force in all the circumstances and was thus an assault.' Goswell also began proceedings for a judicial review of Anderton's decision to reinstate PC Trigg. He told me: 'It's as if the Home Office thought, "He's only a black man. It doesn't matter. Let Trigg have his job back." '

It is a dismal vista: while complainants who may have suffered grievous wrongs are bought off with out of court awards of damages, the police officers who perpetrated these misdemeanors are allowed to continue their careers.

There are too many examples. Alphaeus Reid, another black man of good character, was arrested in 1988 in Brixton whilst driving home from work. He was punched in the eye, handcuffed, bundled (still handcuffed) into the back of a police van, held down and kicked repeatedly in the face. On arrival at Brixton police station, he was bleeding from the mouth, and it became immediately apparent he needed an ambulance. At King's College hospital, doctors noted multiple bruising and swelling to his body; in the words of a statement eventually read in open court, he was injured 'from head to toe'. Five of his teeth – which were said to have been weak as a result of a medical condition – had been kicked out. He was unable to work for two months.

Yet the reason for his arrest remains obscure: he was never charged with an offence. After an inquiry into his complaint, a PC Seymour was charged with the disciplinary offence of 'abuse of authority'. As with PC Trigg, a tribunal ordered his dismissal. He too appealed to the Home Secretary's panel. This is a secretive process: after giving evidence, Alphaeus Reid was forced to leave. He was never informed officially why it was that in March 1992, four months after the hearing, Home Secretary Kenneth Baker announced the reinstatement of PC Seymour. A few months later, four years after his ordeal, Reid accepted damages of £10,000.

The largest out of court settlement to date was the £70,000 paid to Anson King in November 1994. He too is a black man with no convictions. In January 1991, he was assaulted and planted with crack cocaine by PC Mark Carroll and Detective Constable Peter McCulloch of Stoke Newington police station in north London. This was notorious for 'Operation Jackpot', a Metropolitan inquiry into allegations of corruption and the 'recycling' of crack – an investigation described by the former Deputy Commissioner, Sir John Smith, as the largest of its kind for twenty years. Carroll and McCulloch figured in several cases examined by Operation Jackpot, and in an unrelated case before the Court of Appeal, the Crown had to admit they could not be relied upon as witnesses of the truth.

King was hospitalised as a result of an injury to his eye, and eventually acquitted of all charges. But when he wrote to the Commissioner demanding some kind of redress after his trial, he received only a curt note inviting him to sue if he wished. It was only after the 1993 House of Lords judgment giving plaintiffs access to internal inquiry documents that King and his lawyers were given their 'smoking gun': a statement by an inspector recording a conversation in which PC Carroll admitted striking King in the eye with his fist. At King's trial, Carroll had vehemently denied doing any such thing. Shortly afterwards, the police made the first of several, steadily increasing, offers of settlement to King.

★   ★   ★

'One has to assume a rule,' says Raju Bhatt. 'In general, police officers will not be dismissed.'[19] Since 1987, Bhatt estimates he has issued approximately 200 civil actions against the police. Just six of these cases have gone to trial, of which he has lost only three. In every other case, his clients have accepted offers of damages out of court.

Yet despite this volume of payments, officers accused by Bhatt's clients have been dismissed or reduced in rank only *twice* – and one of those was PC Seymour, the officer who assaulted Alphaeus Reid, and was later reinstated. The other case, an attack in 1988 by seven PCs on Gary Stretch, who was left hospitalised with massive head injuries, was somewhat unusual because the officers were off-duty. (On this occasion, an appeal to the Home Secretary notwithstanding, all were sacked.)

In Bhatt's view, there is no mystery as to why this should be so. The observation Lord Scarman made in 1981 remains as apposite as ever: 'The problem stems from the fact that the machinery for the investigation of police misconduct and for maintaining discipline remains in the hands of the police themselves. Until both those functions are carried out by an independent body, confidence will not be restored.'

In Britain, the present systemic failure saps the will to act, without which police deviancy cannot be tackled. Evidence of what such a will can achieve was demonstrated long before the PCA came into being, when the venal culture of the London CID was transformed by a reforming Commissioner, Sir Robert Mark. After *The Times* published tapes of officers attempting to obtain large bribes shortly before he became Commissioner in 1972, he launched a great purge, which saw nearly 500 detectives removed from their jobs.

There were several high profile investigations, the creation of a new complaints department, A10, and a handful of criminal trials. In 1976, he announced that eighty-two CID men (and they *were* all men) had been sacked after formal disciplinary proceedings, and forty-six suspended from duty. Yet Mark's principal weapons in ending the culture of illicit graft were informal and bureaucratic – the early retirement of offending officers on medical grounds; the transfer of others to non-operational posts in charge of pelican crossings. By 1976, no fewer than 301 men had been dealt with in this way. Mark succeeded because he was the man in charge and he was prepared to overcome obstacles. Later attempts to tackle the remaining pockets of corruption, notably 'Operation Countryman', a three-year probe in 1978–81 led by officers from Dorset, ended in ignominious retreat. Later, the Countrymen team was to complain of obstruction within Scotland Yard.[20]

After seven years' membership of the PCA, Jeff Crawford considers that the so-called 'malicious complainant' is a rare phenomenon: 'The police can sue malicious complainants for libel.

If they really believe this is going on on a wide scale, they should use the law. The truth is that many people who could justifiably complain do not do so, because they have no faith in the system.'[21]

Crawford differs from most PCA members – generally retired military men, MPs and lawyers – in several respects. He is black, and worked for many years in community relations. His last post before appointment to the PCA was in Tottenham, during the period before and after the Broadwater Farm riot.

His disillusion with the system he served is palpable:

In the criminal law, the word of witnesses who happen to be friends or colleagues of an accused person is not considered fully independent. Yet the law regards police colleagues' evidence as independent, and it allows them to write up their pocketbooks together. That's an abuse, a perversion.

The PCA has become too police friendly. It lacks focus. As a result, cases are not pursued with sufficient vigour.

Meanwhile, Crawford adds, it is not properly accountable:

Perhaps it should have to report to the Commons Home Affairs Select Committee. But it is a full-time quango, a bunch of people we let loose in an area of basic constitutional importance who are accountable to nobody except for the Home Secretary through their annual report.

There should be a more accountable method of recruitment to membership of the authority. It's very informal. There ought to be a proper selection process. It's too important a job to allow it to become a comfortable sinecure for people coming to the end of their working lives. It needs people with the right attitude to society, and to the people who complain. Most complainants are under twenty-nine years of age, from a working-class background. Do the authority members understand their lives? As you know, we used to get a lot of trouble from Stoke Newington. For the PCA members, that was alien territory.

Crawford backs the analysis made above: that even when investigations disclosed damning facts, 'the PCA suffers from a failure to act'. The PCA was 'conservative with a small "c", and it doesn't want to be seen clashing with the police. That means it doesn't want to be seen ever to lose cases that go to tribunals. It will drop them, rather than take that risk.'

However, if Crawford found the PCA's lack of will frustrating, the passivity displayed by the CPS and Director of Public Prosecutions in the most serious cases of all was almost impossible to bear. As the PCA member responsible for the great West Midlands Serious Crime Squad investigation, Crawford sent no fewer than ninety-six separate case files to the CPS. Nearly twenty of them went with a strong recommendation for criminal prosecution, signed both by Crawford and the West Yorkshire police officers who carried out inquiries. Some contained allegations of the blatant fabrication of evidence. These were convincing enough to satisfy Lord Lane's Court of Appeal: at least thirteen prisoners convicted on Squad evidence of crimes including murder succeeded in having their convictions quashed between 1988–92.

On 19 May 1992, however, Barbara Mills, the Director of Public Prosecutions and head of the CPS, announced that there would not be criminal charges against a single Crime Squad officer, because there was not a realistic prospect of conviction.[22] Crawford says:

I didn't find it difficult to believe because it had happened before, but it was an immense disappointment in such a high-profile investigation, which had already cost nearly £2 million, and was running in tandem with cases in the Court of Appeal. The public needed to be reassured there had not been a camouflage, a cover-up – how could you have all these appeals, and hundreds of thousands being paid in compensation, and yet a message from the DPP that the officers' behaviour was nothing much to worry about?

Mills's decision not to prosecute may have been disappointing to Jeff Crawford, but it was also typical. The CPS has a special department which deals only with allegations against police officers. This handles not only files produced by inquiries into complaints, but also 'ordinary' cases where off-duty officers are said to have committed offences of all kinds. Each year it deals with 3,500 cases. It elects to prosecute no more than 150 – five per cent of the total.[23]

Its caution is, to some extent, understandable. Relatively few police officers plead guilty: they have too much to lose. An officer caught drink driving will normally be sacked. For the tiny number of officers convicted of criminal offences and gaoled, prison is likely to become a living hell, endured at constant risk of attack from other inmates.

As we have seen, the high overall rate of pleading guilty means the CPS can expect more than three-quarters of all people tried in the Crown Courts to be convicted. But the conviction rate for police officers accused of criminal offences is only fifty per cent.[24] There is no evidence that this phenomenon is largely the product of some special reluctance on the part of juries to convict police officers. For every juror who views an allegation that evidence has been fabricated as a kind of rough justice, for which a detective ought not to be made to suffer, there will be another whose predisposition is to put policemen away.

Like organised crime and sexual offences, the criminal trials of police officers disclose a more fundamental difficulty with the very nature of the English system of adversarial justice. In 1994, 60 per cent of all defendants who pleaded not guilty in the Crown Court were acquitted of all offences.[25] Too often factually guilty policemen are likely to walk away from prosecution.

This perspective ought to be borne in mind when contemplating one of the more striking features of the crisis in criminal justice which began with the release of the Guildford Four. *Not one* police officer accused of malpractice arising from the many miscarriages of justice put right by the Court of Appeal since 1989 has been convicted of a criminal offence.

In the Guildford case, three retired detectives, Thomas Style, Vernon Attwell and John Donaldson were accused of perjury and conspiracy to pervert the course of justice, the allegations arising from their record of interviews with Patrick Armstrong. Their trial did not begin until 1993, after years of procedural wrangling. To any lay observer, what followed was a mystery. Although they were accused of lying about Armstrong's 'confession', Armstrong himself was not called to give evidence. Later, contrary to claims made on his behalf at the hearing, he declared publicly he had been waiting and willing to do so.

The officers' defence was based on a single proposition: that Armstrong had been guilty all along. Although he had been cleared by the Court of Appeal, and was not in a position to answer any allegations made during the police officers' trial, the defence for the first time revealed further police interviews in which it was claimed he had 'sung like a canary' and again admitted his guilt. Needless to say, no evidence was heard of Armstong's confused and vulnerable psychological state, nor of other factors which had long cast doubt on the Guildford Four's convictions – the pethidine injection given to Carole Richardson just before she confessed; the suppression of Conlon's possible alibi; the discrepancies between Armstrong's confession and other verifiable facts; and above all, the detailed admissions made by the Balcombe Street gang.[26] After a trial lasting eighteen days, Style, Attwell and Donaldson were acquitted.

A fierce but, until then, largely subterranean polemic burst into the open on the pages of the right-wing press. As Sir John May commented in hs Guildford Four inquiry report, there had been a 'whispering campaign' since 1989 conducted by some senior police officers and lawyers. It claimed the Four had been acquitted on merely 'technical' grounds, and had always been factually guilty.[27]

As the Daily Telegraph leader writer put it after the end of the detectives' trial, 'the acquittal of the three ex-policemen . . . suggests there are reasonable grounds for suspecting that two of the Guildford Four, Mr Patrick Armstrong and Mr Gerry Conlon, might have been guilty after all. This raises the disturbing possibility that the real miscarriage of justice occurred when they walked free.'[28] This was becoming a propaganda war, and there was no room for musing over niceties such as the difficulty in reaching the standard of criminal proof. If the police were innocent, the Guildford Four must be guilty.

Similar conclusions were reached in other cases. Chief Superintendent George Reade and two other officers charged for their part in the Birmingham Six case did not stand trial at all. Mr Justice Garland stayed their indictment after ruling that prejudicial press coverage meant they could not have a fair trial. Some newspapers got so carried away that the Birmingham Six found themselves able to collect substantial damages for libel.

In the spring of 1995, the retired superintendent accused of perverting the course of justice for failing to disclose the evidence which proved the innocence of Stefan Kizsko also learned all charges had been dropped, this time on the grounds of the length of time which had elapsed. Nor was anyone ever prosecuted in respect of the seventeen years of wrongful imprisonment endured by Judith Ward.

The last big trial after a miscarriage of justice of police officers accused of conspiracy to pervert the course of justice and perjury was that of the Metropolitan officers who led the inquiry into the murder of PC Keith Blakelock during the 1985 riot at Broadwater Farm.[29] As the Old Bailey jury was told in July 1994, Esda tests suggested that Detective Chief Superintendent Graham Melvin and Detective Chief Inspector Maxwell Dingle had fabricated Winston Silcott's 'confession'. According to the tests, the genuine notes of the officers' last, crucial interview with Silcott had been destroyed. In this lost 'phantom' interview, which survived in the form of impressions on other sheets of paper detected by the Esda equipment, he made no self-incriminating comments. These, the Crown alleged at the trial, had been interpolated later.

Just as the prosecution in the Guildford police trial failed to call Patrick Armstrong, on this occasion it did not call Winston Silcott. Melvin and Dingle chose to exercise their right not to go into the witness-box to give evidence in their own defence.

The case turned on one issue: whether Melvin and Dingle had lied about what went on in a police interrogation room in 1985. Three people had been there, and only they really knew. But the court heard from none of them.

The only prosecution evidence was oblique, highly technical and indirect: the results of the Esda tests on Silcott's interview notes. The policemen's lawyers, led by Richard Ferguson QC, tackled this head-on, arguing that the test was unreliable, and that Silcott had indeed made the remarks attributed to him. As for the so-called 'phantom interview', Melvin had told the Essex police who were asked to investigate the matter back in 1991 that this amounted to no more than the ghostly record of notes he made to prepare himself for the interview with Silcott. After a two-week trial, Melvin and Dingle were acquitted.

Just as the officers accused in the Guildford case had suggested that Patrick Armstrong had been 'factually guilty' all along, Ferguson also told the Old Bailey jury that Silcott had in fact killed PC Blakelock. The crucial moment came when Ferguson produced an extraordinary document, containing short, anonymous excerpts from statements taken by police over the whole period 1985–94. Some accused Silcott of the most heinous acts: of leading the attack on PC Blakelock; of hacking at him with a machete; and of later holding up his bloodied weapon and boasting it bore 'beast man's blood'.

The effect on the media was electric. The authors of the anonymous statements did not, of course, come to court, and their allegations against Silcott were not tested by cross-examination. Nevertheless, newspapers carried them in full. In their editorial columns, they suggested that the real miscarriage of justice was the quashing of Silcott's conviction by the Court of Appeal.

The conclusions reached by the *Daily Express* were typical. The Court of Appeal which had quashed Silcott's conviction in 1992 'considered narrow, technical details, centred on police notes,' its leading article said. 'The jury that acquitted Melvin and Dingle considered something very different. It was able to hear the evidence of fourteen witnesses, who named Silcott as the killer of PC Blakelock, witnesses who described how he repeatedly stabbed, hacked and slashed the unfortunate officer on that terrible night.'

The impact of Ferguson's document was redoubled by two further sentences from its preamble. The fourteen statements were being given to the court only in excerpted form in order 'to protect the identities of those who provided the information', it said. 'The persons making the statements or supplying the information do not give oral evidence *through fear*' [author's italics].[30]

I have read and re-read these sentences many times. I can derive from them only one meaning: that all the witnesses who had made the allegations against Silcott would have been prepared to stand up at the Old Bailey and repeat them as evidence, had they not been too frightened. It is easy to see why the document achieved its impact. But the preamble was more than misleading. Parts of it were wholly untrue.

There were two sources for the fourteen excerpts. In 1991, after Silcott, together with Mark Braithwaite and Engin Raghip, had his conviction quashed by the Court of Appeal, the Metropolitan Police set up a new investigation into the murder, led by Commander Perry Nove. Its working methods could not have been more different from its predecessor. Where Melvin and his colleagues had proceeded by making waves of arrests – nearly 400 people in all – and attempting to extract confessions, Nove began by seeking the co-operation of Tottenham's black community. He appeared on public platforms with Bernie Grant, the area's black MP, and appealed for assistance.

Over many months of painstaking work, this assistance began to materialise.[31] Nove and his team of twenty-six officers managed to find what Melvin always lacked: informants. They used advanced image enhancement techniques to put names to some of the hundreds of police photographs taken during the riot. Eventually, they considered they knew with some certainty the names of all those who attacked PC Blakelock and the officers around him. Many people were quietly approached and interviewed. Nove proceeded with the utmost ethical propriety: if any interview subject appeared to be at risk of self-incrimination, the interview would be suspended, until the subject had been provided with a lawyer.

Nove secured a vital agreement with the Director of Public Prosecutions. He realised that the only witnesses to the murder were members of the mob – about forty strong – who surrounded PC Blakelock when he fell outside the Tangmere block on the Broadwater Farm estate. Blakelock was killed by fifty-four different stab wounds, not kicks and punches, and under Nove's agreement, people who had joined the attack were offered immunity from prosecution if they had not struck him with a knife.

Furthermore, Nove and the CPS held a series of meetings with senior Treasury counsel, at which the basic evidential standard necessary to achieve a 'realistic prospect of conviction' was agreed. For a person to be charged with murdering PC Blakelock, there would have to be *at least two* eyewitnesses prepared to come to court and give evidence, plus supporting material such as photographic identification. By the end of 1993, when Nove submitted a bulky dossier to the CPS, he had identified no fewer than nine suspects against whom such a case could be prepared. Against most of them were not two but at least three prospective witnesses.

For obvious reasons, Nove's investigations were of great interest to Melvin and Dingle. They believed he would find new evidence of Winston Silcott's guilt, and if this could be produced at their own trial, it was unlikely any jury would convict them, whatever the status of an Esda test on a pile of dusty interrogation notes. Moreover, if Silcott *had* been factually guilty, they could credibly argue that he would have been more likely to have made admissions when he was interrogated in 1985.

Early in 1994, their lawyers made a secret application, heard in camera at the Old Bailey, for unfettered access to the Nove inquiry papers. They also argued that Melvin and Dingle should not be tried until any further criminal proceedings arising from the riot had finished.

Nove, for equally obvious reasons, was determined to prevent this application succeeding. The informants who had helped his investigation had been promised absolute confidentiality. As for those who had agreed to give evidence, they had spoken to Nove in order to solve a savage murder, not to assist the defence of police officers who planned the retrial of Winston Silcott.

In a series of secret hearings before Mr Justice Jowitt spread over many weeks, a compromise was reached. Nove would disclose the relevant passages of any statement by a prospective new witness which mentioned Winston Silcott. The solicitors acting for Melvin and Dingle would then ask, via Nove, if that witness was prepared to give evidence at the detectives' trial. All refused. The judge then ruled that the relevant excerpts of their statements would be read to the jury under sections 23 and 24 of the 1988 Criminal Justice Act. This Act allows statements to be read when witnesses have become unavailable. It is doubtful the drafters of the Act ever envisaged it would be employed when a witness who made a statement for the purpose of a homicide inquiry declined to give evidence for an entirely different purpose.

However, new statements made to Nove accounted for only the first seven of the fourteen excerpts in Richard Ferguson's document. Only one of them claimed Winston Silcott joined the attack on PC

Blakelock. By the standards set by the CPS in 1994, he could not have been accused of the murder.

The first excerpt, 'statement A', said only that on the night of the riot, Silcott was 'incensed' and that he hated the police. The author of statement B said he saw Silcott an hour after the murder, and he 'might have' had something inside his coat. Statement C frankly admitted: 'I did not see the fatal incident' and shed no light upon it. Statement D claimed Silcott had been part of the group around Blakelock's body. However, it did not allege he struck any blow.

Statement E did not mention the Blakelock attack. Statement G came from a prisoner who said he overheard Silcott boasting of 'juking' PC Blakelock while he was on remand at Wormwood Scrubs prison. Nove's team did not consider this to be a reliable account. That left only Statement F from the Nove material. This was more incriminating. Its author claimed he had seen the attack from a 'vantage point', adding that Silcott was 'like a general, sending out his little troops'. He had 'organised' the attack on PC Blakelock, and was one of those who dived upon him.

This too, however, was open to serious doubt. It contained a major discrepancy from other verified facts. The statement said that after slipping and falling, PC Blakelock never rose again: 'He didn't get a chance even to get himself in a press-up position.' In fact, despite his terrible wounds, Blakelock got to his feet and, helped by another officer, staggered fifty yards to police vans parked on the perimeter of the estate. He was still alive when the police there called an ambulance.

Left on their own, the seven excerpts from the Nove inquiry would not have had their overwhelming impact. This required further material: excerpts read to the jury as statements H to N. Their origin was very different. They came from the very statements gathered by Melvin and his team back in 1985.

Some, such as statement H, were horrific. It described how Silcott had been 'fucking hacking the geezer to pieces all over', adding that he and the mob he led were like 'vultures'. The author was said to have been a boy of thirteen, who was terrified of retribution if he gave evidence against Silcott.

Those with long memories recognised the wording as the statement and confession of Jason Hill. He made it after three days of

being held incommunicado, illegally denied access to his parents or a
solicitor, while wearing only his underpants and a blanket stained
with his own vomit. Melvin himself had been disciplined by a police
tribunal for the treatment of this boy, although he succeeded in
reversing the decision on appeal. As to the content of Hill's
statement, the judge who heard the murder case in 1987, Mr Justice
Hodgson, said: 'The end result was an account which seems to me
simply impossible. The ritualistic nature of the account, to me,
shouts: "Fantasy!" Time and again Jason Hill gave the police
warning signs he was straying into make-believe . . . and even when,
to their limited knowledge, what he was saying was plainly
inaccurate, they put it down to deliberate lying.'

What of the claim in the preamble to Ferguson's document that
the reason why fourteen anonymous witnesses would not come to
the Old Bailey now to repeat their allegations against Silcott was
'through fear'? A few days after Melvin and Dingle were acquitted, I
tracked down Jason Hill. He said:

> The first I knew they were going to use my statement was when it
> suddenly flashed up on the telly. It is disgraceful. Last year I
> accepted £30,000 damages from the police because of what
> Melvin and his officers did to me in 1985. I never was a witness to
> the killing and I'm not one now. I was thirteen when I said those
> things: for God's sake, I'm now nearly twenty-three. When do I
> get a chance to live my life away from this? I thought this trial was
> about claims of forged police papers. What did my old, discredited
> statement have to do with that?

Another of the 1985 statements reheated for the 1994 police trial
came from Andrew Pyke, a mentally handicapped juvenile who was
the first person arrested by the Melvin team. His allegations had also
been discredited years earlier. Like Hill, he insisted in 1994 he had no
warning they were about to be aired again, let alone that a court
would be told he was not giving evidence 'through fear'. Another of
the excerpted statements, which had Silcott holding a machete and
boasting he had shed 'beast man's blood', belonged to Perry Kelsey.
He was charged with riot on the sole basis of this statement, and in

1987 was acquitted because the courts would not accept it. He too was appalled when it was dragged out again.

Statement K was made by Mark Pennant, another mentally handicapped juvenile. Like Hill's, his conditions of detention were oppressive and illegal. His confession to murder, in a statement which also alleged that Silcott cut Blakelock with a knife, was thrown out by the 1987 judge. Hill and the other authors of the excerpts dating from 1985 all said separately then that the police led by Melvin had seemed determined to gather evidence against Winston Silcott, questioning them again and again about his supposed role. Their allegations against him had no value in 1985, and they had none nine years later.

Richard Ferguson QC cannot be criticised for the way he used the materials available to him in the trial of Dingle and Melvin. He simply performed the role allotted defence counsel in an adversarial trial: to fight as hard as possible on behalf of his client on the basis of his instructions. The behaviour of Mr Justice Jowitt and the prosecutor, David Calvert-Smith QC, is more puzzling. They knew the text of Ferguson's document in advance, and after the weeks of secret pre-trial hearings, had agreed its content. Why did they let the defence go to trial with material that had already been dismissed in 1987? After the trial, Calvert-Smith made no secret of his disappointment at the result.

Needless to say, the continuing secrecy surrounding the in camera hearings goes on. I tried to discover more from the CPS. All its spokesman would say was: 'It doesn't matter that the material had already been thrown out by one judge. What you're trying to do is apply logic to the legal system.'

Maxwell Dingle had already retired, but after celebrating his acquittal, Detective Chief Superintendent Graham Melvin went back to work. He announced he was looking forward to returning to the 'cutting-edge' of the fight against organised crime. Three months later he quietly bowed out.

But what of the nine suspects for the murder of PC Blakelock named in Commander Nove's dossier to the CPS? On the eve of the Melvin-Dingle trial, the CPS announced no prosecutions were contemplated.

As ever, the service refused to discuss its decision. But as we have seen, leading Treasury counsel had already decided that in these nine cases, the evidence was good enough to provide a realistic prospect of conviction. Accordingly, under the Code for Crown Prosecutors, the decision was made on other grounds. In the view of the CPS, another Blakelock murder trial was 'not in the public interest'.

CHAPTER EIGHT

The Collapse of Criminal Justice

AS CRIME is the first outward and visible sign of a society's pathology, so the study of criminal justice is a valuable diagnostic tool. Like biopsy specimens, samples taken from different layers of the body politic reveal different aspects of its illness.

There are, obviously, wider questions to be asked about the things that so strain and distort the system of justice: the conflicts and suffering produced by deepening inequality, or racism, or the failure of 'community care' for the mentally ill. However, the means by which the system tries to cope with these phenomena can be equally instructive. Sometimes, its failures turn out to be its own inner reflection of the social pressures which bear down on it from without. They also help to explain its resistance to reform.

For example, it is hardly surprising that divisions of social class can be seen in large part to determine the system's raw materials – the crimes, the victims and the perpetrators. As the lawyers in Lucky Deol's murder trial agreed, things go on in places such as Abbey Hulton which do not occur in Kensington. The dramas played out in courtrooms and police stations represent other social and political dramas, with remoter origins. Some have been discussed in this book: the war in Northern Ireland (the Guildford and Birmingham cases); racism and the rise of alienated black minorities (the Deol and Silcott affairs); the formation of impoverished archipelagos of the dispossessed on estates such as Stonebridge Park.

At the same time, class permeates the system's internal structures. The rigidity of the criminal justice hierarchy has long gone out of fashion elsewhere. Like the participants in a famous television sketch starring John Cleese, its actors all look up to someone and down on someone else. Generally speaking, the police are at the bottom (aside, of course, from the criminals), well below the salaried lawyers of the CPS, whose members are in turn looked down on by solicitors in private practice.

In the next layer up, where the wearing of eighteenth-century fancy dress and horsehair wigs maintains an air of the comic and the surreal, no one need be in any doubt of the superiority of Queen's Counsel over mere 'juniors'. Above them again are the judges. Mere members of the circuit bench appear in purple and should be addressed in court by the relatively ungrovelling term 'your Honour'. Only the more serious trials will merit the presence of a red-robed judge of the High Court, and he, of course, will always be 'my Lord'. His status and independence are guaranteed by one of the few parts of the British constitution set down in parliamentary legislation, the 1707 Act of Settlement.

Class accounts for some of the system's most objectionable features. Few prosecuting barristers ever speak to the victim. 'You have only to hear the jargon, the talk of the defendant as a "horrible little oik", and often the rape victim as a "scrubber",' says Geoffrey Robertson QC. 'In the argot of the barristers' robing room, a crime which has had a devastating impact on someone's life can be dismissed as a "tuppeny ha'penny case".'[1]

Among his achievements, Prime Minister John Major numbered the promulgation of a 'Victim's Charter', replete with pledges to keep victims informed of the progress of their case, and the court informed of the impact of the crime on their lives. It has done little to change attitudes in practice. Meanwhile, over half of those summoned to give evidence in court are never called into the witness box, despite often having waited many hours.

It is a truism that law and criminal justice policy are made by those who control the state. Money buys the best lawyers and the most cunning arguments. In the unlikely event that wealthy offenders do go to prison, they appear to receive easier treatment in open gaols as of right. They escape incarceration more easily, even when accused of stealing sums which if demanded over a bank counter at the point of a shotgun would attract a sentence of fifteen years. The Court of Appeal freed Ernest Saunders less than halfway through his seven-year stretch for the 1980s Guinness fraud on the grounds that he suffered from Alzheimer's disease – which miraculously cleared up after his release. Roger Levitt, who conned thousands of investors out of their savings, was punished by being asked to do 180 hours of community service. He still lives in a million-pound house in Hampstead.

Inequalities of this kind are endemic. In themselves they do not indicate a crisis in the justice system, much less a collapse: this is the way the game has been played since the eighteenth-century Black Act and beyond. But as E.P. Thompson argued, their persistence does not *negate* the idea of fairness and equality before the law, although they do conflict with it.[2] The strength of these principles means the law can work as a means of enforcing hierarchies and social control and, more than occasionally, simultaneously deliver social justice, the victory of the weak over the strong. And paradoxically, the period of Tory rule since 1979 has seen the appointment of several members of the high judiciary imbued with liberal, even radical, attitudes which sit most uneasily with the authoritarian approach of the Government. There has been an exponential growth in the number of challenges to the executive by means of High Court judicial review. In a long list of high-profile cases, the judges have quashed Ministers' decisions, finding them unlawful or 'perverse'.

However, while the system's inbuilt stratification is not the source of the crisis which now confronts it, this structure has weakened the system's ability to respond. The demands upon criminal justice have seldom, if ever, been as great. As Chapter Three demonstrated, they have been intensified by the rampant fetish of the free market and consequent social polarisation which developed during the 1980s. The emergence, as Will Hutton puts it, of a 30/30/40 society, in which the bottom segment of 30% of the population has been relegated to the margins, has imposed unprecedented stresses on the administration of justice.[3] The predictions made in the internal Scotland Yard documents in the mid-eighties have been borne out.

In contrast, the fifties and sixties, the era of Keynesian full employment and Butskellite political consensus, was also the era of *Dixon of Dock Green*, that mythical figure of benign justice. These decades also had their violent professional criminals, but thirty years later, they are remembered with nostalgia. The Krays, the legend has it, kept the East End of London free from muggers and rapists. Today 'Mad' Frankie Fraser, who once pulled out his victims' teeth with pliers, is a theatrical showman, who performs his menacing confessions to critical acclaim. It is significant that *Heartbeat*, a rosy-tinted cop show set in the Yorkshire moors of the mid-sixties, is one of the biggest television hits of the 1990s.

But the contemporary crisis in criminal justice is not simply a matter of increasing demands on the system, although they have exacerbated it. The system is failing in its first and most essential task: to separate 'factually guilty' criminals from the falsely accused.

A state which sends innocent people to gaol for life but cannot reliably bring offenders to justice fails to protect its citizens from itself and from themselves. If criminal justice fails this test, its other departments become grotesque parodies of their intended function. How will a prison 'rehabilitate' the innocent? The wrongly-convicted murderer or rapist is forced to endure an Orwellian nightmare: years of 'treatment' to make him 'address his offending behaviour' and so prepare him for release. The latest tool of the prison psychologists is the penile plesythmograph, a metal clip attached to the penis which measures levels of arousal while the prisoner is made to watch videos of violence and deviant sex. In some cases, men who have vehemently and plausibly protested their innocence for many years are being made to submit to this indignity as a precondition to being considered for transfer to lower security gaols.

Perceptions and public confidence now matter almost as much as 'objective' reality – as Lord Denning realised, with his comment about the 'appalling vista' if it were true that the Birmingham Six were innocent. In the criminal law, justice has to be seen to be done in order to command belief and respect. Without that belief, the system is in jeopardy.

The view held widely throughout the 'Dixon' epoch, that British justice was the best in the world, was only one facet of national self-confidence, of the collective self-belief of a society which had only lately won the Second World War. No matter that the secret consensus between the participants in the old criminal justice regime was based on delusions as great as those which masked Britain's broader national decline. Seen from the perspective of a harsher, more cynical age, it is impossible to consider them without envy.

But there comes a point, with any illusion, when it can no longer be sustained. Under pressure for nearly two decades, the fantasy of perfection in criminal justice was dealt its *coup de grâce* with the release of the Guildford Four. In the years since the Guildford appeal, the concern of public discourse has shifted away from miscarriages of justice. Today the principal focus of concern is the discharge or acquittal of factually guilty defendants. Cheered on by the tabloid press, Police Commissioner Condon warns that when guilty men go free, police officers may be tempted to close the legal loopholes by indulging in their own criminal acts, by practising 'noble cause corruption'. Meanwhile, ebbing respect for the rule of law and the rise of vigilantism indicate a dangerous weakness in the State and civil society.

A vicious spiral has become well-established: criminals who get away with their crimes become more confident and aggressive, and more likely to try to intimidate witnesses or juries. According to a 1994 Home Office study, 'on high crime housing estates 13 per cent of crime reported to the police by victims and 9 per cent reported by witnesses resulted in people being intimidated'. As a result, there was 'a general unwillingness of the public to come forward as witnesses, particularly where they were not the direct victim of a crime'. Only 29 per cent of people surveyed had reported crimes which they had witnessed.[4]

Chapter One ended by posing an uncomfortable question: if the old regime's defenders believed its institutionalised malpractice had a functional purpose – of protecting society from crime – could they, after all, have been right? In the descent to near-anarchy found in parts of the country today, that question might seem to be answerable with an emphatic 'yes'.

Yet in the old regime's defeat lay an unprecedented opportunity for renewal and reform. Criminal justice wasn't working, but the time had come to ask why, and to put it right. This chance has not been taken, and the failure to do so is turning crisis into collapse. At the heart of this process is a failure of analysis. As this book has tried to show, wrongful acquittals and wrongful convictions both persist in happening. The argument which public discussion has so far failed to consider is that both outcomes share common, systemic origins. They are two sides of the same debased coin.

It follows that the crisis cannot be resolved by legislative tinkering:

by lurches in the direction of either due process or crime control. It requires a radical reappraisal of both the system's institutional structures, and its underlying philosophy.

★ ★ ★

At a superficial level, the connection between wrongful convictions and wrongful acquittals is clear enough. The steadily rising rate of acquittal by Crown Court juries stems in part from their reluctance to believe police evidence, and their readiness to believe that the police may have lied. But there is a more fundamental link.

Chief Constables such as Charles Pollard and David Phillips have led the Association of Chief Police Officers in a sustained critique of the adversarial trial. As they rightly point out, the adversarial justice of the common law system is not a search for the truth. Each side, prosecution and defence, has its role to play: to construct its case and win. The constraints of legal rules limit the means with which the combatants can pursue victory. Yet at its heart, adversarial justice is not objective. Where gaps in the rules exist, it does not have to be fair.

Sometimes, in defending the adversarial status quo, its staunchest supporters inadvertently highlight its drawbacks. There are few defence counsel with reputations as formidable as Ron Thwaites QC. He says: 'Defendants don't ask for your judgment on them but your advocacy. There is no such thing as a hopeless case, only a hopeless barrister. If there are more acquittals than there used to be, that reflects the commitment and skill of counsel. Am I supposed to do my job half-heartedly? Am I supposed to ignore my best point?'[5]

Yet even Thwaites accepts the potential disadvantages:

I will acknowledge that the witness-box is a very lonely place. It is very hard to withstand good cross-examination, even if you're telling the absolute truth. The art of a good cross-examination is to seal all exits, leaving only the chimney. Then smoke 'em out.

Sometimes police officers do make innocent mistakes. It can be easy to convert mistakes into sinister lies. It's not being hard, it's not being soft. It's only doing my job. You must go to the heart of the case by going for the witnesses – not its big toe.

A point more rarely made by Pollard, Phillips and their ACPO allies is that under the rules of adversarial justice, prosecutors are no less ruthless in the pursuit of victory. The criticisms, made by Commander Williamson from a psychological perspective in Chapter Four, of the adversarial testing of witness evidence also apply to defendants. There are innocent inmates in Britain's gaols who tried to put their case in the witness-box, only for a barrister successfully to portray an innocent hesitation over detail as damning evidence of guilt. If the skill of a defence advocate lies in smoking out the weaknesses of a prosecution, the job of the prosecutor is to cover them up.

Some of the statistics cited in this book further support the argument that the adversarial trial is becoming increasingly inadequate as a mechanism for delivering justice: *vide* the rising acquittal rates in cases of rape and serious violence, and the extreme difficulty of convicting police officers and rich professional criminals. Unacceptably often, defence counsel will secure an acquittal by attempting to put the victim on trial.

The rules of the adversarial contest affect even the behaviour of criminals. 'Serial rapists are quite astute,' comments Mr Justice Stephen Sedley. 'They deliberately look for women whose lifestyle may be slightly chaotic, and before they attack them, they take them boozing. When it gets to court, the victim finds it difficult to give an account which will stand up to fierce cross-examination. The very thing that makes her a target for rapists makes her a target for defence lawyers.'[6]

On top of this defective chassis, a tottering superstructure of statute law and judicial precedent has been built in an attempt to modify the system's more glaring faults. To those outside the siblinghood of legal initiates, its complexities sometimes defy definition or understanding. For example, there is the dictum that evidence which is 'more prejudicial than probative' should not be admitted. But what is prejudicial, what is probative? In the words of a cynical detective who had just lost a case because most of the prosecution case had been thrown out, 'as far as I can see, prejudicial means evidence that proves he did it'.

Then there is the rule against hearsay. Should a court have had the opportunity of considering John Rutter's brother's taped allegation that he had attacked Quddus Ali after all? Should the jury in the Kano case have heard the tapes of the three defendants' arrest? Anyone who spends much time attending criminal trials will be struck by a sense that the version of events being described by the barristers bears only an oblique relationship to reality. For jurors, excluded for hours and days while counsel argue over the admissibility of evidence, this sense of dislocation is even worse.

In the jargon of the English Common Law jurisdiction, lay citizens can barely understand the legal descriptions of the most common offences. In the absence of a modern Criminal Code such as those which exist throughout Europe, the law on assault is still determined by the 1861 Offences Against the Person Act, with its bewildering distinctions between 'actual' and 'grievous' bodily harm. The vagaries of the law on homicide allow wife-killers to evade a life sentence by pleading guilty to manslaughter on grounds they were 'provoked', or that they were experiencing 'diminished responsibility' when they plunged in the knife. Legal definitions of concepts such as 'public place' and 'intent' lie spread across a web of legislation and judicial rulings.

Of course, as Chapter Four demonstrated, only a small minority of cases ever go through a contested Crown Court trial. For most victims and defendants, justice has become an industrialised process, determined by a remote bureaucracy, whose *raison d'être* is to avoid expensive contested trials as often as possible. Police officers who gather evidence know that it will usually never be produced in public or tested by cross-examination. The probability is that it will be discontinued by the CPS, thrown out by a judge, or even more likely, that the defendant will plead guilty, coerced into doing so after a backroom lawyers' deal.

Bureaucratic justice hides the flaws as well as the merits of a prosecution case: for each questionable CPS discontinuance, there is a defendant denied the chance to put his case. Trial by bureaucracy creates the space for the corrupt police officer, who crosses his fingers that a guilty plea will keep the way he bent the legal rules concealed.

However the vital point to grasp is that although the full-blown adversarial contest is relatively rare, its underlying methods and philosophy continue to dominate other parts of the system, including, crucially, the pre-trial phase of police investigation.

The police, just as much as the wily or ruthless counsel for the defence, operate with the rules of adversarial justice constantly in mind. At one level, the investigator of any serious crime must work according to the limits imposed by the adversarial contest and its complex rules of evidence. He must try to second-guess the possible future strategies of the defence, and so, in some circumstances, may leave untouched important lines of inquiry.

The adversarial mindset exerts a further, deeper influence, visible at the very centre of police culture. No less than barristers, the police want and need to win the contest, to 'get a result'. However much chief officers may exhort detectives to work impartially with open minds, every institution within adversarial criminal justice exerts pressure in the opposite direction.

Doreen McBarnet's great insight was to see that the police do not operate in isolation but within the institutional framework of the law, its institutions and the gaps left by its omissions.[7] Here her analysis can be applied to the bedrock of criminal investigation. If police work is to fit with the rest of the system, it can no more be a 'search for the truth' than the contested trial. It has to be about constructing cases, and gathering evidence around a probable suspect.

The collapse of the old regime's distinguishing method, investigation through interrogation, has not altered this. Nor is the CPS an adequate filter: the tests set out by the Code for Crown Prosecutors say nothing about searching for truth. Asking whether there is a 'realistic prospect' of conviction is simply a variant on the same theme.

The recent history of English criminal justice bulges with examples of this process in action. In the case of the Birmingham Six, the police were certain they had caught the bombers within hours because forensic tests – long since discredited – suggested that their suspects had handled explosives. Leaving aside the manner in which the police then obtained confessions, the adversarial approach also meant that they would inevitably ignore available evidence that pointed in other directions.

In the recent case of Colin Stagg, tried and acquitted for the murder of Rachel Nickell on Wimbledon Common, the attempt to construct a winnable case around a plausible suspect led to a vast undercover operation which collapsed disastrously in court. To the eventual fury of the trial judge, the police introduced Stagg to a female detective, who tried successfully to entice him into confessing by pretending she was sexually excited by acts of bloody violence. This scheme had been endorsed not only by the CPS, but by a leading Crown QC.

The Stagg case is a vivid example of the drawbacks of the English approach, measured in terms of the falling rate of convictions. By the time the police reopened the investigation into Rachel's death a year after Stagg was charged, the trail was cold. At the time of writing, a Scotland Yard team has found another possible suspect in New Zealand. But they hold out little hope of eventual success.

The search for truth was no more evident in the byzantine Regional Crime Squad cases involving *agents provocateurs* described in Chapter Five; it is difficult to see how criminal investigations which begin before a crime has been committed could ever be so described. Meanwhile, with huge resources absorbed in such activity, real crimes are not investigated. As Chapter Five noted, the fashion for 'targeting known suspects' instead of investigating crimes now carries the official endorsement of the Audit Commission. It is seen as the way to break not only professional gangs, but local petty thieves, and so convictions won by means of entrapment look set to increase.

Since 1991, when the official police submission to the Royal Commission on Criminal Justice described the professional English detective as a 'neutral investigator', these institutional constraints have been omitted from the argument. In an influential 1995 position paper, the Association of Chief Police Officers claimed the role of the police ought to be seen as 'that of the investigator, impartially and professionally gathering evidence'.[8] And indeed the police critique of the adversarial trial has at times been compelling. But it has failed to take into account the effect of such a style of justice earlier on in the process, and in cases where no trial ever takes place.

Since the Guildford Four appeal, the police have developed a series of internal initiatives aimed at giving the ideal of neutrality substance. Training now urges officers to admit they may not know the answers to every question when they give evidence and to accept that there may be discrepancies between officers' accounts of the same event. A national programme to teach police 'investigative interviewing' seeks to change the aim of interrogation from 'getting a cough' to the collection of any relevant information, including exculpatory facts.

But without changing the law governing criminal justice, and the very structures of that justice, internal reforms of this kind will, for many officers, remain mere exhortation. It is not enough to wish the idea of 'neutral investigation' into being. The system has to change to allow it to become the institutional norm.

$$\star \quad \star \quad \star$$

The alternative to the adversarial model is an 'inquisitorial' system, in which the objective search for truth becomes an avowed public purpose, not a by-product generated by chance. In the halcyon days of 1991, as Home Secretary Kenneth Baker established the Royal Commission, there was widespread speculation that a radical shift in this direction might emerge.

One of the Commission's first acts was to order research into two nearby jurisdictions which broadly follow inquisitorial principles, France and Germany. The authors of this study, published in 1992, reached several immediately striking conclusions. First, they found that in neither country was it likely that miscarriages of justice such as the Guildford or Birmingham cases would occur. Second, in contrast to the stratified and often vexed relationship between the different actors in the criminal process in England, on the continent this relationship was marked by 'a high degree of confidence, and of co-operation and mutual trust'. Finally, public confidence in both systems remained high in their respective countries, and in the German case the conviction rate was as high as 90 per cent.[9]

It is not the intention here to advocate the wholesale adoption of the French or German model. Both, as the Royal Commission study made clear, have their disadvantages, notably long delays before trial during which a suspect may spend an unacceptably long time in custody.

But the Royal Commission elected not even to consider whether it might be possible to adapt and improve existing inquisitorial methods. It dealt with the matter of basic procedural structures in just six paragraphs of a 261–page report, saying: 'Every system is the product of a distinctive history and culture, and the more different the history and culture from our own, the greater must be the danger that an attempted transplant must fail.'

It backed this assertion with the comment that 'hardly any of those who gave evidence to the Commission suggested that the system in another jurisdiction should be adopted in England and Wales'. This was hardly surprising: virtually all the Commission's witnesses came from one or other part of the existing system. All had a strong vested interest in its remaining essentially the same.[10]

Once the Commission had ducked these issues, there was little prospect of their being taken up by anyone else. For most barristers, the structures of English justice have become a fetishistic totem which preserves their own privileges.

Writing in 1915, Weber made observations about the English legal system which have lost none of their applicability:

In England, the reason for the failure of all efforts at a rational codification of law were due to the successful resistance against such rationalisation offered by the great and centrally organised lawyers' guilds, a monopolistic stratum of notables from whose midst the judges of the High Court are recruited . . . they successfully fought all moves towards rational law which threatened their material position.

The consequence, he added, was that court procedures in England 'amounted to a far-going denial of justice to the economically weak groups'.[11]

Today there are more than a hundred barrister MPs, including, at the time of writing, the Home Secretary, Michael Howard QC, the Chancellor of the Exchequer, Kenneth Clarke QC, the Shadow Home Secretary, Jack Straw, and the leader of Her Majesty's loyal Opposition, Tony Blair, husband of Cherie Booth QC. They also include the influential Tory Chairman of the Commons Select Committee on Home Affairs, Ivan Lawrence, QC, MP. He believes English criminal justice is 'democracy at work', and thus 'streets ahead of any other system' adding: 'There are some stones you don't look under. Unless you know what you're going to do to fill the gaps, you're better leaving the old institutions in place. Or else you're going to have a hole.'[12]

By deciding that the existing institutions of English criminal justice were an ineradicable part of the national heritage, the Royal Commission allowed itself to recommend only piecemeal adjustment. Others were soon ready to fill the intellectual vacuum.

In its outright rejection of continental experience, the Commission – and subsequent public debate – have ignored a further important point. It is arguably true that the inquisitorial method of trial used in France could not easily be transplanted across the Channel. In a French court, there is no cross-examination: defence lawyers may not interrupt the witnesses, and all the questioning is done by the judge. It is also arguable that this is the pure inquisitorial model's greatest weakness.[13] But it would be perfectly possible to retain the fundamentals of the English common law trial while at the same time subjecting the entire pre-trial phase to radical reform. The advantages of at least some aspects of the French and German systems are so marked it seems almost inexplicable, Weber notwithstanding, that the possibility of adopting them has been so little explored in Britain.

This is not the place to describe all the details of criminal investigation in Germany and France, and there are big differences between them. But the benefits found by the Royal Commission study and listed above stem from a number of overriding principles. They are all applicable on this side of the Channel.

The first and most important is the supervision of police investigations, especially in serious cases, by an independent body – in France, this is done by the *juge d'instruction*, the examining magistrate; in Germany, by the prosecutor. Their duties include the direction of inquiries into matters which may exonerate the suspect as and when they may occur – or are pointed out by the defence. They are also constitutionally charged to ensure that the minimum standards of a suspect's rights are met, both those set out by statute and those embodied in the European Convention on Human Rights. They must protect the presumption of innocence, and the right against self-incrimination. If they find evidence of police malpractice or brutality during a case, they must appoint an independent prosecutor to investigate it at once.

The contrast with the position in this country, where evidence of malpractice may do no more than weaken the credibility of a prosecution when it comes to trial, is marked. In Germany, the abject failure to redress police scandals set out in Chapter Seven of this book would not be conceivable.

The continental pre-trial method has a further overwhelming advantage. The *juge d'instruction* or prosecutor does not, unlike his counterpart in the CPS, gain only a paper acquaintance with a case. He will meet the victim, suspect and witnesses and often interview them, while at the same time being open to approaches from defence lawyers. If a German prosecutor discontinues a case, it will be on the basis of genuine knowledge, not haphazard speculation based on reading a file. Moreover, the involvement of one official will be continuous throughout a case. There are no fiascos such as that which occurred after Lillian Hedgecock's murder.

Independent supervision undertaken on the basis of guaranteed constitutional rights means the detective's inevitable tendency to look for 'results' meets its foil while inquiries are still in progress, not months later – if at all – in court. The use of undercover methods – probably essential in dealing with organised crime – can be authorised when justified, and then monitored. There should be no blank cheques such as that granted by the CPS to the Midlands Regional Crime Squad in the case of Graham Titley, on the basis of inflated and unverified claims about his crime-busting potential.

The outlines of the first and most vital step to restore the effectiveness of English criminal justice are now discernible. We need a transformed prosecution service. It must operate within the framework of formal constitutional rights, and be constitutionally accountable. Its area boundaries should be coterminous with those of the police, with whom its relationship must be governed not by class-based deference and disdain but co-operation and trust. At the same time, it must be prepared to supervise, modify and stop police inquiries, while automatically referring cases of malpractice to an independent prosecutorial agency. Local prosecutors should be answerable to local authorities, as should the police.

The first dividend would be the return of people's confidence in our justice system. Fewer innocents would go to prison. The changed relationship between police and prosecutors would ensure that cases did not arrive at the door of the Crown Court in such a half-baked state and therefore judges would only seldom direct acquittal before swearing in the jury. The public would know that prosecution evidence could once again be trusted. The acquittal of really guilty criminals would cease to be a common event. In place of the present crisis, a virtuous circle would gradually come into being. Frequent reliable convictions based on reliable evidence would diminish the scourge of witness intimidation: coming forward would not seem so dangerous if cases were less prone to sudden, unpredictable collapse.

There are other measures which could make the trial itself more of a 'search for truth', even short of total structural change. One would be to allow judges to call their own witnesses, if they felt that the court was not being given an adequate account of events, and that the interests of justice were not being served.

There is a rule which prevents either side from casting doubt on the evidence given by a witness which it has called. The only way to this is by applying to make the witness 'hostile', and subject him to full-blown cross-examination – a process which tends to devalue his testimony altogether. The rule should be scrapped. Another outmoded regulation is the ban on allowing courts to hear the evidence of phone-taps. If not for this, Brian Charrington and Curtis Warren would now be serving very long sentences.

The courts should make much more use of audio and video tapes. Police interviews, not only with suspects but with victims and other witnesses, should be filmed and should be made admissible as evidence. The inflation by clever lawyers of minor discrepancies between a statement taken at the time of an offence and a trial months later would diminish.

Another highly desirable change would be to make jury service compulsory. Until the mid-eighties, prospective jurors had to give reasons for declining their public duty. Now, however, it is enough to state that one is unavailable. According to the Lord Chancellor's Department, three-fifths of the 500,000 people asked to serve on juries in 1994 refused. There used to be a property qualification for jury service, and juries were composed of middle-class people who judged their social inferiors. Now the other extreme has been reached: they are made up disproportionately of the retired, the unemployed and the dispossessed.

All of these suggestions for reform, at both the pre-trial and trial stages, share a common characteristic. They represent a move neither towards 'crime control' nor 'due process'. They would reduce the scope for police malpractice, without creating 'technical' loopholes through which criminals might walk free. They would make it easier to convict the guilty and to acquit the innocent. They also represent an opportunity lost. Politically, they lie beyond the far horizon.

★ ★ ★

The 1993 Royal Commission report appeared to have no overall philosophy whatsoever. Its terms of reference exhorted the commissioners to 'have regard' to cost, and its hotch-potch of recommendations appeared to be determined less by justice than by economics. The lack of any overarching analysis severely weakened its impact. This was not a programme, but a *pot pourri*, and it failed to set its stamp on future debate.

Nevertheless, as the aftershocks of the miscarriages of justice began to subside, a new and enlightened attitude seemed to be visible in many of the institutions of English criminal justice: in the Court of Appeal, in parts of the police service, and in the penal policy-making organs of the Home Office.

The 1991 Criminal Justice Act became the embodiment of Home Secretary David Waddington's stated belief that prison was 'an expensive way of making bad people worse', and should be used as a punishment of last resort, primarily for violent and sexual offenders. In the same year, Lord Justice Woolf's report on the riot at Strangeways prison in Manchester became a milestone of sane humanity, recommending comprehensive improvements in prisoners' conditions and their prospects for rehabilitation. Almost all the report's proposals were promptly accepted by the Government.

The new intellectual climate was noticeable in the most surprising quarters. Post-Guildford Four, Lord Chief Justice Lane was a changed man, prepared to overturn convictions on grounds he would once have dismissed. After 1989, no judge was more assiduous in applying the due process 'integrity principle'. If police had breached PACE or committed some other impropriety, that alone would suffice to overturn a finding of guilt. Meanwhile, the advocates of democratic, community-based policing, with their emphasis on quality over quantity of service, were enjoying their brief hour of approval.

But in the context of the unreformed British state, these developments were always vulnerable to abrupt reversal. Not for nothing did the Victorian jurist A.V. Dicey describe the glory of Britain's unwritten constitution as the 'despotism' of the Crown in Parliament. The pre-modern settlement – that compromise between a powerful aristocracy and their merchant, industrial and professional rivals – which originated in 1688 created a polity based not on the concept of universal rights, but immunities: legal freedoms in Britain exist only where gaps between the coercive limits imposed by law leave room for them to flourish.

The prime movers in the treaty which became the 1951 European Convention on Human Rights were Sir Winston Churchill and the Labour Foreign Secretary Ernest Bevin. But Britain did not grant its citizens the right of individual petition to the Human Rights Court at Strasbourg until 1966. All forty-two convention signatories have now 'incorporated' its provisions into their domestic law, so allowing their courts to apply its provisions – except Britain and Ireland, which has its own written constitution and Bill of Rights in any event.

In criminal justice, parliamentary despotism means that any due process safeguards are inherently temporary and expedient. It so happens that the provisions of the British PACE Act relating to police interrogation and access to lawyers are somewhat more stringent than their counterparts in Germany, and especially France. But if Parliament had by this measure made convictions based on confessions more difficult to obtain, it could equally well reverse this trend at any time. In the absence of overarching constitutional standards, there is no theoretical limit to the pursuit of crime control.

By 1992, the window of enlightenment was coming to an end. As the deep recession caused by the overvaluation of the pound in the Exchange Rate Mechanism sent unemployment surging back towards three million, crime totals increased by record margins. In

1991 and 1992, some counties reported increases of over 30 per cent, and for the first time, the annual total for England and Wales was greater than five million offences. The social conflicts inherent in Hutton's 30/30/40 social model – a prosperous top layer of 30 per cent, an increasingly insecure middle group of 40 per cent and an excluded and marginalised underclass of 30 per cent – were becoming unsustainable.

The moment when the Guildford Four ceased to be the primary impulse behind criminal justice policy came in February 1993, with the abduction and murder of the Liverpool toddler Jamie Bulger by two ten-year-old boys. The case brought several acute shared public anxieties into the open, and at once acquired a symbolic importance. On both Left and Right, it was discussed not as the mystifying, isolated act of two aberrant children, but as a signifier of national depravity.

Long before their trial, it was apparent that Jamie's killers came from deeply troubled backgrounds among society's 'excluded' and impoverished bottom 30 per cent. Even before the murder, the tenor of public discourse had been changing rapidly, with fierce tabloid newspaper interest in juvenile crime. Editorials blamed a generation of disaffected youth – not entirely without foundation – for much of the burgeoning car-crime and burglary in city centres and council estates.

The murder also happened to coincide with a period of plummeting political fortunes for the Government, with the Conservatives' prolonged agony over Europe in general and the Treaty of Maastricht in particular. The ERM fiasco had lost voters' trust in the Conservatives to run the economy. Faced with a Labour Shadow Home Secretary, Tony Blair, who was rapidly colonising Conservative home territory with his promise to be 'tough on crime, tough on the causes of crime', Prime Minister John Major signalled a decisive shift to the Right.

On 21 February 1993, less than a month after Jamie's death, he gave a long interview to Jonathan Holborow, editor of the *Mail on Sunday*, one of the few newspapers which could still be relied upon to give him unqualified support. For Major, the paper reported, crime was 'the dominant issue of the hour'. But there was to be no wishy-washy business about getting tough on the causes of crime. As far as he recognised the concept at all, it boiled down to a simple matter of individual moral choice: 'There is a distinction between right and wrong. You know whether what you are doing is right or wrong and other people know it as well. I think the public generally need to draw that distinction in the case of people who are guilty of wrongdoing.'

If crime was no more than what bad people did, the job of the state was to exact retribution: revenge on behalf of the decent majority. Those who were not against the criminals must be for them, Major suggested. He moved on to state the explicitly anti-intellectual, anti-compassionate formula which has already been quoted: 'I believe they should condemn. If they do not condemn they may appear to approve tacitly. Tacit approval will lead to repetition, and that is what we need to avoid. I feel strongly that society needs to condemn a little more and understand a little less.'[14]

Already, punishment, not accurate detection and conviction, let alone possible treatment or rehabilitation, was moving to the centre of the Conservative political stage. Asked about the plight of 'widows who have been robbed and beaten', Major replied: 'We have to protect them. We have to punish severely and we need to safeguard them. I would like a crusade against crime.' No matter that the police detection rate for street robbery in most police areas was 10 per cent or less. The way to protect the victims of crime was to punish the minority who were captured with unprecedented severity.

A few months later, a leaked memorandum from the new Home Secretary, Michael Howard, spoke of the need for 'more austere prisons', apparently pandering to the tabloid legend that Britain's gaols are mostly drink-sodden holiday camps. But the apotheosis of crime control, and retribution had to wait until the Conservative Party Conference.

On 6 October 1993, Jeffrey Archer, the Conservative Deputy Chairman, brought a rape victim to the conference rostrum. Heard in awed silence, she described her experience in harrowing detail. Lord Archer – who would shortly resign his party position after disclosures about his share dealings – used her account to whip the hall into an expectant frenzy. He ended by calling on Howard to wind up the debate, demanding that he 'stand and deliver'. Deliver Howard duly did.

'In the last thirty years, the balance in the criminal justice system has been tilted too far in favour of the criminal and against the protection of the public,' Howard began. 'The time has come to put that right.' As he spoke – almost shouted – his speech, Mr Howard's eyes shone with excitement. For years, Conservative Home Secretaries had found the annual conference an unmitigated ordeal. The supposed 'representatives' of the shires wanted hanging and flogging, and this they never got. But as Michael Howard promised no fewer than 'twenty-seven measures to crack crime', his agenda came from the viscera, and it answered the rumble in the party's stomach. For once, Secretary of State and backwoods Tories were as one.

Crucial to his text was the notion of 'balance'. This was no attempt to examine the failings of criminal justice objectively; to consider the flaws of pre-trial investigation or the retreat from prosecution. Howard's agenda was confined to the stark contrast between due process and crime control. After years of civil libertarian foot-dragging, the time had come to give the police the tools they required: crime control red in tooth and claw.

Here was the very embodiment of Dicey's pre-modern parliamentary despotism. There would be new laws to combat terrorism, and new police powers to stop citizens and vehicles in the street. Howard scorned the anticipated furore from the liberal Left, saying: 'This Government will never put the civil rights of terrorists before the lives of the British people.'

He cited terrorism again to announce the destruction of what the European Convention regards as a fundamental right: that of the suspect to remain silent in police stations. From now on, the prisoner who declined to answer questions would have this held against him in court, as evidence corroborative of guilt. If he subsequently adduced exculpatory evidence which he might have mentioned after his arrest, this too might indicate his guilt.

Months earlier, this change had been rejected by the Royal Commission. It had been introduced in Northern Ireland in 1988, and a challenge was pending in the European Court of Human Rights. A similar action was planned against the special powers of the Serious Fraud Office, which could already require suspects to answer its questions, although their replies were inadmissible in court. But Howard glided effortlessly over these obstacles. Disregarding the awkward fact that terrorists made up only a minute fraction of suspects in custody, and that they were almost all associated with the sectarian conflict in Northern Ireland, Howard justified his proposal by saying the right to silence was being 'ruthlessly exploited by terrorists'.

At last Howard reached his climax. He recognised more people would go to prison, but 'I do not flinch from that. We shall no longer judge the success of our system of justice by a fall in our prison population.' Work would start on six new 'decent but austere' gaols, to be built in partnership with the private sector, at once. 'Prison works,' he said. 'It ensures that we are protected from murderers, muggers and rapists – and it makes many who are tempted to commit crime think twice.' Howard sat down to rapturous applause. Beside him on the platform, Prime Minister John Major beamed, and patted him on the back.

The break with the recent past was complete. William Whitelaw, Margaret Thatcher's first Home Secretary after her election victory in 1979, believed that 'imprisonment is not a cheap way of dealing with offenders. Nor is it the most effective way.' In the view of Douglas Hurd, who held the post in 1985–90, 'the argument that custody should be used sparingly seems to me entirely persuasive'. Even in 1991, as the Thatcherite loyalist Kenneth Baker, Home Secretary 1990–2, accepted Lord Justice Woolf's Strangeways prison report, he said:

> Prison breaks up families. It is hard for prisoners to retain or subsequently secure law-abiding jobs. Imprisonment can lessen people's sense of responsibility for their actions. Some, often the young and less experienced, acquire in prison a wider knowledge of criminal activity. Imprisonment is costly for the individual, for the prisoner's family and for the community.

Without the protection of a modern constitution, the only check on the Government's new policy was the size of its parliamentary majority. Unable to comprehend, let alone repair the damaged social fabric, its response was pure authoritarianism across the broad range of criminal justice.

The 1994 Criminal Justice and Public Order Act tackled the underlying causes of neither crime nor the crisis in criminal justice. It not only abolished the right to silence, it also created new means to outlaw public protest. There was a range of new offences which criminalised trespass for the first time in English history, set down in the name of protecting hunters from saboteurs, landowners from travellers, and villagers from all-night 'raves' with – as the Act so memorably states – their 'music wholly or partly characterised by a succession of repetitive beats'.

Once on the statute book, it became clear that these provisions could be used against other targets, as and when it became appropriate, such as people demonstrating against the export of calves bound for European veal crates. The 1980s had seen the emergence of groups who sought alternative lifestyles, such as 'new age' travellers who preferred the open road to long-term urban unemployment. The State's response was not to attempt to reintegrate them, but surveillance and repression. Criminal justice was being manipulated as a coercive, political tool in a manner not seen since the early nineteenth century, a period of similar social upheaval. In all this, the notion of consensus was dead.

Senior police officers are not to be blamed for seeking policy changes which might make their job easier. In debates about criminal justice, demanding tougher crime control is, in a sense, their allotted role. But with Michael Howard, the Association of Chief Police Officers found itself in the unfamiliar position of actually being asked to draft Government policy. ACPO was not simply pushing at an open door: before the Minister's twenty-seven-point speech, its crime committee was asked to present a shopping list of desirable measures. The dilution of the right to silence had been top of its agenda for many years. At the time of writing, ACPO's next most coveted item is heading for the statute book – restrictions on the duty to disclose evidence to the defence.

Chapter Five demonstrated that disclosure is a vexed area, in which some degree of reform had begun to seem inevitable. Many defence lawyers, led by Richard Ferguson QC, Chairman of the Criminal Bar Association, had come to accept the validity of a proposal made by the Royal Commission – that in order to obtain full disclosure of all material gathered by the police it is reasonable to expect a degree of disclosure by the defence.

But if the change in the right to silence marked a significant move in the direction of crime control, the disclosure proposals presented in a Home Office discussion document in May 1995 were a violent lurch. They conformed exactly to the crime control model, placing extraordinary trust in the integrity and ability of the police. Far from introducing any measure of stronger independent supervision of the police's use of evidence, they loosened the existing weak controls.

Revealing his plans in Parliament, Howard again used the language of 'balance'. There was a 'gap between the demands of the law and the needs of justice', he said. 'I want a statutory framework which does more to convict the guilty, while continuing to protect the innocent.' Running through his Department's document was an implicit act of faith: that the police, in all circumstances, can be trusted not simply to behave ethically, but actively to take steps to protect the interests of the defendant – the fallacy of 'neutral' investigation within a system of adversarial justice.

Thus, while the police previously had an absolute obligation to disclose everything to Crown lawyers, this would end. The police would become the first filter, with the extraordinary responsibility of being able to keep material back unless they made the judgment that it was 'likely to undermine the prosecution case'.

The inherent and unsustainable conflict of interest this would impose appeared not to have troubled the authors of the document. If the police failed to reveal such evidence, who on earth would find out? As the document put it with some understatement: 'There will be a heavy reliance on the investigator to identify material which ought to be disclosed, given that the material will not be scutinised by the prosecutor.'

The document also contained proposals for defence disclosure which went far beyond the Royal Commission, which had suggested that lawyers should tell the court in advance only the basic outline of the defence case, under headings such as alibi, duress and so on. Howard's document said the defence must supply every detail, including the names and addresses of witnesses. 'Even with an honest policeman, that will allow them to unsettle witnesses,' Richard

Ferguson QC commented. 'One shudders to think of the implications with an officer prepared to pervert the course of justice.'

Yet until the police had received these details, the Crown would not have to disclose anything beyond the basic witness statements. Even after revealing its hand, the defence would have to specify what exactly it wanted, while it would be left for the prosecution to decide, in the light of the defence case, whether its requests might be 'relevant' – a subjective judgment which could hardly fail to be influenced by the Crown's interest in getting a conviction. This was very close to a diametric reversal of the burden of proof; the final erosion of the defendant's presumption of innocence. If the onus was not to be on the defendant to prove himself innocent, he was to have to prove in advance why he deserved a fair trial.

Under this proposed system, the Midlands Regional Crime Squad officers who ran Graham Titley would never have told the lawyers acting for David Docker and Bernard Wilson about Titley's true role. Raymond Okudzeto would not have smoked out John Banks. As Presiley Baxendale QC memorably put it during a session of Lord Justice Scott's inquiry into the Matrix Churchill affair: 'If you were not told about something, you don't know if you need to know it.' It was as if the Judith Ward and Stefan Kiszko cases had never taken place. A cornerstone of the old regime has been replaced. Yet ironically, some police leaders have claimed the proposals would improve the 'search for the truth'. Meanwhile, in most inquisitorial jurisdictions such as France and Germany, full disclosure is available as a matter of course. In Germany, defence lawyers often read the full prosecution case file before the trial.

★   ★   ★

The mechanisms of criminal justice can never be a means of tackling the social causes of crime. This lies beyond the scope of the law and its agencies. But the contemporary project of the Right amounts to an attempt to turn this proposition on its head: to recast legal institutions as an authoritarian vehicle for managing the effects of social inequity. It implies a dystopian vision of society in which the impoverished 30 per cent are explicitly excluded from the benefits granted to the majority. For the underclass, the ancient principle of equality before the law is quietly being abandoned.

While shifting the law towards outright crime control is creating the necessary legal process, the police are being made to fall in with this project through the imposition of unheard-of central government control. Under the terms of Britain's pre-modern constitution, the 165-year-old traditions of locally accountable, locally financed police have proved no more resistant to the opportunism of Michael Howard than the right to silence.

The ideology of the Plus Programme, democratic and anti-élitist, as concerned – at least theoretically – with the inhabitants of Stonebridge Park, Harlesden, as with the residents of Belgravia, never chimed easily with traditional Conservative notions of criminal justice. From an early stage, Ministers picked at the place where it was both radical and most vulnerable: at its insistence that the quality of policing, and the relationship of the service with the public, was more important than statistical measures of cleared-up crimes.

The memoirs of Kenneth Baker, Home Secretary 1990–2, record:

> While several of my ministerial colleagues and Tory MPs supported the police in public, they were highly critical of them in private. There was impatience, if not anger, that although we had spent 87 per cent more in real terms since 1979, and had increased police numbers by 27,000, there had still been a substantial rise in crime. 'Where is the value for money?' asked my colleagues.

The first attempt to answer that question was the inquiry into police pay and conditions set up by Kenneth Clarke under the BAT Industries Chairman Patrick Sheehy in 1992. Many of its recommendations – for radical changes to the rank structure, the introduction of performance-related pay and fixed term contracts for all officers, and massive cuts to salaries for recruits – provoked militant hostility from the Police Federation, and most were not initially implemented. But as Clarke gave way to Howard, Sheehy's managerial spirit survived. Much of his core programme has now been enacted.

The Plus Programme and similar initiatives in the counties depended on local autonomy. But the Conservatives under Thatcher and Major had already formed the most centralising Government in modern British history, which had steadily eroded local institutions of every kind. There was no reason to believe that the police were somehow immune.

The main event in this policy of centralisation, the 1994 Police and Magistrates' Court Act, was mauled in Parliament. Two former Conservative Home Secretaries, Lords Whitelaw and Carr, led a significant peers' revolt. Originally, Howard had intended that the Home Office would directly appoint the chairmen of new, remodelled police authorities, creating an umbilical link between government and local policing policy. He was defeated on this, yet the essentials survived in the Act that passed into law. The new authorities were still to contain a substantial bloc of nominated businessmen, ending the former majority of elected councillors.

At the same time, the Home Office was to set each constabulary's annual budget. Chief Constables were henceforth to be employed on fixed term contracts, and to draw performance-related pay. This was to be calculated according to their delivery of national policing objectives, to be fixed not by their reading of their local communities' needs, but by the Home Office. Time and again, Michael Howard insisted that 'the main job of the police is catching criminals', explicitly rejecting the notion of a broader, community-service role. In vain his police critics pointed out that the founder of the service, Sir Robert Peel, had insisted that the first job of the new police was crime prevention, not cure, and that this was in any case much more cost effective.

In 1995, the Audit Commission began publishing crude 'league tables' of each force's performance. In place of Plus's qualitative public service ethic, policing was once again being judged by numerical crime clear-up rates, and the speed at which 999 calls were answered. The old, discredited 'numbers culture' was back. The more liberal police leaders fiercely but vainly protested at the programme of impending change, warning that it would pave the way to the coercive style of American policing which had produced the 1993 Los Angeles riots.

Some chief constables struggled to downplay the importance of numerical measurement. In 1995, the ACPO President, John Hoddinott, began a notable revolt when he refused to sign his new performance-related pay contract, so forgoing the prospect of bonuses of up to £12,000 a year. He had joined the police out of a sense of public service, he said, not to enrich himself. Other liberal police chiefs followed his example.

But in late 1995, centralisation is about to be underlined by the introduction of 'appraisal-related pay' for all ranks, with bonuses tied to the fulfilment of the national targets. A favourite police adage says, 'What gets measured gets done.' Local experiments in community policing, which in towns from Milton Keynes to Tyneside have tried to downplay arrest rates in favour of imaginative approaches to crime prevention, are in jeopardy.

For many years, criticism of the constitutional accountability of the police under the old arrangements had been a shibboleth of the Left. Suddenly, these arrangements were beginning to look like models of democratic virtue. Towards the end of 1995, the local accountability of law enforcement was further weakened by John Major's announcement of the first national crime squad, in which MI5 was to play a central role. The recent experience of MI5's leadership of the fight against Irish terrorism has provided vivid illustration of the probable consequences. MI5 officers give their evidence in court behind screens, under *noms de guerre*.

There is one 'reform' introduced by Michael Howard which is certain to have serious and lasting effects on the culture of policing. In the autumn of 1994, following the Sheehy report's claim that police officers' pay was 'more than the market' indication of their worth, Howard cut the pay for police recruits by between 19 and 30 per cent, according to geographical area. In London, a fully-trained PC would earn only £15,000: not an attractive prospect for a graduate in his late twenties.

By July 1995, the Police Federation was reporting that married new constables with children were applying for state benefits to supplement their salaries. The years which had seen the average age and educational qualifications of police officers steadily rising were now at an end. According to the federation, 'high living costs in London mean only young, single people can afford to join the Metropolitan Police'. For the first time in nearly a decade, the

Metropolitan Police was forced to begin recruitment advertising outside the south-east, hoping to attract applicants from areas where the economy was still in recession.

The last element in the Right's authoritarian project is penal policy. Howard's claim at the 1993 Conservative conference that 'prison works' provoked a furore from the judiciary, led by the author of the Strangeways report, Lord Woolf. Over the next two years, the prison population rose by nearly a quarter, to a record 52,000. Many of the new inmates were not serious violent or sexual criminals but inadequates of varying hue: individuals unable to pay their television licence fees, petty thieves and the mentally ill.

Undeterred by the fact that Britain – having briefly lost this dubious accolade – was again incarcerating a higher proportion of its population than any other country in Europe, Howard promised a still greater expansion at his party's conference in 1995. Within two hours of his speech, his promise to abolish remission and to bring in harsh minimum sentences for repeat offenders provoked a stinging rebuke from Lord Chief Justice Taylor.

Lord Taylor's attack went straight to the heart of the new penal strategy, and hinted at the true nature of criminal justice's impending collapse. Longer sentences would have no effect on the crime rate as long as the detection and conviction rates were so low: why should a burglar worry about serving an extra six or twelve months when the prospect of his being convicted was so remote?

In his great work *Discipline and Punish*, the French philosopher Michel Foucault described the replacement at the end of the eighteenth century of ghastly public tortures and executions with invisible imprisonment. According to Foucault, the shift in policy by which punishment 'became the most hidden part of the criminal process' depended on a view spread through society that crime would not pay. The effectiveness of punishment administered by bureaucrats in place of executioners required the 'certainty of being punished'.[15]

In Britain today, people no longer believe in that certainty, and as this book has shown, their scepticism is well-founded. Acute as Lord Taylor's observation was, his mistake was to assume that a policy conceived under the rubric of 'understanding a little less' might conform to conventional rationality. For its logic had nothing to do with the principles and ethics which have underlain criminal justice for many decades, nor with empirical evidence.

Having failed to restore confidence in criminal justice by means of rational reform, so recreating the 'certainty of being punished', the Right has instead chosen to reassert State power through exemplary punishment for the minority who have been convicted. The inspiration for this strategy does not lie within the criminal justice system at all. Its purpose is entirely political: as a blatant appeal to the relatively comfortable majority, based on the promise that if they fear the excluded underclass, the State will deliver revenge.

Taylor's reaction to Howard's 1995 speech — which swiftly produced the accusation that he was meddling in politics — also reflected his outrage that in his rigid sentencing proposals, the Home Secretary was trampling on the constitutional doctrine of the separation of powers, abolishing judges' discretion to fit punishment to crimes and criminals. Again, this was exactly the point. Having nationalised the police, Howard was attempting to overcome the final obstacle to an unfettered authoritarian state. He was attempting to nationalise the judiciary.

'He who thirsts for vengeance', Max Weber said, 'is not interested in motives.' Weber was describing justice in primitive, tribal societies. These had no interest in 'the idea of degrees of guilt', he said, nor in the offender's background and attitudes. A criminal justice system in which revenge becomes the operating penal principle dehumanises its subjects: it sees no division between the harmful acts of criminals and animals.[16]

Contemporary political rhetoric recasts this formulation only slightly. Like its primitive predecessor, the revenge justice of the 1990s has no interest in the psychological state of the offender. Born into the underclass, he is beyond redemption. It sees only acts which must be punished, in the name of the victims and the property-owning, law-abiding majority. The ancient principle governing the law on intent is being reversed: it is now the deed, not the motive, which counts.

Inevitably, revenge justice has been developed to a higher level in the United States, whose social inequalities make our own seem relatively trivial. In October 1995, the proportion of black males aged twenty to forty in gaol or on probation reached a staggering one third: there, prisons have become the warehouses of the poor. If

rehabilitation was no longer the object of penal polic
deterrence. States with the death penalty had a murd
average 50 per cent higher than those without. Florida,
most murders of all, spent more on prisons than on schoo

Meanwhile, the eighteenth-century 'theatre of punishment'
described by Foucault is making a comeback. In the spring of 1995,
as New York became the thirty-eighth state to restore capital
punishment, the Alabama prison commissioner placed a $17,000
order for leg irons, and heralded the return of the chain gang. 'With
leg shackles, we can put higher-risk inmates to work on the outside,'
he said. Alabama's law-abiding citizens could see them degraded on
the very streets where they committed their crimes.

The echoes in Britain, however, are already disturbingly loud.
When Singapore birched the American teenager Michael Fay for
vandalising cars, Britain's right-wing tabloids called for such
methods to be re-adopted here. In America, State legislatures rushed
to do just that. In 1995, bills were pending in at least nine states, and
in some cases proposed legislation would allow offenders to be
beaten in public. Meanwhile in Britain, despite overwhelming
evidence of their failure in America to divert young offenders from a
criminal career, Michael Howard was preparing the first of a series of
US-style 'boot camps'.

For Labour, apparently on the verge of power for the first time in a
generation, the dilemma is pressing. It would not be fair to Tony
Blair to blame Michael Howard's strident populism on his success as
Shadow Home Secretary. Nevertheless, it is a factor in the constantly
rising stakes in the political auction. The summer of 1995 saw the
present Shadow Home Secretary Jack Straw pledging to 'reclaim the
streets' from the 'aggressive begging' of 'winos, addicts and squeegee
merchants'. No amount of later explanation – he claimed he was
trying to address the fear of crime by suggesting ways of reducing
street disorder – could altogether mitigate the initial impact of his
rhetoric, which seemed to owe more to the Republican Mayor of
New York, Rudy Giuliani, than to British social-democratic
thinking on homelessness.

Lord Lester QC, the Liberal Democrat peer, human rights jurist
and constitutional reformer, once noted that 'power is delightful,
absolute power is absolutely delightful'. Tony Blair's New Labour

Party has to decide whether it wishes merely to inherit the enhanced powers of the pre-modern criminal justice system and state, or dismantle them and replace them with more humane and democratic institutions.

Yet even as the Right has rushed so swiftly to destroy the more benign structures which accompanied the old regime, it has created new opportunities for reform. It will be harder for a Labour Government to sink back on the ropes of the status quo, because that left behind by Michael Howard is so deeply unacceptable. The door is open to a new settlement between the State and the citizen. The institutions of policing, the law, the courts and the prisons will never be a means of restoring an equitable society. But at the same time, in the absence of *criminal* justice, social justice will remain an unattainable goal.

Equally, if the project of the Right is carried through to fruition, English criminal justice will in all meaningful senses collapse, reduced to the status of a machine for national coercion.

In an article in the *Sunday Times*, expressed in terms more candid than those available to a politician, Barbara Amiel, the influential columnist and wife of the media magnate Conrad Black, set out this project's nightmare vision: 'We do have problems of crime and violence. How do we eliminate them? First, by acknowledging where the problem exists: in the underclass. By the end of the last century, this underclass was actually called the 'residuum', which suggests it was a shrinking phenomenon.'

Now, she went on, it was back.

From the 1960s on the family was seen as too restrictive. We whittled away at its authority, made a two-parent family with a stay-at-home mother a fiscal liability through tax policies, created the conditions for children to parent children (by removing taboos on teenage sex), and made it a civil if not criminal offence to describe such loose morality pejoratively. In effect, we subsidised and financed an enlarged underclass, pooh-poohed the bootstrap mentality of the poor as Uncle Tom-ish, described the bettering of oneself as yuppie behaviour or greed, and promoted envy as the common currency. Together with indiscriminate immigration policies from Asian and African countries at levels too high to allow assimilation, we allowed the nightmares of Enoch Powell to come true (though without the blood in the streets) . . .

In summary: we cannot deport people who are now here. But we can segregate the underclass and forget about egalitarian principles. We should try to reintroduce the best of our values while getting rid of the worst. We must stop ruining our free society by enacting rules appropriate for a zoo. Just because some of the rooms in our house have been taken over by pigs and donkeys does not mean we should turn the entire kingdom into a place appropriate for the housing of animals.[17]

Underclass, *untermensch*. What price due process when an entire class is guilty? Why should it matter if their convictions are safe and satisfactory? Where better to segregate them than in prison?

It is a glimpse into hell: the 30/30/40 society mediated by violence, with all pretence of equality before the law removed. It must not come to pass.

Chapter One: The Old Regime and its Passing

1 'Estoppel' is the ancient regal power to halt an action dead in its tracks, whatever its merits.

2 Full details of the progress of the Avon and Somerset inquiries, and of the long delay in acting upon them, are contained in the official inquiry report into the case by Sir John May, published by HMSO in June 1994.

3 Interview with the author.

4 The fictional presentation of the Guildford case in the feature film *In the Name of the Father* suggested the appeal rested on the discovery by defence lawyers of an alibi statement which had never been seen before, marked 'not to be seen by the defence'. In this and in other respects too numerous to mention, the film is a travesty of the facts, which manages to weaken the drama of what really happened.

5 *Independent*, 18 October 1989.

6 *Guardian*, 24 October 1989.

7 For a full account, see David Rose, *A Climate of Fear: The Murder of PC Blakelock and the Case of the Tottenham Three*, Bloomsbury, 1992.

8 *Independent*, 26 January 1990.

9 *A Climate of Fear*, op. cit. In English trials, juries are normally excluded from court when lawyers make submissions on the law or the admissibility of evidence, and when the judge makes his ruling.

10 *Observer*, 25 September 1990.

11 *Independent*, 21 April 1994.

12 Sir John Woodcock, speech to International Policing Exhibition and Conference, 13 October 1992.

13 *Independent*, 25 March 1993.

14 *Panorama*, BBC1, 5 April 1993.

15 *Criminal Injustice*, BBC2, 12 March 1995.

16 *Guardian*, 11 March 1995.

17 E.P. Thompson, *Whigs and Hunters*, Penguin, 1977.

18 The 'Judges' Rules' were the code of practice governing police behaviour

before the 1984 PACE Act. The rules were the result of various judges' rulings, collected and codified.

19 John Baldwin and Michael McConville, *Confessions in Crown Court Trials*, HMSO, 1980.

20 Interview with the author, 22 March 1995.

21 J. Walkley, *Police Interrogation: A Study of the Psychology, Theory and Practice of Police Interrogations and the Implications for Police Training*, unpublished MSc thesis, Cranfield Institute of Technology, 1983.

22 Interview with the author, 22 December 1994.

23 Baldwin and McConville, op. cit.

24 *Police Review*, 14 August 1992.

25 Interview in prison with the author.

26 *Brighton Evening Argus*, 27 October 1976.

27 I pressed the Metropolitan Police for an explanation for months. Finally Scotland Yard appointed a chief superintendent as a special spokesman, who said the destruction was 'unfortunate': so unfortunate, that as a result of my inquiries, the Metropolitan Police issued a new policy directive that interview notes and similar original documents must be kept for at least twenty-five years.

28 Interview with the author, 15 November 1994.

29 Interview with the author, 8 February 1995.

30 Sir John May, op. cit.

31 May Inquiry, transcripts of oral evidence, 15 July 1993.

32 May transcripts, 1 June 1993.

33 Herbert Packer, *The Limits of the Criminal Sanction*, Stanford University Press, 1968.

34 Andrew Sanders and Richard Young, *The Rule of Law, Due Process and Pre-Trial Criminal Justice; Current Legal Problems*, vol. 47, Oxford University Press, 1994.

35 Doreen McBarnet, *Conviction*, Macmillan, 1981.

36 For a fuller, at times hilarious critique of this type of 'Left idealism', see Jock Young, 'Incessant Chatter: Recent Paradigms in Criminology', *The Oxford Handbook of Criminology*, Oxford University Press, 1994.

Chapter Two: Race, Class and Justice

1 A shorter version of the Deol story was published in the *Observer* on 30 October 1994. This account is based on interviews with the family, their lawyers, local residents and on legal documents, especially Dave and Lucky's proofs of evidence to their solicitor, Gareth Beynon, of Howell and Partners, Small Heath.

2 *Evening Sentinel*, 19 October 1994.

3 Peter Fryer, *Staying Power: The History of Black People in Britain*, Pluto Press, 1984.

4 David Rose, *Guardian*, 24 May 1985 and 17 July 1985.

5 Ibid, 11 July 1985.

6 Ibid.

7 Robert Reiner, *The Politics of the Police*, second edition, Harvester, 1992.

8 GLC Police Unit, *Policing London*, October 1982.

9 Simon Field et al., 'Ethnic Minorities in Britain', Home Office Research Study no. 68, HMSO, 1981.

10 'Future Strategic and Policy Issues', Metropolitan Police Force Appraisal, September 1986, part II, pp. 110 ff.

11 *Police Review*, 8 November 1985.

12 *Guardian*, 16 January 1987.

13 Unmesh Desai, *Racial Harassment, Housing and Community Action, Race and Class*, Autumn 1987.

14 *Observer*, 7 October 1990.

15 Interview with the author, 28 October 1994.

16 Interview with the author, 27 October 1994.

17 *Guardian*, 13 January 1995.

18 *Guardian*, 16 November 1994.

19 Helena Kennedy, *Eve Was Framed*, Chatto & Windus, 1992.

20 Ibid.

21 *Evening Sentinel*, 19 October 1988.

22 Ibid, 'Crimewave in "Chicago" ', 10 September 1991.

23 Ibid, 'Abbey Gangs on Rampage', 9 January 1992.

24 Ibid, 'We'll Sort Out Terror Estate – Police Chief', 11 January 1992.

25 Ibid, 'Estate Sets Up Vigilantes', 25 August 1992.

26 Ibid, 1 March 1993 and 3 March 1993.

27 Ibid, 'Jeering Yobs in Attack on Crimefighters', 31 March 1993.

28 Interview with author, 22 February 1995.

29 *Guardian*, 17 January 1995.

30 *Daily Mirror*, 25 January 1995.

31 *Sunday Times*, 26 February 1995.

32 *Daily Telegraph*, 30 January 1995.

33 *Daily Express*, 15 October 1994.

34 Max Weber, *Economy and Society*, University of California Press, 1978.

35 British Crime Survey, HMSO, 1993.

36 A. Sivanandan, *Communities of Resistance*, Verso, 1990.

Chapter Three: The Rising Tide of Crime

1 Under the terms of my agreement with the Metropolitan Police, I have not

published the real names of any of the Kilburn officers quoted or observed.
For the sake of convenience and readability, I have occasionally used
pseudonyms.

2 *Guardian*, 11 January 1994.

3 *Spectator*, 17 April 1994.

4 *Mail on Sunday*, 21 February 1993.

5 *Independent*, 11 November 1993.

6 *Guardian*, and *Independent*, 27 April 1994.

7 *Today*, 19 February 1992.

8 When British Gas was privatised, its chairman, Cedric Browne, earned less
than the Commissioner of the Metropolitan Police. By the middle of 1995, he
was getting seven times as much.

9 'Over the side': common police slang for committing adultery.

10 David Hare, *Asking Around*, Faber & Faber, 1993.

11 Metropolitan Police Force Appraisal, September 1986, part II, pp. 85 ff.

12 Metropolitan Police Force Appraisal, September 1987, pp. 145 ff.

13 Metropolitan Police, Commissioner's Conference, 1991.

14 'Inquiry into Income and Wealth', Rowntree Foundation, 1995.

15 *Financial Times*, 11 February 1995.

16 *Sunday Telegraph*, 12 February 1995.

17 *The Times*, 11 February 1995.

18 'Demographic Characteristics of Stonebridge', Foresight Strategic Consultants, 1993.

19 Northumbria Police, Chief Constable's Report, 1980.

20 Simon Field, 'Trends in Crime and their Interpretation', Home Office
Research Study 119, HMSO, 1990.

21 See John Wells, 'Crime and Unemployment', Employment Policy Institute
Economic Report, February 1995.

22 *Observer*, 29 October 1994.

23 *Sunday Times*, 22 May 1994.

24 Norman Dennis, *Rising Crime and the Dismembered Family*, Institute of
Economic Affairs, 1993.

25 Robert Reiner, 'Policing by Numbers: The Feel-Good Fallacy', *Policing
Today*, February 1995.

26 The statistics in the following section are drawn from successive volumes of
the annual Home Office Criminal Statistics, and of the British Crime Survey,
both published by HMSO.

27 Malcolm Young, *An Inside Job*, Oxford University Press, 1993.

28 *Observer*, 8 December 1991.

29 Commissioner of Police for the Metropolis, Annual Report, 1993–4.

30 Geoffrey Pearson, *Hooligan: A History of Respectable Fears*, Macmillan, 1983.

31 Peter Hennessey, *Never Again*, Jonathan Cape, 1992.

32 Jock Young, 'Recent Paradigms in Criminology', op. cit.

33 Beatrix Campbell, *Goliath: Britain's Dangerous Places*, Methuen, 1993.

Chapter Four: The Retreat from Prosecution

1 *Spectator*, 27 May 1995.
2 Interview with the author, 7 February 1995.
3 See Chapter One, pp. 47–8
4 Interview with the author, 26 January 1995.
5 See Chapter One, pp. 48–9
6 Interview with the author, 2 November 1994.
7 See, for example, Michael McConville, Andrew Sanders and Roger Leng, *The Case for the Prosecution*, Routledge, 1992, and Andrew Sanders and Richard Young, *Criminal Justice*, Butterworths, 1994.
8 Michael McConville, 'Corroboration and Confessions: The impact of a rule requiring that no conviction can be sustained on the basis of confession evidence alone', Royal Commission Research Study 13, HMSO, 1993.
9 David Brown, 'The incidence of right to silence in police interviews: the research evidence reviewed', Home Office Research Bulletin 35, HMSO, 1994.
10 The story of the murder of Lillian Hedgecock is taken from legal documents.
11 CPS 1994 Discontinuance Survey, CPS, 1995.
12 A. Brown and D. Crisp, 'Diverting Cases from Prosecution in the Public Interest', Home Office Research Bulletin 7, HMSO, 1992.
13 *Guardian*, 30 May 1995.
14 I have changed all the names in the story of the attempted rape of 'Patricia Freely', which is derived from interviews and the prosecution case file.
15 *Guardian*, 30 May 1995
16 Brian Block, Claire Corbett and Jill Peay, 'Ordered and Directed Acquittals in the Crown Court', Royal Commission Research Study 15, HMSO, 1993.
17 Michael Zander and Paul Henderson, 'The Crown Court Study', Royal Commission Research Study 19, HMSO, 1993.
18 Crown Prosecution Service, Annual Report 1993–4, HMSO, 1994.
19 For further details see Andrew Ashworth, *The Criminal Process*, Oxford, 1994.
20 Interview with the author, 15 December 1994.
21 Crown Prosecution Service, Annual Report, 1986–7, HMSO, 1987.
22 Doreen McBarnet, *Conviction*, op. cit.
23 Judicial Statistics, Lord Chancellor's Department, 1994.
24 Zander and Henderson, op. cit.
25 Michael McConville, Jacqueline Hodgson, Lee Bridges and Anita Pavlovic, *Standing Accused*, Oxford, 1994.
26 Metropolitan Police, Case Disposal Manual, 1995.
27 Zander and Henderson, op. cit.
28 Ibid.
29 Metropolitan Police, Case Disposal Manual, 1995.

Chapter Five: The Problem of Organised Crime

1 The story of Bramble and his associates is taken from case papers and legal documents. I have changed the Kanos' surname.
2 Sir Peter Imbert, 'Trust in the Police: the Search for Truth', address to International Police Exhibition and Conference, 1992.
3 *The Times*, 15 March 1987.
4 Interview with the author.
5 See Andrew Jennings, Vyv Simpson and Paul Lashmar, *Scotland Yard's Cocaine Connection*, Jonathan Cape, 1990.
6 The account of the Charrington case is drawn from legal papers, court proceedings and interviews with confidential sources.
7 Jennings et al., op. cit.
8 Interview with the author, July 1994.
9 Parts of this account are to be found in an article I wrote about the Okudzeto case, *Observer*, 11 April 1993.
10 The intelligence logs were disclosed to the defence in the arms case.
11 This account is drawn from legal documents. See *Observer*, 25 September 1994 and 18 December 1994.
12 The story of the Norris murder is based on confidential documents and interviews.

Chapter Six: The Culture of Policing

1 Robert Reiner, *The Politics of the Police*, op. cit.
2 Malcolm Young, *An Inside Job*, op. cit.
3 David Powis, *The Signs of Crime: A Field Manual for Police*, McGraw Hill, 1977.
4 Andrew Sanders and Richard Young, *Criminal Justice*, op. cit.
5 Robert Chesshyre, *The Force*, Sidgwick & Jackson, 1989.
6 *Guardian*, 9 July 1994.
7 Robert Reiner, op. cit.
8 Alan Smithers, Susan Hill and Geoff Silvester, *Graduates in the Police Service*, School of Education, Manchester University, 1989.
9 For a gripping account of the tense battles between the police and Lord Callaghan's Labour Government which preceded the Edmund-Davies award, see Tony Judge, *The Force of Persuasion: the Story of the Police Federation*, Police Federation, 1994.
10 Interview with the author.
11 'Skipper': police argot for sergeant.
12 Ron Hope, 'Copper and Black', *Policing*, Spring 1995.
13 David J. Smith and Jeremy Gray, *The Police in Action, Police and People in London*, vol. 4, Policy Studies Institute, 1983.
14 Carolyn Hoyle, doctoral thesis in progress, Oxford University.

15 See, for example, Helena Kennedy, op. cit.

16 Lord Scarman, op. cit.

17 Interview with the author, 13 April 1995.

18 Ian Beckett and James Hart, 'Neighbourhood Policing: The Theory and Hypothesis, A Systems and Behavioural Study of Police Operations in the Urban Environment', Police Staff College, 1981.

19 Sir Kenneth Newman, Annual Report, 1984.

20 Tom Williamson, 'Strategic Changes in Police Interrogation', University of Kent PhD, 1991.

21 Metropolitan Police 1986 appraisal, op. cit.

22 For a scorching critique of Neighbourhood Watch see Mike McConville and Dan Shepherd, *Watching Police, Watching Communities*, Routledge, 1992.

23 These articles quoted in David Rose, *A Climate of Fear*, op. cit.

24 Sir Kenneth Newman, Annual Report, 1985.

25 Sir Ian MacGregor, *The Enemies Within*, Methuen, 1987.

26 Interview with the author, 2 August 1994.

27 Interview with the author, 20 March 1995.

28 Sir Peter Imbert, speech to the International Police Exhibition and Conference, 13 October 1992.

29 'The Plague of the Blue Locusts: Police Reform and Popular Resistance in Northern England', 1840–57, *International Review of Social History*, 20, 1975.

30 Interview with the author, 8 December 1994.

31 Wolff Ollins, *A Force for Change*, Metropolitan Police, 1988.

32 *Observer*, 31 January 1993.

Chapter Seven: Policing the Police

1 All details of the Treadaway case are taken from evidence given in the High Court before Mr Justice McKinnon, and from his judgment. The preface to this book has already made clear that this chapter could not have been written without the assistance of Raju Bhatt, solicitor, of Birnberg and Co. The disclosures it contains are of some constitutional importance, and they are essentially the product of his diligence and commitment.

2 See Chapter Five above.

3 *Hornal v. Neuberger Products Ltd, 1957* 1 QB 247.

4 The Dandy case was the first time Esda was used by the defence in a criminal trial: later it was employed to historic effect in the Birmingham Six and Tottenham Three cases.

5 Quoted in Robert Reiner, *The Politics of the Police*, op. cit.

6 Lord Scarman, op. cit., part VII, D.

7 The following passages are drawn from the correspondence in the autumn of 1994 between the PCA, Mr Bhatt and the West Midlands police.

8 *Independent*, 30 June 1991.

9 M. Maguire and C. Corbett, *A Study of the Police Complaints System*, HMSO, 1991.

10 The quotation came from a brochure explaining the PCA's work.

11 Maguire and Corbett, op. cit.

12 See, for example, *Police and People in London*, Policy Studies Institute, op. cit., and S. Holdaway, *Inside the British Police*, Oxford, 1983.

13 Reiner, *Politics of the Police*, op. cit.

14 I reported Hanney's trial in the *Observer*, 11 November 1990. The details of his subsequent action against the police are taken from legal documents.

15 Unpublished figures from Metropolitan Police solicitors' department.

16 *The Times*, 14 October 1993.

17 Parliamentary answer to Chris Mullin MP.

18 *Independent*, 30 July 1992.

19 Interview with the author, 14 December 1994.

20 The definitive account of the main phases of this process is to be found in Barry Cox, John Shirley and Martin Short, *The Fall of Scotland Yard*, Penguin, 1977.

21 Interview with the author, 12 January 1995.

22 *Independent*, 20 May 1992.

23 Previously unpublished figures supplied by CPS officials.

24 Ibid.

25 Judicial Statistics, Lord Chancellor's Department, HMSO, 1995.

26 See Chapter One above. For an account of the 'Guildford Three' police case, see Ronan Bennett, *Double Jeopardy: The Retrial of the Guildford Four*, Penguin, 1993.

27 In March 1990, I published an article in the *Guardian* disclosing that after his trial in 1975, Conlon made further 'confessions' about his supposed role in the bombings, in interviews with none other than Peter Imbert, the later Metropolitan Commissioner. I have since come deeply to regret what amounted to a grave error of judgment. I failed to spot internal evidence that these additional admissions were fictitious: for example, an account of seeing a 'bomb' festooned with flashing lights, which resembled no known IRA device. Although Conlon's new 'confessions' mentioned two men later convicted of terrorist offences, they were well-known local 'characters', whom any Catholic nationalist moving around England in the early 1970s might easily have met. The Imbert interviews contained many other names of no significance.

28 *Daily Telegraph*, 19 May 1993.

29 David Rose, *A Climate of Fear*, op. cit.

30 *Daily Express*, 26 July 1994.

31 The information here and in the following paragraphs was supplied by confidential police sources.

Chapter Eight: The Collapse of Criminal Justice

1 Interview with the author, 22 March 1995.

2 See Chapter One, p. 15.

3 Will Hutton, *The State We're In*, Jonathan Cape, 1995.

4 Warwick Maynard, 'Witness Intimidation: Strategies for Prevention', Police Research Group Crime Detection and Prevention Series Paper 55, HMSO, 1994.

5 Interview with the author, 23 March 1995.

6 Interview with the author, 1 March 1995.

7 Doreen McBarnet, *Conviction*, op cit. See Chapter One, pages 48–9.

8 John Hoddinott and Peter Neyroud, *In Search of Criminal Justice*, Association of Chief Police Officers, September 1995. The authors are the Chief Constable of Hampshire and his Superintendent staff officer.

9 Leonard H. Leigh and Lucia Zedner, 'A Report on the Administration of Criminal Justice in the Pre-Trial phase in France and Germany', HMSO, 1992.

10 Royal Commission on Criminal Justice, Report, Chapter One, pp.3–4, HMSO, 1993.

11 Max Weber, *Economy and Society*, Part Two, Chapter XI, translation published by the University of California Press, 1978.

12 Interview with the author, 22 December 1994.

13 For a scholarly examination of all these issues, see Jenny McEwan, *Evidence and the Adversarial Process*, Blackwell, 1992.

14 *Mail on Sunday*, 21 February 1993.

15 Michel Foucault, *Discipline and Punish*, Penguin edition, 1977.

16 Weber, *Economy and Society*, op cit.

17 *Sunday Times*, 28 April 1994.

INDEX

Ackner, Lord 161
Act of Settlement (1707) 307
Ahmed, Mukhta 73, 74, 77, 78, 79, 80, 81, 82, 105
Alderson, John 237
Ali, Quddus 73, 77, 78, 80, 81, 82, 85, 105, 313
Altaf, Mohammed 70, 71
Amiel, Barbara 336
Amlot, Roy, QC 5, 6
Andersen, Arthur 145, 146
Anderson, Digby 98
Anderson, Jim 193
Anderton, Chief Constable James 43, 68, 237, 243, 291
Animal Liberation Front 189
Anti-Racist Alliance 74
Archer, Lord Jeffrey 324-5
Argyle, Michael 173
Armstrong, Patrick 1, 2, 6, 18, 296, 297, 298, 299
Association of Chief Police Officers (ACPO) 11, 164, 257, 311, 312, 315, 327, 332
Audit Commission 207, 315, 331

Baker, Kenneth 9, 16, 277, 292, 316, 326, 330
Ball, Superintendent John 71
Banks, John 192-201, 329
Bar, failings of 9, 38, 41, 44, 117, 118, 157
see also CPS, Criminal Justice
Barker, Brian, QC 131, 132
Baxendale, Presiley, QC 329
Baxter, Robert 4
Beackon, Derek 79
Beards, Detective Superintendent R. 202

Bevin, Ernest 322
Bibby, Michael 46-7
Biggs, Ronnie 170
Bill of Rights, proposals for 17
Birmingham Six 3, 5, 7, 8, 9, 11, 12, 22, 31, 34, 44, 49, 116, 297-8, 306, 309, 314, 316
'Black Act' 15, 108
Black, Conrad 336
Black Police Association 230, 231
Blair, Tony 14, 93, 317, 323, 335, 336
Blakelock, PC, murder case 8, 10, 11, 24, 242-3, 257, 298-305
Blom-Cooper, Louis, QC 21
Bonczosek, Detective Constable Noel 67
Booth, Cherie, QC 317
Bradford football stadium fire 47
Bradford Twelve 67, 83
Braithwaite, Hiram 167
Braithwaite, Mark 8, 300
Bramble, Keith 166, 167, 169, 172
Brent (Borough of) 85, 98
Briggs, Commander Michael 38, 39, 146, 237, 249, 251, 252
British Broadcasting Company (BBC) 9, 13, 14, 30, 36, 114, 289
British Crime Survey 85, 105, 106, 111
British Medical Association (BMA) 97
British National Party (BNP) 79
Brittan, Leon 145
Broadwater Farm see Blakelock, PC
Bulger, Jamie, case of 47, 92, 323

Calvert-Smith, David, QC 304
Campaign for Nuclear Disarmament (CND) 248
Campbell, Beatrix 112, 113

Campbell, Duncan 30, 42
capital punishment 325; in US 335
Carlo, Francesco di 170–1
Carlos the Jackal 193
Carr, Lord 331
Cartwright, John 278, 279
Cartwright, Chief Inspector Norma 76
Caruana, Alfonso 170–1
Chalkley, Caroline 141
Chandler, Raymond 94
Charrington, Brian 174–85, 207, 208, 320
Charter 88 16–17
Chesshyre, Robert 215–16, 225, 226
Chiesa, General Dalla 170
Church of England 97
Churchill, Sir Winston 322
Clark, Commander Roy 171, 172, 189
Clarke, Kenneth 37, 253, 317, 330
Commons Select Committee on Home
　　Affairs 13, 22
community care 90
Condon, Sir Paul, Commissioner of
　　Metropolitan Police 13, 14, 109, 110,
　　231, 233, 245, 291, 310
Confait, Maxwell, case of 21–2, 42, 119
confessions see police
Conlon, Gerard 1, 2, 4, 7, 45, 46, 297
Connelly, Assistant Chief Investigator
　　Philip 198, 199
Conservative Party 9, 17, 88, 92, 107, 110,
　　308, 323, 324–7, 330–1
Cope, Sir John 182
Cornwall, Micky 25, 26, 28, 29, 31
Court of Appeal 2, 3, 5, 8, 10, 21, 24, 25,
　　31, 34, 35, 36, 37, 45, 46, 120, 122, 188,
　　260, 265, 280, 292, 295, 296, 297, 299,
　　307, 321
Craik, Detective Superintendent Michael
　　81
Crawford, Jeff 277, 293–5
crime: armed robbery 105, 173–4; arson
　　105, 113; assault 69, 104–5, 107, 154–5,
　　159, 162; burglary 76, 89, 91, 96, 102–3,
　　104, 107, 109, 111, 112, 141–2, 145,
　　154, 160, 162, 172, 323; car crime 76,
　　78, 106, 112, 113, 161, 172, 323; child
　　abuse 242; domestic violence 74, 91,
　　218, 234–5; and drugs 76, 89, 93, 98,

100, 111, 125, 162, 172, 173, 244; and
　　the family 100, 101; fear of 69, 75, 96,
　　98, 109, 335; gene for 100; juvenile 323,
　　335; mugging 89, 96, 99, 105, 106, 111,
　　112, 145, 172; organised crime 16,
　　169–210; and poverty 85, 86, 88–9,
　　92–100, 112, 163; racially-motivated see
　　racism; rise in 87–113, 114, 161, 330;
　　rape 89, 103, 104, 107, 137–9, 140–1,
　　145, 158–9, 160, 168, 242, 307, 312;
　　surveillance 173, 179–80, 190, 327;
　　terrorism 1, 7, 25–6; and
　　unemployment 95, 96, 99, 100, 101,
　　112, 244, 322–3; and young men 101,
　　111, 112, 113, 244; vandalism 76, 77,
　　99; vigilantism 76–7, 83–5, 115, 310
crime, victims of 73, 75, 82, 83, 86, 115,
　　153, 221, 222; police crime 280, 282,
　　324; 'Victim's Charter' 307
crime statistics 91, 112–13, 149–50;
　　acquittals 143, 158–60, 311, 312; 'clear-
　　ups' 107–10, 160, 163, 330, 331;
　　convictions 38, 48, 102–7, 112, 114,
　　115, 124, 149, 158, 160–1, 223, 311,
　　313, 333
Criminal Appeal Act (1968) 3; (1995) 35
Criminal Bar Association 327
Criminal Investigation Department (CID)
　　69, 70, 94, 103, 114, 227–8, 229, 255,
　　268; corruption in 26, 43, 108, 236, 239,
　　293
criminal justice: advantages of
　　'inquisitorial' system 316–21, 329;
　　authoritarianism of 17, 327, 329 'crime
　　control' model 47–8, 49, 50, 73, 74, 75,
　　83, 112, 116, 120, 207, 215, 244, 321,
　　322, 324, 325, 327, 328, 330; criminal
　　informants and supergrasses 172–4, 177,
　　188–9, 192, 207–8; 'due process' model
　　48, 49, 73, 75, 116, 119, 120, 168, 207,
　　215, 222, 239, 253, 321, 325; and
　　economic inequality 94–100, 112, 306,
　　308, 329–30, 334–5, 336–7;
　　encouragement of malpractice by
　　system 13, 19–25, 38–41, 44, 50, 310,
　　314, 319; failings of adversarial system
　　149–158, 311–16; jury service 320–1;
　　Left-Liberal views on 14, 15, 73, 74, 75,

77, 83, 86, 93, 101, 102, 112, 335–6;
legal aid 155; maintenance of class
structure 15, 50, 306–8, 327;
miscarriages of justice 3, 4, 5, 7, 8–9, 25,
34, 35–7, 44, 45, 46, 47, 115, 140, 215,
309, 310, 316, 321 (see also Birmingham
Six; Blakelock murder case; Guildford
Four; Kiszko, Stefan; Maguire Seven;
Torso murders case; Ward, Judith); 'old
regime' 1–49, 108, 119, 222, 309, 310,
314, 329, 336; outlawing of public
protest 327; proliferation of convictions
quashed 8–9; rhetoric and reality 47–50;
right to silence 17, 19, 325–6, 327, 328,
330; Right views on 16, 86, 92, 93, 99,
100, 102, 323–6, 329, 330, 334, 336;
severity in sentencing 1–2; and society
15–16, 84, 306–310, 323, 327, 329–30,
336; women and 74; see also crime
criminal informants see criminal justice
Criminal Justice Act (1988) 161, 301, 321
Criminal Justice and Public Order Act
    (1994) 17, 327
Crown Courts 17, 24, 39, 81, 119, 123,
    142, 149, 151, 152, 153, 154, 156, 158,
    160–1, 168, 296, 311, 313, 320
Crown Prosecution Service (CPS) 5, 45,
    119, 161, 164, 181, 202, 204, 223, 271,
    279, 280, 284, 285, 287, 295–6, 300,
    302, 304–5, 307, 313; failures in 131–7,
    139–49, 153–8, 258, 313, 314, 315, 319
'cusum' test 32

Daily Express 84, 233, 299
Daily Mirror 79
Daily Telegraph 192, 216, 297
Dandy, Paul, 271, 278
Davies, Christopher 140
Davies, Howard 97
Dear, Chief Constable Geoffrey 31, 32,
    265
death penalty 15
Denning, Lord 3, 4, 5, 31, 49, 266, 309
Dennis, Norman 101
Deols, case of 51–66, 72, 73, 75, 76, 77,
    83, 85, 115, 306
deregulation in the City 97
Desai, Unmesh 70

Devlin, Lord 2
Devlin, Tim, MP 181, 182, 184, 185
Dicey, A.V. 322, 325
Dingle, Chief Inspector Maxwell 298,
    299, 301, 303, 304
Diplock, Lord 120
Disraeli, Benjamin 97
divorce, increase in 100, 101
Dixon of Dock Green, myth of 38, 42, 43,
    238, 308, 309
domestic surveillance 248–9
domestic violence see crime
Donaghue, Aidan 137–140, 141
Donaldson, Sir John 2
Donellan, Austin 140, 141
Dudley, Reg 25, 26, 27–8, 29, 30, 31, 32,
    33, 34

Edwards, Patrick 74
Ealing vicarage rape case 103
East End 78, 79, 171, 308
Esda (electrostatic document analysis) 3, 8,
    32, 44, 122, 271, 288, 298, 301
eugenics 100
European Convention on Human Rights
    (1951) 17, 318, 322
European Court of Human Rights 325
Evans, Andy 36
Evans, Chief Constable John 124
Evening Sentinel 76, 77
Everett, Anthony 109

Farquharson, Lord Justice 6, 8, 11
Faulkner, David 88, 145
Ferguson, Lynn 159
Ferguson, Richard, QC 298, 299, 301,
    303, 304, 327, 328–9
Financial Times 98, 226
Fingret, Judge 199
Fisher, Sir Henry 21, 22
Fisher, Mark, MP 65, 72, 75, 77
forensic science service: failings of 9;
    evidence 19
Foucault, Michel 333, 335
Fox, Alf 35, 36
Fraser, Frankie 170, 308–9
Freely, Patricia 137
Fuller, Nicky 73, 77, 79

Garland, Mr Justice 297
Garner, Roy 177
GCHQ trade union ban (1983) 248
Gerty, Assistant Chief Constable David
    268, 272
Getting Away With Rape (Channel 4) 159
Gibbs, Richard 204, 207
Gill, Ranjit 141, 142
Gillie, Detective Sergeant 67
GLARE 74
Glidewell, Lord Justice 6
Goldberg, Jonathan, QC 27, 28
Gompertz, Jeremy, QC 266, 270
Goswell, Daniel, case of 290–1
Graef, Roger 104, 242, 255
Grant, Bernie, MP 257, 300
Gray, Gilbert, QC 183
Great Depression 101
Greater London Council (GLC) 67
Greater London Council Police
    Committee 43
Green, David 98
Greenham Common peace-camp 248
Griffiths, Courtenay 70
Guardian 7, 14, 30, 70, 73, 74, 78, 85, 212,
    226
Guildford Four 1–9, 17, 18, 22, 25, 34, 35,
    45, 47, 49, 115, 116, 119, 123, 296–7,
    298, 299, 306, 310, 315, 316, 321, 323
Guinness case 188, 253, 307

Hadfield, Chief Constable Ron 11
Halley, Mario 176, 180, 181, 186, 187
Hanney, Roy, case of 282–7
Hare, David 95
Havers, Michael, QC 2, 45
Hawkesworth, Simon, QC 45
Haywood, Derek 76
Hedgecock, Lillian, case of 125–33
Hellawell, Chief Constable Keith 13, 116,
    182
Henry, Mr Justice 188
Herod, Judge, QC 191
Hill, Jason 10–11, 302–3
Hill, Michael, QC 45, 46
Hill, Paul 1, 2, 4, 6, 18
Hoddinott, John 332
Hodgson, Mr Justice 303

Holborow, Jonathan 323
homosexuality *see* policing
Hooligan: A History of Respectable Fears
    (Pearson) 110
Hope, Chief Inspector Ron 230–1
Howard, Michael 17, 33, 83, 87, 92, 93,
    94, 99, 107, 233, 291, 317, 324–6, 327,
    328, 330, 331, 332, 333, 334, 335, 336
Human Rights Court 322
Hume, Cardinal Basil 2, 4, 5
Hurd, Douglas 2, 3, 4, 5, 9, 92, 326
Hutton, Will 308, 323

illegitimacy 101
Imbert, Sir Peter, Commissioner of
    Metropolitan Police 2, 71, 97, 168–9,
    253–9, 290
Independent 10
Inspector Morse 252
Institute of Economic Affairs 98
Institute of Race Relations 85
Irish Republican Army (IRA) 1, 84, 192,
    194, 201, 255

Jenkins, Roy 2
Job, The 256
Johnson, Chief Constable Brian 47
Johnson, Rebecca 248
Jones, John 125, 132
Jones, Assistant Commissioner Wyn 231
Jowitt, Mr Justice 301, 304
'Judges' Rules' 19, 20, 48
judiciary 117, 333, 334; criticism of police
    11; malpractice 38, 40, 44, 117; *see also*
    criminal justice
Justice (pressure group) 37

Kano family, case of 165–8, 172, 313
Kassar, Joseph 175, 179, 187
Kelly, Chief Constable Charles 76
Kennedy, Helena, QC 74
Kent, Bruce 248
Kilburn 88, 89
King, Anson, case of 292
Kinnock, Neil 212
Kiszko, Stefan, case of 8, 46, 47, 124, 298,
    329
Krays, the 22, 170, 308

Labour Party 14, 17, 21, 22, 93, 94, 101, 256, 335–6
Lane, Lord 1, 3, 4, 5, 6, 8, 9, 37, 142, 295, 321
Lattimore, Colin 21
Laughland, Judge Bruce, QC 20
Lawrence, Ivan, QC 22, 40, 317–18
Lawson, Nigel 97, 146
Lawton, Lord 173
Ledbrook, Detective Constable Alan 201, 202, 204, 205
Lederman, David, QC 159
legal aid 69, 287
Leighton, Ronald 21
Lester, Lord, QC 325–6
Levine, Sir Montague 133
Levitt, Roger 307
'lifers': gain access to case files 37; protestations of innocence hinder release 25, 33, 34, 36
Londonderry 84
Lundy, Tony 177
Lyell, Sir Nicholas, Attorney-General 182, 183

Maastricht Treaty 323
McCallion, Glen 36–7
McCowen, Mr Justice 30
MacDonald, Ian, QC 66
McGoldrick, Maureen 85
MacGregor, Sir Ian 246–7
McIlkenny, Richard 44
McKenna, Sir Brian 37
McKinnon, Mr Justice 65, 260, 261, 263, 265, 266, 267, 268, 270, 272–4, 277, 278
MacLagan, Graham 30
McNee, Commissioner David 43, 68, 236
Mafia 170–1, 180
Magistrates' Courts 136, 149, 150, 151, 152, 153, 154, 155, 223, 246, 290
Maguire Seven 8
Mail on Sunday 236, 323–4
Major, John 92, 110, 307, 323–4, 326, 331, 332
Makanji, Narendra 74
Mandela, Winnie 201
Manning, Bernard 233
Mark, Sir Robert 26, 43, 168, 212, 213, 228, 236, 293
Marnock, Commander Alex 250, 251, 256
Matrix Churchill, case of 183, 184, 329
May, Mr Justice 185, 186, 187
May, Sir John 9, 45, 46, 297
Maynard, Bob 25, 26, 28, 29, 30, 31, 32, 33
Maxwell, Kevin 253
Mbuto, General 193
media 4, 9, 42, 50, 68, 83, 101, 110, 236, 297–8, 299, 335
Melvin, Chief Superintendent Graham 298, 299, 300, 301, 303, 304
mentally ill, the 90–1, 93, 235–6, 306
Merriam, Joy 78, 81, 82
MI5, British 248–9, 332
MI6, British 248
Mills, Barbara, Director of Public Prosecutions 144, 295
miners' strike (1984–5) 229, 246–7, 249, 250
Moorhouse, Peter 286–7
Morgan, Keith 261
Morton, Dr Andrew 32–3
Moseley, Billy 25, 28, 29, 30, 31
M62 coach bomb 8, 46, 188
Murmuring Judges (Hare) 95
Murray, Charles 100, 101
Murshid, Kumar 73

National Coal Board 246
National Criminal Intelligence Service (NCIS) 170
Natt, Malkjit, case of 289–90
Neighbourhood Watch 240
News of the World 115
Newberry, Ted 83
Newham Eight 67, 83
Newham Monitoring Project 67, 70, 71
Newham Seven 67, 69, 83
Newman, Sir Kenneth, Metropolitan Police Commissioner 68, 69, 70, 239, 240, 242, 243, 244, 245, 255
Nickell, Rachel 314
Norris, David 208, 209
Nove, Commander Perry 257, 300, 301, 302
NYPD Blue 123

Observer 11, 30, 34, 109, 215, 236
O'Connor, Patrick, QC 269
Offences against the Person Act (1861) 313
Okudzeto, Raymond, case of 196–9, 329
'Operation Bumblebee' 103, 109
organised crime *see* crime
Ortiz, Camillo Jesus 176, 180, 181, 186
Orwell, George 110
Oxford, Chief Constable Kenneth 43, 247

Packer, Herbert 47, 48
Panorama (BBC) 13
Patten, John 36, 92, 93
Peach, Blair 42
Peach, Sir Leonard 278
Pearson, Geoffrey 110
Peel, Sir Robert 217, 331
Pender, John 269, 270, 272
Penrose, Roy 170
Perrin, Chief Superintendent Keith 72
Philip, HRH Prince 110
Phillips, Chief Constable David 115–16,
    119, 168, 311, 312
police: attitudes towards the Conservatives
    91, 93–5, 237, 331; attitudes towards
    Labour and the Left 42, 43, 67, 70, 93,
    98, 112, 237, 243; authoritarianism 17,
    212, 215, 216, 243; brutality 3, 20, 21,
    40, 229, 262–3, 269, 270, 274, 284,
    290–2, 293; cautioning 103, 135–6, 161,
    163; centralisation in 330–2; civil
    awards against 271, 274, 287–8, 292,
    303; coercion 13, 19, 20, 40, 212, 219;
    Conservative policy 328–9, 330–2;
    criminal charges against 6, 45, 296–7;
    culture 211–59; disillusion with legal
    system 11, 14, 102, 115–19, 124, 149,
    157; and firearms 173; freemasonry in
    230; gays and lesbians in 230;
    ineffectiveness 75, 76–7, 78, 84, 161;
    and mentally ill 90–1, 93, 235–6;
    pressure on 8, 107–8, 330; and racism
    42–3, 67–72, 73, 77–82, 121, 214, 216,
    230–4, 242, 243, 245, 289–90, 291 (*see
    also* Deols case); radicalism 252–3, 254,
    255–6; reform within 9–10, 217,
    236–42, 255–9; regarded as infallible 41,
    42, 44; secrecy 19, 20, 191; and sexism

70, 104, 216; verbals (verbal
    confessions) 22–4, 27, 28, 40, 44, 124,
    236; violent attacks on 42, 113, 218–19,
    281; *see also* policing
Police (journal) 243
Police (TV documentary) 104, 242
Police Act (1976) 275
Police Case Disposal Manual 162–4
Police Complaints Authority (PCA) 9, 31,
    35, 109, 185, 204, 265, 276–80, 285–6,
    288–9, 293–5
Police Complaints Board 278
police corruption 1, 3, 6, 9, 10, 42, 108,
    109, 116, 207, 212, 228, 229, 236,
    283–4, 292; falsification and fabrication
    of confessions 4, 6, 9, 12, 18–25, 27,
    31–2, 50, 108, 124, 236; 'noble cause
    corruption' 12–13, 14, 22, 38–40, 116,
    310; *see also* West Midlands Serious
    Crime Squad
Police and Criminal Evidence Act (PACE)
    (1984) 36, 42, 119, 120–4, 163, 187,
    217, 221, 223, 240, 261, 264, 271, 275,
    276, 322
Police Federation 124, 237, 243, 251, 275,
    288–9, 330, 332
Police and Magistrates Court Act (1994)
    331
Police Review 70, 243
policing: community 75, 237–42, 243,
    322, 332; of homosexuals 211, 214; of
    miners' strike 246–7, 249–50; of
    political protest 42, 282–3; of
    prostitution 214; underfunding of 75–6,
    84, 113, 161
Policing London 43
Policy Studies Institute (PSI) 231, 233, 234
Poll Tax riot (1990) 282–3
Pollard, Chief Constable Charles 13, 14,
    116, 143–4, 168, 311, 312
Powis, David 211, 213–14, 222, 254
Prosecution of Offences Act (1985) 119,
    125
prostitution *see* policing
Pridige, Chief Superintendent Patrick 72
prisons 17, 309, 321, 324, 325, 326, 333,
    335; in US 334–5; *see also* 'lifers'

racism 16, 51–86, 306; assaults on Asians and Afro-Caribbeans 68, 70, 73, 78, 84; and Bengali community 69, 78; and class 85–6; in Deols case 51–66; and education 85; harassment 68, 69, 70, 71, 77, 84, 85; need for new legislation 74; number of racial incidents reported 69, 84–5; and police 42–3, 67–72, 73, 77–82, 121, 214, 216, 230–4, 242, 243, 245, 289–90, 291; and unemployment 101; in Virk brothers case 67

Raghip, Engin 8, 300

rape *see* crime

Read, Chief Inspector Euan 39

Read, Detective Chief Superintendent George 44

Reid, Alphaeus, case of 291–2

Rees, Merlyn 2

Richardson, Carole 1, 2, 4, 35, 45, 297

Richardson, Judge 167

riots: inner city 8, 43, 59, 68, 92, 112, 113, 236, 237, 242–3, 250, 282–3; Poll Tax 282–3; Strangeways prison 321

Roach, Colin 229

Roberts, Norwell 231, 232

Robertson, Geoffrey, QC 307

Robinson, Andrew 84

Rogaly, Joe 98

Ronson, Gerard 253

Roskill, Lord Justice 25, 29

Rough Justice (BBC) 9, 36, 114

Rowntree Foundation 97, 98

Royal Commission: on Criminal Justice (1993) 9, 16, 123, 143, 168, 315, 316–17, 318, 321, 325, 328; on Criminal Procedure (1981) 22, 42, 145, 275; on Crown Courts (1993) 150, 152, 156; on Police Powers (1928) 20

Royal Ulster Constabulary (RUC) 243–4

Ruddock, Joan 248

Runcie, William, Archbishop of Canterbury 3

Rutter, John, case of 73, 77, 80, 81, 82, 312–13

Saatchi & Saatchi 71

Salih, Ahmet 21

Sampson, Mr 132, 133

Sanders, Andrew 214, 215

Saunders, Ernest 188, 307

Saward, Jill 103

Scargill, Arthur 246

Scarman, Lord 2, 7, 68, 97, 237–8, 239, 242, 243, 244, 275–6, 293

Scott, Lord Justice 329

Sedley, Mr Justice Stephen 312

Serious Fraud Office 325–6

Shawcross, Lord 135

Sheehy, Patrick 330, 332

Shepperdson, Peter 200, 201

Signs of Crime, The (Powis) 211, 213–14

Silcott, Winston 8, 10, 298, 299, 300, 301–2, 304, 306

Simey, Margaret 43, 247

single parent families 98, 100

Sivanandan, A. 85

Skellhorn, Norman, Director of Prosecutions 173

Smalls, Bertie 173

Smith, David 173

Smith, Sir John, Deputy Commissioner of Metropolitan Police 12, 292

Social Affairs Unit 98

Solley, Stephen, QC 65, 85

Somoza, Antonio 192

Special Branch 255

Spectator 114

Spence, Judge 189

Spencer, Sir Derek, Solicitor-General 183

Stagg, Colin, case of 314–15

Sterne, Chester 236

Stevens, David 93

Stevens, John 109

Stoke-on-Trent 72

Stokes, Michael, QC 65

Straw, Jack 315, 335

Stretch, Gary, case of 293

Sunday Telegraph 98

Sunday Times 83, 336

'supergrasses' *see* criminal justice

Swanwick, Mr Justice 25, 29

Tansey, Rock 192

Taylor, Dean 70, 71

Taylor, Michelle and Lisa 35–6, 81

Taylor, Lord Chief Justice Peter 37–8, 47,

Taylor, Lord Chief Justice Peter (Cont.)
  189, 333, 334
Territorial Support Group (TSG) 282, 283
terrorism *see* crime
Thatcher, Lady Margaret 9, 17, 88, 91, 92,
  94, 97, 98, 146, 239, 246, 249, 326, 331
Thompson, E.P. 15, 16, 308
Thwaites, Ron, QC 43, 311
'Tiger Committee', the 248–9
Times, The 10, 43, 293
Titley, Graham, 201–7, 208, 265, 319, 329
Torso murders 25–34, 42
Tottenham Three *see* Blakelock murder
  case
Tower Hamlets (Borough of) 69, 73, 79,
  81
Tower Hamlets Anti-Racist Committee
  73
Treadaway, Derek John, case of 260–74,
  275, 277, 278, 279, 280, 287
Turner, Kelly 79, 80, 82
Twitchell, Keith 277–8, 280

Ulster Defence Association (UDA) 209,
  210
unemployment 93, 95, 96, 98, 99, 100,
  101, 112, 229, 244, 322–3
USA, signals intelligence treaty with 248

Vagrancy Act (1824) 43
Vaz, Valerie 70
Verney, Judge Lawrence 209, 210
violent crime *see* crime
Virk brothers, case of 66–7

Waddington, David 321
Walsh, Brian 47
Ward, Judith, case of 8, 46, 47, 124, 188,
  298, 329

Ware, John 114, 115
Warren, Curtis 176, 178, 179, 180, 185–8,
  320
Weber, Max 84, 334
Wells. Chief Constable Richard 41–2,
  251, 257
West Midlands Serious Crime Squad 9,
  24, 31, 32, 122, 260–74, 277–8, 279–80,
  295
Wheatley, Lord 49
Whigs and Hunters (Thompson) 15
Whitehouse, Paul 251, 256
Whitelaw, William 326, 331
Whyte, Simon 167
Wickstead, Commander Albert 26–7, 28,
  29, 30
Wild, Tony 29, 30
Wilkinson, Asst. Chief Constable Frank 11
Willesden 88
Williams, George 173
Williams, Hugh 207
Williamson, Commander Tom 117, 168,
  312
Winson Green prison 33, 63
Women Against Rape and Legal Action
  for Women 140
Woodcock, Sir John, Chief Inspector of
  Constabulary 12, 13, 38
Woolf, Lord Justice 321, 326, 333
World in Action (Granada) 233

Yorkshire Television 2
Young, Hugo 7
Young, Jock 112
Young, Malcolm 212, 222, 245
Young, Richard 214, 215
Youth Connections 73
youth groups 73